Conflict Between India and Pakistan

Roots of Modern Conflict

Conflict Between India and Pakistan
Peter Lyon

Conflict in Afghanistan
Ludwig W. Adamec and Frank A. Clements

Conflict in the Former Yugoslavia
John B. Allcock, Marko Milivojevic, and John J. Horton, editors

Conflict in Korea
James E. Hoare and Susan Pares

Conflict in Northern Ireland
Sydney Elliott and W. D. Flackes

Conflict Between India and Pakistan

An Encyclopedia

Peter Lyon

A B C CLIO

Santa Barbara, California   Denver, Colorado   Oxford, England

Library of Congress Cataloging-in-Publication Data

Lyon, Peter, 1934–

    Conflict between India and Pakistan : an encyclopedia / Peter Lyon.

      p.   cm. — (Roots of modern conflict)

    Includes bibliographical references and index.

    ISBN 978-1-57607-712-2 (hard copy : alk. paper)

    ISBN 978-1-57607-713-9 (ebook)

    1. India—Foreign relations—Pakistan—Encyclopedias.   2. Pakistan-Foreign relations—India—Encyclopedias.   3. India—Politics and government—Encyclopedias.   4. Pakistan—Politics and government—Encyclopedias.   I. Title.

DS450.P18L86   2008

954.04-dc22

2008022193

12 11 10 9 8   1 2 3 4 5 6 7 8 9 10

Production Editor: Anna A. Moore
Production Manager: Don Schmidt
Media Editor: Jason Kniser
Media Resources Manager: Caroline Price
File Management Coordinator: Paula Gerard

This book is also available on the World Wide Web as an eBook.
Visit www.abc-clio.com for details.

ABC-CLIO, Inc.
130 Cremona Drive, P.O. Box 1911
Santa Barbara, California 93116–1911

This book is printed on acid-free paper ∞
Manufactured in the United States of America

Contents

Conflict Between India and Pakistan
An Encyclopedia

Preface

This encyclopedia is about relations between India and Pakistan from 1947 to today, and it endeavors to trace and account for the principal vicissitudes in these relations in their several dimensions—political, military, economic, and cultural. It does not purport to be a detailed account of all aspects of India and/or Pakistan in these years, but it does make occasional reference to earlier history (e.g., of Akbar, Babar, or Aurangzeb) when doing so seems relevant to an understanding of more recent or even contemporary events.

Arguably Indo-Pakistan relations since 1947 have been in a state of Cold War, but such a description is inadequate because there have been diverse armed clashes between the principals (as in 1948, 1965, and 1971). Furthermore, on occasion (such as in 2003–2004) the dominant motif in official Indo-Pakistan relations has been the search for détente and the prospect of a lasting entente. Although this study is primarily about official, that is, intergovernmental relations between these two countries, I am aware and desire to indicate that this subject has its important nongovernmental dimensions and that treating the subject fairly involves taking due account of public moods, fears, hopes, and aversions.

As in any encyclopedia, this work presents entries arranged alphabetically. Cross-references are given where appropriate to indicate related entries, and most entries are followed by bibliographical pointers, listed in author–date form. These abbreviated references are included in the expanded bibliography. The biographical sketches do not claim to cover all aspects of the persons concerned but rather to refer principally to how they relate to Indo-Pakistan relations. The chronology conveys information about principal events in date order in some detail, especially for the past decade or so, for it is a familiar paradox that it is often easier to see the more remote than the recent past in perspective.

A cautionary remark seems appropriate: Statistics, whether emanating from governmental sources or from their challengers, should be treated cautiously and with some skepticism, especially about deaths from terrorism or the incidence and mortalities from communal violence. The temptations to massage such figures are strong and not always resisted. Furthermore, both India and Pakistan are themselves so complex and diverse that virtually every general proposition can find some verifying evidence—but also some for its opposite.

Historical Patterns

According to the University of Chicago's superb geopolitical synopsis in *A Historical Atlas of South Asia* (published in 1978), of 63 distinct and considerable powers whose authorities waxed and waned during the past 1,500 years, 28 had their principal centers and bases on the northern Indian plain, only 9 actually achieved pan-Indian status, and of these 7 were centered on the plain.

The general deduction is made that

> control over much or all of the north Indian plain, then, clearly allows the surest regional basis for the attainment of undisputed hegemony in the Indian sub continent. The explanation is not far to seek. No other comparably large area of South Asia affords the ease of movement and hence the opportunities for rapid conquest and integration that are encountered on the Indo-Gangetic Plain. None has a comparable population base or, as a corollary, comparable agricultural productivity. (Schwartzberg, 259)

The same overall analysis amply demonstrates the point that the existence of a pan-Indian state, even for decades on end, often has not precluded the concurrent existence of a number of quite sizable and durable lesser states. Thus the coexistence of India with Pakistan, Bangladesh, and other countries in South Asia is not without some suggestive precedents or parallels.

Heavy preoccupation with internal security is not a new priority for the Indian (or indeed for the Pakistani) army after 1947 and into the early 21st century. According to the Simon Commission report of 1930 and the prevailing British orthodoxies of the late 1920s and early 1930s, approximately 35,000 British and 30,000 Indian troops were deemed to be the minimum numbers considered necessary to secure peace within India's own borders. Thus, more than half the total number of the British troops and one-fifth of the Indian troops of the entire army were so designated.

The reason offered by the Simon Commission for the greater number of British than Indian troops being earmarked for internal security is that "the British soldier is a neutral and is under no suspicion of favoring Hindu against Muhammadans, or Muhammadans against Hindus" and "as the vast majority of the disturbances which call for the intervention of the military have a communal or religious complexion, it is natural . . . that the intervention which is mostly likely to be authoritative should be that which has no bias, real or suspected to either side" (Spear 1961).

Before the Vasco da Gama era (which inaugurated European interventions in South Asia from the late 16th century onward), land power (the resultant of population military technology and mobility) rather than sea power was the basis for the erection of such powerful pan-Indian systems as emerged. When northern India was strong, potential invaders were kept beyond the Indus. Historians have often recorded that India was in fact invaded a number of times and that northern India ruled from bases on the Iranian plateau or from Afghanistan. It is more often forgotten that on occasion invaders were driven back—as when Chandragupta Maurya (from which time—the 4th century BCE—we have India's classic *realpolitik*-style treatise on statecraft, the *Arthasastra* of Kautilya) drove back the Seleucid Greeks, or when Pushyamitra beat the Bactrian Greeks, or the Sultans of Delhi evicted the Mongols.

The late Percival Spear, in his wide-ranging *India: A Modern History* (University of Michigan Press 1961) summed up the lessons of these trends thus:

> A strong Iran and weak India might mean incursions into India like that of Nadir Sha, the Persian, and Ahmad Shah, the Afghan, in the eighteenth century. A strong India with a weak Iran meant that India might still be exposed to attack from central Asia, as in the time of the Mongols in the thirteenth century.

Spear concluded that

> the Indian position today is unstable because the Iranian power is weak and divided (between Iran, Afghanistan and Pakistan) while the central Asian power is formidable. Security from the latter can only be obtained by reliance on a transoceanic source of power which means that the Indian destiny may be affected by many forces and accidents beyond the reach of the most skilful diplomacy.

This analysis by Spear was published, however, in the 1960s, not the early 21st century, and an up-to-date analysis has to factor in not only the United States and Russia (and the Soviet Union's central Asian successor states) but China as well.

A main principle of defense for Imperial Britain in India was to stave off a potential enemy's advance by interposing protective zones and maintaining land and sea frontiers. The long maritime frontiers of India furnished an analogy between the principle by which a seashore is defended and by which a system of protectorates is applied to the defense of a land frontier. In both cases, the main objective is to keep clear an open space beyond and in front of the actual boundary.

The British in India did this for their land frontiers by belts of protected land thrown forward in front of a weak border. The assertion of exclusive jurisdiction over the belt of water immediately surrounding the seacoasts is founded on the same principle. Whereas, however, throughout the decades of the Raj, British claims (in common with those of other maritime powers) were to a maximum territorial waters of three nautical miles from the shorelines. However, since the late 1950s there has been a virtual revolution, fueled by new technologies and politicoeconomic ambitions in the nautical domains of patrimonial sea claims made and conceded, especially through the work of various sessions of successive United Nations Conferences on the Law of the Sea (UNCLOS). This has now become a worldwide phenomenon, with each of the South Asian countries with a maritime face extending their claims to territorial waters and to exclusive economic zones and/or fishing zones, whether or not they have adequate naval power to protect their claims to extended patrimonial sea space successfully.

In addition to the duties of defense and security within the British Raj in India, the Indian army was frequently employed for imperial purposes outside the subcontinent. It provided contingents for operations in Ceylon, Manila, Macao, Java, Egypt, Ethiopia, the Sudan, South Africa, and especially in China in 1865, 1900, and 1926. In each of these instances, the ostensible justification for the use of Indian troops was, in part at least, geostrategic—that India was geographically much more favorably situated for the dispatch of troops to the scene of action than the other camps and garrisons of the Empire, and the proposed and actual use was made when no danger immediately threatened either Britain or India. The Indian exchequer paid all the expenses connected with the maintenance of the troops, including their pay. This is what imperial peacekeeping, willingness to wage "savage little wars for peace" (to cite a convenient phrase from Kipling) meant in practice within the British Empire while the Indian Ocean was treated in effect as a British lake.

Since 1947 India, Pakistan, Bangladesh, and Nepal have sent troops abroad to serve in international peacekeeping operations, though no authoritative comparative study of these South Asian experiences and their domestic "feedbacks" exists.

Indo-Pakistan Relations and Polymorphous Violence

Conflict in the early 21st century may be characterized as polymorphous, multidimensional, and highly volatile, that is, it takes many forms and has several dimensions, and these forms and dimensions can interact or shade into each other rather rapidly. Classic warfare before the 20th century was only two-dimensional: It was fought either on land or at sea, though rather primitive amphibious capabilities occasionally were demonstrated, and in the late 19th century Gambetta's famous escape from Paris by balloon, during the Franco-Prussian war, in a sense foreshadowed subsequent developments in air power.

World War I experienced a quantum leap in the development of air power and of submarine warfare capability. World War II saw both these dimensions very much developed and refined, as well as the awesome inauguration of the atomic age at Hiroshima and Nagasaki. Warfare-related technology since 1945 has led to the most sophisticated strategic power nowadays being capable of operating in and across five or six spatial dimensions—on the seabed, in and through submarine space, on the surface of the oceans, on land, in the air, and in or through space. No war, as yet, has involved the simultaneous or concurrent use of all these dimensions and, at most, only the United States currently has such a capability. Furthermore, in 1998 both India and Pakistan conducted tests that demonstrated to the world that they had nuclear weapon capabilities. And it is very likely that both countries have chemical and bacteriological weapons in their armories.

Warfare between India and Pakistan since 1947 generally has widened in scope, technological inputs, and destructiveness. The 1947–1948 raids by guerrillas into Kashmir resulted in India's counterinsurgent use of troops and air power; the 1965 Indo-Pakistan War was virtually a classical World War II type of tank war; the 1971 Indo-Pakistan War had a serious naval and enhanced air dimension. Each of these wars tended to be basically encounters between the professional forces of the combatants. Prophets of future Indo-Pakistan wars fear that they may take on a nuclear dimension.

Indo-Pakistan relations since 1947–1948, however, display many examples of internal violence—communalism, caste and class conflict, insurgency and terrorism—where civil-military distinctions tend to get elided. Pakistan in 1958, 1977, and 1998, like Bangladesh in 1975 and after, has experienced military coups and has remained prone to coups, whereas India so far has not. Furthermore, on a number of occasions large-scale military exercises and maneuvers conducted by India or Pakistan have seemed likely to erupt into large-scale fighting, and there have been many skirmishes and exchanges of gunfire between India and Pakistan forces, on the Siachen glacier, for example, and elsewhere.

For a number of years, relations between India and Pakistan have been in a condition of Cold War memorably expressed by the English writer Thomas Hobbes in the mid 17th century, in *Leviathan*, Chapter 13, in the following terms:

> The war, consisteth not in battle only, or the act of fighting; but in a tract of time, wherein the will to contend by battle is sufficiently known; and therefore the notion of time is to be considered in the nature of war; as it is in the nature of weather. For as the nature of foul weather, lieth not in a shower or two of rain; but in an inclination thereto of many days together: so the nature of war, consisteth not in actual fighting; but in the known disposition thereto, during all the time these is no assurance to the contrary.

Intermesticity

An ugly neologism, intermesticity, has acquired considerable currency lately to draw attention generally to the symbiosis—and perhaps the inherent volatility—between so-called international (or transnational) and domestic affairs. This neologism applies with considerable, and perhaps increasing, force to contemporary South Asia, as it does to the world generally. While it would be unhistorical and naive to assume that intermesticity is novel to the early 21st century, it does seem plausible to say that the intermesticities of the Punjab, Kashmir, Afghanistan, Assam, and Waziristan, to cite only some of the most obvious current examples, have not only lately acquired heightened salience but are likely to persist in the immediate future.

In a world where increasingly questions regarding their performance on human rights, good governance, and democracy are being levied at incumbent governments by their own citizens, autocracies such as that in Pakistan today are particularly subject to scrutiny and strictures, from at home and abroad.

Mounting evidence of religious and communal clashes (whether in the name of Islamic fundamentalism, Hindu revivalism, militant Buddhism, or an assertive Baloch or Kashmiri identity) all cast shadows and indicate that violence that originates within a particular state but that may be fomented and made to escalate because of external intervention or other process of internationalization will very likely continue to trouble India and Pakistan in the years immediately ahead. Thus attention to de-escalation, to combating communalism, to insurgency and ter-

rorism, to conflict amelioration and resolution will need to remain high on the agendas of South Asian governments and peoples.

Since the mid 1980s, the problematic nature of the relationships between South Asia and its general international environment changed considerably, for two main reasons: (1) South Asia began to develop some regional infrastructure and organization, notably through SAARC (the South Asian Association for Regional Cooperation), and (2) the main constellations of power and influence on the world stage at large underwent some striking changes. In general terms, these latter changes are much more important and consequential than the former, but they are too obvious and well-known to require much elaboration here. World economics has witnessed the clear emergence of three principal powers—the United States, Germany, and Japan [or, more generally, North America, the European Union (EU), and the East Asian Newly Emerging Countries (the NECs)].

The world's military balance has experienced the virtual eclipse or self-immolation of Soviet military power and the abandonment of some of the structures, notably the Warsaw Pact, which earlier had multilateralized and institutionalized Soviet power. South Asia in the early 21st century is thus relatively securely anchored regionally in a world system that has become, rather suddenly, remarkably fluid. The South Asian jigsaw has jelled, for the time being at least into a SAARC-approved pattern, at a time when the world's many diplomatic-strategic patterns are in flux or becoming blurred. Conflict over Kashmir or along and within Afghanistan's borders (to cite merely two of the most suppurating wounds) might result in the breaking of present political molds—but not easily and not yet.

Thus, South Asia today exhibits neither an excessive nor a negligible integration into the current world system, but rather a lopsided set of involvements. It is often insufficiently strong and influential to satisfy the ambitions or hopes of many South Asians and frequently has been the prey or victim of outsiders' interferences and meddling. If such factors are evident in the early 21st century, they are nevertheless not new.

The equivocations of status for India and for Pakistan (though the multiple nuances of these cannot be pursued here) attest to the mutations and volatilities currently at work within the new and unstable hierarchy of values in the world system (where, for example, India aspires to recognized great power status and Pakistan seeks to restrict this), of conditions unfavorable for decisive South Asian impacts, of highly uneven production and exchange networks, and of the uncertain and at times markedly unsure contribution to international equilibria. SAARC certainly so far has proved to be a rather frail vessel and one that requires India's support, or at least acquiescence, to survive.

From the late 1940s until the late 1980s, South Asians were able to capitalize to a considerable degree on the dynamics of decolonization, which placed less value on the economic importance of states than on their political or diplomatic activity. Thus Indians, Pakistanis, and from 1972 onward Bangladeshis, were prominent in the activities of the United Nations (UN) or in one or more of its sprawling subsets, The World Bank, the International Labour Organisation, UNCLOS, or in peacekeeping endeavors, for instance.

In short, one can say that on world stages, such as at the UN, Indians and Pakistanis could and did compensate to some considerable extent for their economic handicaps and lack of a resilient South Asian regionalism. Multilateralism was, and is, relatively serviceable for both India and Pakistan in their quests on the international scene.

India's Composite Dialogue with Pakistan yielded dividends in 2004–2006. There were increasing people-to-people and institutional contacts, as well as renewed transportation and communication links. In the wake of the severe earthquake of October 8, 2005, in Pakistan-occupied Kashmir (POK) and other areas, India announced relief assistance worth US$25 million to Pakistan. In addition, assistance worth US$10 million was sent by private sources from India. Five crossing points on the Line of Control (LoC, the cease-fire line between the two zones of Kashmir) were opened. The Indo-Pakistan Joint Commission was revived after 16 years, and the Munabao–Khokrapar rail service was reestablished after more than 40 years.

Indian Prime Minister Dr. Manmohan Singh (who was born in India) has offered a Treaty of Peace, Security and Friendship to Pakistan. He told President Pervez Musharraf that, while borders could not be redrawn, cooperative work could be done to make borders less relevant to the two countries. He expressed the hope that Pakistan would take decisive action against terrorism.

At a meeting in Islamabad, on February 16, 2005, India's minister for external affairs, K. Natwar Singh, and Pakistan's foreign minister, Mian Kurshid Mahmud Kasuri, agreed to open a direct bus route between Srinagar and Muzaffarabad, the capital of Pakistan-administered (Azad) Jammu-Kashmir, the service commencing on April 7. This accord, reported by some commentators as the most significant advance between the two countries, had been delayed because India had initially stipulated that passengers carry passports to cross the LoC. However, the two sides eventually agreed on the use of entry permits. Singh and Kasuri also agreed on other transport links, including a bus service between Lahore, the capital of Pakistan's Punjab province, Amritsar in the Indian state of Punjab, and a rail link between Pakistan's southern Sind province and India's northwestern state of Rajasthan. Natwar Singh also agreed to exploratory talks on building pipelines to India from Iran and Turkmenistan that would run through Pakistan.

Modalities

The soldier, the diplomat, and the trader are the archetypical professions and roles in the conduct of Indo-Pakistan relations. The conception and conduct of Indo-Pakistan relations has involved many of the nationals of the two countries, with many ups and downs, though it should be remembered that millions of Indians and Pakistanis spend their whole lives with no direct involvement in Indo-Pakistan relations, except perhaps rhetorically.

The armed forces of both countries have mostly assumed and reacted to the notion that their neighbor is or could be their principal adversary, though this is more true of Pakistan than of India. And adversarial relations actually involving fighting was the most pronounced between the early 1960s and 1971. Nuclear tests in both countries in 1999 served awesome reminders of the potential destructiveness that could be wielded by either country.

Diplomacy, the art of convincing without use of force, may be said to be the principal modality governing Indo-Pakistan relations other than their brief periods of open war. Reference to the Chronology of this book shows that the conversations and negotiations between India and Pakistan have been much more continuous and frequent than is often popularly believed. True, there is generally an acute disproportion between the number of these contacts and their rather slender accomplishments. But for both countries their bilateral encounters constitute a major aspect of their external relationships.

Economic relations between the two newly independent countries began with fierce argument about the division of the assets of the Raj and their reapportionments. Subsequently Indo-Pakistan economic relations have been on the whole meager. However, India and to a lesser extent Pakistan have generally liberalized their economies and widened their trade and investment links since the early 1990s and continue to do so at present.

A Note on India and Pakistani Names

There is no generally accepted scheme of transliteration of many Indian or Pakistani names into roman script. There are, for instance, at least five common variants of the English spelling of Muhammad. The name of the same individual may be spelled in several different ways in different publications. What the author of this book has done is to choose one commonly used spelling of the name of each person and to stick to that version throughout. A comparable difficulty arises in the order in which the several names of an individual are placed and in the choice of one or more of these names as what we might call key names corresponding to an English surname. There is no intrinsic logic in this and generally an arbitrary choice has to be made.

References

Schwartzberg, J., ed. *A Historical Atlas of South Asia.* 2nd ed. Chicago: University of Chicago Press, 1992

Spear, Percival. *India: A Modern History.* Ann Arbor: University of Michigan Press, 1961

Prime Ministers of India

Jawaharlal Nehru*	Congress	1947–1964
Lal Bahadur Shastri**	Congress	1964–1966
Indira Gandhi	Congress	1966–1977
Moraji Desai	Janata	1977–1979
Charan Singh	Janata	1979–1980
Indira Gandhi	Congress	1980–1984
Rajiv Gandhi	Congress	1984–1989
V. P. Singh	Janata Dal	1989–1990
Chandra Shekhar	Samajwadi Janata Party	1990–1991
P. V. Narasimha Rao	Congress	1991–1996
Atal Bihari Vajpayee	Bharatiya Janata Party	May 16–29, 1996
H. D. Deve Gowda	Janata Dal	June 1996–April 1997
I. K. Gujral	Janata Dal	April 1997–1998
Atal Bihari Vajpayee	Bharatiya Janata Party	March 1998–2001
Manmohan Singh	Congress	May 2004–

*When Nehru died, Gulzari Lal Nanda became acting prime minister (May 27–June 9, 1964).

**When Shastri died, Nanda was once again acting prime minister (January 11–24, 1966).

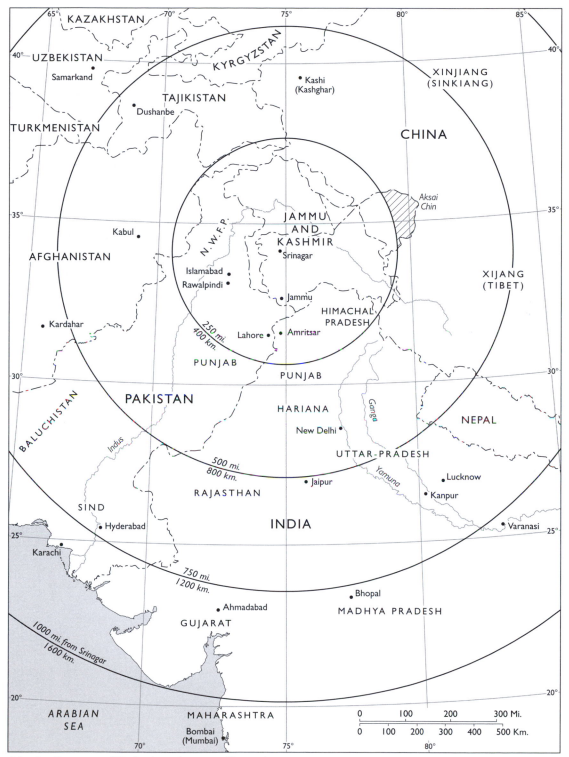

Map 1   Jammu and Kashmir and surrounding regions.

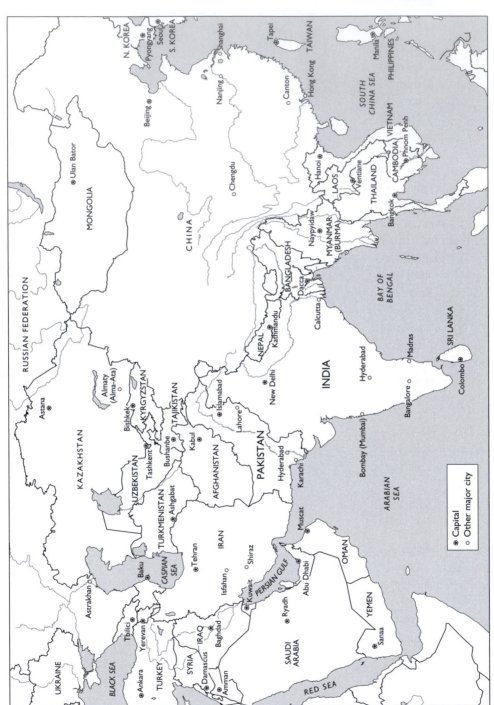

Map 2   *India, Pakistan, and surrounding nations.*

ABDULLAH, DR. FAROOQ (1937–)

Dr. Farooq Abdullah has been a major figure in Indian-administered Kashmir for several decades and chief minister three times. He first emerged prominently onto Kashmir's political scene in 1976 when he campaigned for his father, the legendary Sheikh Abdullah. Four years later he was elected to Parliament representing Srinagar, the state's winter capital. He became chief minister after his father died in 1982, and he has been in and out of office ever since. Throughout his political life he has always urged that Kashmir should remain part of the Indian Union. He campaigned vigorously, however, for greater autonomy within India and for more central funds for the ailing Kashmiri economy, ensuring an often difficult relationship with Delhi. His detractors accused him of abandoning the state and going to live in the United Kingdom when militancy was at its peak in Kashmir.

He is also criticized for shifting allegiances. He was allied with the Indian National Congress (INC) Party in 1987 when it was in power in Delhi but switched sides in 1996 to support the United Front government. He then became an ally of the ruling coalition led by the Hindu nationalist Bharatiya Janata Party (BJP).

See also Azad Jammu-Kashmir (AJK); Abdullah, Sheikh Mohammad; Bharatiya Janata Party (BJP).

References
Bose, Sumantra. *The Challenge in Kashmir: Democracy, Self-Determination and a Just Peace.* Thousand Oaks, CA: Sage Publications, 1997

ABDULLAH, OMAR (1970–)

Son of Dr. Farooq Abdullah and an English mother, Mollie Abdullah, Omar Abdullah is a third-generation member of his family to be active in Kashmiri and Indian politics. He was born in Essex, England, on March 10, 1970. He married Payal Abdullah, September 1, 1994, and they have two sons. Omar Abdullah was educated at Sydenham College in England, Mumbai (Maharashtra), and the University

of Strathclyde, Scotland, where he earned his B.Com and MBA degrees. Subsequently, he became a consultant in his fields of expertise.

He was elected to 12th Lok Sabha (lower house of India's Parliament) for Srinagar and reelected to the 13th Lok Sabha for a second term in 1999. From October 13, 1999, onward, he was Union Minister of State, Commerce and Industry and then Minister of State for External Affairs. On June 23, 2002, Omar Abdullah formally took over as president of the state's ruling National Conference and was expected shortly to replace his father as Jammu and as Kashmir's chief minister as well. He records his special interests as "Finding long-term solution to the problem of unemployment in Jammu and Kashmir." Omar Abdullah lost his seat in Kashmir's state assembly elections, which were held in September–October, 2002.

See also Abdullah, Dr. Farooq; Azad Jammu-Kashmir (AJK).

References
Bose, Sumantra. *The Challenge in Kashmir: Democracy, Self-Determination and a Just Peace.* Thousand Oaks, CA: Sage Publications, 1997

ABDULLAH, SHEIKH MOHAMMAD (1905–1982)

Sheikh Mohammad Abdullah was a Kashmiri politician and close but uneasy friend of Jawaharlal Nehru, with whom he debated and often disagreed about the future of Kashmir. A Muslim, he led the struggle for constitutional government against the Maharajah of Kashmir from 1930 onward, first as a Muslim and later as an advocate of a secular political future for India and Kashmir. He was imprisoned in 1931 and on his release formed the All Jammu and Kashmir Moslem Conference (renamed the National Conference in 1938). Popularly known as the Lion of Kashmir, Sheikh Abdullah was imprisoned again in 1946 after launching the Quit Kashmir Movement but was released and appointed chief minister in 1947 in an emergency administration. He agreed to the accession of the State to India to halt tribal infiltration but was charged with treason and imprisoned again (1953–1968), when he publicly reaffirmed the right of the people of Kashmir "to decide the future of the State." In 1963 he seemed to be brokering new relations between India and Pakistan on Kashmir, but Nehru's death abruptly terminated these moves. He was chief minister again from 1975 until his death. His son, Dr. Farooq Abdullah (1937–) succeeded him as chief minister.

See also Abdullah, Dr. Farooq; Abdullah, Omar; Nehru, Jawaharlal.

References

Abdullah, Sheikh Mohammad. *Flames of the Chinar: An Autobiography.* Translated by Khuswant Singh. New York: Viking, 1993

Bose, Sugata, and Jalal Ayesha, eds. *Modern South Asia Delhi.* New York: Oxford University Press, 1997

ABELL, SIR GEORGE EDMOND BRACKENBURY (1904–1989)

Sir George Edmond Brackenbury Abell was on the staff of the last three viceroys (Britain's senior officers) of India, was private secretary to the last two, and thus intimately involved in the British departure in 1947 and the subsequent emergence of India and Pakistan as independent states. Abell joined the Indian Civil Service (ICS) as a district officer in the Punjab in 1928, becoming deputy secretary of cooperative societies and a settlement officer. In 1941 he was appointed to be private secretary to the governor of the Punjab, and in 1943 he was promoted to deputy secretary to the viceroy, the second Marquis of Linlithgow. In 1945 he took over as private secretary to the viceroy, Viscount (later First Earl) Archibald Percival Wavell, and he continued to hold this post under Louis Mountbatten (later First Earl Mountbatten of Burma) until the end of the Raj, thereafter serving as Mountbatten's secretary when he became first governor-general of independent India in 1947.

Abell's roles in government during the critical years leading up to the partition and transfer of power in India were important. Although Hindus regarded his Punjab background with suspicion, Wavell, whom he liked and admired, used him as an intermediary for discussions with M. K. Gandhi. Abell wrote the first draft of the handover plan to be presented to the new British Labour government and was on the small committee used by Wavell to work out details of his plan.

Abell tended to moderate Wavell's tough telegrams but respected his soldierly directness. He came, however, to believe that the British position in India was untenable, that partition was inevitable, and that the British should extricate themselves quickly. Although less comfortable with Mountbatten's personality, he nonetheless worked loyally to implement his policies. Abell drafted the partition plan for the viceroy with General (later Baron) Hastings Ismay and helped him avoid or to handle some of the potential mistakes in the rush to comply with looming deadlines. On his return to England in 1948, Abell joined the Bank of England as an adviser, serving as a director from 1952 until 1964.

See also Gandhi, Mohandas Karamchand; Mountbatten of Burma; Raj, the; Wavell, Archibald Percival, First Earl Wavell.

References

Schofield, V. *Wavell: Soldier and Statesman.* London: John Murray, 2006

Ziegler, P. *Mountbatten: A Biography.* New York: Alfred A. Knopf, 1985

ADVANI, LAL KRISHNA (1927–)

Lal Krishna Advani was the Indian leader of the Bharatiya Janata Party (BJP) and home minister in 2004, with a reputation for being tough on Indian Muslims and Pakistan. Born in Karachi (now in Pakistan) on November 8, 1927, he married Kamla Advani on February 25, 1965, and has one son and one daughter. He was educated at St. Patrick's High School, Karachi; at DG National College, Hyderabad, Sind (now in Pakistan); and at Government Law College, Mumbai (Maharashtra). He organized local work for the Rashtriya Swayamsevak Sangh (RSS) from 1947 to 1951. He was chairman of the Metropolitan Council, Delhi (1967–1970) and president of the Bharatiya Jana Sangh (BJS) in Delhi (1970–1972). He was a member of the Rajya Sabha (upper house of India's Parliament) for four terms, from 1970 to 1989. He was detained under the Maintenance of Internal Security Act (MISA) during the Emergency (June 1975–January 1977). He was a member of the RSS from 1942 onward and of the Press Council of India (1990). He played a prominent part in Ayodhya in 1989–1990, which exacerbated Hindu–Muslim relations within northern India.

In 1984 Advani's party was reduced to two seats out of 542 and seemed to be on the brink of extinction. As president he invigorated his party so successfully that by 1998 it became the leading political party in the country's multiparty system. Indeed, Advani is credited with turning the BJP into a significant force in Indian politics by undertaking a *Ratha Yatra* (chariot tour) to mobilize support to build a temple dedicated to Lord Rama in Ayodhya, believed to be his birthplace, which was razed and converted to a mosque by Babar, the first Mughal ruler in India who arrived from Afghanistan in 1528.

According to some sources, a criminal case is still pending against Advani and 17 others for allegedly conspiring to kill Pakistan's first governor-general, Mohammad Ali Jinnah and other leaders. Successive Pakistan governments, however, have not sought actively to indict him on this matter.

On June 1, 2005, Advani offered his resignation from his post as BJP's president amid controversial comments he is said to have made during a visit to Pakistan in 2005. He became the first major Indian political leader to visit Jinnah's mausoleum. On June 4, he wrote in the visitor's book:

> There are many people who leave an irreversible stamp on history. But there are few who actually create history. Quaid-e-Azam Mohammad Ali Jinnah was one such rare individual. In his early years, leading luminary of freedom struggle, Sarojini Naidu, described Jinnah as an ambassador of Hindu–Muslim unity. His address to the Constituent Assembly of Pakistan on 11 August 1947 is really a classic and a forceful espousal of a secular state in which every citizen would be free to follow his own religion. The State shall make no distinction between the citizens on the grounds of faith. My respectful homage to this great man.

He was president of the BJP (1973–1977); Union Cabinet Minister of Information and Broad-casting (1977–1979); leader of the house, Rajya Sabha (1977–1979); leader of the opposition, Rajya Sabha (1979–1981); general secretary, BJP (1980–1986); and concurrently leader of the BJP, Rajya Sabha. In 1989 he was elected to the 9th Lok Sabha (lower house of the Indian Parliament). In 1989–1991 and 1991–1993, he was leader of the opposition, Lok Sabha. In 1991, he was reelected to the Lok Sabha for a second term. He was president of the BJP, 1993–1998, and in 1998 was elected to the 12th Lok Sabha for a third term (1998–1999). He served as Union Cabinet Home Minister from October 13, 1999 until the 2004 elections.

One of Advani's most striking plans, though organized principally by Pramod Mahajan, was the *Ratha Yatra* in 1990, a slow cavalcade procession through India to Ayodhya. Advani rode in an exotic chariot as part of a caravan bedecked with images from Hindu mythology while delivering speeches with pronounced Hindu themes. The trail of the weeks-long procession was punctuated by anti-Muslim riots in which large numbers died. At the end of 1990, the Indian government said that 890 people had been killed and almost 4,000 injured in the 15 weeks of Hindu–Muslim riots provoked by the Hindu militant campaign against the Ayodhya mosque. India's junior interior minister, reporting to Parliament on some of India's worst communal violence since 1947, said that 332 people had died in the first two weeks of December alone. The mosque was demolished by Hindu fanatics.

In part because of Advani's journeying, the BJP successfully pandered to Hindu sentiments, which, in turn, translated into votes for the BJP. The party assumed power in 1998 and remained in office for six years, with Advani as home minister and deputy prime minister throughout. He records his favorite pastimes and recreations as reading, watching films, sports, and music. Widely traveled, he says that his special interest is electoral reforms, though he is not famous for specifying exactly what these should be. Reputedly a hard-liner in India's relations with Pakistan, he supported A. J. Vajpayee's moves toward détente in 2003–2004 until the BJP's electoral defeat in the general election of May 2004. Advani was widely regarded as A. J. Vajpayee's most likely successor as head of the BJP, but he resigned from his senior post in the party in 2005. A Tamil Nadu court convicted over 150 people connected with a series of explosions in 1998 that killed nearly 60 people.

Eight people were acquitted. L. K. Advani was said to have been a prime target of the bombs.

Advani is generally known for his tough-minded views on the issues of terrorism and Pakistan. In 2005, however, while visiting Pakistan (and revisiting his birth town of Karachi), he made conciliatory remarks about Jinnah, the founder of Pakistan, resulting in much reactive controversy in India and Pakistan. For his remarks, Advani was soon forced to resign from his post as BJP president. This was reported in the Indian media as Advani's calling Jinnah a "secular" leader. Hindu nationalist groups that were aligned with the BJP and officials from the ruling Indian National Congress (INC) Party lashed out against Advani for his statements. Some leaders of the BJP tried to persuade Advani not to resign, a suggestion he rejected. A memorandum was presented to Advani by the party members hailing his trip to Pakistan without any reference to the Jinnah speech. Advani also rejected this memorandum.

Visiting Lahore in 2005, he inaugurated the renovation project of Karasraj Temple, the most ancient temple in Pakistan. Early in 2007, Advani met archaeologists from Pakistan who had been visiting Indian temples to acquaint themselves with Hindu architecture.

In a television interview in December 2006, L. K. Advani stated that, as the leader of the opposition in a parliamentary democracy, he considered himself the prime ministerial candidate for India's next general election scheduled for early 2009. This public statement irritated colleagues within the party who were not supportive of his candidacy. Earlier, a leading party spokesperson, Muktar Abbas Naqui, told the press that the BJP would fight the next elections under a second-generation leader. Naqui also said that Advani had not managed to repair his relationship with the RSS following his remarks about Jinnah. Advani would be 82 by the time of the next general election. The chief of the RSS, K. S. Sudarshan, made it clear that he wants Vajpayee and Advani to step aside for younger leaders.

See also Ayodhya; Babar; Bharatiya Janata Party (BJP); Mahajan, Pramod; Rashtriya Swayamsevak Sangh (RSS); Vajpayee, Atal Bihari.

References
Advani, L. K. *Ram Janmabhoomi: Honour People's Sentiments.* New Delhi: Bharatiya Jana Sangh, 1989
Advani, L. K. *Ayodhya Before and After.* New Delhi: Janadhikar Samiti, 1992
Hardgrave, R. L., and S. A. Kochanek. *India: Government and Politics in a Developing Nation,* 6th ed. Fort Worth, TX: Harcourt College Publishers, 2000
Khilnani, Sunil. *The Idea of India.* London: Hamish Hamilton, 1997

AFGHANISTAN

This landlocked country in central Asia roughly took on the simulacrum of a single state from the mid 18th century, though it has been subsequently plagued right down to today by endemic internal violence and pressure from outside powers. The population of Afghanistan, according to United Nations estimates for 2004, was about 23 million. Pashtans comprised about 24 percent of this total and predominated in the south and west, the Tajiks about 25 percent, the Hazaras 10 percent in the center, the Uzbeks 8 percent in the north, the Baluchis 0–5 percent. The principal languages are Dari (a form of Persian) and Pashtu.

Afghanistan today has six contiguous neighboring countries: (1) Iran (to the west), (2) Pakistan (east and south), (3) Tajikistan, (4) Uzbekistan and (5) Turkmenistan (to the north), and (6) China (to the northeast). A thin sliver of Afghanistan's territory in its northeast in the Hindu Kush Range, known as the Wakhan Panhandle, separates Tajikistan from Pakistan and China, and it is geographically significant though a formidable terrain. Mountains cover three-quarters of the country, with plains in the north and southwest. The climate is arid to semiarid with extreme temperatures. Summers are hot and dry, and winters cold with heavy snowfalls, especially in the north. The weather conditions, especially the severe winters, much affect fighting in this land.

Afghanistan has been a crossroads for religion and trading between Europe and Asia since the days of Alexander the Great. Buddhism flowed west and north from India, and Islam spread eastward from Arabia. Being such a transit zone has made Afghanistan repeatedly exposed to internal disputes and external pressures—in this latter respect by competition between the extensive British Empire in Asia and imperial Russia and then, after World War II right down to today, by Russia, China, and the United States.

In late December 1979 troops from the then Soviet Union invaded Afghanistan and installed a

Soviet soldiers ride aboard an airborne combat vehicle in Kabul, Afghanistan, in March 1986. (Department of Defense)

pro-Soviet government. Armed Islamic resistance groups, the mujahedeen, fought against Soviet and Afghan forces until the puppet government collapsed in April 1992. Mujahedeen forces swiftly overran Kabul and declared an Islamic state. Between 1994 and 1998, divided mujahedeen forces met with heavy defeats inflicted by Taliban forces (armed Islamic students), who soon extended their power across more than 90 percent of the country. Remnant forces of the former pro-Soviet regime were driven northward. A United Islamic Front for the Salvation of Afghanistan (UIFSA) or Northern Alliance was formed by the four main mujahedeen factions. The Taliban, widely believed to be supplied and supported by Pakistan and by other Islamists, imposed Shari'ah law, though inevitably patchily.

On September 11, 2001, terrorist attacks on the United States were boastfully and suicidally carried out by Osama bin Laden's al-Qa'ida (the base) organization. Afghanistan subsequently refused to surrender bin Laden and the al-Qa'ida leadership to the U.S. authorities, U.S. and UK forces began military operations against al-Qa'ida and Taliban elements in early October 2001. Under intensive U.S. air bombardment, conducted from bases in Uzbekistan, Tajikistan, and Pakistan, and under attack by U.S. and UK ground troops

and by Northern Alliance forces, the Taliban regime swiftly collapsed.

Moves to form an alternative government from among the anti-Taliban factions began in 2001. Various Afghan leaders met near Bonn, Germany, and a multiethnic interim government was patched together. Attempts to capture Osama bin Laden and Mullah Omat, the Taliban leader, were unsuccessful, however. Pockets of al-Qa'ida and Taliban forces remained actively at large in the country.

At the end of 2002 India reopened four consulates in Afghanistan. Pakistan's reaction to India's consular staff arriving in Jalalabad and Kandahar was comparable to that of the Americas when Soviet advisers turned up in Cuba in 1961. But relations between India and Pakistan were palpably easier in 2002 than in earlier decades. Even so, some Pakistanis still accuse so-called Indian spies of whipping up secessionist sentiment among ethnic Pushtuns in Pakistan and also of financing would-be secessionist insurgents in Baluchistan. And ethnic Tajiks who are prominent in the Afghan government are castigated as anti-Pakistani Indian stooges.

Tensions stayed high throughout the years 2002–2005. A 5,000-strong UN-mandated peacekeeping force, the International Security Assistance Force (ISAF) was set up and, by late 2004, about 8,000 U.S. troops remained in the country, ostensibly part of the American-led "war against terrorism." Following the collapse of Taliban rule in December 2002, an interim government for Afghanistan was to assume office for six months, pending the holding of a *Loya Jirga* (tribal council) to appoint a transitional government. In June 2002 the *Loya Jirga* selected Hamid Karzai as transitional president of the country pending presidential elections. A new government was sworn in and charged with preparing for nationwide elections, which were held in October 2004. A new constitution was adopted in January 2004, establishing Afghanistan as an Islamic republic.

The North Atlantic Treaty Organization (NATO), in 2007, avowedly was a key component of the international community's engagement in Afghanistan, assisting the Afghan authorities in providing security and stability and paving the way for reconstruction and effective governance. NATO took command and coordination of the ISAF in August 2003, which was NATO's first mission outside the Euro-Atlantic area. ISAF operates in Afghanistan under a UN mandate and is intended to work according to current and future UN Security Council (UNSC) resolutions. ISAF's mission was initially limited to Kabul. Resolution 1510, passed by the UNSC on October 13, 2003, opened the war to a wider role for ISAF to support the government of Afghanistan beyond Kabul.

NATO's Three-Tiered Engagement

- Through leadership of the UN-mandated ISAF, an international force of some 41,000 troops (including National Support Elements), NATO assists the Afghan authorities in extending and exercising their authority and influence across the country, creating the conditions for stabilization and reconstruction.
- A senior civilian representative, responsible for advancing the political-military aspects of the Alliance's commitment to the country, works closely with ISAF, liaises with the Afghan government and other international organizations, and maintains contacts with neighboring countries.
- A substantial program of cooperation with Afghanistan concentrates on defense reform, defense institution-building, and the military aspects of security sector reform. Neither India nor Pakistan is involved in these NATO arrangements, but both are closely interested, albeit Pakistan more so than India.

See also al-Qaeda/al-Qa'ida; Taliban.

References

Adamec, L. W., and F. A. Clements. *Conflict in Afghanistan: An Encyclopedia. Roots of Modern Conflict.* Santa Barbara, CA: ABC-CLIO, 2003

Marsden, P. *The Taliban: War, Religion and the New Order in Afghanistan.* New York: Zed Books, 1999

Saikal, A. "The Changing Geopolitics of Central West and South Asia After 11th September." In Ramesh Thakur and Oddny Wiggen, eds. *South Asia in the World: Problem Solving Perspectives on Security. Sustainable Development and Good Governance.* Tokyo: United Nations University Press, 2004

AFGHANS

The origin of the name "Afghan" is obscure but has been in use since its first known appearance in a Sanskrit text of the 6th century. In the 20th and 21st centuries, the inhabitants of the country are divisible into four main ethnic or cultural groups: (1) the Pashtans (Pathans), (2) the Tadzhiks, (3) the Uzbeks, and (3) the Hazaras. The Pathans (the Afghans proper) form about 60 percent of the population. The Tadzhiks (or Tajiks) represent the next largest ethnic group, comprising about 30 percent, followed by the Uzbeks (or Usbegs) at 5 percent and the Hazaras at 3 percent. The remaining 1–2 percent consists of Hindus, Jews, Sikhs, and a congeries of central Asian tribal elements.

Members of the four principal groups are scattered throughout the country, but the bulk of the Pathans occupy its eastern and southeastern parts, as well as Herat and Kabul. The Uzbeks are in northern and central Afghanistan. The Hazaras live in the mountainous district of Hazarajar, south of the main range of the Hindu Kush and in the region west of Anardarra (Gardarra) bordering Iran.

See also Afghanistan; Pathans.

References

Adamec, L. W., and F. A. Clements. *Conflict in Afghanistan: An Encyclopedia. Roots of Modern Conflict.* Santa Barbara, CA: ABC-CLIO, 2003

Maley, William. *Fundamentalism Reborn? Afghanistan and the Taliban.* New York: New York University, 1998

Nomadic Afghans in Afghanistan seated in a tent with camels nearby. (Library of Congress)

AIR DEFENSES
India
Units of the Indian Air Force are organized into five operational commands: western at Delhi, central at Allahabad, eastern at Shillong, southern at Thruvananthapuram, and southwestern at Jodhpur.

In mid 2005, its principal equipment included 774 combat aircraft in over 40 squadrons of aircraft and 34 armed helicopters.

The major combat types included Su-30s, Mig-21s, Mig-27s, Mig-29s, Jaguars, and Mirage 200s.

Air Force reserves numbered 140,000 in 2004.

Pakistan
The Pakistan Air Force came into being on August 14, 1947. It has its headquarters at Peshawar and is organized into three air defense sectors: the northern, central, and southern areas of the country. There is a flying college at Risalpur and an aeronautical engineering college at Korangi Creek. The total strength in mid 2005 was 389 combat aircraft, 45,000 active personnel, and 8,000 air force reservists.

The equipment included Mirage IIIs, Mirage 5, F-16s, J-6s, and J-7s.

Air warfare was not a major dimension of Indo-Pakistan clashes in 1948 or even in 1965. In 1971,

India soon assumed air superiority, and Pakistan's air force was held back for city protection.

Since 1999 both countries have had military nuclear capabilities.

See also Armed Forces.
References
The Military Balance. Washington, DC: International
    Institute for Strategic Studies (IISS), annual

AKALI DAL
The Akali Dal is both regionally and communally confined to the Punjab and open only to members of the Sikh community, of which it claims to be the sole representative. The Akali Dal was first organized as a reform group to bring the *gurdwaras* (Sikh shrines) under the control of the orthodox Sikh community.

The Akali Dal is thus the paramilitary political party of Sikh nationalism and has long demanded a Sikh state in the Punjab if not the independent Sikhistan it sought at the time of partition in 1947. The demand for a separate State of the Punjab (Punjabi Suba) was based not on community but on language. There was no major language problem in the Punjab, however; differences revolved principally around a problem of script and fundamentally of religion.

Punjabi is the mother tongue of Sikhs and Hindus alike for those living in the Punjab, but communal passions have led large sections of the Hindu community to renounce the Punjabi language by naming their mother tongue as Hindi for census purposes. The languages, as spoken, are very alike, but Punjabi is distinguished by the use of Gurmukhi, the script of the Sikh holy books. Hindus in the Punjab write in Urdu or in Devanagari script. Akali Dal has never had widespread electoral support even among the Sikhs, though Sikhism is a considerable factor in the public life of Indian Punjab, with an understandably active interest in Indo-Pakistan relations.

See also Communalism; Punjab; Sikhism.

References

Hardgrave, R. L., and S. A. Kochanek. *India: Government and Politics in a Developing Nation,* 6th ed. Fort Worth, TX: Harcourt College Publishers, 2000

AKBAR, EMPEROR (JALAL-UD-DIN MOHAMMED) (1542–1605)

Akbar was the greatest of the Mogul emperors in India, and his life and works showed that Muslims and Hindus could coexist amicably. He was born in October or November 1542 at Umarkot in Sind when his father, Humayan, driven from the throne of Delhi by the Afghan usurper, Sher Shah, was escaping to Iran. Not until 1555 did Humayan undertake to reconquer Hindustan, and, when he died in 1556, the Mogul empire was still only an idea or aspiration. Succeeding his father, Akbar first overthrew all rivals and then embarked on a career of conquest. By 1562 his kingdom included the Punjab and Multan, the basin of the Ganges and Jumna rivers from Panipat to Allahabad and, in Afghanistan, the province of Kabul. Another 14 years of warfare resulted in the acquisition of further extensive territories, including Gujerat and Bengal. Between 1586 and 1595 he added Kashmir, Sind, Baluchistan, Kandahar, and parts of Orissa to his domains. With his power firmly established in the north, he moved southward into the Deccan. By 1605 his empire comprised 15 *subahs* (provinces) and stretched from the Hindu Kush to Godavari River and from Bengal to Gujarat.

Akbar did much more than achieve Mogul political hegemony in northern India. He stabilized and prolonged it by imposing a framework of administrative and military institutions and a foundation of political and social order. He provided the inspiration as well as the opportunity for the burgeoning of a remarkable synthetic Mogul culture extending over art, architecture, literature, history, gastronomy, dress, and pastimes, which dominated the imagination and engaged the sympathies of Indians of diverse communities until the mid 19th century and in some respects down to today. His system of provincial administration is still discernible in present-day India and Pakistan, drawn in its details from the experience of nearly 400 years of Muslim rule.

Under vigorous management, which Akbar himself provided, the military system of recruiting cavalry by *mansabdars* (imperial officers) provided an army that was loyal, effective, and large enough for Indian conditions before the second half of the 18th century. The reform of the traditional method of land revenue collection, by which the state's demand for one-third of the gross produce was commuted into a cash payment carefully assessed by reference to average local prices and yields, provided Akbar with the resources that his plans for conquest required, without oppressing the cultivator. Akbar deliberately founded his empire on an understanding with the Hindu Rajputs and on respect for Hindu religion and culture. In 1562 and 1570 he married Rajput princesses. He conferred important *mansabs* on Rajput chiefs and appointed some to high positions in revenue departments. Not favoring a militant orthodox Islam, he formally abolished, in 1564, the *jizya* (poll tax) on non-Muslims and rescinded the taxes previously levied on Hindu pilgrims. He discouraged cow slaughter, participated in Hindu festivals, and encouraged the study of Sanskrit classics, ordering their translation into Persian.

In his personal religious life, though he was often regarded as purely opportunistic politically, Akbar stood at the confluence of many contemporary streams of thought, all militating against a strict Sunni orthodoxy and in favor of toleration. His famous *mahzan,* or declaration, of 1579, to which a group of religious scholars at his court subscribed, allowed Akbar certain powers of religious interpretation as a *mujthid* of Islam in matters not already explicitly covered by a clear scriptural text or by agreement among religious scholars. In 1575 Akbar built an *ibadat-khana* (house of worship) at Fatehpur-Sikri in which Muslims of many hues, Jesuit fathers from Goa, Zoroastrians, Hindu pandits, and yogis discussed religion with Akbar himself. After 1582 he and his mentors at court formulated the *tauhid-i-ilahi* or divine monotheism, compounded of ideas from Sufism and observances from Zoroastrianism, with Akbar himself as the adherents' *pir* or spiritual leader, but Akbar did not compel adherence to his beliefs in the empire at large. He died at Agra on October 16, 1605.

See also Afghanistan; Aurangzeb; Azad Jammu-Kashmir (AJK); Babar; Baluchistan; Hindustan.

References

Spear, P. *India: A Modern History.* Ann Arbor: University of Michigan Press, 1961

Stein, B. *A History of India.* New York: Macmillan, 1998

ALI, CHOUDHURY MUHAMMAD (1905–1980)

Choudhury Muhammad Ali was a civil servant and, briefly and controversially, Pakistan's prime minister from October 1955 to September 1956. Born in Jullundur, he qualified and practiced as an accountant before independence. In 1947 he became secretary-general to the government, the most important bureaucratic post and principally responsible for organizing Pakistan's civil service. Unlike Muhammad Ghulam, his close friend and associate, he nourished no personal political ambition.

In 1951 he became minister of finance and then in October 1955 succeeded Mohammad Ali Bogra as prime minister. He presided over the introduction of the One Unit Scheme and the 1956 Constitution, but he was uneasy in Pakistan's political world of shifting allegiances, especially after the creation of the Republican Party. Following the elections in 1956, Mirza did not want Suhrawardy to replace him as prime minister and tried energetically but unsuccessfully to dissuade Choudhury Muhammad Ali from resigning. But Suhrawardy's appointment as prime minister was nonetheless forthcoming on September 8, 1956.

During the early years of the Mohammed Ayub Khan regime, Ali acted as an adviser to the National Bank of Pakistan. In 1962 he joined the opposition, but soon increasing frailty prevented him from playing an active or formal role in the post-Ayub political scene. His lucid memoir, *The Emergence of Pakistan,* was soon recognized as a classic account of the birth of this country and its immediate aftermath, with fair-minded treatment of Pakistan's relations with India.

See also Ayub Khan, Mohammed; Bogra, Muhammad Ali; Mirza, Iskander; Muhammad, Ghulam; Suhrawardy, Huseyn Shaheed.

References

Ali, Chaudhri Muhammed. *The Emergence of Pakistan.* New York: Columbia University Press, 1967

Talbot, I. *Pakistan: A Modern History.* New York: Hurst and Company, 1998

ALI, CHOUDHARY RAHMAT (1897–1951)

Often regarded as a putative father of Pakistan and inventor of the name Pakistan, Rahmat Ali was an Indian Muslim living in Cambridge, England. Ali was born in Jalandhar in eastern Punjab. Educated in Lahore, he trained as a legal adviser and went to England in 1930 to study law at Cambridge University. He and a small circle of friends then started to lobby for the millions of Muslims in the five northern provinces of India, believing they should have their own nation. It was from Ali's small backstreet house, 3 Humberstone Road, Cambridge, on January 28, 1933, that his Pakistan declaration pamphlet *Now or Never: Are We to Live or Perish Forever?* was issued. In it he coined the word "Pakistan." "Pak" means spiritually pure in Urdu—Ali expected Pakistanis to become known as Paks—and "Stan" means land. The name was also a near acronym for Punjab, Afghania (North-West Frontier Province), Kashmir, Iran, Sind, Tukharistan, Afghanistan, and Balochistan. The name did not come into common use until 1940. Even the March 1940 resolution of the Muslim League from Lahore, calling for a separate state for India's Muslims, did not mention it, despite the fact that this resolution is often referred to as the Pakistan Resolution. When Ali visited Pakistan in 1948, his reputation foundered because he had no following or organization in Pakistan. One of his Cambridge tutors, Edward Welbourne, wrote in an obituary that "Ali's invention was seized by men of perhaps greater political gifts." Back in England, Ali worked as a lawyer and returned to Cambridge, where he died during a flu epidemic in 1951.

See also Afghanistan; Kashmir; Lahore; Muslim League; North West Frontier Province; Punjab.

References

Cohen, S. P. *The Idea of Pakistan.* Washington, DC: Brookings Institution Press, 2004

Gauhar, A. *Ayub Khan: Pakistan's First Military Ruler.* Lahore, Pak.: Sang-e-Meel Publications, 1993

ALIGARH

Aligarh is a town and headquarters of the district of the same name in Uttar Pradesh, India, and is famous as a center for Islamic culture and learning. Lying about 80 miles southeast of Delhi on the Grand Trunk Road, it has rail connections with Delhi, Calcutta (Kolcatta), and Bombay (Mumbai). The city itself lies west of the railway and is generally called Koil or Kol, Aligarh being the name of a fort beyond the civil station east of the railway. In and about the town are several tombs of Muslim saints. A large part of the city is built on swampy land around the fort; there are a number of good black-topped roads. Aligarh town has a number of degree colleges, but it is chiefly celebrated for the Aligarh Muslim University, founded in the late 19th century by Sir Sayyid Ahmad Khan. The university consists of a number of allied institutions, of which the engineering college, the polytechnic, and the ophthalmic institute are outstanding. The Azad Library, named after the central education minister in Jawaharlal Nehru's cabinet, has a fine building in the heart of the university campus.

See also Nehru, Jawaharlal; Uttar Pradesh.

References

Spate, O.H.K. *India and Pakistan: A General and Regional Geography,* 2nd ed. New York: Methuen, 1960

ALLIANCES AND ALIGNMENT

For at least 20 years from the mid 1950s until the mid 1970s, Pakistan seemed to be a quintessential aligned state, while India appeared to be quintessentially nonaligned. Alliances are instruments of national security; they are sought to supplement or save the national armed forces. The military support that is promised usually, but not always, requires the use of allied forces in time of need. Other forms of assistance may be involved too. One country may give its allies permission to station troops and weapons on its territory and to conduct maneuvers and other military exercises.

Alliances may extend to forms of cooperation other than military ones, but they are unlikely to survive in any substantial way if the military reason disappears or proves insufficient to prompt reciprocal planning and action—as Pakistan's experience with the Southeast Asia Treaty Organization (SEATO) and the Baghdad Pact showed. No alliance is likely to be an unqualified blessing. In some cases it may prove more of a drain than a supplement to a country's strength, and uncertainty is inherent in any promise of future assistance. The outstanding asset of an alliance is the military assistance expected in case of need and its deterrent effect on the enemy, even preceding an armed conflict. Moreover, a country may gain prestige as well as protection from having powerful allies or from denying them its actual or potential opponents. The chief international liability of an alliance, other than its effect on a country's reputation, is the obligation to assist an ally possibly under conditions that from a narrowly national point of view might suggest abstention from a conflict. A country fearing that the cost of involvement or entanglement in the quarrels of others will not be compensated by gains from the alliance may decide to go it alone, which in effect means inactivity, doing nothing with respect to a particular war.

A weak country often fears that it may become totally dependent on a more powerful ally; the stronger country fears that it will unduly restrict, and perhaps lose, its freedom of action by supporting a weak ally. Thus alliance obligations cannot be assumed to operate automatically. It is a recurrent argument of modern international politics whether great-power alliances are conducive to war, and the argument in general is as inconclusive as it is familiar. On the one hand it is claimed that alliances are regulatory mechanisms, devices bringing an element of order, of system, of predictability, even of restraint into the otherwise fluid and anarchical reality of interstate relations—that alliances thereby reduce the Hobbesian atmosphere of a war all against all. On the other hand, it is claimed, with almost equal plausibility, that alliances by their nature express, canalize, and institutionalize antagonisms and enmities in ways that serve to structure international relationships into patterns of conflict and into hostile coalitions and combinations.

In serious policy terms, however, such arguments never take place apart from and immune to the ideological and practical compulsions of time and place. In South Asia from the late 1940s onward, first the Soviet–American Cold War and then the Sino-American and Sino-Soviet Cold Wars intruded into and complicated attitudes and behavior toward alliances and alignments. An alignment is something less formal than an alliance. In the vocabulary of current international politics, an alignment means a diplomatic (and perhaps an economic or ideological) inclination or orientation; so, strictly, nonalignment means abstention from alignments. But in fact in contemporary usage, nonalignment came to mean something more formal, in a negative sense, namely nonalliance.

The collapse of the Soviet Union led to the end of the Cold War and to new fluidities in the world's patterns of alliances. Ironically the nonaligned movement (the NAM) also became more diffuse, and India's and Pakistan's roles in the NAM diminished in significance for their governments.

Furthermore, Indian and Pakistani relations within the Commonwealth continued in the 21st century to be rather placid for India and volatile for Pakistan—the latter coming under Commonwealth censure when it practiced military rather than civilian government. Zulfikar Ali Bhutto took Pakistan out of the Commonwealth in 1972, ostensibly as protest against what he regarded as the premature recognition of an independent Bangladesh. Pakistan rejoined the Commonwealth in 1989 after spells of military or capriciously civilian government with Benazir Bhutto, in effect overturning this aspect of her late father's policies. During these years Pakistan mostly experienced military rule and was openly criticized by India for this.

Following General Pervez Musharraf's coup in October 1999, Pakistan was suspended from the Commonwealth's councils. This suspension was ended in May 2004, and Pakistan resumed full membership. Pakistan was again suspended from the councils of the Commonwealth in October 2007 in direct reaction to President Musharraf's declaration of an emergency. In the 21st century, the government of India has been loath to criticize Pakistan's government openly whether within the Commonwealth or otherwise.

See also Baghdad Pact; Nonalignment; Southeast Asia Treaty Organization (SEATO).
References
Lyon, P. "India's Foreign Policy." In F.S. Northedge, ed. *The Foreign Policies of the Powers.* London: Faber and Faber, 1967
Mortimer, Robert A. *The Third World Coalition in International Politics.* Westport, CT: Praeger, 1980
Singham, A. W., and Shirley Hune. *Non-Alignment in an Age of Alignment.* London: Zed Books, 1986
Wight, Martin, Hedley Bull, and Carsten Holbraad. *Power Politics.* Leicester, UK: Leicester University Press, 1978

ALL INDIA ANNA DRAVIDA MUNNETRA KAZHAGAM (AIADMK)

The AIADMK is the ruling Tamil nationalist party in the Indian state of Tamil Nadu, led by a former film star, Jayalalitha. Jayalalitha has shown a recurrent ability to win state elections despite being enmeshed in a series of corruption cases. She led her party to landslide victories in the 2001 and 2004 state elections in Tamil Nadu to become, once again, chief minister of the state.

References
Hardgrave, R. L., and S. A. Kochanek. *India: Government and Politics in a Developing Nation,* 7th ed. Fort Worth, TX: Harcourt College Publishers, 2002

ALL-PAKISTAN MOHAJIR STUDENTS ORGANISATION (APMSO)

Founded in Karachi in June 1978 by Altaf Hussain and his close colleagues, the APMSO was a precursor of the Mohajir Qaumi Mahaz (MQM). Its formation sprang from mohajir anger over fraud in the application of admissions policies to colleges and universities. The APMSO soon outpaced the student wing of Jamaat-I-Islami and acquired a reputation for militancy. In 1980 Altaf Hussain was expelled from Karachi University following a preceding spell in prison. Many former APMSO students joined the MQM in March 1984. Subsequently the APMSO acted as a quasi-independent student wing of the MQM.

See also Ershad, Hussain Muhammad; Jamaat-I-Islami (JI); Karachi; Mohajir Qaumi Mahaz (MQM).
References
Talbot, I. *Pakistan: A Modern History.* New York: Hurst and Company, 1998

ALMATY MEETING (2002)

Almaty, Kazakhstan, was the venue for a security conference June 4–9, 2002, convened by Russian Prime Minister Vladimir Putin and attended by both General Pervez Musharraf and Atal Bihari

Vajpayee. At the latter's insistence, there were no bilateral face-to-face discussions between the leaders of Pakistan and India. This illustrated the desire of the leaders of both countries to publicize their case and their unwillingness to engage in direct discussion, still less in serious negotiations, at this time.

See also Musharraf, Pervez; Vajpayee, Atal Bihari.

AL-QAEDA/AL-QA'IDA

In Arabic, "al-Qaeda" means "The Base." It is the name of an Islamic network of organizations committed to the use of terrorism for the attainment of their aims. It was formed by the wealthy Saudi-born terrorist Osama bin Laden in the late 1980s to rally and mobilize Sunni Arabs who had fought in Afghanistan against the Soviet Union. It was based in Afghanistan until the removal of the Taliban regime there in late 2001, but it resumed as a major fighting force in Afghanistan in 2004–2007. The avowed agenda of al-Qaeda is the replacement of so-called heretic governments by Islamic governments based on the rule of Sharia (Islamic Law)—an ambition that encompasses several Arab regimes (especially Saudi Arabia), as well as the United States, whose influence throughout the Middle East it wishes to eliminate.

Bin Laden has issued several *fatwas* (religious rulings) calling on Muslims to take up arms against the United States and in a 1998 statement asserted that it was the duty of all Muslims to kill U.S. citizens and their allies. The number of members in the organization is unknown, but it probably totals several thousand. Since 1998 it has served as an umbrella organization called The Islamic World Front for the Struggle against the Jews and the Crusaders, which includes several Sunni Islamic extremist groups, such as the Egyptian al-Gama'a al-Islamiyya and the Islamic Movement of Uzbekistan.

The most notorious terrorist act of al-Qaeda was the suicidal attack by 19 of its members who hijacked and crashed four U.S. commercial planes onto U.S. sites on September 11, 2001—two into the World Trade Center in New York City, one into the

Smoke clouds the remaining structure at ground zero, the site of the World Trade Towers destroyed in an attack on September 11, 2001. (U.S. Air Force)

Pentagon in Washington, D.C., and one into a field in Shanksville, Pennsylvania, killing a total of more than 3,000. Al-Qaeda was also responsible for the bombing of U.S. embassies in Nairobi, Kenya, and in Dar es Salaam, Tanzania (both nearly simultaneously in 1998); the attack on the USS *Cole* in the port of Aden (2000); other attacks on U.S. military personnel in Kuwait and Yemen (2000–2002); and the bombing of a hotel in Mombassa, Kenya (2002). It may also have been implicated in several other terrorist acts, such as the nightclub bombings in Bali, Indonesia (in 2002 and 2005), and in central London on July 7, 2005.

See also Afghanistan; Taliban; Terrorism.

References

Adamec, L. W., and F. A. Clements. *Conflict in Afghanistan: An Encyclopedia. Roots of Modern Conflict.* Santa Barbara, CA: ABC-CLIO, 2003

Rappoport, D. C. *Inside Terrorist Organizations.* New York: Columbia University Press, 1988

Zahab, Mariam A., and Roy Olivier. *Islamic Networks: the Afghan-Pakistan Connection.* New York: Hurst and Company, 2004

AMRITSAR

Amritsar is the largest and most important city in India's state of Punjab. It is close to the India–Pakistan border on the main road from Delhi to Lahore. It is the center of Sikhism and the site of the Sikh's principal place of worship, the Golden Temple. The city was founded by Ramdas, the fourth guru, on a site granted by the emperor, Akbar. Ramdas also ordered the excavation of the sacred tank (lake), or *Amrita Saras* ("pool of nectar"), from which the city derives its name. In the middle of this tank on a small island, the fifth guru, Arjun Dev, built a temple. During the reign of Ranjit Singh (1792–1839), the upper part of the temple was decorated with a gold foil–covered copper dome, and since then it has been known as the Golden Temple, alternately called the *Darbar Sahib* ("court divine") by the Sikhs.

Amritsar became notorious in April 1919 when the local British commander, Brigadier General Reginald Dyer, ordered his troops to fire on those taking part in a prohibited political demonstration in a public enclosure, the Jallienwalla Bagh. At least

India's Golden Temple in the Punjabi city of Amritsar is Sikhism's holiest site. Located on a tract of land between the Ravi and Beas rivers, the Golden Temple is also a symbol of spiritual freedom, as it is open to all people, regardless of race, sex, or religion. (iStockPhoto.com)

370 Indians were killed and 1,200 wounded. A British government enquiry subsequently censured Dyer, and he resigned.

The massacre left a legacy of bitter resentment against the British among many Indians, and for many of them this episode demonstrated the moral bankruptcy of British imperial rule. In June 1984 and in May 1988, there was severe rioting in Amritsar with heavy losses of life when the Indian army sought to seize Sikh extremists demanding autonomy. In 1984 Sikh militants found refuge in the Golden Temple (and more than 30 other shrines), which suffered severe damage in Indian military operations, code-named Operation Bluestar. The leader of the Sikhs in the Golden Temple, Jarnail Singh Bhindranwale, a charismatic and puritanical preacher, was killed in the siege.

See also Bhindranwale, Sant Jarnail Singh; Gandhi, Indira; Gandhi, Rajiv; Sikhism.

References

Talbot, I. *India and Pakistan: Inventing the Nation.* London: Arnold Publishers, 2000

Tully, M., and S. Jacob. *Amritsar: Mrs. Gandhi's Last Battle.* New Delhi: Rupa and Company, 1985

ARMED FORCES

Historically there were two main British Imperial armies. The first was the British Army proper with its headquarters in London. In 1838 it was about 100,000 strong, with more than half of it usually stationed abroad. Most of its officers were rich men of fashion who bought their commissions. The rank and file enlisted for 21 years, and a large proportion of them were Irish Catholics or recruited from the Scottish Highlands, the southwest counties, and mid-Wales.

The second British army in India originated with the forces of the East India Company, was an agent of British power and influence, and lasted as such until the so-called Indian Mutiny (or War of Independence in current Indian historiography) of 1857. Thereafter, from 1858 until 1947, the armed forces in India played active roles as instruments of British power in South Asia and indeed throughout the Indian Ocean and its shore lines. Britain's Indian army played significant roles in several theaters during World Wars I and II.

Thus, before 1947, the armed forces of India were instruments of the Raj. They served to help maintain British imperial rule or paramountcy throughout the subcontinent and also were employed for British imperial policing and peacekeeping tasks in and around the India Ocean. In the two world wars of the 20th century, the contribution of Indian forces to Britain's war efforts was considerable and consequential. After 1947, those who had served the Raj before independence were, in the view of some nationalists, tinged as having been collaborators with the British. This was in comparison to those who joined the renegade self-styled Indian National Army, led by Subhas Chandra Bose, which had collaborated with the Japanese in World War II. These were regarded by some as brave patriots and by others as contemptible traitors. From 1947 until 1962, India's armed forces were relatively neglected and preoccupied with Pakistan. The Chinese attacks in 1962, at three difference positions along the de facto Sino-Indian boundaries, rapidly changed all that.

Henceforth India's armed forces were, and are, regarded as vital auxiliaries of the nation's integrity, security, and reputation. The chances of a successful coup in India mounted by the military have perhaps increased in recent years, but not by much because a civilian ethos and the subordination of the armed forces to civilian rule are well-entrenched features of the political system. A coup is unlikely to be seriously mounted, still less to succeed, for two major reasons. First, India is such a vast and complex country that even a well-planned and efficiently executed takeover plot carried out in New Delhi would not guarantee that the would-be coup makers could command support and exercise authority in such large urban and regional centers as Bombay (Mumbai), Calcutta (Kolcatta), Madras (Chennai) and elsewhere in the country. Put simply, there are formidable functional and logistical difficulties in the way of a successful military takeover.

Secondly, an ingrained professionalism of training and tradition throughout the upper echelons of India's armed forces predisposes the officer corps to accept and prefer civilian rule in the nation's government, with Pakistan often regarded as an "avoidance" model. Before 1947, most of India's army was recruited from the Punjab. Since 1947 recruitment has been much more variegated, and top-ranking army, navy, and air force commanders have been recruited, for example, from Bengal, from Madras, and from the Sikhs. In other words, recruitment is related to wide-ranging "nation building." (By contrast, Pakistan's armed forces are overwhelmingly recruited from the Punjab and from the Pushstuns with very little recruitment from Baluchistan or from the Sindh.)

Some commentators add a third consideration inhibiting a possible military takeover in India: the well-tried and working commitment of most Indians to a civil, indeed democratic, polity, demonstrated at many general elections since 1947 and especially in the widespread opposition to Mrs. Gandhi's Emergency between 1975 and 1977. Even so, it is also said, plausibly by some commentators, that this entrenched disposition of India's armed forces to respect a civilian system and ethos of government and administration has been undermined in recent years by two unwelcome trends: (1) the increasing use of the army in internal law-and-order operations (to quell civil unrest and communal violence—unwelcome tasks for any army); (2) from the 1980s especially, the alienation of some Sikhs from serving in the armed forces (where their presence and influence have been greatly in excess of their relatively small proportion in India's population).

India

Ever since 1947, but especially since 1962–1965, the governments of India and Pakistan have paid close attention as to the capacities and potential of each others' armed forces and this remains true today, though in the early 21st century India is more concerned with China's capabilities than with Pakistan's.

The supreme command of India's armed forces is vested in the president. In addition to armed forces of 1.325 million personnel in 2004, there were nearly 1.090 million active paramilitary forces, including 174,000 members of the Border Security Force based mainly in the Jammu-Kashmir regions. Military services are voluntary, but under the amended constitution it is regarded as a fundamental duty for every citizen to perform National Service when called upon.

Defense expenditures in 2003 were US$15.508 billion (US$15 per capita and 2.6 percent of GDP). In the period 1999–2003, India's spending on major conventional weapons was second to that of China, whose 2001–2002 expenditure was higher, although in 2003 that of India (at US$3.6 billion) was high. In

September 2003 India announced that it would be buying 66 Hawk trainer fighter jets, with delivery expected by 2009. In October 2003 agreement was reached for India to purchase Israel's sophisticated Phalcon early warning radar system. India has nuclear and chemical weapons, and its biological weapons research program is another awesome indicator of what future conflict between India and Pakistan might entail.

Army   The Army is organized into five commands, each divided into areas, which in turn are subdivided into subareas. The strength of the Army in 2004 was 1.1 million. There are four RAPID divisions, 18 infantry divisions, three armored divisions, and two artillery divisions. In all, there are 355 infantry battalions, 300 artillery regiments, 62 tank battalions, and 22 helicopter squadrons. Officers are trained at the Indian Military Academy, Dehra Dun (Uttaranchal). An Aviation Corps of 14 squadrons operates helicopters that are locally built under license. Army reserves number 300,000, with a further 500,000 personnel available as a second-line reserve force. There is a volunteer Territorial Army of 40,000. There are also numerous paramilitary groups, including the Ministry of Defence Rashtriya Rifles (numbering 40,000), the Indo-Tibetan Border Police (32,400), the State Armed Police (400,0000), the Civil Defence (453,000), the Central Industrial Security Force (95,000), and the Ministry of Home Affairs Assam Rifles (52,500)

Navy   The Navy has three commands: Eastern (at Visakhapatnam), Western (at Bombay), and Southern (at Kochi), the last a training and support command. The fleet is divided into two elements, Eastern and Western; and well-trained, all-volunteer personnel operate a mix of Soviet and Western vessels. In May 2003 India held joint naval exercises with Russia in the Arabian Sea for the first time since the collapse of the Soviet Union.

The principal ship is the light aircraft carrier, *Viraat*, formerly HMS *Hermes*, of 31,976 tons, completed in 1959 and transferred to the Indian Navy in 1987 after seeing service in the Falklands War. In 2003 India began construction of another aircraft carrier and began negotiations to purchase a third from the Russian navy. The fleet includes 12 Soviet-built diesel submarines and four new German-designed boats. There are also 24 destroyers and frigates. The Naval Air force, 5,000 strong, operates 35 combat aircraft (including 20 Sea Harriers) and 32 armed helicopters. The main bases are at Bombay (Mumbai, the main dockyard), Goa, Visakhapatnam, and Calcutta (Kolcatta) on the subcontinent and at Port Blair in the Andaman Islands. Naval personnel in 2004 numbered 55,000, including 5,000 Naval Air Arm and 1,200 marines.

Air Force   Units of the Indian Air Force (IAF) are organized into five operational commands: (1) Central at Allahabad, (2) Eastern at Shillong, (3) Southern at Thruvananthapuram, (4) South Western at Gandhinagar, and (5) Western at Delhi. The air force has 170,000 personnel.

The equipment includes nearly 690 combat aircraft, in 46 squadrons of aircraft, and about 40 armed helicopters. Major combat types include Su-30s, MiG-21s, MiG-23s, MiG-27s, MiG-29s, *Jaguars,* and Mirage 2000s. Air Force reserves numbered 140,000 in 2004.

Pakistan

A Council for Defence and National Security was set up in January 1997, disbanded in February 1997, and revived and took on wider scope in October in 1999 following General Pervez Musharraf's assumption of power. Pakistan's defense expenditure in 2003 totaled US$3.129 million (US$21 per capita representing 4.5 percent of GDP).

Army   Army strength in 2004 was 550,000, with about 292,000 personnel in paramilitary units: National Guard, Frontier Corps, and Pakistan Rangers. Army reserves number around 500,000. In April 2004 the army announced a cutback of 50,000 soldiers. Most armored equipment is of Chinese origin, including over 2,400 main battle tanks. There is an air wing with fixed-wing aircraft and 21 attack helicopters.

Navy   The combatant naval fleet includes seven French-built diesel submarines, three midget submarines for swimmer delivery, and eight ex-British frigates. The Naval Air wing operates six combat aircraft and nine armed helicopters. The principal naval base and dockyard are at Karachi. Naval personnel in 2004 totaled 24,000. There is a marine force estimated at 1,400 personnel and naval reserves of 5,000.

Air Force   The Pakistan Air Force came into being on August 14, 1947. It has its headquarters at Peshawar and is organized within three air defense sectors, in the northern, central, and southern areas of the country. There is a flying college at Risalpur and an aeronautical engineering college at Korangi Creek. Total strength in 2004 was 415 combat aircraft and 45,000 personnel. Equipment included Mirage IIIs, Mirage 5s, F-16s, J–5s, and J-7s. There were 8,000 Air Force reservists.

Nuclear Weapons   Pakistan began a secret weapons program in 1972 to reach parity with India but was restricted for some years by U.S. sanctions. The Stockholm International Peace Research Institute (SIPRI) estimates that Pakistan has manufactured between 30 and 50 nuclear weapons. In May 1998, Pakistan carried out six nuclear tests in response to India's tests earlier in the month. Pakistan is known to have a nuclear weapons program and, like India, has not signed the Comprehensive Nuclear-Test-Ban Treaty, which is intended to bring about a ban on any nuclear explosions. Pakistan has both chemical and biological weapon research programs.

References

Anthony, Ian. "Arms Exports to Southern Asia: Policies of Technology Transfer and Denial in the Supplier Countries." In Eric Arnett, ed. *Military Capacity and the Risk of War. China, India, Pakistan and Iran.* New York: Oxford University Press, 1997

Hackett, James. The *Military Balance.* Washington, DC: International Institute for Strategic Studies (IISS), annual, 1963 et seq.

Lyon, P. "The First Great Post-colonial State: India's Tryst with Destiny." In James Mayall and Anthony Payne, eds. *The Fallacies of Hope: The Post-colonial Record of the Commonwealth Third World.* Manchester, UK: Manchester University Press, 1991

Mason, P. *A Matter of Honour: An Account of the Indian Army, Its Officers and Men.* London: Jonathan Cape, 1974

Various annual publications. Solna, Sweden: Stockholm International Peace Research Institute

ARTHASHASTRA

Arthashastra is a treatise on the uses of power, dating from the early Mauryan state, whose authorship is usually ascribed to Kautilya (321–296 BCE) but which was not rediscovered until the early 20th century. Resembling, in some respects, the famous treatise of Niccolo Machiavelli, *The Prince*, the *Arthashastra* cynically instructs a would-be ruler in the devious tricks of the political world, including the use of spies and secret agents and various ways to commit murder. It is now believed by scholars to be more a theoretical treatise than a description of an actual court. In the 20th and 21st centuries, Kautilya's *Arthashastra* has been lauded by some Indian nationalists as evidence of an indigenous Indian realist approach to politics with a long pedigree. Renowned from its rediscovery and translation into English in the early 20th century, the tract by Kantilya (also named *Vishnuigupta* or *Chanakya*) is an exposition of the art of government, of the duties of kings, ministers, and officials, and of the methods of diplomacy.

References

Kautilya. *Arthasastra*. Translated by R. Shamasastry. Mysore, Ind.: Mysore Printing and Publishing House, 1915

Stein, B. *A History of India*. New York: Macmillan, 1998

ARYA SAMAJ

Literally the "society of the Aryans," this movement within Hinduism was founded by Dayanand Saraswati in 1875. Rejecting among other matters the "accretions" to the Vedas of caste, idol worship, and ritual, adherents campaigned for the "reconversion" of Muslims and others to Hinduism. The movement's greatest strength has been in the Punjab.

ASHOKA, EMPEROR (CA. 268–231 BCE)

Ashoka, or Asoka, was the last major Mauryan emperor. He was a convert to Buddhism and organized it as a recognized principal religion, while granting freedom to other religious sects. He convened the third great council of Buddhists at Patna and proclaimed his faith as far as his influence extended. He gave up armed conquest in favor of disseminating *dharma* (broadly moral principles) and inscribed his moral precepts and pronouncements widely on rocks and pillars. He founded hospitals, arranged for wells to be dug, and had avenues of trees planted. "Ashoka" is a name more revered today in India than in Pakistan.

References

Spear, P. *India: A Modern History*. Ann Arbor: University of Michigan Press, 1961

Stein, B. *A History of India*. New York: Macmillan, 1998

ASSAM

"Assam" is the name for a substantial part of northeastern India, almost cut off from the rest of the country on the west by West Bengal, on the north by Bhutan and then Arunachal Pradesh, on the east by Nagaland, Manipur, and Myanmar, on the south by Meghalaya, Bangladesh, Mizoram, and Tripura. From 1947 to 1971, Assam was a close and in part contiguous neighbor of East Pakistan. The territorial definition of Assam has changed considerably over the past 200 years. Assam first became a British protectorate at the close of the first Anglo-Burmese War in 1826. In the next decade extra portions of territory were included in the East India's Company's dominions, and in 1839 Assam was annexed to Bengal. In 1874 Assam was detached from Bengal. Upon the partition of Bengal in 1905, it was united to the eastern districts of Bengal.

From 1912 the chief commissionship of Assam was revived, and in 1921 a governorship was created. Upon the partition of India in 1947, almost the whole of the predominantly Muslim district of Sylhet was merged with East Bengal, which from then until 1971–1972 was East Pakistan. Dewangiri in North Kamrup was ceded to Bhutan in 1951. The Naga Hill district, administered by the Union government of India since 1957, became part of Nagaland in 1962, as India's relations with China worsened.

The autonomous state of Meghalaya within Assam, comprising the districts of Garo, Khasi, and Jaintia hills, came into existence on April 2, 1970, and achieved full independent statehood in January 1972 (just as an independent Bangladesh was emerging to the south). At the same time it was also decided to create a new Indian Union Territory Mizoram (now itself a state of the Union) from the Mizo Hills district.

During British imperial rule the province of Assam included also the district of Sylhet in the south, most of which is now part of Bangladesh (and also a major source of emigration to Britain and elsewhere). The British governor of Assam had supervision over Manipur, which upon partition in 1947 became an Indian Union territory and in 1972, as already noted, a state of the Indian Union. The population of Assam is heterogeneous and includes many people of distinctly Mongoloid physical type, among them such tribal groups as the Khasis and the Nagas. According to the 1961 census about 40 percent were recorded as speaking Assamese and about 24 percent Bengali. About 65 percent were Hindu and 22 percent Muslim; most of the rest professed Christianity or tribal beliefs. Today the state government within the Indian Union has a unicameral legislature under a governor and cabinet.

See also Bangladesh; Myanmar; West Bengal.

References

Spate, O.H.K. *India and Pakistan: A General and Regional Geography.* New York: Methuen, 1954

ASSASSINATION AND ATTEMPTED ASSASSINATIONS

Assassination is the deliberate killing of a person or persons to promote political aims, and it has a long history in South Asia. Political life in India and Pakistan since 1947 has been much punctuated by assassinations and would-be assassinations, but not much by Pakistanis killing Indian leaders or Indians killing Pakistani leaders. The list of top leaders—such as Mahatma Gandhi, Indira and Rajiv Gandhi, and Liaquat Ali Khan, not to mention unknown or little known victims who have been assassinated—is thus considerable.

Indeed, throughout South Asia, certainly including Bangladesh and Sri Lanka, the record of deliberate killings to eliminate rivals and to promote assassins' political purposes is extensive and thereby challenges political change by election, referendum, or other peaceful methods. Assassinations of political leaders tend to occur especially when there are no settled and practical rules for political succession and/or where political polarization within a particular country is so intense that opposed political leaders tend to regard themselves as playing a zero-sum game.

Attempted assassinations are more frequent than actual assassinations. Obviously not all attempted assassinations succeed, but the frequency of attempts provides serious indications of stasis (that is, civil unrest) and political instability in a society. Thus assassinations and, even more, attempted assassinations are much more commonplace than is often realized, and regrettably they must be expected to punctuate public, especially political, life in South Asia in the future.

The terrorist attacks on American symbols of power on September 11, 2001, began a much stepped-up campaign against terrorists by the United States and others, including moves, where possible, to foresee and forestall acts of suicidal destruction. Political assassinations in independent India have generally occurred in crowded public places, whereas in Pakistan such killings of political leaders, as with Liaquat Ali Khan or Zia-ul-Haq, have more often involved personnel from the armed forces or have targeted military or political leaders such as Pervez Musharraf or Benazir Bhutto in October 2007.

The Hindu extremist who shot Mahatma Gandhi in January 1948 killed him at a prayer meeting. Rajiv Gandhi was killed by a Tamil suicide bomber at an election meeting in 1991. Generally, assassinations of top leaders have not been instigated by people authorized by the state to bear arms. One invidiously dramatic exception to this was Mrs. Indira Gandhi's assassination in 1984 by two of her personal bodyguards. These were Sikhs seeking vengeance for the Indian army's assault earlier that year on the Sikhs' sacred Golden Temple in Amritsar, which had led to the death of Jarnail Singh Bhindranwale, damage to the shrine, and extensive anti-Sikh violence—the latter described by some as the most serious communal violence in India since partition.

Whilst assassination is not a major feature of Indo-Pakistan relations, the frequent incidence of this form of political violence reveals the fissures and pathology at work within each of these two countries.

See also Abdullah, Dr. Farooq; Arthashastra; Communalism; Gandhi, Indira; Gandhi, Rajiv; Khan, Liaqat Ali; Musharraf, Pervez; Terrorism.

References

Adamec, L.W., and F. A. Clements. *Conflict in Afghanistan: An Encyclopaedia. Roots of Modern Conflict.* Santa Barbara, CA: ABC-CLIO, 2003

Khilnani, Sunnil. *The Idea of India.* London: Hamish Hamilton, 1997

Rappoport, D. C. *Assassination and Terrorism.* Toronto: Canadian Broadcasting Corporation, 1971

ATTLEE, CLEMENT RICHARD (1883–1967)

C. R. Attlee was Britain's prime minister from 1945 to 1951 and a major influence in determining the nature and timing of India's independence. Despite his terse and dry speech and prose style, he was a convinced and at times impassioned believer in the potential of the Commonwealth, of international organization, and even of world govern-

As prime minister of Great Britain from 1945 to 1951, Attlee played a key role in bringing about Indian and Pakistani independence and shaping their initial relations. (Library of Congress)

Attlee was born in Putney (London), educated at Haileybury (a British public school famous for educating boys who later went on to careers in India), and University College Oxford. He became a barrister but spent much of his early adulthood helping with social problems in the poorer part of London's East End. A major in World War I, he served at Gallipoli and in Mesopotamia as well as in France.

He entered Parliament as a Labour MP in 1922 and remained in the Commons until he was created Earl Attlee in 1955. For the last 20 of his years in the Commons, he led the Labour party and was prime minister of the first Labour government to enjoy parliamentary majorities. While serving as deputy prime pinister in Sir Winston Churchill's wartime coalition government, Attlee was also dominions secretary (February 1942 to September 1943). Becoming prime minister in 1945, he pushed for the independence of India and Pakistan in 1947 and soon came to recognize the general need for postwar decolonization, beginning with independence for Burma and dominion status for Ceylon—both achieved in 1948. A principal architect of the partition of British India, Attlee got on well with Jawaharlal Nehru but not with Mohammad Ali Jinnah.

Attlee regarded the British Empire and the Commonwealth as "the creation of sea-power," arguing (in 1945) that in "the air age" it was strategically indefensible, except through the United Nations. Britain assumed trusteeship for Italy's former colonies in Cyrenaica and Somaliland and sought energetically to end Britain's Palestine mandate. In May 1947, Attlee set up a cabinet committee on the future of the Commonwealth, chairing its meetings himself: "We want no unwilling partners in the British Commonwealth," he said. His views on the looser structure of the Commonwealth links prevailed in the London Declaration of April 1949, and while he was Britain's prime minister he chaired meetings of an 8- to 10-member Commonwealth, which from 1949 included India and Pakistan as full members.

ment. He was a deft and businesslike chair of the many committees he led in his extensive public life. As a member of the special commission set up by the British government in the interwar period to examine developments in India—the Simon Commission—Attlee visited India (and Burma) twice, February to April 1928 and October 1928 to April 1929. The Simon Report, published in June 1930, recommended an immediate grant of responsible government in the provinces and negotiations with the princely rulers over the structure of central government. These proposals fell short of dominion status because the commissioners felt this should not be accorded until Hindu–Muslim communal relations had improved and sufficient Indian officers had been trained for senior posts in the armed forces. In 1935, as the Labour Party's newly elected leader, Attlee devoted an early radio broadcast to India's claim for dominion status. As prime minister, Attlee selected First Earl Louis Mountbatten as viceroy and personally piloted the India Independence Bill through every stage of the House of Commons until it became law on July 18, 1947.

See also Churchill, Sir Winston L. Spencer; Jinnah, Mohammed Ali; Mountbatten of Burma; Nehru, Jawaharlal.

References

Beckett, F. *Clem Attlee: A Biography.* London: Richard Cohen Books, 1997

Moore, R. J. *Escape from Empire: The Attlee Government and the Indian Problem.* Oxford, UK: Clarendon Press, 1983

AURANGZEB (1618–1707)

Aurangzeb (Mohi-ud-Din Mohammad, also called Alamgir I) was the last of the great Mogul emperors of India. He was a zealous Muslim during whose reign (1658–1707) the empire reached its greatest extent but lost its inner cohesion. Born in early November 1618 at Dohad in Gujerat, he was the third son of the Emperor Shah Jahan by Mumtaz Mahal. He was well educated and had scholarly knowledge of Arabic and Persian, of the Koran, and of the Hadith, or traditional sayings of the Prophet. His mother tongue was Urdu, but he also conversed in Hindu and Chagatai Turki.

His appointment in 1636 as viceroy of the Deccan provinces first brought him into prominence, but tense relations with his father and the rivalry of his elder brother, Dara, led to his resignation in 1644. In 1645, however, he was appointed governor of Gujerat. In 1647 he was sent to be governor and commander-in-chief in Balk and Badakshan, as Shah Jahan was attempting the reconquest of the Mogul's ancestral lands in central Asia. Operations against the Uzbeks were indecisive, however, and a severe drain on the imperial finances. Aurangzeb repeatedly demonstrated his courage and skill, but the war-torn lands could not support his army, and he was ordered to retreat before the winter.

In 1648 he was made governor of Multan, to which Sind was added in 1649. In 1649 he was also ordered to relieve Kandahar, besieged by the Persians, but it had surrendered before his arrival, and, lacking heavy siege artillery, he was unable to dislodge the Persian garrison. He had but nominal command of a second attempt with greater force in 1652, which also failed. In summer 1652 he was again appointed viceroy of the Deccan. There he reformed the administration and sought to increase revenues. His aggressive wars against Golconda (1656) and Bijapur (1657) were both halted by Shah Jahan.

Shah Jahan's serious illness in September 1657 was the signal for a war of succession, in which Aurangzeb ruthlessly supplanted his brothers. Shah Jahan himself was closely confined in the fort at Agra from June 1658 until his death in 1666. On July 31, 1658, Aurangzeb crowned himself emperor with

Mughal prince Aurangzeb takes his father, Jahan Shah, prisoner in 1658. When Jahan Shah became ill the previous year, he had chosen another son, Dara Shikoh, as his successor. The brothers' power struggle turned into civil war, and when Jahan Shah recovered from his illness, he was imprisoned by Aurangzeb, who then claimed the throne for himself. (Library of Congress)

the title Alamgir (Conqueror of the World). The first half of Aurangzeb's long reign was devoted to consolidating his power in northern India. He seized western Assam in 1662 but lost it again in 1667. He quelled the pirates of Chittagong in 1666, and pacified but could not crush the Pathan tribes in the province of Kabul (1667 and 1672–ca.1680).

The second half of his reign from 1681 was spent fighting in the Deccan, principally against the Marathas. By his conquest of the Muslim Shiah kingdoms of Bijapur (1685–1686) and Golconda (1685–1687), the Mogul empire, by this time at its most vast, was extended to reach from the Coromandel coast to Chittagong and the Hindu Kush. Within the empire, however, the Marathas, unsubdued, grew in strength.

Aurangzeb's Deccan campaigns proved both a military and a political miscalculation: By long absence from the centers of power and wealth in the north, he lost control there; by continuous wars he exhausted the imperial treasury and desolated his lands. Despite his narrow and ruthless efficiency as a general and administrator, his authority was everywhere in dispute when his last illness came upon him. This failure was considerably due to his reversal of Akbar's policy of conciliating the subject Hindu population. Unlike Akbar, Aurangzeb was a militant orthodox Sunni Muslim, who had claimed the throne as the champion of orthodoxy against the heretical views of his elder brother, Dara. Aurangzeb's accession was followed by increasingly puritanical ordinances enforced by *Muhtasibs,* or censors of morals, and courtiers were forbidden to salute in the Hindu fashion.

Aurangzeb's treatment of Hindus was severe: Their fairs were prohibited and religious festivals restricted; their idols, temples, and shrines were often destroyed; the employment of Hindus in the administration was discouraged; the defiant Sikh guru Teg Bahadur was arrested and, refusing to embrace Islam, beheaded; and in 1679 the *jizya,* or poll tax on non-Muslims that had been abolished by Akbar, was reimposed. Eventually his harsh inflexible policies produced a widespread Hindu reaction in the Deccan, and the Maratha revolt spread; in northern India the Rajputs, Jats, Sikhs, and others joined the revolt. In effect his empire had become rotten at its core, and it crumpled to pieces in the hands of his sons, among whom he had tried to divide it before his death. Aurangzeb died on March 3, 1707 in Ahmednagar.

See also Akbar Emperor (Jalal-Ud-Din-Mohammed); Islam; Sikhism; Sind.

References

Spear, P. *India: A Modern History.* Ann Arbor: University of Michigan Press, 1961
Stein, B. *A History of India.* New York: Macmillan, 1998

AURORA, JAGJIT SINGH (1916–2005)

Lieutenant General Jagjit Singh Aurora led the Indian army, which defeated Pakistan in a 13-day war in December 1971 and produced an independent Bangladesh. Jagjit Singh Aurora was born the son of an engineer in Jhelum in what is now Pakistan. He was commissioned into the 2nd Punjab Regiment in 1939, after his graduation from the Indian Military Academy, and went on to command it during the 1947–1948 hostilities with Pakistan in Kashmir. He had reached the rank of brigadier by the time he was involved in border hostilities with Chinese troops in 1961–1962.

In 1970–1971, as relations between West and East Pakistan worsened and Indo-Pakistan relations deteriorated appreciably, it seemed to many observers that the breakup of Pakistan had become unavoidable. This seemed very likely from Pakistan's national elections of December 1970, in which the electorate of East Pakistan voted overwhelmingly for Bengali nationalism. Pakistani troops intervened to stop the nationalist Awami League from taking power—virtually a hopeless task given that their lines of supply were stretched over 1,000 miles from West Pakistan, from which they were separated by Indian territory, and given that the Indian government and people were sympathetic to the Bengali cause. Thousands of civilians died at the hands of Pakistan before the outbreak of war.

East Pakistan seceded from West Pakistan, so that in less than two weeks Pakistan had lost 55,000 square miles of its territory and 70 million of its people—Bangladesh's immediate inheritance—in an operation meticulously prepared months in advance by Aurora and others. Aurora had also been closely involved in training and equipping the Mukhti Bahini, a ragtag group (or groups) of Bengali freedom fighters who were transformed into an effective guerrilla force that harassed and demoralized the Pakistanis.

All in all, this softened up the Pakistanis in readiness for India's strike, which was launched after West Pakistan carried out bombing raids on several Indian airfields on December 3, 1971. The raids had been preceded by several Pakistani attacks on Mukhti Bahini camps inside India. An Indo-Pakistan war was now inevitable. Aurora had helped to oversee the logistical preparations for the coming battles, including the improvement of roads, communications, and bridges, as well as the movement of 30,000 tons of supplies close to the border of East Pakistan. Even so, the Indian Army could not have anticipated how quickly the Pakistani troops in the east would be routed. Instead of attacking Pakistani positions head-on, Aurora ordered his troops to bypass them wherever possible and head straight for Dhaka (earlier Dacca). The key breakthrough came when thousands of forces succeeded in crossing the Meghna River, which the Pakistanis had left unguarded, having blown up the only major bridge. Local people ferried Indian troops across the river in huge numbers of small boats under cover of darkness. "That was the turning point," Aurora later recalled.

After his retirement from the army, Aurora spent several years as an MP in the Rajya Sabha (upper house of India's parliament) for the Sikh party, the Akali Dal. He fiercely criticized the Indian army's attack on the Golden Temple in Amritsar in 1984, the Sikhs' holiest shrine. This action was planned and justified by Prime Minister Indira Gandhi's government to flush out armed Sikh militants who had taken up positions inside the temple. He was also a leading activist on behalf of the victims of anti-Sikh riots in Delhi in 1984, which followed the assassination of Indira Gandhi by her Sikh bodyguards. Aurora was born on February 13, 1916, and died on May 3, 2005, aged 89.

See also Azad Jammu-Kashmir (AJK); Amritsar; Awami League (AL); Bangladesh.

References
Obituary. *The Times, India* (May 3, 2005)

AUTONOMY

Autonomy is the power or right of self-government, especially partial self-government. In recent South Asian history, autonomy is an idea or formula for something less than full independent statehood. The avowed quest for autonomy generally proposes a reformist program, stopping short of secession or a full breakaway from an existing political system, though thwarted ambitions for autonomy may escalate into secessionist demands—as occurred with the Awami League in East Pakistan, eventually becoming Bangladesh. Ever since 1947–1948, there have been recurrent, though in detail different, proposals for Kashmir to be less than fully independent but vested with distinctive autonomy. Autonomy can thus seem to be an opposite of centralization, though it is most often a particular recipe for decentralization.

See also Awami League (AL); Azad Jammu-Kashmir (AJK); Bangladesh.

References
Hardgrave, R. L. Jr., and S. A. Kochanek. 2000. *India: Government and Politics in a Developing Nation*, 6th ed. Fort Worth, TX: Harcourt College Publishers, 2000

AWAMI LEAGUE (AL)

A party, political organization, and movement founded by H. S. Suhrawardy in 1950, the Awami League (AL) soon became centered in Dhaka (earlier Dacca), gaining considerable support during and after the 1952 Bengali language disturbances. It campaigned during the 1954 East Pakistan provincial elections in a united front alliance with the Krishak Praja Party (KPP) following the dismissal of the United Front government. Fazlul Haq split the Awami League. One sector took up a 6-Point Programme calling for the establishment of full provincial autonomy for East Pakistan in light of the Lahore Resolution of 1940. Under this plan the center would be left only with responsibility for foreign affairs and national defense. An Awami League government, led by Atwar Rahman Khan, was established in Dhaka in August 1956. Tension soon grew between it and the national coalition of the Awami League and Republican Party of Suhrawardy. The party was in opposition during the Mohammed Ayub Khan era (1958–1969).

Following Suhrawardy's death in 1963, Mujib-Ur Rahman became the AL's leading figure. The party secured a massive victory in the 1970 East Pakistan polls, securing 160 of the 162 National Assembly seats, thus also polarizing emphatically the differences between East and West Pakistan. The failure to evolve working relations between the two wings of Pakistan led to growing tension and to the emergence of Bangladesh under the AL's leadership. Since Sheikh Mujib-Ur's assassination in August 1975, the AL has been one of the two major parties in Bangladesh [the Bangladesh National Party (BNP) being the other] that have alternated in office. Mujib-Ur Rahman's daughter, Sheikh Hasina, has been head of the AL and prime minister when the AL is in office.

See also Ayub Khan, Mohammed; Bangladesh; Bhutto, Zulfikar Ali; Lahore Resolution; Rahman, Sheikh Mujib-Ur; Suhrawardy, Huseyn Shaheed.

References
James, Morrice Sir. *Pakistan Chronicle*. New York: Hurst and Company, 1993
Maniuzzaman, T. *The Bangladesh Revolution and Its Aftermath*. Dhaka, Bang.: University Press Ltd., 1988

AWAMI NATIONAL PARTY (ANP)

The Awami National Party (ANP) was founded in 1988 following the merger of the National Democratic Party, the Awami Tehrik of the Sindh, and the Pakistan National Party led by a Baloch nationalist. Wali Khan, son of the so-called Frontier Gandhi,

Abdul Ghaffar Khan, became its first president. This coalition party split shortly after its launching and its influence was limited mostly to the Frontier, though even there dissidents broke away to form the Pakhtun Liberation Front. The ANP aligned itself with former leading opponents, the Muslim League and Janaat-I-Islami, in the Islamic Democratic Alliance (IDA) in 1990.

One of its leaders held office in Nawaz Sharif's federal cabinet. The ANP maintained its anti-Pakistan People's Party (PPP) alliance with Nawaz Sharif in the 1993 elections. Then it had more support than the Pakistan Muslim League-Nawaz (PML-N) and gained 31 out of 83 Frontier Assembly seats along with nine National Assembly constituencies. It finally split with the PML-N, accusing Nawaz Sharif of betrayal regarding the remainder of the North West Frontier Province (NWFP) at Pukhtoonktiwa.

See also Jamaat-I-Islami (JI); Muslim League; North West Frontier Province; Pakistan People's Party (Shaheed Bhutto) PPP (SB).

References

Talbot, I. *Pakistan: A Modern History.* New York: Hurst and Company, 1998

AYODHYA

Ayodhya is a town in northern India in the State of Uttar Pradesh, where in 1992 the 16th-century Babri mosque was demolished by Hindu zealots, who claimed it to be the exact birthplace of their god, Lord Rama. The mosque's destruction triggered off nationwide Hindu–Muslim riots that left more than 2,000 people dead.

One of the leaders of the campaign to demolish the mosque was L. K. Advani, who went on to be deputy prime minister in Atal Bihari Vajpayee's government (2004). Many blamed India's prime minister in 1992, P. V. (Pamulaparti Venkata) Narasimha Rao, of inexcusable inaction toward the baying Hindu mobs surrounding the mosque, maintaining that he could have prevented the catastrophe by mobilizing the security forces on standby waiting to be deployed. For his hesitation and inactivity Rao was dubbed by his detractors *mauri baba,* or Silent Old Man. Harsher critics asserted that Rao gratuitously allowed the mosque to be demolished, believing that with its destruction the problem would disappear. If so, the assessment could not have been more flawed because the issue lingers and hovers menac-ingly over Indian politics and Hindu–Muslim relations even today.

See also Advani, Lal Krishna; Rao, P. V. Narasimha; Uttar Pradesh.

References

Advani, L. K. *Ayodhya Before and After.* New Delhi: Janadhikar Samiti, 1992

Bharatiyajanat Party. *White Paper on Ayodhya and the Rama Temple Movement.* New Delhi: Author, 1993

Guha, Ramachandra. *India after Gandhi. The History of the World's Largest Democracy.* New York: Macmillan, 2007

AYUB KHAN, MOHAMMED (1907–1974)

Ayub Khan Mohammed, a Pathan and Pakistani soldier, was president of Pakistan for 11 years (1958–1969), a time that included the war with India in 1965. Born in Abbottabad, he was educated at Aligarh Muslim University and Britain's Royal Military Academy at Sandhurst. He served in World War II and in 1951 became the first Pakistani commander-in-chief of Pakistan's army and field marshal in 1959. He became president of Pakistan in 1958 after mounting a bloodless army coup, soon establishing a stable economy and political autocracy, tempered by what he called basic democracy at local levels. In May of 1965, he led Pakistan during the armed clashes with India over the Rann of Kutch and again in a harsher conflict in September in the immediately subsequent Indo-Pakistan war—a war that seemed to produce a military and political stalemate but whose long-term economic and social costs were much heavier for Pakistan than for India.

In March 1969, after widespread civil disorder and violent opposition from both right and left wings, Ayub relinquished power and martial law was reestablished under a government headed for just over two disastrous years by General Yahya Khan. In 1967 Ayub published an autobiography entitled *Friends Not Masters.*

See also Khan, Agha Muhammad Yahya; Kutch (Cutch), Rann of; Pathans.

References

Ayub Khan. *Friends Not Masters: A Political Autobiography.* New York: Oxford University Press, 1967.

Gauhar, A. *Ayub Khan: Pakistan's First Military Ruler.* Lahore, Pak.: Sang-e-Meel Publications, 1993

AZAD, (MAULANA) ABUL KALAM (1888–1958)

Abul Kalam Azad was a leader among Muslim thinkers and politicians who advocated a pan-Indian

Pakistani president Ayub Khan and Jacqueline Kennedy meet in 1962. Khan sought American support during a critical year for India.
(Library of Congress)

nationalism based on the comfortable coexistence of all religious and ethnic communities and thus was initially opposed to partition. Azad was one of the earliest political thinkers of 20th-century India to advocate secularist democracy for an independent India. Abul Kalam Ghulam Muhiyuddin (pseudonym, Azad) was born in Mecca. His mother was Arab, and his father, Maulana Khairuddin, was a Bengali Muslim of Afghan origin. From a very early age, Azad showed an active interest in politics. He developed an interest in the pan-Islamic doctrines of Afghani and the Aligarh thought of Sir Syed Ahmed Khan.

He traveled widely, visiting Afghanistan, Iraq, Egypt, Syria, and Turkey before returning to his family home in Calcutta. Azad believed that Indian nationalism had to be well grounded in secular concepts of politics and statehood. As a leading congressman, he supported the Khilafat Movement not with the aim of restoring Ottoman rule, but rather to strengthen the hands of the Young Turks who, according to him, represented the true spirit of the original Khilafat. After World War I, Azad became a member of the central leadership of the All India National Congress and a colleague of Motilal Nehru, Jawaharlal Nehru, and Chitta Ranjan Das. Soon he was recognized by Mahatma Gandhi as one of his most trusted followers. He was elected the president of the special session of Congress in Delhi in 1923 and again in Ramgarh in 1940, and he was president of Congress from 1940 to 1946.

In all the negotiations with the British, from the Cripps Mission of 1942 to Cripps Cabinet Mission of 1946, Azad was closely consulted by the Mahatma Gandhi especially on matters of communality and constitutionality. Azad was also one of the negotiating members during both missions, but, with the strengthening of the Pakistan movement and worsening Hindu–Muslim relations, Azad's influence waned somewhat.

Later, in his autobiography, he recorded a frustration of his that the partition of British India could have been avoided had the Congress High Command respected his idea about the accommodation of the viewpoint of Jinnah and the Muslim League. He served long periods in prison during the Raj. After 1947 Azad stood for India as a secular state, one in which Hindu–Muslim relations were peaceful with due respect for India's Muslims. Like Mahatma Gandhi, he favored cordial Indo-Pakistan relations, but his influence after 1947 was diminishing and marginal, despite being India's minister for education from 1947 to his death.

See also Afghanistan; Aligarh; Cripps Mission; Gandhi, Mohandas Karamchand; Jinnah, Mohammed Ali; Nehru, Jawaharlal; Muslim League.

References

Azad, Abul Kalam. *India Wins Freedom.* New York: Longman, 1959

Clarke P. *The Cripps Version: The Life of Sir Stafford Cripps.* London: Allen Lane, 2002

Guha, R. *India after Gandhi. The History of the World's Largest Democracy.* New York: Macmillan, 2007

AZAD JAMMU-KASHMIR (AJK)

"Azad" (meaning free) is the Pakistani title for its Kashmiri territorial holdings, that is, Azad Jammu-Kashmir (AJK), which India calls Pakistan-occupied Kashmir (POK). It was established in 1949 after Kashmir was split as a result of the partition of what was called British India. AJK had an estimated population of approximately 3 million by the end of 2004 living in its six districts: Muzaffarabad (the capital), Mirpur, Bagh, Kotti, Rawalakot, and Poonch. AJK has its own institutions, but its political life is heavily controlled by Pakistani authorities, especially the military.

References

Jones, O. B. *"Pakistan": Eye of the Storm.* New Haven, CT: Yale University Press, 2002

AZIZ, SHAUKAT (1949–)

Following his election on August 27, 2004, Shaukat Aziz was sworn in as Pakistan's 23rd prime minister and leader of the lower house of the federal legislature, the 342-member National Assembly. Aziz was elected by 191 votes, with all the opposition members boycotting the election in protest against the speaker's refusal to allow the candidacy of Javed Hashmi of the Alliance for the Restoration of Democracy (ARD), who had been imprisoned in April for sedition.

The caretaker prime minister, Chaudry Shujaat Hussain, had already resigned on August 25. The way had been cleared for Aziz to become prime minister by his victories on August 19 in two separate by-elections to the National Assembly, in the constituencies of Attock in Punjab province and Tharpaarkan in Sind province. In both constituencies, Aziz contested the elections as a candidate for the ruling Pakistan-Muslim League–Qaid-I-Azam (PML-QA); the parliamentarian candidates of the Pakistan People's Party (PPP) took second place. Appointed finance minister in Pervez Musharraf's first cabinet after the October 1999 coup and returning to Pakistan from a 30-year career in the United States as a Citibank executive, Aziz was credited with subsequently stabilizing Pakistan's economy. However, with his lack of political experience or popular support, Aziz was regarded as essentially a bureaucrat, chosen by the president to carry on Musharraf's policies, and he ceased to play that role in 2007 when Musharraf replaced him as prime minister.

See also Musharraf, Pervez; Muslim League; Pakistan People's Party (Shaheed Bhutto) PPP (SB); Punjab; Sind.

References

Musharraf, Pervez. *In the Line of Fire: A Memoir.* New York: The Free Press, 2006

B

BABAR (1483–1530)

Babar (sometimes Babur) the conqueror, Zahir al-Din Muhmmad, was the first Mughal emperor of India and is well-known to all historically minded Indians and Pakistanis. The nephew of Sultan Mahmud Mirza of Samarkand, he sought—unsuccessfully—as a young man to establish himself as ruler there, but from 1504 turned his attention with greater success toward Afghanistan, invading Kabul in that year. A further attempt to win Samarkand in 1511 was again unsuccessful.

The death of Sikandar Lodi in 1517 brought civil war to the Afghan Lodi empire in India, and Babar took advantage of the conflict to invade India, defeating Ibrahim Lodi decisively at the Battle of Panipat in 1526 and laying the foundation for the Mughal empire. The following year he defeated the Hindu Rajput confederacy and, despite continuing resistance from the Hindus and from the Afghans, the military strength of the Mughal enabled him to consolidate his gains. A soldier of great talent, he was also a cultured man with interests in architecture, music, and literature. Himself a Muslim, he initiated a policy of toleration toward his non-Muslim subjects that was continued by most of his successors and became a hallmark of the Mughal empire at its height.

See also Akbar, Emperor (Jalal-Ud-Din Mohammed); Afghanistan; Aurangzeb.

References
Kaur, Surinder, and Sanyal, Tapan. *The Secular Emperor Babar.* Sirhind, Ind.: Lokgeet Pradashan, 1987
Kaur, Surinder, and Sher Singh. *The Secular Emperor Babar, a Victim of Indian Partition.* New Delhi: Genuine Publishers, 1991
Spear, P. *India: A Modern History.* Ann Arbor: University of Michigan Press, 1961
Stein, B. *A History of India.* New York: Macmillan, 1998

BAGGE TRIBUNAL

A judicial tribunal was set up by an Indo-Pakistan agreement of December 14, 1948, to resolve boundary disputes between East and West Bengal and between East Bengal and Assam. The tribunal, of three members, under the chairmanship of Justice Bagge (Sweden) had as its other members a retired judge of the Madras high court (India's nominee) and a justice of the Dacca high court (Pakistan's nominee).

The tribunal's report, published on February 1950, settled two of the disputes in India's favor, one in favor of Pakistan, and the fourth in favor of neither. The report proposed that Indian and Pakistani experts should demarcate the boundary lines within one year from February 5, 1950, and that no unilateral action should be taken in the interim by either side.

References
Razvi, Mujtaba 1971. *The Frontiers of Pakistan.* Karachi, Pak.: Dacca National Publishing House Ltd.

BAGHDAD PACT (1955–1958)

The Baghdad Pact was the journalistic label for the complex formal linkages made among Iran, Iraq, Turkey, Pakistan, and Britain in 1955 with the United States informally associated. Comembership of alliances with the United States and/or with other Western powers in the mid 1950s [as well as with the Southeast Asia Treaty Organization (SEATO) from 1954] was regarded by Pakistani leaders as strengthening their country against a possible threat from India. Nuri-e-Said, who was prime minister of Iraq in 1955 (and long associated with Britain) until his assassination at the same time as his monarch King Faisal, failed to recruit any Arab states to the pact. Instead, the Baghdad Pact became widely regarded throughout the Arab world as a tool of Anglo-American policy (a view that Egypt's new

Four Middle East premiers pose with Harold Macmillan, British foreign secretary, at the inaugural meeting of the Baghdad Pact in Baghdad, Iraq, in November, 1955. Signed in 1955 by Iraq and Turkey, the pact established a defense coalition between Iraq, Turkey, Pakistan, Iran, and Great Britain. Iraq withdrew from the pact shortly after the 1958 coup that brought down King Faisal II and put Abdul Karim Qassem in power. (AP/Wide World Photos)

leader Gamal Abdel Nasser and Jawaharlal Nehru shared). Though the United States gave bilateral economic and military aid to the signatories of the pact, it did not formally join this basically short-lived and ostensibly multilateral association. With Iraq's withdrawal from the Baghdad Pact in 1958, it was renamed the Central Treaty Organization (CENTO).

See also Alliances and Alignment; Nehru, Jawaharlal; Southeast Asia Treaty Organization (SEATO).

References

Jansen, G. H. *Afro-Asia and Non Alignment.* London: Faber and Faber, 1966

BALUCHISTAN

Situated within the southwestern extremities of Pakistan and deriving its name from its chief inhabitants, the Baloch or Balochi (Baluchi). Baluchistan

(or Balochistan) is Pakistan's biggest and least populated province. In terms of area, Baluchistan is the largest of Pakistan's provinces (134,050 square miles). Though the land is rich in coal and gas, it is mostly desert, and the people are poor. The province stretches from the Gomal River in the northeast to the Arabian Sea in the south and from the borders of Iran and Afghanistan in the west and northwest to the Suliman Mountains and Kirhar Hills in the east. Its coastline is known as Makran, which continues into Iran.

Balochistan was an independent state in the early 18th century and then entered into treaty relations with British India in 1854 and 1876. The British then obtained a small area around Quetta and named it British Balochistan. They also gained the right to fortify and administer Quetta and Bolan and to bring troops into the territory of the paramount Baloch chief, the khan of Kalat, who in return received a subsidy. Kalat, which lay outside Quetta, Bolan, and British Balochistan, was an independent state and an independent northern area, which was not ruled by the Khan and was mainly Pathan.

In 1887, British Balochistan was incorporated into British India. In 1947, as Pakistan came into being, the whole of Balochistan was incorporated into the newly independent state, an action that was then, and in varying degrees ever since, a cause of unrest and Baluchi discontent. Baluchis are nearly all Sunni Muslims, speaking the Baluchi language. The main concentrations of Baluchis are in the Baluchistan provinces of Iran and Pakistan, with smaller communities living in the provinces of the former Soviet Union and in Afghanistan. Since the mid 1970s some 2,500 Baluch guerrillas have been sheltering in southern Afghanistan, many of them refugees from the struggles for Baluch autonomy in Pakistan.

See also Afghanistan; Bugti, Nawab Akbar; Pathans.
References

Shah, Mehtab Ali. *The Foreign Policy of Pakistan: Ethnic Impacts on Diplomacy 1971–1994.* London: I.B. Tauris, 1997

Wilcox, W. *Pakistan: The Consolidation of a Nation.* New York: Columbia University Press, 1963

BANDUNG CONFERENCE (APRIL 1955)

This was the first plenary intergovernmental conference of Asian and African States after World War II and was in part notable for the contrasting attitudes conveyed by Indian Prime Minister Jawaharlal Nehru, in favor of nonalignment and of Pakistan's Prime Minister Mohammad Ali, in favoring membership in alliances. But the dominant theme of the conference was anticolonialism. China was ably represented at the conference by its foreign minister Zhou Enlai.

This conference of mostly independent Asian and Arab states was organized and convened by the five Colombo Powers. It opened at Bandung on the island of Java in Indonesia on April 18 and was attended by representatives of all the 29 countries invited, except the Central African Federation. Unofficial observers who attended the conference included Archbishop Makarios of Cyprus (then a leader of the Enosis Movement), the ex-Mufti of Jerusalem, and spokespeople for the African National Congress. In view of the large number of observers, it was decided that none of them should be allowed to address the conference.

During the discussions in the committees and especially in the political committee, a cleavage became apparent between the pro-Western and anticommunist group led by Pakistan and Turkey (comembers of the recently formed Baghdad Pact) and the nonaligned and procommunist groups led by India, China, and Egypt. Two notable features of this discussion were (1) the split among the Colombo Powers, Pakistan, and Ceylon, which were pro-Western, and India, Burma, and Indonesia, the nonaligned stance; and (2) the unexpected adherence of Cambodia and Laos to the nonaligned group under the influence of Nehru and of assurances given by Zhou Enlai. On the question of world peace, several resolutions were submitted. U Nu of Burma proposed a resolution based on the five principles of peaceful coexistence (first authoritatively defined by India and China as the Panch Sheel, or Panch Shila, a year earlier) with the addition of clauses on human rights and the principles of the United Nations (UN) charter.

For Pakistan, Mohammed Ali put forward a so-called seven pillars of peace formulation including commendation for alliances if they added to a country's national security and independence. Nehru, for India, submitted a resolution appealing to the great powers not to test or use atomic or thermonuclear weapons and to stop producing them. Nehru denounced both the Southeast Asia Treaty Organization (SEATO) and the Cominform as dangerous to peace, saying that he was surprised by the timing of the Manila Treaty, which he described as "an angry reaction" to the success of the Geneva Conference on Indochina a year earlier. The fact that at Geneva the great powers had agreed that the states of Indochina should not align with any power bloc showed them that nonalignment was the way of peace.

Mohammad Ali also criticized Sir Winston Churchill's phrase "peace through strength," which, he said, had resulted in "strength" being underlined but not "peace." At the final plenary session on April 24, Nehru claimed that the conference had achieved considerable success, adding that "we want to be friends with Europe and America and cooperate with them, but they are in the habit of thinking that their quarrels are world quarrels, and that therefore the world must follow them this way or that." He demanded rhetorically, "Why should we be dragged into their quarrels and wars?" He said he would like Australia and New Zealand, which did not belong to Europe and much less to America, to come nearer to Asia. He added that there was "nothing more terrible and horrible than the infinite tragedy of Africa," dating from the time of the slave trade, and that it was "up to Asia to help Africa to the best of her ability, because we are sister continents." "We have made some history here," he concluded, "and must live up to what the world expects of us."

During the next decade, as decolonization proceeded rapidly, especially in 1960, differences among those who had assembled in 1955 increased (not the least being tensions between India and Pakistan), and so the claims to Asian–African solidarity became less and less convincing. Major fissures among the sponsors of the original Bandung Conference became more manifest in 1961 (the year of the first plenary summit conference of the nonaligned, with India playing a leading role and Pakistan excluded) and again in 1964–1965, when China and Indonesia pressed for a second Asian–African summit conference. In both instances India (in conjunction with Yugoslavia and the United Arab Republic-Egypt) succeeded in organizing meetings of nonaligned states rather than of the militantly anticolonial anti-Western rivals advocated by China and Indonesia. In November 1965 a second Asian–African conference that was to be held in Algeria was indefinitely postponed. It appeared unlikely that a genuine Bandung Conference would ever be held again.

On the 50th anniversary of the original conference, leaders from Asia and Africa met in Jakarta and Bandung, ostensibly to launch a New Asian–African Strategic Partnership (NAASP). They pledged to promote political, economic, and cultural cooperation between the two continents, sentiments that subsequently remained patchy aspirations rather than achieved actualities.

See also Ali, Chaudhri Muhammad; Colombo Powers; Nehru, Jawaharlal.

References

Best, Antony, J. M. Hanimaki, J. A. Maiolo, and K. E. Schulze. *International History of the Twentieth Century.* New York: Routledge, 2004

Guha, R. *India after Gandhi: The History of the World's Largest Democracy.* New York: Macmillan, 2007

Jansen, G. H. *Afro-Asia and Non Alignment.* London: Faber and Faber, 1966

BANGLADESH

"Bangladesh" literally means Land of the Bengalis, though for strict accuracy it should be designated the land of the Bengali Muslims. Today the People's Republic of Bangladesh comprises 144,000 square kilometers (55,585 square miles) of territory and occupies the northeastern sector of the Indian subcontinent. It is bounded on the west and north by India, on the east by India (which almost encircles Bangladesh on its land boundaries) and by Myanmar, and on the south by the Bay of Bengal. Its capital is Dhaka (previously Dacca). In 1992 India granted a 999-year lease of the Tin Bighra Corridor linking Bangladesh with its enclaves of Angarpola and Dahagram. The second most populous country in the Commonwealth (after India) with a total population in the early 21st century of about 130 million, it has also the third largest Muslim population in the world (after Indonesia and India).

Both the circumstances of its origin as an independent state in 1971–1972 and its geopolitical position make Bangladesh very attentive to relations with India, first and foremost, then China, the United States, and Pakistan. A Ganges water sharing accord was signed with India in 1997, ending a 25-year dispute, which had hindered and irritated relations between the two countries.

Until 1947 Bangladesh (together with parts of Assam) formed the province of East Bengal in the British Raj. Upon partition in 1947, the region became the Eastern Province of Pakistan, separated from Pakistan's western province by about 1,000 miles of the Indian Republic. Complaints that the Bengali Pakistanis were being exploited by the Punjab-dominated central government, located in Karachi since 1947, prompted the formation in 1954 of a movement for autonomy, the Awami League, led by Sheikh Mujib-Ur Rahman.

As late as 1968–1969, there was only one Bengali among 12 lieutenant generals and only one Bengali among 20 major generals in the Pakistan Army. In the civil bureaucracy, the representation of the Bengalis at the central secretary level was 14 percent, 6 percent at the joint secretary level, and 18 percent at the deputy secretary and class I officer levels (the latter the rank below that of central secretary). These discrepancies of representation become even more blatant in light of the fact that the total population of East Pakistan in 1969–1970 was greater than that of West Pakistan. Despite a crushing electoral victory for the Awami League throughout East Pakistan in December 1970, the central government refused to modify the constitutional relationship between the two wings. On March 26, 1971, the Sheikh formally proclaimed Bangladesh's secession from Pakistan and a government-in-exile was set up in Calcutta three weeks later. This move led to civil war and, in December 1971, to a wider war—a fortnight's conflict between India and Pakistan. Bangladesh was formally recognized as an independent state by its external patron India and by the patron's protectorate Bhutan within 10 days of the defeat of the central Pakistan forces on December 16, 1972.

Soon the Pakistan central government found that it was militarily impossible to hold onto the dissident province (then and subsequently there was controversy as to the significance of the roles of the Indian army and of the local guerrillas, or the so-called freedom fighters). Most countries recognized Bangladesh's independence early in 1972.

The newly independent republic of Bangladesh was the most densely populated country in Asia with just over 70 million people in 1972, less than 30 percent of whom were literate, all living on a land that was about the size of England and Wales and that was recurrently prone to catastrophic cyclones and floods. Given these conditions and a rather factious political public, Mujib-Ur Rahman could not set up and sustain the socialist parliamentary democracy favored by his Awami League. In January 1975 Rahman made himself president and assumed autocratic powers. Seven months later, in August, he was murdered in a military coup, the alleged leader of the rebels being assassinated soon afterward.

Major General Zia Rahman became president in April 1977 and prepared the country for democratic elections in February 1979, which were won by his Bangladesh Nationalist Party (BNP). President Zia was assassinated at Chittagong in May 1981, while seeking to stamp out a secessionist movement among the tribes in the hilly southeastern region of the country.

Bangladesh's national politics since the late 1970s may be characterized as those of martyrology, with

Sheik Mujib's surviving daughter, Sheik Hasina Wahed as leader of the Awami League, being implacably opposed to Begum Khaleda Zia, the leader of the Bangladesh National Party and widow of former President, Ziaur Rahman. The Awami League is generally said to be closer to India and the BNP closer to Pakistan, but these alleged affinities are nothing compared with the rivalry and mutual mistrust displayed by the two leaders toward each other.

Even in the first decade of the 21st century, over 30 years after Bangladesh gained independence, various small disagreements with India persist—involving the delimitation of river boundaries, the exchange of miniscule enclaves in both countries, the allocation of divided villages, sporadic communal violence, and the transit of terrorists through porous borders. A joint Bangladesh-India boundary inspection in 2005 discovered that 92 boundary pillars were missing. And disputation with India impeded agreement regarding the delimitation of maritime boundaries in the Bay of Bengal.

See also Awami League (AL); East Bengal; East Pakistan; Ershad, Hossain Muhammed; Myanmar; Rahman, Sheikh Mujib-Ur.

References

Maniruzzaman, T. *The Bangladesh Revolution and Its Aftermath.* Dhaka, Bang.: University Press Ltd., 1988

O'Donnell, C. P. *Bangladesh: Biography of a Muslim Nation.* Boulder, CO: Westview Press, 1984

Rahman, M. *Emergence of a New Nation in a Multi-Polar World: Bangladesh.* Dhaka, Bang.: University Press Ltd., 1979

BEAUMONT, CHRISTOPHER (1912–2002)

Christopher Beaumont was one of a few top civil servants in the last days of the Raj who retained a lifelong dislike of Lord Louis Mountbatten and a suspicion of some of his doings while viceroy. Some 50 years after the transfer of power and the partitions of 1947, then an elderly retired circuit judge, Beaumont asserted that, under Jawaharlal Nehru's influence, the viceroy had put pressure on the head of the boundaries commission to alter some boundaries in India's favor. As private secretary to the senior British judge, Sir (later Lord) Cyril Radcliffe, the chair of the Indo-Pakistan Boundary Commission, Beaumont was well-placed to observe the partitions of 1947.

Herbert Christopher Beaumont was born in Wakefield, West Yorkshire, the son of a lawyer.

His childhood was spent in Hatfield Hall, the family home, and he was educated at Uppingham and Worcester Colleges, Oxford, where he studied history.

After spending a year in Germany, where he saw the rise of Nazism firsthand, Beaumont joined the Indian Civil and Political Service in 1936, initially serving as a district officer in Punjab, and stayed until independence in 1947. Beaumont was famous among his close colleagues for his strong personality, devastating wit, and candor. His frankness and dislike of humbug led him to speak publicly about Mountbatten in 1992, casting doubts on the viceroy's impartiality in India. Beaumont had been appointed private secretary to Sir Cyril Radcliffe, the day after Radcliffe became chair of the commission. The commission's deliberations were supposed to be secret, impartial, and impervious to political persuasion. But Beaumont said that, after Radcliffe had drawn the line in Punjab, he was persuaded to change his mind about the transfer of the subdistricts Ferozepur and Zira from Pakistan to India at a lunch with Mountbatten, a meeting from which he said he was excluded.

See also Nehru, Jawaharlal; Radcliffe, Sir Cyril; Raj, the.
References
Dictionary of National Biography. New York: Oxford
   University Press, 2002

BENGAL

The name "Bengal," or "Bangala," derives from the ancient deltaic kingdom of Vanga, or Banga. Its early history is obscure until the 3rd century BCE, when it formed part of the extensive Maurya Empire inherited by Ashoka. The heartland of a distinct culture and language, Bengal was formerly a province of British India and is now a region of northeastern India and Bangladesh, and it is a somewhat variable term today designating primarily West Bengal (a state of the Republic of India) and Bangladesh (formerly East Pakistan). The geographical limits of Bengal have varied throughout the centuries. Its boundaries have been altered either as a result of conquest or for administrative reasons. Before the partition of 1947, it stretched from the Duars immediately south of Sikkim and Bhutan to the Sundarbans, then north of the Ganges. It was bounded on the west by Bihar and on the east by Assam and by the part of Burma that lay to the east of the Chittagong coastal tract. The most distinctive topographical feature of the area is its entwining network of rivers, most notably the Ganges and Brahmaputra, with their affluents and distributaries.

The first British settlements were East India Company (EIC) factories, dating from 1633. A center of trade was established on the Hooghly River at Calcutta in 1690. The EIC's presidency of Bengal was formed in 1699, but the territory remained under the overlordship of the Mogul emperors until 1740, when the ruling nawab asserted his independence. Sixteen years later, resentment at the EIC's commercial penetration provoked the nawab to launch a surprise attack and overrun the fortress of Fort William. In June 1757 Robert Clive recovered Calcutta and defeated Siraj-ud-Dowlah at the Battle of Plassey. Thereafter pliant nawabs accepted the acquisition by EIC's soldiers and officials of a vast dominion, which included Oudh and Agra (until 1833) as well as the modern Indian provinces of Bihar and Orissa and present-day Bangladesh. By the end of the 19th century, Bengal had a population twice that of the United Kingdom. Almost all the people were Bengali speaking, but there were some 78 linguistic variants. In 1905 Lord George Curzon, the imperious viceroy, imposed partition on the huge province: 31 million people formed the new province of East Bengal and Assan, in which Muslims outnumbered Hindus by 3 to 1, while Bengal proper (including Bihar) retained 50 million people overwhelmingly Hindu. Curzon's partition provoked fierce opposition, stimulating Bengali nationalism but intensifying sectarian divisions. In 1912 all Bengali-speaking peoples were reunited in a revived Presidency of Bengal. There was, however, no longer any genuine political unity.

Under the Government of India Act 1935, Bengal was constituted an autonomous province in 1937. The partition of 1947 detached East Pakistan (1947–1971 and since 1971, Bangladesh). Boundary disputes arising out of the Radcliffe award of August 1947 were settled by the report of the Bagge Tribunal in February 1950. Since 1947, West Bengal has remained one of India's most substantial constituent states—twelfth in area but ranking third in population.

See also Ashoka, Emperor; Assam; Bangladesh.
References
Roy, Ajit. "West Bengal: Not a Negative Vote." *Economic and Political Weekly* (July 2, 1977).

BHARATIYA JANATA PARTY (BJP)

The Bharatiya Janata Party (BJP) was formed from the Janata Party elements of Jana Sangh, with support mainly from Hindi-speaking northern India, under the initial leadership of Dr. Shyama Prasad Mookerjee, a former cabinet minister. It favors a Hindu nationalist identity and ideology and has a somewhat variable relationship with the Rashtriya Swayamsevak Sangh (RSS).

Its strength is greatest in the western and northern states of Delhi, Gujerat, Himachal Pradesh, Mahya Pradesh, Maharashtra, Rajasthan, and Uttar Pradesh. The BJP provided the all-Union government from March 1998 until May 2004 when, contrary to the predictions of many electoral pundits, it lost decisively to the Indian National Congress (INC) Party, which became the core of the new government with the BJP the principal opposition party in India's parliament.

See also Jana Sangh; Rashtriya Swayamsevak Sangh; Uttar Pradesh.

References

Hardgrave, R. L. Jr., and S. A. Kochanek. *India: Government and Politics in a Developing Nation*, 7th ed. Fort Worth, TX: Harcourt College Publishers, 2002

Lyon, P., and D. Austin. 1993. "The Bharatiya Janata Party of India." *Government and Opposition* 28, 1 (Winter 1993): 36–50

BHINDRANWALE, SANT JARNAIL SINGH (1947–1984)

Sant Jarnail Singh was a Sikh extremist leader. Born into a poor Punjabi Jat farming family, he trained at a leading Sikh missionary school, becoming its head in 1971 and assuming the name Bhindranwale. Initially encouraged by Sanjay Gandhi (1946–1980), the younger son and close political adviser of Indira Gandhi, who sought to divide the Sikh Akali Dal movement, Bhindranwale campaigned violently against the heretical activities of Nirankari Sikhs during the late 1970s. His campaign broadened into a demand for a separate state of Khalistan during the early 1980s, precipitating a bloody Hindu–Sikh conflict in Punjab.

After taking refuge with about 500 devoted followers in the Golden Temple complex at Amritsar and building up an extensive cache of arms there for

Atal Bihari Vajpayee, the prime minister of India and the leader of the Bharatiya Janata, sits with former U.S. secretary of defense Donald H. Rumsfeld in 2002. (Department of Defense)

terrorist activities, he was killed by Indian army forces who stormed the temple in Operation Blue Star in June 1984.

See also Amritsar; Gandhi, Indira; Punjab; Sikhism.

References

Sandhu, Singh Ranbir. *Struggle for Justice: Speeches and Conversations of Sant Jarnail Singh Khalsa Bhindranwale.* Dublin, OH: Sikh Educational and Religious Foundation, 1999

Sidhu, Singh Choor. *Amar Shaheed Sant Jarnail Singh Bhindranwale: Martyr of the Sikh Faith.* Chandigarh, Ind.: European Institute of Sikh Studies, 1997

BHUTTO, BENAZIR (1953–2007)

Benazur Bhutto was a Pakistani stateswoman and prime minister (1988–1991, 1993–1996). Born in Karachi the daughter of the former prime minister Zulfikar Ali Bhutto, she completed her formal education at Oxford, when her father was prime minister. She returned to Pakistan and was placed under house arrest (1977–1984) after the military coup led by General Zia-ul-Haq, who deposed and imprisoned her father. She moved to England (1984–1986), becoming the joint leader in exile of the opposition Pakistan People's Party (PPP), and then returned to launch a nationwide campaign for open elections. She married a wealthy landowner, Asif Ali Zardari, in 1987.

In 1988 Benazir Bhutto was elected prime minister, shortly after giving birth to her first child. She and her supporters won a slender electoral victory in November of that year, and she became prime minister, defense minister, and finance minister on December 2. On October 1, 1989, in a reversal of her father's policy, she brought Pakistan back into the Commonwealth. Early in 1990 she became the first head of government to give birth to a child—her second—while in office.

Her modern Westernized practices lost her support in rural areas, especially in the Punjab, and she fell from office in October 1990, after the Islamic Democratic Alliance (IDA) won the elections. She won a further election in 1993 but was ousted by presidential decree in 1996, ostensibly for misgovernance and the corruption of her government. Subsequently she lived in exile abroad, principally in Britain and Dubai, but continued to be a prominent focus of opposition discontent, especially to General Pervez Musharraf's rule.

Opposition leader Benazir Bhutto flashes victory signs to welcoming crowds shortly after her return from exile on April 10, 1986. In 2007 she returned to Pakistan and was assassinated in December at an election rally in Rawalpindi. (Reuters/Corbis)

As a Western-educated woman from the relatively poor province of Sindh, Benazir Bhutto never had the sure-footed claim to power of politicians from Punjab. Although she recast herself as a Sunni in the 1990s, she came from a Shia family, albeit a wealthy one. Shias make up about a fifth of Pakistan's population. Mohammad Ali Jinnah, Pakistan's founder, was a Shia, but the national self-image became more Sunni through the 1990s, though Benazir Bhutto's heritage was of no marked help to her political standing. She was assassinated at an election campaign rally on December 27, 2007, in Rawalpindi.

See also Bhutto, Zulfikar Ali; Karachi; Musharraf, Pervez;
    Pakistan People's Party (Shaheed Bhutto) PPP (SB).
References
Bhutto, Benazir. *Daughter of the East: An Autobiography.*
    London: Hamish Hamilton, 1988

Zulfikar Ali Bhutto at United Nations press conference in 1965. He became leader of the Pakistan Peoples Party (PPP) in 1971 and was executed by Zia-ul-Huq in 1979. (Library of Congress)

BHUTTO, ZULFIKAR ALI (1928–1979)

Zulfikar Ali Bhutto was a Pakistani statesmen, president of Pakistan (1971–1973), and prime minister (1973–1977). He was a doughty opponent and critic of India, though he signed the Simla agreement with Indira Gandhi in 1972, formally concluding the 1971 Indo-Pakistan war. Born in Larkana, Sind, into what had been an aristocratic Rajput dynasty, he entered Pakistan's politics after 1947, establishing the Peoples Party in 1967 to promote a form of moderate Muslim Socialism. "Zulfi" Bhutto graduated from the Universities of California and Oxford and became a lawyer. He was minister of commerce in 1958 and a flamboyant foreign minister from 1963 to 1966.

He founded the Pakistan People's Party (PPP) in 1967, which won the army-supervised elections in West Pakistan in 1971, polarizing relations between West and East Pakistan, the latter with its substantial Bengali-speaking Muslim majority under the aegis of the Awami League led by Mujib-Ur Rahman. As Foreign Minister under Mohammed Ayub Khan, from 1963–1966, Zulfi Bhutto took a strongly anti-Indian stance in the Kashmir dispute. Immediately after Pakistan's defeat by India, in the short war over Bangladesh's secession, Bhutto became president and took Pakistan out of the Commonwealth on January 30, 1972. After amending the constitution to make the prime minister chief executive of the republic, Bhutto resigned the presidency in August 1973 but continued to head the government, as well as holding the portfolios of defense, foreign affairs, and atomic energy.

Victory in the election of March 1977 was followed by accusations of vote rigging from opponents who were alarmed at Bhutto's policy of nationalizing basic industries. After four months of rioting and virtual anarchy in several cities, the chief of the army staff, General Zia-ul-Haq (1924–1988) carried through a military coup on July 5, 1977. Bhutto was arrested in September 1977, and on March 18, 1978, he was sentenced to death for conspiracy to murder. Despite appeals for clemency from various world leaders, he was hanged at Rawalpindi on April 4, 1979, after being held for 13 months in a death cell.

See also Awami League (AL); Ayub Khan, Mohammed;
    Bangladesh; Bhutto, Benazir; Gandhi, Indira;
    Pakistan People's Party (Shaheed Bhutto) PPP (SB).
References
Burki, Shahid Javed. *Pakistan Under Bhutto 1971–1977.*
    New York: Macmillan, 1980
Schofield, Victoria. *Bhutto: Trial and Execution.* New
    York: Cassell, 1979
Wolpert, S. *Zulfi Bhutto of Pakistan: His Life and Times.*
    New York: Oxford University Press, 1993

BIHARIS

Biharis were Urdu-speaking Muslims who opted to migrate, mostly from Bihar, to East Pakistan in 1947. When in 1971 East Pakistan seceded to become Bangladesh, the so-called Biharis were loyal to the main base in the west but were captured and imprisoned in the east. Following the secession of the east wing, the government of Pakistan refused to take most of them back or, more precisely, to offer a future in Pakistan. Most of those who did not flee immediately after the war found themselves stateless and incarcerated in internment camps in Bangladesh. In the early 21st century over a quarter of a million Biharis are still in Bangladesh, mostly in camps around Dhaka. Bangladesh and Pakistan cannot agree on any substantial settlement regarding their future beyond some token repatriation agreements.

See also Bangladesh; East Pakistan.

References

Cohen, Stephen P. *The Idea of Pakistan*. Washington, DC: Brookings Institution Press, 2004

BLACK, EUGENE (1898–1992)

Banker and president of the International Bank for Reconstruction and Development (commonly known as The World Bank), Eugene Black was born in Atlanta, Georgia. He studied at the University of Georgia and became a banker on Wall Street. He joined The World Bank in 1947 as executive director, becoming president in July 1949 and remaining until December 1962. He was personally influential in altering the emphasis of the bank from post–World War II reconstruction, to providing loans for economic development, especially to the Third World, and notably to India and Pakistan regarding the division of the Indus Basin Waters.

In the Indus Basin Waters dispute, an offer from The World Bank to arbitrate was accepted in 1952. The Indus Waters Treaty, signed in 1960, granted the waters of the three main western rivers, the Indus, the Jhelum, and the Chenab, to Pakistan and the waters of the three eastern rivers to India. Financial help toward the engineering costs of the necessary irrigation works was made available to Pakistan from The World Bank, and a consortium of countries pledged to help Pakistani's development. In 1968, the Mangla Dam was completed and the larger Tarbela project begun. The World Bank has also provided assistance at times of natural disasters.

In November 1970, giant tidal waves from the Bay of Bengal pounded the Ganges–Brahmaputra delta and its offshore islands and coastal districts, causing as many as 600,000 deaths. The bank's affiliate, the International Development Association (which Black had helped to set up) advanced a US$25 million credit to finance key elements in a US$180 million reconstruction program.

See also Indus Waters Treaty.

References

Black, E. *The Diplomacy of Economic Development*. Cambridge, MA: Harvard University Press, 1961

Guha, R. *India after Gandhi. The History of the World's Largest Democracy*. New York: Macmillan, 2007

BOGRA, MUHAMMAD ALI (1909–1963)

Muhammad Ali Bogra was a Bengali diplomat, foreign minister, and prime minister whose career illustrated the main ups and downs of East Pakistan's relations with the politically dominant west wing right up until his death in 1963. He served as a parliamentary secretary and minister before independence, then in the diplomatic service as ambassador to Burma (1948), as high commissioner to Canada (1949), and as ambassador to the United States (1952–1955).

Whilst serving in Washington, D.C., he acquired a pro-American reputation, as his country joined the Baghdad Pact and the Southeast Asia Treaty Organization (SEATO), and this was an important factor in his appointment as prime minister upon Khwaja Nazimuddin's dismissal in April 1953. Bogra carried on as prime minister after Ghulam Muhammad's dismissal of the Constituent Assembly, although power lay with Mohammed Ayub Khan as defense minister and Iskander Mirza as minister of the interior. Bogra was replaced as prime minister in October 1955, largely because he opposed Mirza's replacement of Ghulam Muhammad as governor-general. After another period as ambassador in Washington, Bogra served from 1962 until his death in 1963 as minister of foreign affairs under Ayub.

See also Ayub Khan, Mohammed; Baghdad Pact; Manila Treaty; Mirza, Iskander.

BOMBAY. *SEE* MUMBAI.

BUGTI, NAWAB AKBAR (1927–2006)

Architect and later saboteur of Pakistan, Bugti's active controversial and seemingly contradictory life moved in many political and ideological directions: Pakistan patriot and one-time establishment figure, traditional Baluchi nationalist, rebel leader, and guerrilla fighter. As chief of 250,000 Baluchis of the Bugti clan, he was the ruler of a state-within-a-state and the commander of a 10,000-man army. Bugti began his political career as an all-Pakistan establishment figure. He was governor-general of Pakistan after the country's formation in 1947. He became interior minister of Baluchistan and also its governor. Despite his early pan-Pakistan offices, his Baluchi nationalism was never far beneath the surface. He was involved in insurgencies, each crushed with huge losses of life, in the 1950s, 1960s, and 1970s.

Early in 2004 the nawab launched his latest and what proved to be his last Baluchi freedom struggle, as he called it, which involved his supporters fighting a series of intense battles with Pakistan's security forces. Pakistan's governmental spokespeople alleged that Bugti was able to step up his guerrilla operations thanks to financial aid from India, an allegation that Delhi denied.

As a *sardar,* or chief, Bugti ran a fiefdom rooted in centuries of tradition. Loyalty to the clan is the main social political and military cement in Baluchistan. As clan chief, Bugti was revered by his followers. To oppose him might be to die or to end up in one of his two private prisons: one reserved for "commoners," the other for high-ranking tribals. Bugti could be charming, eloquent, and polite. He could also be brutal, a killer of many men, and an oppressive ruler through the ancient *sardar* system. Fluent in English, he was well educated in Pakistan and Britain. Legend had it that he killed his first victim at the age of 12. When his youngest son Salal was assassinated by progovernment tribals in 1992, he was said to have ordered the murder of 100 men in reprisal. After that he moved his base from Quetta, the capital of Baluchistan to Deva Bugti, 150 miles to the southeast. The cave in which he died, courtesy of Musharraf's Air Force, was nearby.

As a tribal chief Akbar Bugti voted in 1946 in favor of the creation of Pakistan (ordinary Baluchis were not invited to vote) and in favor of Baluchistan's membership of it—hardly a clear indication of what he would do for the rest of his life. Bugti's power came not only from the *sardar* system; he also grew wealthy on the commissions he received from Pakistan for the right to extract gas and coal from vast areas of Baluchistan under his control, in particular the gas-rich area of Sui. In the early 21st century, he received 120 million rupees (just over £1 million) each year as rent for land used by Pakistan Petroleum for natural gas extraction. He also received two million rupees (approximately £17,500) a month, ostensibly to provide security to the very gas operations his own soldiers were sabotaging.

Indeed, at the time of his death, Bugti was probably the single most dangerous internal enemy of the state of Pakistan's industry—as well as a key disrupter of domestic life in millions of homes across the country. For instance, the supply of gas was cut off in January 2006 when the gas fields in Sui, the biggest in Pakistan, were sabotaged. Akbar Bugti sent waves of heavily armed men to capture Sui, and in fierce gun battles they occupied several buildings before eventually being forced back. Bugti also became associated with a violent organization, the banned Baluchi Liberation Army, which first surfaced in the 1980s. Its aim is the establishment of an independent greater Baluchistan, fashioned out of Baluchi areas in Pakistan, Afghanistan, and Iran. Bugti was its most visible and audible leader for the three years or so before his death.

See also Baluchistan.

References

Wilcox, W. *Pakistan: The Consolidation of a Nation.* New York: Columbia University Press, 1963

Wirsing, R. G. *The Baluchs and Pathans.* New York: Macmillan, 1987

BUSH, GEORGE WALKER (1946–)

The 43rd president of the United States, George W. Bush has embroiled his administration in Iraq and Afghanistan, with repercussions on his country's substantial involvement with Pakistan and generally much lower-key connections with India.

Bush took office as president in 2001, in succession to Bill Clinton, after one of America's most controversial and closely run presidential elections. He is the first president since 1888 to reach the White House despite losing the popular vote. Not noted for his knowledge of and skills in foreign affairs, with much controversy still surrounding his election, he immediately struck a conciliatory stance, declaring, "I was not elected to serve one party, but a nation."

Within nine months of taking office, Bush was subjected to one of the most challenging episodes of any presidency as the United States suffered unprecedented attacks by Islamic terrorists on September 11, 2001. In February 2003, following a controversy within the United Nations about how to respond to terrorism and whether Saddam Hussein's regime had acquired weapons of mass destruction, Bush authorized U.S.-led forces to attack and remove Saddam Hussein from power. Bush was reelected for a second term as president in November 2004 and was inaugurated in January 2005, and he has determinately sent many messages of approval or criticism on aspects of India's and Pakistan's policies.

George W. Bush was born in New Haven, Connecticut, on July 6, 1946, and grew up in Maine and Houston, Texas. He attended Yale University and the Harvard Business School, being awarded a degree in history and an MBA. Bush served as a pilot in the Texas National Guard in the 1960s and then set up his own—financially successful—oil and gas company in the mid 1970s, which he sold in 1986.

In 1988, he campaigned energetically for his father George H. W. Bush to become president of the United States. In 1994, he was elected Republican governor of Texas. When George W. Bush was inaugurated as president in January 2001, he became only the second son of a former president (the first was John Quincy Adams) to reach the White House.

In the face of open criticism from India and muted comment from Pakistan, Bush initiated a highly controversial plan to replace the 1972 Anti-Ballistic Missile Treaty with a new accord so that he could introduce a U.S. missile defense system. After discussing this proposal with Russian President Vladimir Putin, the two leaders agreed in May 2002 to reduce their respective strategic nuclear warheads by two-thirds over the next 10 years.

Bush's presidency and the United States' relationship with the rest of the world were battered and transformed by the events of September 11, 2001. Two hijacked passenger airlines were crashed into the World Trade Center towers in New York City, another hit a wing of the Pentagon building in Washington, D.C., and a fourth came down in a Pennsylvanian field short of its intended target, which may have been the White House. The total number of people killed was about 3,000, including many rescue workers.

The 9/11 attacks had widespread international political and economic repercussions. Bush declared a war against terrorism. With evidence pointing to the involvement of Osama bin Laden and his al-Qaeda organization, Bush threatened action against Afghanistan's Taliban regime, which he accused of sheltering the terrorist network. He sought to establish a global alliance to put pressure on Afghanistan and to receive some support from Europe, especially the United Kingdom, as well as cooperation from Pervez Musharraf's Pakistan (as well as from Uzbekistan and at least the acquiescence of Iran).

In October 2001, mainly U.S. and British forces attacked Taliban and al-Qaeda forces in Afghanistan, and in the following months the Northern Alliance, an Afghan group opposed to the Taliban, retook the capital of Kabul. Meetings of various Afghan leaders were organized by the United Nations (UN) to produce a new interim government (headed by Hamid Karzai) and to ratify an agreement allowing the UN peacekeeping force to enter Afghanistan.

President Bush visited both India and Pakistan in March 2006. In Pakistan his visit appeared to be principally designed to keep his host country as an active ally in the so-called war on terrorism. Despite issuing an agreement to establish a strategic partnership, it was clear that the American government regarded Pakistan as a somewhat ambiguous ally. The Bush visit to India appeared, by contrast, to be initiating newly cordial relationships between the two countries. Most notably this applied to American willingness to assist India's civil nuclear capability. Given how strongly the United States had criticized India's nuclear tests in 1998, this marked a significant change, in effect showing American willingness to accept India as one of the world's nuclear powers. Toward the end of 2006, one of the biggest business delegations ever sent abroad by the United States visited India to discuss future cooperation and investment.

By 2007, President Bush was repeatedly saying that he wanted Pakistan to hold genuinely free and fair elections and to return to democracy while discouraging Islamic militias and other forms of internal violence. While proffering much gratuitous political advice, there has been no warning that the United States would cease or severely reduce its extensive military assistance to President

Musharraf. Meanwhile, India's government, headed by Dr. Manmohan Singh, has generally maintained a mostly circumspect calm vis-á-vis events in Pakistan.

See also Afghanistan; al-Qaeda/al-Qa'ida; Nuclear
    Weapons; Taliban.

References
Guha, R. *India after Gandhi. The History of the World's
    Largest Democracy.* New York: Macmillan, 2007

Saikal, Armin. "The Changing Geopolitics of Central,
    West and South Asia After 11th September." In
    Ramesh Thakur and Oddny Wiggen, eds. *South
    Asia in the World: Problem Solving Perspectives on
    Security, Sustainable Development and Good
    Governance.* Tokyo: United Nations University
    Press, 2004
Sathasivam, K. *Uneasy Neighbours: India, Pakistan
    and US Foreign Policy.* Aldershot, UK: Ashgate,
    2005

CARTER, JAMES (EARL) (1924–)

The 39th president of the United States (1977–1980), popularly known as Jimmy Carter, was born in Plains, Georgia, and eventually became something of an Indophile. He trained at the U.S. Naval Academy and served in the U.S. navy until 1953 when he took over the family peanut business and some other enterprises. As an activist Democrat and governor of Georgia (1970–1974), he championed the rights of African Americans and women. In 1976 he won the Democratic presidential nomination and went on to win a narrow victory over Gerald Ford. He brokered a peace treaty between Egypt and Israel in 1979 and devoted much attention to human rights at home and abroad. His administration ended mired in difficulties, especially over the taking of U.S. hostages in Iran and the widely ramifying consequences of the Soviet invasion and occupation of Afghanistan.

He was beaten by Ronald Reagan in the 1980 U.S. presidential election and subsequently set up an institute to promote peace projects. Arguably and ironically, Carter's agenda of attention to human rights and to matters affecting free and fair elections and good government became more influential within the United States and internationally after his presidency. He and his family—including his mother, Miss Lillian—showed considerable interest in India both during and after his presidency. He was awarded the Nobel Prize for Peace in 2002.

See also Afghanistan; Human Rights.

References

Kux, Dennis. *India and the United States: Estranged Democracies, 1942–1991.* Washington, DC: National Defense University Press, 1992

CASTE

For centuries a rigid caste system, determining rank in society deriving from birth or origin and governing social mobility, has prevailed among Hindus in India. Highly ranked Brahmin priests,

C

for example, were forbidden to share food, water, or even shadows with Dalits—sweepers and laborers often called outcasts or untouchables, or, by Mohandas Karamchand Gandhi, *harijans* (children of God). Pakistanis are inclined to criticize India as caste ridden.

After India became independent in 1947, untouchability was officially abolished, and in 1990 the government reserved 22 percent of state university places and at least 12.5 percent of government jobs for Dalits and members of the lower castes. Caste continues, however, to be assertive and divisive in India's political and social life. In late May 2006, the Congress-led government reserved an additional 27 percent of university seats for groups officially known as the Other Backward Classes (OBCs) that took effect as of June 2007. that decision provoked demonstrations in many Indian cities and towns. University staff staged walkouts, students protested, and public hospitals shut their doors to all but emergency cases. Officials claimed that fresh quotas are necessary because the lower castes are still marginalized, but critics said that the government is pandering to the OBCs because they are a big voting bloc. Caste functions often as a surrogate for class in a society in which class identity is weak. As Robert Hardgrave (2000) has tellingly and rightly asserted, "Caste conflict cuts deeply in India's fragmented society."

See also Gandhi, Mohandas Karamchand; Harijans; Hinduism; Hindutva.

References

Hardgrave, R. L., and S. A. Kochanet. *India: Government and Politics in a Developing Nation,* 6th ed. Fort Worth, TX: Harcourt College Publishers, 2000

CHINA

China's leaders, while never defining their country as part of South Asia [and not ever seeking to join South Asian Association for Regional Cooperation (SAARC)], have evinced close interest in India and Pakistan ever since 1949, but with variable intensity and different calculations of interest.

After China's reoccupation of Tibet in 1950 and despite India's acute concern over this, in April 1954 Jawaharlal Nehru and Zhou Enlai signed a broad agreement regarding trade and transit into Tibet, which also enunciated five principles of peaceful co-existence (also labeled the Panch Sheel or Panch Shila), which inaugurated mutual cordialities that lasted only four years.

In the mid 1950s, India became notably a leading exponent of nonalignment, while the post-Stalin Soviet Union cultivated good relations with New Delhi and was critical of Pakistan's membership of U.S.-led alliances. Despite formally good relations between the Soviet Union and China (as for instance symbolized in the 1950 Sino-Soviet accord), the former refused to aid the latter's nuclear weapon's program to the extent that Beijing thought appropriate.

In 1958 the Soviet Union proposed a summit conference to discuss Middle Eastern problems to which it proposed India should be invited (as a participant) but did not suggest that China should attend. Thus the Sino-Soviet accord had patent limitations, which gradually became more obtrusive until, as many said, by the end of the 1960s a Sino-Soviet cold war was widely apparent. Undoubtedly, however, the Sino-Indian War of October 1962 was a major event, a severe shock, and setback for India, revealing New Delhi's unpreparedness for war, especially mountain warfare. And the diplomatic fallout from this war resulted in heightened Indian reliance on Soviet support and encouraged Pakistan to be more activist in cultivating Chinese assistance vis-à-vis India. The 1962 war was as big a setback for India as the 1971 war was a military defeat and setback for Pakistan.

References

Ali, S. Mahmud. *Cold War in the High Himalayas: The USA, China and South Asia in* the 1950s. New York: St. Martin's Press, 1999

Anthony, Ian. "Arms Exports to Southern Asia: Policies of Technology Transfer and Denial in the Supplier Countries." In Eric Arnett, ed. *Military Capacity and the Risk of War: China, India, Pakistan and Iran.* New York: Oxford University Press, 1997

Kapur, A., and Jeyaratnam A. Wilson. *Foreign Policies of India and Her Neighbours.* London: Macmillan, 1996

Lamb, Alastair. *The China-India Border.* New York: Royal Institute of International Affairs. New York: Oxford University Press, 1994

Maxwell, Neville. *India's China War.* London: Jonathan Cape, 1970; New York: Penguin, 1992

CHITRAL

Chitral is a former Princely State making up the most northerly section of what was the Malakand Agency in the frontier region that is now Pakistan. In their 19th-century rivalry to assert control over the northwest passes between the British Empire to India and the Russian Empire, the British established an agency in Gilgit in 1889 with a subsidiary for Chitral. A British garrison was maintained until the state was ceded to Pakistan, following the partition of the subcontinent in 1947. In July 1969 Chitral, together with Dir and Swat, was incorporated as a district into the newly formed Malakand Division. It is bounded north and west by Afghanistan, the Wakham Valley dividing it by the Gilgit Agency, and to the south and southeast by the former Dir state and by Kalan in the Swat Kohislan.

The administrative center, Chitral (or Kashkar) is 205 kilometers (128 miles) north of Peshawar on the Chitral River in a valley that is only 2 miles wide. It can be reached by road in motor vehicles during the summer via Malakand, Dir, and the Lowari Pass. It is connected with Gilgit by the Shandur Pass and is linked with Peshawar by air service. The valley is said to have been subdued by the Chinese in the 1st century BCE and was ruled by them for several centuries. Muslims from Afghanistan first entered Chitral early in the 11th century and converted the population to Islam, the people of upper Chitral being members of the Isma'ili sect.

See also Afghanistan; Azad Jammu-Kashmir (AJK); Gilgit; Islam.

References

Spate, O.H.K. *India and Pakistan: A General and Regional Geography,* 2nd ed. New York: Methuen, 1960

Yearbook of the North West Frontier Province. New Delhi: Government Press, Annual

CHUNDRIGAR, ISMAEL IBRAHIM (1897–1960)

A lawyer from Ahmadabad who was a close supporter of Mohammad Ali Jinnah in the Pakistan movement and who briefly became prime minister in 1957 as parliamentary government in Pakistan tottered. He served in 1937–1946 as a member of the Bombay Legislative Assembly. In 1946 he served in the interim government as commerce minister. After the emergence of Pakistan, he was ambassador to Afghanistan. In 1950–1953 he was governor of the Frontier Province and then of the Punjab.

He became prime minister on October 1957, not because of his political standing in the Muslim League, but because of his close friendship with President Iskander Mirza. Chundrigar's coalition ministry lasted just two months in office, thereby serving only to further discredit the failing political process.

See also Jinnah, Mohammed Ali; Muslim League; North West Frontier Province; Punjab.

References

Talbot, I. *Pakistan: A Modern History.* New York: Hurst and Company, 1998

CHURCHILL, SIR WINSTON L. SPENCER
(1874–1965)

Winston Churchill, twice Britain's prime minister, from 1940 to 1945 during World War II and again from 1951 to 1955, had a long and active public life, quite a lot of which involved him in active controversy about India and its future. Churchill was born on November 30, 1874, at Blenheim Palace, near Oxford. Through his father, Lord Randolph Churchill, he was directly descended from John Churchill, first duke of Marlborough. His mother, Jennie Jerome, was the daughter of a self-made New York businessman. As well as being a prominent leader of a group of would-be reformist Conservatives, his father was secretary of state for India for about eight months (1885–1886) and for a short while chancellor of the exchequer and leader of the House of Commons. Among his extensive biographical and historical writing, for example, Winston published lives of his father (in 1906) and of his ancestor John Churchill (in 1933–1938); in 1953 he was awarded the Nobel Prize for Literature. After schooling with governesses and at preparatory schools and then at Harrow and the Royal Military College, Sandhurst, Churchill entered the army, in the 4th Hussars, in 1895, the year of his father's early death.

In 1896 his regiment went to India, where he saw service as both soldier and journalist in the cam-

paign with the Malakand field force in what is now Pakistan's North West Frontier Province. Churchill arrived in India just eight months before Queen Victoria's Diamond Jubilee, an imperial climacteric. Churchill was in India only just over 18 months, but in this time he traveled extensively and met many of the top men of the British Raj. Basically he took the view that British retention of control over India was fundamental to the maintenance of an extensive British Empire and of Britain's prominent role in the world. Churchill left India in March 1899 and never returned. Although India was for some years in the early 1930s to dominate his political activities and considerably limit his political standing, he never revisited the subcontinent, which he regarded as a mere geographical expression and "no more a country than is the equator."

Throughout his political career, right up to 1967, Churchill was opposed to moves toward greater autonomy for India, much less its full independence. In the late 1920s and for the first half of the 1930s, Churchill campaigned and voted against what became the federalist Government of India Act of 1935 in the company of those who were often described then as die-hard Tories.

Throughout World War II, Churchill, as Britain's prime minister, refused to countenance Indian nationalistic claims for eventual independence, though he certainly recognized the importance of the Indian Army in his overall strategic calculus. By the mid 1940s, however, and after he had ceased to be prime minister immediately following Britain's general election of 1945, Churchill accepted the inevitability of partition and the emergence of India and Pakistan as independent states from 1947 onward. Churchill was old and intermittently ill during his second administration, but he presided over two meetings of Commonwealth prime ministers in 1953 and 1955. These were both attended by Jawaharlal Nehru for India and Mohammad Ali Jinnah, Pakistan's prime minister, but Indo-Pakistan relations were not discussed formally, primarily because of Nehru's refusal to participate generally in what he regarded as essentially bilateral business.

See also Mountbatten of Burma; Nehru, Jawaharlal; Raj, the; Wavell, Archibald Percival, First Earl Wavell.

References

Gilbert, Martin. *Churchill: A Life.* London: William Heinemann Ltd., 1991

Jenkins, R. *Churchill.* New York: Macmillan, 2001

CITIZENSHIP

Citizenship means the condition of being or of having the rights and duties of a citizen and of conducting oneself in relation to these duties. Thus citizenship is contextually defined and understood in relation to particular political systems. Given the complexity and heterogeneity of India and Pakistan citizenship, its entailments constitute a deeply controversial matter in both countries.

In general terms, citizenship is the nexus that, in any state, links civil society and the individual. According to one well-known definition by T. H. Marshall in 1950, citizenship includes at least three components: civil rights (that is, rights under law to personal liberty, freedom of speech, association, religious toleration, and freedom from censorship), political rights (that is, rights to participate in the political processes), and social rights—contemporary definitions tend to give prominence to human rights (within social rights) as well.

References

Marshall T. H. *Citizenship and Social Class.* Cambridge, UK: Cambridge University Press, 1950

CLINTON, WILLIAM JEFFERSON (1946–)

William Jefferson Clinton, 42nd president of the United States (1993–2001), nicknamed Bill, was born in Hope, Arkansas. He studied at Georgetown University, Oxford (as a Rhodes Scholar), and Yale Law School. He entered Arkansas politics as state attorney general and became Democratic governor (1974–1981) and (1983–1992). He defeated the incumbent president George H. W. Bush in 1992 and was elected to a second term in 1996. Clinton was not notably interested in South Asia during his first term as president except for his opposition to the development of nuclear capabilities there, as manifested in his outspoken criticism of India and Pakistan's nuclear testing in 1999.

With regard to Indo-Pakistan relations, two factors were especially prominent during Clinton's second administration: (1) nuclear issues, again most notably as focused by India and then by Pakistan's detonations in May 1998, and (2) sustained efforts to discourage fighting between the two South Asian countries and to encourage an Indo-Pakistan détente. On March 18, 2000, Clinton made a weeklong trip to India, Pakistan, and Bangladesh; taking a large number of American businesspeople with him, many of them with South Asian family ties. In his memoirs, Clinton said he was going to India to "lay the foundations" for what he hoped would be a positive long-term relationship. He added that "we had wasted too much time since the end of the Cold War, when India had aligned itself with the Soviet Union principally as a counterweight to China. Clinton's stop in Pakistan was the most controversial because of the October 1999 coup there, which brought General Pervez Musharraf to power. Clinton later wrote that he decided that he had to go for several reasons: to encourage an early return to civilian rule and a lessening of tensions over Kashmir, and to urge General Musharraf not to execute the deposed prime minister, Narwaz Sharif, who faced a number of charges that may have carried the death penalty. In particular, Clinton sought to press Musharraf to cooperate with the U.S. campaigns against Osama bin Laden and al-Queda.

The American Secret Service was strongly opposed to President Clinton's going to Pakistan or Bangladesh because the CIA had intelligence indicating that al-Qaeda wanted to attack Clinton on one of these stops, either on the ground or during takeoffs or landings. Clinton felt that he had to go because of the adverse consequences to American interests of going only to India and because he did not want to appear to be giving in to a terrorist threat. So he went despite far-reaching Secret Service advice about the conditions of the visit, and this Clinton later wrote was the only substantial request that the Secret Service made that he refused or at least heavily modified throughout his presidency. While Clinton was in Bangladesh, 35 Sikhs were murdered in Kashmir by unknown assassins intent on getting publicity from his visit.

In Delhi, during his meeting with Prime Minister Atal Bihari Vajpayee, Clinton expressed outrage and deep regret at this recent act of terrorism. Clinton later claimed to have gotten on well with Vajpayee and expressed the hope that he would have an opportunity to "re-engage" Pakistan before he left office. The two political leaders did not agree on the test ban treaty, but that was known beforehand, not least because Strobe Talbot had been working with India's Foreign Minister Jaswant Singh and others for months on nonproliferation issues. However, Vajpayee did pledge to forgo future tests and agreed on a set of positive principles that would govern their bilateral relationship, "which had been cool for so long."

Clinton also had a meeting with the leader of the then opposition Indian National Congress (INC) Party, Sonia Gandhi. Clinton addressed a joint session of the Indian parliament. He spoke of his respect for India's democracy, diversity, and impressive strides in building a modern economy. He discussed frankly Indo-American differences over nuclear issues and urged a peaceful solution to the Kashmir problem. In his memoirs, Clinton later expressed his surprise at getting "a grand reception" on this occasion.

See also Al-Qaeda/al-Qa'ida; Azad Jammu-Kashmir (AJK); Bangladesh; Talbott, Nelson "Strobe."

References
Clinton, W. J. *My Life.* New York: Random House, 2004
Talbot, Strobe. *Engaging India: Diplomacy, Democracy and the Bomb.* Washington, DC: Brookings Institution Press, 2004

COLD WAR

A phrase invented by Americans in the mid 1940s (and soon thereafter gaining prodigious currency and use) to characterize what they saw as the predominant nature of their country's relations with the Soviet Union and the communist world generally. Paradoxically, and contrary to the thermometer-like metaphor that "Cold War" implies, as relations became colder, the opponents often tend to approach "hot war"—that is, actual direct fighting. Thus the phrase can apply to aspects of Indo-Pakistan relations, literally and metaphorically.

Experience of U.S. relations with the Soviet Union, and from 1949 on with China, soon showed that the Cold War had most of the features of rivalries between traditional great powers that just stopped short of direct assault on the homeland territory of one or both of the principals—as seemed likely during the Cuban missile crisis of October 1962.

Similarly, the governments and populaces of India and Pakistan regarded each other as adversaries and rivals on occasions, especially around the times of their localized limited "hot" wars of 1947, 1965, and 1971. In some sense, a Cold War had been a recurrent condition of Indo-Pakistan relations since 1947—though this is not an idiom much used by either Indians or Pakistanis among themselves to describe their relations.

The condition of the Cold War is, in its many variants, as old as international relations, as readers of Thucydides' *History of the Peloponnesian War* are soon made aware. A classic description of the state of Cold War, eminently applicable to aspects of Indo-Pakistan relations, was made by Thomas Hobbes in Chapter 13 of his *Leviathan* (1651) in the following terms:

> For war consisteth not in battle only, or the act of fighting; but in a tract of time, wherein the will to contend by battle is sufficiently known; and therefore the notion of time is to be considered in the nature of war; as it is in the nature of weather. For as the nature of foul weather lieth not in a shower or two of rain; but in an inclination thereto of many days together. So the nature of war consisteth not in actual fighting but in the known disposition thereto, during all the time there is no assurance to the contrary. All other time is peace.

References
Ali, S. Mahmud. *Cold War in the High Himalayas: The USA, China and South Asia in the 1950s.* New York: St. Martin's Press, 1999

COLOMBO PLAN (1950)

This plan, founded in Ceylon's capital of Colombo in 1950 to promote the development of newly independent Asian countries, was one of very few regional organizations at the time [South Asian Association for Regional Cooperation (SAARC) came later in the mid 1980s], and it had both India and Pakistan as members from its inception. (Ceylon was officially renamed Sri Lanka in 1977.) Indeed, the Colombo Plan grew from a group of seven Commonwealth member states into an organization of 24 countries. Originally the plan was intended for a period of six years. This was renewed from time to time until its Consultative Committee gave the plan an indefinite life span in 1980. The plan is multilateral in approach and bilateral in operation: multilateral in that it recognizes the problems of development of member countries in the Asian and Pacific region and endeavors to deal with them in a coordinated way; bilateral because negotiations for assistance are made directly between a donor and a recipient country.

The Consultative Committee is the principal policy-making body of the Colombo Plan. Consisting of all member countries, it meets every two years to review and renew the economic and social progress of members, to exchange views on technical cooperation programs, and generally to review the activities of the plan. The Colombo Plan Council represents each member government and meets several times a year to identify development issues, to recommend measures to be taken, and to ensure implementation. The Colombo Plan Council is assisted by the Colombo Plan Secretariat (headquartered in Colombo), who participates in an advisory capacity at meetings of the Consultative Committee and assists the Council in the discharge of its functions, servicing committees and providing administrative support. The Secretary-General of the Colombo Plan Secretariat gives guidance to the programs and is in overall charge of all financial and administrative matters on which he reports to the council.

References

Jansen, G. H. *Afro-Asia and Non Alignment.* London: Faber and Faber, 1966

COLOMBO POWERS

"Colombo powers" was a term used journalistically in the 1950s to designate the occasional ad hoc meetings of five independent southern Asian powers, starting with their meeting in Colombo at the end of April and the beginning of May 1954 (though, in terms of economic diplomacy, they had begun to work together in the early 1950s). The prime ministers of Burma, Ceylon (renamed Sri Lanka in 1977), India, Indonesia, and Pakistan met in Colombo on April 29–30 and in Kandy on May 1–2, 1954, to exchange views and discuss problems of common interest and concern to them all. It was a rare opportunity for the prime ministers of India and Pakistan to meet together and to discuss a broad agenda—such as Indo-China, great power rivalries, ending colonialism—as was indicated in their joint communiqué, though there was no specific reference to bilateral Indo-Pakistan disagreements, as over Kashmir. It was from the Colombo powers that the idea of holding a general Afro-Asian conference emerged, which eventuated as the Bandung Conference.

See also Bandung Conference.

References

Jansen, G. H. *Afro-Asia and Non Alignment.* London: Faber and Faber, 1966

COMMUNALISM

Communalism is the advocacy and projection of a group identity based on religion, language, and/or ethnicity, and it has played a prominent part in the political and social life of India and Pakistan, at times perturbing or worsening their relations. Tensions and violence between various religious, ethnic, and linguistic groups have been endemic in India and Pakistan sporadically ever since 1947—and even earlier. Indeed, the very fact that Pakistan was created ostensibly to provide distinct homelands for the Muslims of the subcontinent and that it was created by partition and boundary redrawing meant that there were bloody clashes between Hindus and Muslims and between Muslims and Sikhs from the start. Estimates of the killings occasioned by the partitions of 1947 suggest that up to one million people lost their lives and perhaps as many as 20 million people were rendered homeless.

Eruptive violence in society is a major potential destabilizing force in both India and Pakistan. This was dramatically and bloodily evident by the mass communal killings in Gujarat in 2002. Violence in society has the potential to foment further political economic and religious frenzy, particularly in large urban areas such as Mumbai, Karachi, and Delhi, all three of which have suffered major instances of communal violence in recent decades. Communal tensions strongly influence the expectations and behavior under which Indo-Pakistan relations are conducted. Tensions between Hindus and Muslims can significantly influence Indian public perceptions of Pakistan and vice versa.

Some parallels can be drawn between afflictions of communal violence across Pakistan and India and violence within Jammu-Kashmir. Communalism there, although sporadic and usually highly localized, punctuates and affects political outcomes. Events such as the temple attack at Akshardam are blamed by Indians on Pakistani/Kashmiri terrorist organizations, such as Lashkar-e-Taiba. Linkages between Gujerat, Jammu-Kashmir, and India's northeast, with the potential for their violence to spill over into other areas, carry with them risks that conflict in any of these areas could undermine constructive social and economic efforts in India and Pakistan.

See also Azad Jammu-Kashmir (AJK); Karachi; Mumbai.

References
Brass, Paul. *Ethnicity and Nationalism: Theory and Comparison*. Thousand Oaks, CA: Sage Publications, 1991

CONFIDENCE-BUILDING MEASURES (CBMS)

Confidence-building measures (CBMs) are intrinsically intended to build confidence. They have gained prominence in the declaratory, and some would say in the operational, aspects of Indo-Pakistan relations, and the phrase has become much used, especially since the late 1990s.

Drawing on their experience and planning, senior Irish leaders have suggested, since the beginning of 2006 [see, for example, *Asian Age* (January 12, 2006)], that a common electricity grid like the one being designed for Ireland could be a constructive and confidence-building measure for India and Pakistan. Thus, Teresita Schaffer, Ireland's ambassador in Washington, D.C., recommended, in her report entitled "Kashmir: The Economics of Peace Building," that a common electricity grid for Jammu-Kashmir, including Pakistan-occupied Azad Jammu-Kashmir, could further the cause of peace between India and Pakistan. CBMs are intrinsic to improving Indo-Pakistan relations.

See also Azad Jammu-Kashmir (AJK); Karakoram Nature Park.

References
Schaffer, Teresita C. *Kashmir: The Economics of Peace Building: A Report of the CSIS South Asia Program with the Kashmir Study Group*. Washington, DC: Center for Strategic and International Studies, 2005

COUP D'ÉTAT

A term of French origin, coup d'état literally means a stroke or blow of state, but it more often and significantly means the illegal display or use of force to seize governmental authority. Strictly, a successful coup requires not only the displacement of the ruling person and authority (this could be achieved by assassination) but also the emplacement by the coup makers of a new person or regime in power.

One suggestive analysis, by the late S. E. Finer in a book entitled *The Man on Horseback,* argued plausibly that there is an inverse relation between levels of political culture and the propensity of the military to coup. When political culture is low, the propensity of the military to coup is high; when a country's political culture is high, then the propensity of the military to coup is low. A corollary follows

from these propositions: The violence required to carry through a successful coup in a country of high political culture is liable to be extensive, whereas the violence in a coup carried out in a country of low political culture may need only to be light.

The historical record shows that there have been many more unsuccessful coups than successful ones, though not in Pakistan, perhaps because of the generally embedded political power of the army. Coupology has some suggestive examples from Pakistan since 1947 (in 1958, 1977, and 1999), but not from India. Although there were loud rumors in India of an impending coup by segments of the army in 1962, these remained rumors. The nearest India has come to a coup d'état was Indira Gandhi's proclaimed Emergency in 1975—in effect an incumbency coup, which lasted two years and ended when she called and lost her parliamentary seat and overall support in parliament at the general election in March 1977.

References
Finer, S. E. *Man on Horseback*. London: Pall Mall Press, 1963
Lyon, P. "The First Great Post-colonial State: India's Tryst with Destiny." In James Mayall and Anthony Payne, eds. *The Fallacies of Hope: The Post-colonial Record of the Commonwealth Third World*. Manchester, UK: Manchester University Press, 1991

COUPLAND, SIR REGINALD (1884–1952)

Sir Reginald Coupland was an academic, publicist, classical scholar, and member of several important British commissions. He was educated at Oxford and appointed lecturer in ancient history at Trinity College, Oxford, in 1907. He became an early member of the board of the prestigious journal *The Round Table* and edited its quarterly journal twice (1917–1919 and 1939–1941).

Persuaded by the egregious advocate of imperial federation, Lionel Curtis, to study colonial history, Coupland soon succeeded his mentor as Oxford's Beit Lecturer in Colonial History in 1913. He was appointed to the Beit Chair in Colonial History in Oxford from 1920. This included a professorial fellowship at All Souls College. Coupland held both posts until his retirement in 1948.

Coupland first visited India in 1923, as a member of the British Royal Commission on the Higher Civil Services. In the interwar years he visited and wrote extensively about Ireland, Burma, and Palestine. He was an adviser to the Burma Round Table Conference in 1931. In 1936–1937, he was a member of the Royal Commission on Palestine, chaired by Lord William Wellesley Peel, and wrote much of the chairman's, report, which recommended partition. This report was utilized by the United Nations in 1947.

During World War II, Coupland in effect acted as if, in the words of one historian, he was "a one-man" royal commission on India's future. His study of India's constitutional developments was under the auspices of Nuffield College but was encouraged by Leo Amery, secretary of state for India, who arranged that Coupland should accompany the Sir Stafford Cripps Mission in 1942. When Cripps announced in a press conference of March 29, 1942, that a future Indian Union would be a dominion that could stay in or leave the Commonwealth and that any province could opt out if it dissented from the constitution produced by an Indian constituent assembly, Coupland described the announcement as India's Declaration of Independence. Coupland

Mahatma Gandhi walking down steps with Sir Stafford Cripps in New Delhi, India, following the Cripps Mission in 1942. The Cripps Mission was the British government's unsuccessful attempt to secure Indian support for its efforts in World War II. (Library of Congress)

published four volumes on India, which helped to prepare interested British opinion for partition and the possibility of Pakistan, though he personally hoped unity could be preserved by a new confederate plan formed from groups of states and provinces.

See also Cripps Mission.
References
Coupland, R. *The Indian Problem.* New York: Oxford University Press, 1944
Dictionary of National Biography. New York: Oxford University Press, 2002

CRICKET

Cricket matches, and especially "Test" (i.e., internationally approved) matches between India and Pakistan, act as indices of the state of public relations between the two countries. At times of strained relations, Indo-Pakistan Test matches were not and are not possible. When the matches are held, it is reasonable to deduce that relations are at least in moderately good condition.

India's Test victories in Pakistan (over the host country) early in 2004 were applauded by the usually fiercely partisan crowds, and Indian commentators reported approvingly on the sportsmanship of Pakistan's crowds, saying that this was also evidence of public support for the Indo-Pakistan détente processes then under way.

See also Khan, Imran.
References
Cashman, Richard. *Patrons, Players and the Crowd: The Phenomenon of Indian Cricket.* Mumbai: Orient Longmans, 1980

CRIPPS MISSION

Sir Stafford Cripps (1889–1952) was a leading British politician who twice led unsuccessful high-level missions appointed by the British government, once under Sir Winston Churchill and the second under Clement Attlee, in the hope of negotiating India's independence by agreement. In March 1942, Churchill sent Cripps on a special mission to India in the hope, which proved to be vain, that he would win the support of Jawaharlal Nehru, Mohandas Gandhi, and the Indian National Congress (INC) Party in the war against Japan by promising that India should have an assembly with powers to draft the constitution of an independent state once the war was over.

Cripps conceived of a federal India with semi-autonomous states, able to choose freely whether to remain within or to leave the Commonwealth. Gandhi sought immediate independence instead, saying that the British offer was a "post-dated cheque on a crashing bank." In March 1946, while Cripps was president of the Board of Trade in Attlee's government, he headed a second cabinet mission to South Asia in the hope of establishing a united federal India, but the Muslim concept of an independent Pakistan was by then too far advanced for this second mission to succeed.

See also Indian National Congress; Nehru, Jawaharlal.

References
Clarke, Peter. *The Cripps Version: The Life of Sir Stafford Cripps.* London: Allen Lane, 2002
Schofield, V. *Wavell: Soldier and Statesman.* London: John Murray, 2006

DAWN

Dawn is Pakistan's most prestigious and widely circulated English language newspaper. It was founded by Quaid-i-Azam Mohammad Ali Jinnah, with headquarters in Karachi and offices in most of Pakistan's major cities. It is also read by Pakistanis in the Diaspora overseas.

DEFENSE FORCES. *SEE* ARMED FORCES.

DELHI AGREEMENT. *SEE* LIAQUAT-NEHRU AGREEMENT (1950).

DESAI, MORAJI RANCHODJI (1896–1995)

A long-serving Indian politician who was briefly prime minister in the late 1970s, Moraji Ranchodji Desai was critical and suspicious of Pakistan's policies but came in his later career to be even more suspicious and critical of Indira Gandhi. Born in Gujerat and educated at Bombay University, Desai was a civil servant for 12 years before embarking on a long and varied political career. He joined the Congress Party in 1930 but was twice imprisoned as a supporter of Mahatma Gandhi's Civil Disobedience Campaign, before becoming revenue minister in the Bombay government (1937–1939).

He was again imprisoned in 1941–1945 for his part in the Quit India Movement before again serving as Bombay's revenue minister (in 1946) and later as home minister and chief minister (1952). Four years later he entered central government, first as minister for commerce and industry (1956–1958), then as finance minister, resigning in 1963 to devote himself to party work. Austere and proud of his integrity, he was always more interested in India's internal economic and financial issues than in foreign affairs.

He was a candidate for the premiership in 1964 and again in 1966, when he was defeated by Indira Gandhi. Appointed deputy premier and minister of finance in her administration, Desai resigned in

D

1968 over differences with the premier. In 1974 he supported political agitation in Gujerat, and the following year he began a fast in support of elections to the state, being detained when the Emergency was proclaimed by Gandhi in 1975. After his release in 1977, he was appointed leader of the Janata Party, a coalition opposed to Gandhi's rule. He finally became prime minister after elections that same year. The Janata government was, however, afflicted by much internal strife, and Desai was forced to resign in 1979.

See also Gandhi, Indira; Gandhi, Mohandas Karamchand; Janata Party; Mumbai.
References
Desai, Moraji. *The Story of My Life*, 2 vols. New Delhi: Macmillan of India, 1974

DEVALUATION

Devaluation is the reduction of the exchange value of a currency. Specifically, it is a fall in the amount of foreign currency that can be obtained per unit of a country's own currency. Since 1947, devaluation of their currencies has twice been a factor shaping Indo-Pakistan relations. Both occasions occurred when the great majority of the world's currencies were regulated by fixed exchange rates, especially since 1945 in relation to the American dollar and the Bretton Woods system.

In 1949, the pound sterling was devalued, and the currencies of most of the rest of the nondollar world, including India, followed suit. The Pakistani rupee was, however, maintained at its existing level. The Indian government was very critical of Pakistan's decision, and direct trade between the two countries almost came to a standstill. The economy of Pakistan was able to survive, however, mostly because of the great increase in export prices stimulated by the Korean War.

Pakistanis expressed great pride in being able to maintain the formal value of their rupee and were openly resentful of India's policy and its repercussions on Indo-Pakistan trade. The Pakistani rupee was devalued in its turn in 1955. The many-sided vulnerabilities of India's economy in the 1960s led to another draconian devaluation in 1966. The Sino-Indian War of 1962, followed by the 1965 Indo-Pakistan War, forced a doubling of military expenditure. The failure of two successive monsoons in 1965 and 1966, together with longer-term inadequacies of food production, storage, and transportation, exposed the economy as highly vulnerable to pressures from The World Bank and the International Monetary Fund. Devaluation of the rupee became a condition of further emergency aid.

After 1973 most countries, including India and Pakistan, allowed their currencies to float, that is, their exchange rates were determined by the market. But ascendant protectionism continued for several years before giving way gradually to more open economic policies, first by India and then to some extent by Pakistan, though in the 21st century the latter country seldom displays much confidence about its economic competitiveness via-à-vis India.

References

Black, E. *The Diplomacy of Economic Development.* Cambridge, MA: Harvard University Press, 1961

Srinivasan, T. N. *Eight Lectures on India's Economic Reforms.* Oxford, UK: Oxford University Press, 2000

DIASPORAS

Diaspora generally means the dispersal of a people or peoples—an extensive and continuing experience for India and Pakistan. Some commentators have made much of the potentially benign and positive influence of various South Asian diasporas as an aspect of, say, UK and/or U.S. policies in South Asia. As a long-term factor assisting economic development and investment, this is not a negligible matter. But three caveats need to be entered:

1. The diasporas are not homogeneous, organized, or easily mobilized, but they tend to be focused on particular issues.
2. The dominant attitudes held by those affected by the diasporas tend to judge events and policies historically rather than

contemporaneously and with a future orientation. Their attitudes thus tend to be more anachronistic than up-to-date.

3. Stay-at-home indigenes in India and Pakistan (especially in Kashmir) are inclined to complain that outside powers listen to the people or spokespersons in the diasporas more seriously than they do the stay-at-homes.

Among the many elements making up the diasporas from South Asia are Kashmiris from both sides of the Line of Control (LoC). Mirpuris from Azad Jammu-Kashmir have voted with their feet, whole families have migrated elsewhere in Pakistan (notably in the Punjab) but also abroad—especially to the United Kingdom and the United States. One, Farooq Kathwari, an expatriate from Srinagar now well installed in business in the United States, is the founder and funder of the Kashmir Study Group.

References

Malik, K. N., and P. Robb, eds. *India and Britain: Recent Past and Present Challenges.* New Delhi: Allied Publishers Ltd., 1994

Parekh, B., Gurharpal Singh, and S. Vertovee, eds. *Culture and Economy in the Indian Diaspora.* Oxford, UK: Taylor & Francis, 2003

Singh, Gurmukh. *The Rise of Sikhs.* New Delhi: Rupa and Company, 2003

DIPLOMACY

Both India and Pakistan built up professional diplomatic services after their independence in 1947, though India more swiftly and intensively than Pakistan. From the start, both countries often made political appointments to their embassies or high commissions abroad, and India soon acquired a reputation for the abilities of her diplomats. Both India and Pakistan practiced multilateral diplomacy, notably through membership in the United Nations and the Commonwealth.

Top diplomats in both countries invariably have to acquire detailed knowledge of the twists and turns of Indo-Pakistan relations, and they must expect their ups and downs. As this book's chronology indicates, senior diplomats from the two countries have met much more often than is popularly supposed by foreigners, sometimes meeting even when their intergovernmental relations are ostensibly badly strained. The main differences are that Pakistan wanted to internationalize or multilateralize the Kashmir issue, whereas India insisted that it was and should remain essentially a bilateral matter. In recent years reference is sometimes made to second- or third-track diplomacy to refer to quasi diplomatic meetings or dealings involving personnel who are not officially diplomats.

See also Azad Jammu-Kashmir (AJK); Dixit, J. N.
References
Kissinger, Henry. *Diplomacy.* New York: Simon & Schuster, 1994

DIVIDE AND RULE

"Divide and rule" is a capacious phrase expressing the idea that overall rule in a system is facilitated and maintained by dividing it into various component parts and keeping them separate. The British have often been accused of deliberately engaging in such tactics in their empire, especially in India from the 19th century to 1947. Since 1947 to some extent, the rulers of both India and Pakistan have been accused by others as engaging in deliberate divisiveness.

References
Moon, P. *Divide and Quit.* London: Chatto and Windus, 1961

DIWALI

Diwali is the Hindu festival of lights, held in October or November each year, in honor of Lakshmi, goddess of wealth and luck, and Rama, an incarnation of the god Vishnu. Lamps are lit and gifts exchanged. Sikhs associate Diwali with the sixth Guru's release from prison. Diwali is also a Jain religious festival.

See also Hinduism; Sikhism.

DIXIT, J. N. (1936–2005)

Jyotindra Nath "Mani" Dixit was a former foreign secretary of India and an ambassador to Bangladesh, Afghanistan, Pakistan, and Sri Lanka, and from May 2004 until his death, principal national security adviser to Manmohan Singh's government. During his 36-year-long career as a diplomat, as of 1994 he had dealt directly with Pakistan four times. He was undersecretary at the Pakistan desk briefly in 1964. He was the director of the special task force dealing with the East Pakistan crisis between November 1970 and January 1972. He was the head of

India's mission in Pakistan from the beginning of 1989 to the end of 1991, and Pakistan remained an important part of his responsibilities as foreign secretary from 1991 to 1994.

More generally, during his career Dixit served in various capacities in South America, Japan, Europe, the United States, and South Asia. He served on India's delegations to the United Nations Security Council and participated in a large number of multilateral conferences, political and technical, including summits of the Non Aligned Movement (NAM), the Commonwealth, and the South Asian Association for Regional Cooperation (SAARC). In 1995, he published an analysis of Indo-Pakistan relations from 1971 to 1994.

See also Afghanistan; Bangladesh; South Asia.
References
Dixit, J. N. *Anatomy of a Flawed Inheritance: Indo-Pak Relations 1970–1994.* Delhi: Konark Publishers Ltd., 1995

DIXON, SIR OWEN (1886–1972)

Sir Owen Dixon was an Australian jurist and United Nations (UN) mediator on Kashmir in the 1950s. He became justice of the Supreme Court of Victoria (1926), of the High Court of Australia (1929–1952), and then chief justice of that court (1952–1964). He served also as Australian minister to the United States (1942–1944). In 1950 Dixon was appointed the UN's representative for India and Pakistan. It was a frustratingly thankless task, inviting obloquy and recrimination. Each party was determined to hold on to what it had of Kashmir and to claim the rest. Dixon's report (UN Security Council document 5/1791, submitted September 15, 1950) was a succinct and well-argued case study. But nothing apparently could then, or later, convince Jawaharlal Nehru to hold a plebiscite that he might lose or to accept any de jure partition of the territory he wholly claimed.

By 1950, the Kashmir dispute had gotten bogged down because of the fixed and mutually suspicious attitudes of the principals. Nehru's official biographer, Sarvepalli Gopal, was later to write that Dixon's impartiality was "beyond doubt" but that he was too legalistic and impractical. Dixon sought to arrange zonal plebiscites and to replace the regular government of Kashmir by an administrative body consisting of officers of the United Nations. Nehru promptly rejected these proposals. Liaquat

Ali Khan told Dixon that public opinion in Pakistan would never permit him to concede the Vale of Kashmir to India and that there was nothing Pakistan could offer to India to induce her to give up the valley.

See also Azad Jammu-Kashmir (AJK); Khan, Liaquat Ali.
References
Gopal, S. *Jawaharlal Nehru.* Cambridge, MA: Harvard
    University Press, 1976–1984

DRUGS

Afghanistan supplies most of the world's opium, which is processed to make heroin, accounting for about 92 percent of illicit production. The annual crop in the early 21st century generated a third of the country's economic output. In 2005–2007 the government of the United States admitted that counternarcotic efforts in Afghanistan were failing in large areas of the war-torn country. U.S. officials claimed that there is a growing problem in the south of Afghanistan, with acute instability as the Taliban continued its offensive against U.S. and North Atlantic Treaty Organization (NATO) troops. Intensified antiopium eradication efforts focused on the southern province of Helmand, which U.S. officials say accounts for half of Afghanistan's production. Some 75 percent of the poppy growing in Helmand has developed since American and British troops became active in Afghanistan.

The U.S. government wants to use aerial spraying as one way to tackle eradication, but it has met strong opposition from many European, Afghan, and NATO officials who fear it will undermine counterinsurgency efforts.

DULLES, JOHN FOSTER (1888–1959)

U.S. secretary of state from 1953 to 1959, John Foster Dulles established a reputation as a tough negotiator and staunch anticommunist who cultivated close relations with Pakistan as a formal ally while being critical of India, and of Nehru in particular, for its "neutralism" and nonalignment. Dulles was born in Washington, D.C., into a family of marked legal and diplomatic distinction. Educated as a lawyer, he served as legal counsel to the U.S. delegation at the 1919 Peace Conference in Paris. Toward the end of World War II, he assisted in the drafting of the United Nations (UN) charter. Appointed as a

An opium poppy field in Afghanistan. Afghanistan produces and supplies almost 90 percent of the world's opium. (Ash Sweeting/ Courtesy of the Senlis Council)

John Foster Dulles was a U.S. diplomat and senator. He also served as secretary of state in the Eisenhower administration. He became famous for his strong anticommunist views, was critical of Nehru's India, and favored the United States' alliance with Pakistan. (Library of Congress)

State Department adviser by President Harry S. Truman, Dulles was the principal American drafter of the Japanese Peace Treaty that was signed at San Francisco in 1951 and that took effect in 1952, a role that brought him into some clashes with India's leaders. Dulles's general attitude in his foreign policy was that you are either for us or against us, which is why he regarded Pakistan as friendly and India with suspicion. Dulles became a cancer victim, resigning as secretary of state in April 1959 and dying the next month.

See also Eisenhower, Dwight David; Nehru, Jawaharal; Southeast Asia Treaty Organization (SEATO).
References
Gopal, Sarvepalli. *Jawaharlal Nehru.* Cambridge, MA:. Harvard University Press, 1976–1984

DURAND LINE
The boundary between Britain in India and Afghanistan was delimited by the Durand Agreement of 1898, named after the chief British negotiator, in an attempt to stabilize insurrectionary tribal areas at a time of mounting British and Russian maneuvers to extend their influence in central Asia.

In July 1949 the Afghan national assembly repudiated its treaties with Britain regarding the tribal territories of Pakistan and specifically disavowed the Durand line as an international boundary. Afghanistan's attempts to promote Pathan separation were increased in 1955 when the North West Frontier Province (NWFP) was integrated with West Pakistan (from 1971, Pakistan) and led to armed incursions of the tribes across the Durand line in September 1960 and again in March 1961.

For a time immediately afterward, diplomatic relations between the two countries were broken off. From about 1963, however, specific agitation for an independent Pakhtunistan ceased, though turmoil, Soviet occupation, and then civil war in Afghanistan have meant that the Durand line has become a very porous boundary for self-styled mujahedeen and refugees.

See also Afghanistan; Pathans; North West Frontier Province.
References
Caroe, O. *The Pathans.* New York: Oxford University Press, 1958
Khan, Hayat A. *The Durand Line—Its Geo-Strategic Importance.* Peshawar, Pak.: University of Peshawar and Hanns Seidel Foundation, 2000
Maxwell, N. *India's China War.* London: Jonathan Cape, 1970; New York: Penguin, 1992

DYARCHY
Dyarchy (or diarchy) is a form of government in which two persons, bodies, or states are jointly vested with supreme power. More generally, the term is used of a system where political authority is divided. The term was particularly associated with constitutional reforms introduced by the British into India in 1919. Under the reforms, some departments of provincial government were subject to Indian control, and others, including finance and security, remained under British control. The reforms did not extend to central government.

See also Autonomy; Raj, the.
References
Tully, M., and Z. Masani. *From Raj to Rajiv: 40 Years of Indian Independence.* New York: BBC Books, 1988

DYNASTICISM

Dynasticism means rule by a family with the clear implication that this dominance will be exercised over more than one person's period of governance. It is a notion expressed in monarchism (as in Bhutan or Nepal in present-day South Asia). But the term is used contemporaneously and, usually polemically, in a metaphorical sense to mean rule by a particular family such as the Nehru-Gandhi family in India or the Bhutto family in Pakistan.

Strictly speaking, political succession is not formally guaranteed by family ties in either India or Pakistan, because high political office is gained primarily by election and popular support or, in addition, as in Pakistan, by military seizure of power by coup d'état.

See also Coup d'État.

References

Ali, Tariq. *An Indian Dynasty: The Story of the Nehru–Gandhi Family.* New York: Putnam, 1985

EAST BENGAL

East Bengal was the designation utilized twice in the 20th century for a partitioned territory that roughly anticipated the modern state of Bangladesh. The first partition of the sprawling state of Bengal was from 1905 to 1912; the second partition took place from 1947 to 1971.

British rule in India centered in Bengal, especially after Robert Clive's victory at the Battle of Plassey in 1757, which gave the British East India Company dominance in Bengal. After the Indian war of national liberation of 1857 (known to the British as the Indian Mutiny), the British government took control from the East India Company and established its imperial capital at Calcutta (now Kalcotta).

By 1900 the British-fashioned province of Bengal was a huge territory, stretching from the Burmese border to extensively up the valley of the great Ganges River. With the assumption of the imperious Lord George Curzon as viceroy of India in 1905, the decision was taken, primarily for administrative conveniences, to partition Bengal. Calcutta and Bengal's hitherto western territories (approximately the equivalent of modern West Bengal, Bihar, and Orissa) was to be named simply Bengal. Eastern Bengal and Assam, a newly carved province, roughly anticipated modern Bangladesh excluding also the northeastern states of India (then all grouped under the name of Assam with its capital at Dacca, later Dhaka).

The partition of Bengal, begun in July 1905, provoked by nationalist protests and opposition from Bengalis. The partition was reversed in 1912, but this was accompanied by the separation of the non-Bengali–speaking portions of the province (in effect creating two additional provinces—Assam and Orissa—both of which were first subdivided after 1946) and the shifting of India's capital from Calcutta to Delhi.

Bengal was divided into two provinces in July 1946 in preparation for the end and partitioning of

British India. With a large Hindu majority in West Bengal and an extensive Muslim majority in East Bengal, in August 1947 West Bengal became part of India and East Bengal became part of Pakistan. Tensions between East Bengal and the western, politically dominant wing of Pakistan led to the One-Unit Scheme in 1955.

In 1955, two more areas of the western wing were put together to form the new province of West Pakistan. This system lasted until 1971 when East Pakistan declared independence during the Liberation War of Bangladesh and the new nation of Bangladesh was launched. The government of Pakistan did not recognize Bangladesh until 1974, and full diplomatic relations were not established until 1976.

References
Zaheer, Hasan. *The Separation of East Pakistan. The Rise and Realization of Bengali Muslim Nationalism.* New York: Oxford University Press, 1994

EAST PAKISTAN

Strictly, the term "East Pakistan" applied only from mid August 1947 until late December 1971 or early 1972: from the independence of Pakistan until the emergence of Bangladesh from what had hitherto been East Pakistan.

The territorial configuration of East Pakistan was defined predominantly by the Radcliffe Award of 1947. It produced an East Pakistan jutting out from the Bay of Bengal like a promontory almost entirely surrounded by Indian territories. Except for a small stretch of border with Burma in the extreme southeast (which first became a formal international boundary with the separation of Burma from British India in 1937), and with the further exception of the state of Tripura in the east, all of East Pakistan's land boundaries were those of the Radcliffe Award. The border with Assam, located in the Garo and Khasi Hills, also was adjudged by Sir Cyril Radcliffe, and, with the exception of Sylhet, the old provincial boundary between Assam and Bengal also became the Radcliffe boundary of 1947. The southern frontier was, of course, the Bay of Bengal. East Pakistan's northern border was not contiguous with China but was very close to it.

This East Pakistan comprised the extensive territories of the eastern flanks of Pakistan, officially between 1955 and 1971. East Pakistan was fashioned from Bengal by partition based on plebiscite and mostly conducted by British India in 1947. The predominantly Bengali-speaking Muslims chose to join Pakistan and thereby became part of that province of Pakistan with the name "East Bengal."

This East Bengal was renamed East Pakistan in 1956. But the next five years increasingly demonstrated alienation between West and East Pakistan. Then in 1971 warring Bangladeshi elements, aided extensively by Indian forces, enabled East Pakistan to break away from West Pakistan and to declare independence.

Severe tension between East and West Pakistan developed soon after 1947 because of their considerable geographic, economic, and cultural differences. East Pakistan's Awami League, a political party founded by the moderate Bengali Muslim nationalist Sheik Mujib-Ur Rahman in 1949, sought first great autonomy and then independence from West Pakistan. Although by the early 1950s about 56 percent of Pakistan's population lived in the eastern wing, the west held and wielded the predominant political and economic power.

After elections in 1970, East Pakistanis secured a majority of the seats in the national assembly. President Yahya Khan postponed the opening of the national assembly in an attempt to circumvent East Pakistan's demand for greater autonomy. Consequently East Pakistan's government proclaimed the independent state of Bangladesh on March 26,1971. Rahman (Mujib) and many of his supporters were imprisoned, and civil war broke out. Massive and professional help from Indian troops, openly provided in early December, swiftly led to the defeat and surrender of West Pakistani forces in East Bengal, by December 16. An estimated 1 million Ben-

galis were killed in the fighting and perhaps as many as 10 million more took refuge in India from March 1971 onward. Not until February 1974 did the rump state of Pakistan agree to recognize the independent state of Bangladesh.

See also Radcliffe, Sir Cyril.

References

Zaheer, Hasan. *The Separation of East Pakistan. The Rise and Realization of Bengali Muslim Nationalism.* New York: Oxford University Press, 1994

EISENHOWER, DWIGHT DAVID (1890–1969)

Dwight David Eisenhower was a U.S. general and 34th president (1953–1961), nicknamed Ike. His presidency occurred during some of the coldest years of the United States–Soviet Cold War, which affected relations with the formal ally Pakistan and nonaligned India.

Born in Denison, Texas, Eisenhower trained at the West Point Military Academy and by 1939 had become chief military assistant to General Douglas MacArthur in the Philippines. In 1942 he commanded the Allied forces for the amphibious invasion of French North Africa. He was selected as supreme commander for the cross-channel invasion into France in 1944. In 1950, he was made the supreme commander of the Combined Land Forces in the North Atlantic Treaty Organization (NATO). In 1952 he was swept to victory in that year's presidential elections, standing as a Republican, and he was reelected in 1956. Throughout his presidency, he and his government were preoccupied with foreign and defense policies and with campaigning against Communism, though in the latter respect with less doctrinairism than Secretary of State John Foster Dulles.

Dulles advocated military pacts and openly preferred Pakistan to India, whereas Eisenhower dealt more evenhandedly with the two largest South Asian countries. Eisenhower visited India in December 1959, the first serving American president to do so while in office, and he enjoyed a spectacularly popular welcome. Indeed, of the four successive American presidents when Jawaharlal Nehru was India's prime minister, he got on best with Eisenhower. Nehru's official biographer, Sarvepalli Gopal, commented that "Truman's cocky vulgarity had grated on him; and so did the affluence and glitter with which Kennedy was surrounded. Lyndon Johnson he hardly knew. But Eisenhower's sincerity and goodwill, especially in contrast to the blinkered preachiness of Dulles, struck a chord." However, it was in vain that Eisenhower urged Mohammed Ayub Khan to respond to Delhi's repeated offers of an Indo-Pakistan no-war declaration.

See also Ayub Khan, Mohammed; Dulles, John Foster ; Kennedy, John Fitzgerald.

References

Wolpert, S. *Nehru: A Tryst with Destiny.* New York: Oxford University Press, 1996

EMERGENCY (1975–1977)

"Emergency" was the term utilized by Indira Gandhi in June 1975 to impose a draconian regime that lasted 21 months. Opposition leaders were imprisoned, severe press censorship imposed, and the Constitution amended to restrict the powers of the judiciary. Eventually the Emergency proved to be Indira's rather than India's, for it ended with the abruptly called general election and conclusive defeat of Indira Gandhi and her supporters in March 1977.

The Janata Party opposition coalition won a decisive victory. For the first time the Indian National Congress (INC) Party lost control of the national government, winning only 34 percent of the popular vote, and it was the first time it had obtained less than 40 percent of the popular vote.

See also Gandhi, Indira.

References

Frank, K. *Indira: The Life of Indira Nehru Gandhi.* New York: HarperCollins, 2001

Hardgrave, R. L., and S. A. Kochanet. *India: Government and Politics in a Developing Nation,* 6th ed. Fort Worth, TX: Harcourt College Publishers, 2000

Tully, M., and Z. Masani. *From Raj to Rajiv: 40 Years of Indian Independence.* New York: BBC Books, 1988

ERSHAD, HOSSAIN MUHAMMAD (1930–)

A leading Bangladeshi soldier and subsequently a politician who played a prominent role as president and minister of defense in the 1980s. Born February 1930, son of the late Malebul Hussain and Mojida Begum, he married Begum Raushad in 1956, and they had one son and one adopted daughter. Ershad was educated at Carmichael College, Rangpur, and Dhaka University. He then joined the army, attending initially the staff course of the Defence Service Command and Staff College at Quetta in Baluchistan, Pakistan, in 1966 and later the war course of

Hossain Muhammad Ershad led a military takeover of Bangladesh in 1982. He ruled the country until two months of student protests against his regime and accusations of widespread corruption forced his resignation in 1990. (AFP/Getty Images)

the National Defence College, New Delhi, India, in 1975. An infantryman, he rose by various promotions until he became commanding officer of the infantry battalion (1969–1971); adjutant general of the Bangladesh Army (1973–1974); deputy chief of army staff, Bangladesh Army; chairman coordination and control cell for national security (1975–1978); and chief of army staff, Bangladesh Army (1978–1986). Lacking significant support from either of Bangladesh's two main political parties, he sought without much success to form his own government party, named the Jatiya party.

Taking control of power in a bloodless coup in March 1982, he was chief martial law administrator, Bangladesh (1982–1986), president of the Council of Ministers (1986–1990), president of Bangladesh (1983–1990), and minister of defense (1986–1990). Ershad, as leader of the country's third largest party, became eligible to stand in elections after a judge declared, on January 17, 2007, that he had served sufficient time in prison following a conviction for corruption. Ershad, who had been banned from taking part in the judicial hearings, was greeted by thousands of Jatiya Party supporters outside the court.

See also Bangladesh.

References

Rose, Leo O., and Richard Sisson. *War and Secession: Pakistan, India and the Creation of Bangladesh.* Berkeley: University of California Press, 1990

EXECUTIVE RULE. *SEE* EMERGENCY

F

FAMILY. *SEE* DYNASTICISM

FEREZEPUR

Ferezepur in the north Punjab was an area awarded to India by the Radcliffe Commission in 1947. It was important because it contained major headwaters that were vital for the irrigation of the agriculturally productive state of Bikaner, which was ceded to India. As with Gurdaspur, some allegations were made from the Pakistan side that Mountbatten had influenced the issue in India's favor, but there is no conclusive evidence to substantiate this claim.

See also Gurdaspur; Mountbatten of Burma.
References
Menon, V. P. *The Story of the Integration of the Indian States.* New Delhi: Orient Longmans, 1956
Ziegler, P. *Mountbatten: A Biography.* New York: Alfred A. Knopf, 1985

FLOODING

Flooding and the ravages of natural disasters recurrently afflict India, Pakistan, and Bangladesh. Northeastern India and Bangladesh are repeatedly prone to great natural disasters. About half a million people died in one night in November 1970 when a terrible cyclone struck the Ganges Delta. Cyclones and monsoonal floods are an annual affliction, and death tolls often have to be numbered in the tens of thousands. Such catastrophes bring in their wake the diseases that poverty and chronic malnutrition foster: cholera, small pox, typhoid, yellow fever, and many others. Undoubtedly many deaths result from disease, and thousands of other people exist precariously during their often short lives in hunger and illness. While natural disasters crudely and cruelly reduce and restrict the impact of demographic pressure, no neat quasi Malthusian forces are at work to keep population growth at manageable proportions and compatible with the level of food production from the land.

Instead, agricultural saturation, or so-called involution, often sets in. The density of the population has passed the point where the land is no longer capable of sustaining it with the staple, rice, given the domestic levels of production and the traditional types of seeds and methods. Occasionally, India and Pakistan help each other when afflicted by natural disasters. This help has varied quite a lot since 1947, but their reaction to this or that disaster is an indication of the prevailing state of Indo-Pakistan relations.

References
Spate, O. H. K. *India and Pakistan: A General and Regional Geography,* 2nd ed. New York: Methuen, 1960

GALBRAITH, JOHN KENNETH (1908–2006)

John Kenneth Galbraith was a professor, lifelong American liberal, public servant, anglophile, and U.S. ambassador to India (1961–1963). He was born at Iona Station, Ontario, Canada, near Lake Erie and the U.S. border, of Scottish Calvinist ancestry. Educated first in Canada and then extensively in the United States, he served in various jobs in academe and in the federal government from 1934 onward.

He became an American citizen in 1939. In 1949 he was appointed Paul M. Warburg Professor of Economics at Harvard, which was to be his main base for the rest of his life. He became emeritus professor in 1975. Galbraith was an active Democrat and a consultant-adviser to successive Democratic presidents, from Franklin Delano Roosevelt to William J. Clinton. He was an adviser to John F. Kennedy's election campaign for president in 1960

and was rewarded with the post of ambassador to India. Soon he was on cordial terms with India's Prime Minister Jawaharlal Nehru. "You realize, Galbraith," Nehru once said to him, "that I am the last Englishman to rule in India."

Apart from a brief period of intense behind-the-scenes activity during the Sino-Indian border conflict late in 1962, Galbraith did not find his official duties onerous. While in Delhi, he continued to write and publish extensively, including the coauthorship of a book about Indian painting, and compiled a daily diary that was later published as *The Ambassador's Journal*. Galbraith was a prolific and elegant writer who published more than 20 books, including his autobiography, *A Life in Our Times* (1981). He was a Keynesian in economics and a classical American liberal in politics.

See also Kennedy, John Fitzgerald; Nehru, Jawaharlal.
References
Galbraith, J. K. *Ambassador's Journal: A Personal Account of the Kennedy Years.* Boston: Houghton-Mifflin, 1969

John Kenneth Galbraith (1908–2006), Canadian American economist and U.S. ambassador to India under John F. Kennedy. (National Archives and Records Administration)

GANDHI, FEROZE (1912–1960)

Feroze Ghandi was a Parsi by birth and upbringing and an activist in the Indian Congress from his student days in Allahabad, where and when he first became friendly with Kamala Nehru. He studied in London and was close to Indira Gandhi in Switzerland, Paris, and England. He married Indira Gandhi in 1942, and they had two sons, Sanjay and Rajiv. Feroze Gandhi became a Congress member of Parliament for Rae Bareilly in Uttar Pradesh after independence and a fierce critic of corruption. He separated from his wife, Indira, as she became full-time political helper and hostess for her

father, Jawaharlal Nehru. Feroze Gandhi was no relation of Mahatma Gandhi.

See also Gandhi, Indira.
References
Frank, Katherine. *Indira: The Life of Indira Nehru
    Gandhi.* New York: HarperCollins, 2001

GANDHI, INDIRA (1917–1984)

Indira Gandhi was prime minister of India from
1966 to1977 and again from 1980 to 1984. She was
the daughter and only child of independent India's
first prime minister, Jawahawalal Nehru, and
mother of Rajiv Gandhi. Kashmiri-born, she was
unrelated to Mohandas Gandhi, though with him
she sought to curb or reduce communal violence
between Hindus and Moslems in partitioned Bengal
in 1947. Her mother died in 1936, and from early
adulthood Indira Gandhi was the close companion,
confidante, and helper of her father, Jawaharlal
Nehru. In 1942 she married a Parsi, Feroze Gandhi,
but soon it was clear that her husband was less important to her than her father. As long as her father
was alive, she was widely thought not to have political ambitions of her own, but at his death she became minister of broadcasting and information
from 1964 to 1965 and was thus responsible for pre-
senting much of India's case against Pakistan in
their two wars of 1965. On the death of Prime Minister Lal B. Shastri (1966), she was elected leader of
Congress and became prime minister.

Her two periods in the premiership were marked
by active social and economic reform but also by
tension and war, in 1971, with Pakistan. She was at
the zenith of her power and popularity in 1971–
1972, but her assumption of almost dictatorial powers with the declaration of the Emergency in 1975
quickly polarized India's politics and caused mounting determination from her critics and opponents
to topple her. In March 1977 the Indian National
Congress (INC) Party was defeated for the first
time—by the Janata coalition, united only in their
opposition to Gandhi. Within a few months she was
back on the path to power, winning the general election of 1980 with a promise of firm government and
demonstrating her renewed appeal with much of
the electorate.

All in all, throughout her two terms as prime
minister, she combined the basic policies of her father, but in a more abrasive way and with mounting
difficulties: Her motifs were socialism, industrializa-

*Indira Gandhi broke traditional gender boundaries and helped
lead India through its formative years of independent,
democratic government. She was assassinated by her Sikh guards
in 1984. (Library of Congress)*

tion, and nonalignment though the latter policy, in
her hands, exhibited a distinct leaning toward the
Soviet Union and the development of India's nuclear capacity, albeit justified entirely in terms of
India's national interests. She dealt highhandedly
with the fissiparous tendencies and regional dissi-
dence that had cumulatively afflicted India since independence.

She was assassinated in October 1984 by some of
her personal Sikh bodyguards, ostensibly in revenge
for her tough line against Sikh would-be secession-
ists and for ordering Operation Bluestar in the
Sikh's holy city of Amritsar within its famous
Golden Temple. Indira Gandhi was succeeded as
India's prime minister by her second son, Rajiv
Gandhi.

See also Amritsar; Gandhi, Feroze; Gandhi, Rajiv; Janata
    Party; Nehru, Jawaharlal.
References
Frank, Katherine. *Indira: The Life of Indira Nehru
    Gandhi.* New York: HarperCollins, 2001
Gopal, S. *Jawaharlal Nehru.* London: Jonathan Cape,
    1975–1983
Masani, Zareer. *Indira Gandhi: A Biography.* London:
    Hamilton, 1975

GANDHI, MOHANDAS KARAMCHAND
(1869–1948)

Mohandas Karamchand Gandhi [Mahatma, or Great Soul] was a foremost Indian national leader who devoted most of his life, certainly from 1915 onward, to help India achieve independence, through a campaign based on nonviolence and civil obedience but also, especially in the last years of his life, by enjoining fellow Hindus to be fair to Muslims and to the new country of Pakistan. He was very reluctant to see the partition of the Raj in 1947 and did what he could to minimize communal violence in 1947–1948, seeking to persuade Indian leaders to be generous and conciliatory toward the newly independent Pakistan. He was assassinated by a Hindu fanatic on January 30, 1948.

Gandhi was born in Porbandar in western India, the son of Karamchand Gandhi, the chief minister of Porbandar and his fourth wife Putlibai, a deeply religious Hindu. From her, he developed a firm moral belief in nonviolence and in fasting as a means of spiritual cleansing. An undistinguished

student in his adolescence, he was married at the age of 12, and at 19 his family sent him to London to study law at the Inner Temple. On his return to India from Britain in 1891, he was unable to find suitable employment as a lawyer, so he accepted a year's contract in Natal, South Africa, in 1893. Encountering the humiliation of racial prejudice there, he was persuaded to remain in South Africa to protest proposed legislation that would deprive Indians of the right to vote. His mission met with mixed successes and failures, but he was instrumental and influential in publicizing the rights of Indians in South Africa, and in so doing he launched himself as a skillful and tenacious political campaigner.

Shedding his Anglicized ways (both figuratively and literally), Gandhi adopted a simple ascetic life. He organized boycotts of British goods (both as a symbolic protest against India's subordinate colonial status and to stimulate India's local industries). His nonviolent campaigns of civil disobedience to British rule provoked the British to imprison him

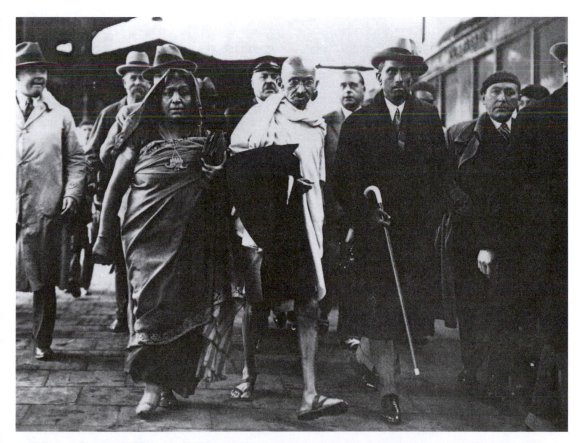

Indian nationalist leader Mohandas Gandhi (center) with Indian poet Sarojini Naidu (left) in England in 1931. (Library of Congress)

on four different occasions (1922, 1930, 1933, and 1942). He also went on hunger strikes to focus attention on, and to generate sympathy and support for, the cause of Indian independence.

He stayed in South Africa for 29 years opposing further discriminatory legislation by means of nonviolent defiance. His law practice funded his political activities, and, with the support of his wife, he threw his home open to political colleagues. During the South African War (1899–1902), he aided the British by raising an ambulance corps of more than 1,000 Indians for which he was awarded the War Medal. Gandhi showed great interest in the Khilafat movement and helped to keep it broadly nonviolent.

Gandhi returned to India in 1914, and, while supporting the British in World War I, he became a dominant personality in the National Congress Movement (which had been formed in 1885), reshaping it and thereby becoming a widely recognized public figure. His basic policies to achieve independence remained unchanged: nonviolent means and noncooperation. During his Civil Disobedience Campaign, however, British soldiers killed nearly 400 people at Amritsar in 1919. Gandhi was jailed for conspiracy for two years. On his release, the Hindu and Muslim factions of the Indian National Congress (INC) Party were at loggerheads, and reasoning with them proved unproductive. In an attempt to reactivate the nonviolent campaign, Gandhi undertook a much publicized personal fast for three weeks. By 1928, he was back at the head of the Congress Party.

In 1930, he launched his spectacular campaign against the punitive salt taxes imposed by the British, leading a 320-kilometer (200-mile) march to collect salt, in symbolic defiance of the government monopoly. More than 60,000 were imprisoned, and he was rearrested. On his release in 1931, Gandhi negotiated a truce between Congress and the British government in India and traveled to London to participate in the Round Table Conference on Indian Constitutional Reform. Returning to India, he renewed the civil disobedience campaign and was arrested again—a pattern, along with his fasts unto death, of his political activity for the next six years. He assisted in the adoption of the constitutional compromise of 1937, by means of which Congress ministers accepted office in the new provincial legislatures.

Portrait of Mahatma Gandhi in 1946. (Library of Congress)

With the outbreak of World War II, Gandhi was convinced that only a fully free India could give Britain effective moral support. He thus urged complete independence more and more strongly. Presented with the Cripps proposal in 1942 for a constituent assembly with the promise of a new constitution after the war, he described it as a "post-dated cheque on a crashing bank." In August 1942, he was arrested for concurring in disobedience action to obstruct the war effort and for supporting the Quit India Movement. He was not released from prison until May 1944. British policy changed under the Clement Attlee government, and Gandhi sought to collaborate with the last two viceroys (Sir Archibald Percival Wavell and (later Lord) Louis Mountbatten) but could not reach agreement with the Muslim leader Mohammad Ali Jinnah. Gandhi regarded the partition of India "as potentially disastrous" and accepted it with reluctance. He welcomed the grant of Indian independence as the noblest act of the British nation. He began fasts in order to shame the perpetrators of communal violence into accepting his pleas for mutual tolerance, but his moderation alienated radical nationalists. Accompanied by Indira Gandhi, he was in Bengal at the time of India's independence in mid August 1947, endeavoring to damp down communal violence, efforts that continued in various parts of India for the rest of his life. He survived one assassination bid, but ten days later, on January 30, 1948, he was shot dead in Delhi by a young Hindu journalist.

See also Abdullah, Sheikh Mohammad; Amritsar; Gandhi, Indira; Nehru, Jawaharlal; Wavell, Archibald Percival, First Earl Wavell.

References

Schofield, V. *Wavell: Soldier and Statesman.* London: John Murray, 2006

Tidrick K. *Gandhi: A Political and Spiritual Life.* London: I. B. Tauris, 2006

Wolpert, Stanley. *Nine Hours to Rama.* New York: Random House, 1962

Wolpert, Stanley. *Gandhi's Passion: The Life and Legacy of Mahatma Gandhi.* New York: Oxford University Press, 2001

Zeigler, P. *Mountbatten: A Biography.* New York: Alfred A. Knopf, 1985

GANDHI, RAJIV (1944–1991)

Indian statesman and prime minister (1984–1989), Rajiv Ghandi was born in Mumbai (Bombay). Initially a nonpolitical member of modern India's most famous political family, he became prime minister of India (1984–1990) and attempted, with only minor fleeting success, détente in India's relations with Pakistan, especially by meeting with his opposite number, Benazir Bhutto. The eldest grandson of Jawaharlal Nehru (and second son of Indira Gandhi and Feroze Gandhi), Rajiv Gandhi was an engineering student in Cambridge, where he met his Italian-born future wife, Sonia. He left without taking a degree and went on to have a career as a pilot in India. Following the death of his younger brother Sanjay (1946–1980) in a flying accident in 1980, his mother persuaded him to enter politics, hoping to groom him as her successor. Following her assassination in 1984, he won a record majority in India's general elections that year.

Rajiv Gandhi identified India's internal strife as his major problem and attempted to reduce tensions in Punjab, Assam, and Gujerat, but he was only fleetingly successful, particularly in the Punjab, where Sikh militants revived their campaign for greater autonomy in 1986. As prime minister Gandhi also sought (with limited success) to improve relations with neighboring governments— notably with Pakistan and Sri Lanka, making use where possible of comembership in the Commonwealth and in the South Asian Association for Regional Cooperation (SAARC).

Initially there were high hopes within India and abroad of a new regime led by a man with modern ideas, free from the taint of corruption and perhaps capable of defusing and improving Indo-Pakistan relations. Such expectations were soon sadly disappointed. In the face of renewed Sikh violence in the Punjab and Tamil violence in Sri Lanka, Rajiv Gandhi appeared hesitant, and his regime was tainted with a corruption scandal.

Although he introduced a vigorous policy of technological innovation, he was hampered by the legacy of his mother's campaign against Sikh militancy, and he ordered further military action at Amritsar in May 1988. In 1989 he and his supporters suffered an electoral defeat as devastating as victory had been massive in 1984. During a subsequent electoral campaign he was assassinated on May 21, 1991, by a Sri Lankan sailor, ostensibly on ceremonial guard duty. His widow, Sonia Gandhi, subsequently entered politics to further Rajiv's work and that of his family.

See also Amritsar; Gandhi, Indira; Gandhi, Sonia; Sikhism.

References

Mehta, Ved. *Rajiv Gandhi and Rama's Kingdom.* New York: Penguin, 1995

Tully, Mark, and Masani Zareer. *From Raj to Rajiv: 40 Years of Indian Independence.* New York: BBC Books, 1988

GANDHI, SONIA (1946–)

Sonia Ghandi is an Indian political leader and present head of the Nehru dynasty. She has also been president of the Indian National Congress (INC) Party since 1998 and minister to parliament (MP) for the Congress Party from Raebaeli in Uttar Pradesh, Lok Sabha, since 2004. Earlier she was MP for Amethi, Uttar Pradesh, 1999–2004.

Born in Italy on December 9, 1946, daughter of Stefano and Paola Maino, in 1968 she married Rajiv Gandhi who was assassinated in 1991 and whom she had first met when they were students in Cambridge, England; they had two children, one daughter, Priyanka, and one son Rahul. Sonia adopted Indian nationality in 1983. She is president of the Rajiv Gandhi Foundation and a member of the Congress Party since 1997.

Leader of the opposition in the Lok Sabha (1999–2004), she refused to become prime minister of India after the May 2004 general elections, despite the fact that many of her party supporters wanted her to. Nonetheless, she exerts considerable influence from behind the scenes and from the wings of India's political stages. Sonia Gandhi has notably not taken a pronounced interest in Indo-Pakistan relations.

See also Gandhi, Rajiv; Uttar Pradesh.

References

Kidwai, Rasheed. *Sonia: A Biography.* New York: Viking Penguin, 2003

Tully, M., and Masani, Z. *From Raj to Rajiv: 40 Years of Indian Independence.* New York: BBC Books, 1988

Wilkinson, S. *Votes and Violence: Electoral Competition and Ethnic Riots in India.* New York: Cambridge University Press, 2004

GILGIT

Gilgit is the name of a mountainous territory in the northwest of Kashmir, containing the town of Gilgit, which gives its name also to (1) the Gilgit River; (2) the Gilgit Wazarat lying to the south; and (3) the Gilgit agency now comprising four political districts, two subdivisions of Gilgit and Astor, the two states of Hunza and Nagar, and the subagency of Chilas. These territories extend toward Chitral, Afghanistan, Tajikistan (formerly part of the USSR), and Xinjiang (Singiang, China). Since 1947 the whole area has been administered by Pakistan.

The ancient name of the land once under its Hindu rulers that today comprises Gilgit was Sargin; later it was known as Gilit, which the Sikhs and Drogas corrupted into Gilgit. To the local people the region is still named Gilit or Sargin Gilit. The remains of Buddhist carvings suggest that Gilgit was once a center of Buddhism. The Sikhs entered Gilgit in the early 1840s and built a garrison there. When the British granted Kashmir to Maharaja Gulab Singh of Jammu in 1846, Gilgit was transferred with it, and a boundary commission was sent, which included the first known English visitors.

The Dogras (Gulab Singh's people) were driven out for eight years (1852–1860). For the next 30 to 40 years, there were armed skirmishes for control of the Gilgit Basin. In 1889, in an attempt to guard against the advance of Russia, the British government, acting as the suzerain power of Kashmir, established the Gilgit agency. With the British withdrawal in 1947, the place of the political agent was taken by a Kashimiri governor. In November 1947 the Gilgit scouts rose in revolt, imprisoned the governor, and proclaimed Gilgit's accession to Pakistan.

When the fighting between India and Pakistan ceased in Jammu-Kashmir in 1949, a cease-fire line was established. The whole of Gilgit, including the agency and the *wazarat,* lay north of this line of Pakistan, which appoints a political agent as head of the administration. The population is Muslim, mainly Shia.

See also Azad Jammu-Kashmir (AJK); Chitral; Russia.

References

Knight, E. F. *Where Three Empires Meet.* New York: Longmans, 1895

Spate, O. H. K. *India and Pakistan: General and Regional Geography,* 2nd ed.. New York: Methuen, 1960

GOA

Goa is a territory on the west coast of India, bounded on the north by Maharashtra and on the east and south by Karnataka. It has a coastline of 65 miles, an overall area of 1,429 square miles, and, according to 1991 census population, 1.7 million inhabitants. The coastal area comprising present-day Goa was captured by the Portuguese in 1510, and the inland area was added in the 18th century. Despite the growing appeal and strength of decolonization after 1945, the Portuguese strongly disapproved of retroceding to India and mounted and maintained a stance in favor of their continued colonial rule. For Nehru, India was opposed not only to the continuance of colonial enclaves such as Goa in South Asia, but to West European colonialism generally.

In December 1961 Portuguese rule was ended by the Indian Army, and Goa was immediately incorporated into the Indian Union as a Territory, together with Daman and Diu. Goa was granted statehood as a separate unit on May 30, 1987; Daman and Diu remain Union Territories. Pakistanis generally condemn India's seizure of Goa, saying that this was further evidence of India's expansionist and militaristic character.

See also Nehru, Jawaharlal.

References

Gopal, Sarvepalli. *Jawaharlal Nehru.* Cambridge, MA:. Harvard University Press, 1976–1984

GOKHALE, GOPAL KRISHNA (1866–1915)

A leading Indian politician and social reformer, Gopal Krishna Gokhale was born in Kotluk, Bombay. He became professor of history at Fergusson College, Poona, resigning in 1904, when he was selected as a representative of the Bombay legislative council at the supreme council. He founded the Servants of India Society in 1905 to work for the relief of the underprivileged and in that same year was elected president of the Indian National Congress (INC) Party. He was a leading protagonist of Indian self-government and influenced Mahatma Gandhi, advocating moderate and constitutional methods of agitation and gradual reform.

See also Gandhi, Mohandas Karamchand; Savarkar, Vinayak Damodar; Tilak, Bal Gangadhar.

GORBACHEV, MIKHAIL SERGEYEVICH (1931–)

Soviet statesman, general secretary of the Communist Party of the Soviet Union (1985–1991), and president of the Supreme Soviet of the USSR (1988–1991), Mikhail Gorbachev was born in Privolnoye in eastern Russia and studied at Moscow State University and Stavropos Agricultural Institute. He began work as a machine operator and joined the Communist Party in 1952. He rose steadily in the ranks of the party and became general secretary of the Central Committee (1985–1990). In 1988 he also became chairman of the Presidium of the Supreme Soviet and in 1990 the first (and last) executive president of the USSR.

On becoming the party's general secretary, he launched a radical program of reform and restructuring, popularly known as *perestroika*. A reassessment of Soviet history was encouraged under the label of *glasnost* (openness). In foreign and defense policies he reduced military expenditure and practiced a policy of détente and of nuclear disarmament with the West. He ended the Soviet military occupation of Afghanistan in 1989. Briefly surviving a coup in August 1991, he was forced to resign following the dissolution of the Soviet Union in December 1991. Since 1992 he has been president of the International Foundation for Socio-Economics and Political Studies (the Gorbachev Foundation), which he established in 1991. He failed to attract a significant vote in Russia's 1996 presidential elections.

In his executive years, Gorbachev showed considerable interest in promoting and maintaining good relations with India, a country he visited several times. Gorbachev was relatively uncritical of the

Portrait of Mikhail Gorbachev, former president of the Soviet Union, who favored good relations between India and the Soviet Union. (Library of Congress)

nuclear tests detonated by India (and by Pakistan) in 1999, and he was disposed to support the notion that India was, and should be, accorded recognition as a power of consequence on the world stage within a remodeled world order. He was awarded the Indira Gandhi Prize in late November 1988 during his second official visit to India.

See also Khrushchev, Nikita; Putin, Vladimir (Vladimirovich).

References
Gorbachev, M. *Memoirs.* New York: Doubleday, 1996

GOVERNMENT OF INDIA ACT (1935)

The Government of India Act was largely the lengthy consequence of the Round Table Conferences of 1931–1932, much parliamentary debate in Britain, and a white paper of 1933 on the Indian government. The act proposed an all-India federal structure, including the Princely States but with an administration based on diarchy, in which the viceroy and the council retained "reserved" topics, including defense, foreign affairs, and any issue endangering financial stability or threatening civil peace. At the same time the act extended the authority of regional legislatures, to which provincial ministers were to be responsible.

This latter provision was put into operation within two years, but it still gave the provinces no more than limited democratic rights: the electoral system allowed 43 percent of the people (about 7 percent of them women) to vote. Discord between the various communities of the subcontinent prevented agreement on a federal structure before the spread of World War II led to calls for greater independence. When after 1947 India devised its own constitution (a process that produced a full text by 1950), much of that document was based on the Government of India Act of 1935.

See also Dyarchy.

References

Hardgrave, R. L., and S. A. Kochanet. *India: Government and Politics in a Developing Nation,* 6th ed. Fort Worth, TX: Harcourt College Publishers, 2000

Morris-Jones, W. H. *The Government and Politics of India.* London: Hutchinson & Co., 1964

GRACEY, GENERAL SIR DOUGLAS DAVID (1894–1964)

Sir Douglas David Gracey was a senior British soldier who served in South Asia for much of his career and who was chief of staff of the Pakistan army (1947–1948) and commander-in-chief of the Pakistan army from 1948 until his retirement in 1951. Son of a member of the Indian Civil Service and educated at Blundell's School and at the Royal Military College, Sandhurst, Gracey served in France in 1915 and then in Iraq, Palestine, Syria, and Egypt 1916–1920, latterly with the Gurkha Rifles. He was an instructor at Sandhurst (1925–1927) and then a student at the Staff College, Quetta, in Baluchistan (1928–1929). He served in India (1930–1934) with Gurkha Rifles again and in North West Frontier operations in 1939. He served in many different theaters during World War II, including Burma and Indochina. He was commander-in-chief northern command in India (1946) and commander First Indian Corps (1946–1947), before becoming successively vice deputy and then head of the Pakistan army.

References

Schofield, V. *Wavell: Soldier and Statesman.* London: John Murray, 2006

Who Was Who. 1961–1970. London: A&C Black Publishers, 2007

GREAT GAME, THE

For almost a century the world's two most extensive empires—those of Victorian Britain and czarist Russia—waged a secret war of espionage, intelligence, and counterintelligence in the remote and bleak mountain passes and deserts of central Asia. Some of those engaged in this shadowy struggle called it the Great Game, a phrase invented in the mid 19th century by British spies and officials and immortalized in Rudyard Kipling's famous novel, *Kim,* about northwest India, first published in 1901. When the game first began, the two rival empires lay nearly 2,500 kilometers (1,553 miles) apart. By the end of the century, some Russian outposts were within 33 kilometers (20 miles) of British India across the Wakhan panhandle. And in the first half of the 20th century, the Great Game proved to be very volatile, even if its frontline principals were few.

Since the end of the Cold War and the collapse of the Soviet Union, the central Asian successors states have become actively involved in the rivalries among Russia, China, and the United States, especially regarding energy resources. The phrase "the Great Game," on occasion, has been revived contemporaneously to characterize the interplay among the great and minor powers in the extensive region of central Asia, affecting also the outlook, calculations, and geopolitics of India and Pakistan.

See also Afghanistan; Raj, the; Russia.

References

Brobst, Peter J. *The Future of the Great Game: India's Independence and the Defence of Asia.* Akron, OH: University of Akron Press, 2005

Kipling R. *Kim.* New York: Macmillan, 1901

Undeland, Charles, and Nicholas Platt. *The Central Asian Republics. Fragments of Empire. Magnets of Wealth.* New York: Asia Society, 1994.

GREAT POWER ASPIRATIONS

To be regarded and recognized as a great power is a widely held ambition within India, whereas Pakistanis, though not expecting or even aspiring to such status themselves, are deeply apprehensive that India might achieve such status and that this will turn out to be to Pakistan's disadvantage. However, though there has been much talk about enlarging and reforming the United Nation's Security Council (UBSC) and this has happened once (by increasing the number of nonpermanent members from 6 to

11), successive Indian governments, especially from the mid 1990s to today, have sought in vain to achieve permanent status—and possibly also the veto power—for their country.

Both India and Pakistan have served several terms of office as nonpermanent members of the UNSC, but not simultaneously. Reform of the UN generally is not easy to accomplish and it may be that, despite its demographic weight and growing economic strength, India will not achieve permanent membership on the UNSC in the immediate future.

As well as controversies about the size and powers in the contemporary world of the permanent members of the United Nations (currently known as the P5), informal hierarchies are manifested mainly in their conference diplomacy and illustrated especially in the activities of the Group of Seven or Eight (G7 or G8) in world economic matters. Neither India nor Pakistan is a member of these top hierarchies of the contemporary world system, but India is very much a candidate member in the event of reform of the composition and workings of the UNSC or the G7, whereas Pakistan is not.

References
Hardgrave, R. L., and S. A. Kochanet. *India: Government and Politics in a Developing Nation,* 6th ed. Fort Worth, TX: Harcourt College Publishers, 2000
Wight, Martin, Hedley Bull, and Carsten Holbraad. *Power Politics.* Leicester, UK: Leicester University Press, 1978

GREEN REVOLUTION

"Green revolution" is a colloquial phrase that acquired a considerable currency, especially in the 1960s and 1970s, to designate dramatic increases in cereal outputs (especially rice and wheat) per unit of land in a number of developing countries, including India and Pakistan. These rapid increases in cereal output were pioneered by Borlaug's plant breeding research in Mexico, which produced high-yielding dwarf wheat varieties, and by the work at the International Rice Research Institute in the Philippines, which did the same for rice varieties. Success with these new varieties depended on a monoculture integrated production system, with high fertilizer applications, considerable water supplies, fossil fuels, and agrochemical weed and pest controls. Easier storage of wheat rather than rice meant that some traditional rice growing areas such as Bengal switched in part to wheat production and consumption. But the Green Revolution benefited a relatively small number of farmers.

References
Frankel, F. R. *India's Political Economy 1947–1977.* Princeton, NJ: Princeton University Press, 1978

GUJRAL, INDER KUMAR (1919–)

This Indian politician and former prime minister was born in Jhelum (part of Pakistan since 1947). Educated at the Forman Christian College, Harley College of Commerce in Lahore, and Punjab University. He was imprisoned by the British in 1930–1931 and again in 1942 for his active involvement in India's independence movement. He and his family settled in India upon its partition in 1947. He became a member of parliament in 1959 and served as minister of external affairs (1989–1990 and 1996–1997). He became India's prime minister (1997–1998) as head of a United Front coalition and sought actively to improve relations with Pakistan. In 1998 he became chairman of the Parliamentary Committee on External Affairs.

References
Who's Who 2005. New York: Palgrave Macmillan, 2005

GURDASPUR

A district and town in northeast Punjab that in 1947 Radcliffe's boundary commission controversially awarded to India (i.e., East Punjab) in the face of bitter objections by Pakistan's leaders. In 1947, Gurdaspur contained Hindu and Muslim populations of roughly equal sizes. Gurdaspur was essential to India if the Amritsar district was not to be cut off from the rest of the country. Subsequently it was alleged by Pakistanis, probably wrongly, that Mountbatten had awarded Gurdaspur to India to make possible land links with Kashmir. According to his official biographer, Mountbatten did not interfere in this decision and in any case the future of Kashmir had not been decided at the pertinent time.

See also Abell, Sir George Edmond Brackenbury; Beaumont, Christopher; Mountbatten of Burma; Radcliffe, Sir Cyril.
References
Schofield, V. *Wavell: Soldier and Statesman.* London: John Murray, 2006
Ziegler, P. *Mountbatten: A Biography.* New York: Alfred A. Knopf, 1985

GWADAR

Gwadar is a port on Pakistan's Arabian Sea coast in Baluchistan. It is strategically located because it is near the Strait of Hormuz through which about 40 percent of the world's oil passes. China contributed about US$200 million for construction of Gwadar Port's first phase, which was completed in April 2005 when Prime Minister Wen Jiabao visited Pakistan.

It was reported then that China will also finance the second phase, which will have nine more berths, an approach channel, and storage terminals. President Pervez Musharraf, while on a five-day state visit to China, said, "we are interested in setting up a trade and energy corridor for China," through which oil imports from Iran and Africa can be transported to China's Sinkiang Uygur Autonomous Region by land. He also said that the route on which a feasibility study is being conducted is a shortcut compared with the present main route via the Strait of Malacca to East Asia's seaboard.

See also Baluchistan; Musharraf, Pervez.
References
Asian Age (February 23, 2006).

"HAIR OF THE PROPHET" REVOLT

Serious disorders in Kashmir were caused by the theft of a hair, said to be a relic of the Prophet Mohammed, from a mosque at Hazratbal (near Srinagar) on December 26, 1963.

The hair that was reputedly brought to Srinagar by the Mogul Emperor Aurangzeb (1658–1707) was kept in a small glass tube in a wooden box that was locked in a cupboard and that was ritually exhibited about ten times a year. The fact that the thief had ignored valuable silver that was kept in the shrine suggested that the theft had a political motive. This theft of a relic precipitated the gravest political unrest in Kashmir for several years and led to serious riots in Srinagar.

Khwaja Shamsuddin, who had succeeded Bakshi Gulam Muhammad as prime minister of Kashmir on October 12, resigned in consequence on February 28, 1964 and was succeeded by Ghulam Muhammad Sadiq. The latter announced on March 31 that the treason charges against Sheikh Abdullah and his codefendants would be withdrawn. The Sheikh was unconditionally released on April 8, 1964, after having been more than 10 years in detention.

The unrest in Srinagar, together with an earlier announcement that the state's constitution would be amended to strengthen integration with India, accentuated the tension between India and Pakistan over Kashmir, leading to an increase in the number of incidents on the cease-fire line.

HAQ, FAZLUL (1873–1962)

Maulvi Abul Kasem Fazlul Haq (or Huq), colloquially known as the Tiger of Bengal, was a lawyer and prominent and volatile figure in Bengali and Pakistani politics. He was born in the Barisal district of East Bengal and educated in Calcutta. He was active in Muslim League politics from 1913 and president of the All India Muslim League from 1916 to 1921. He was a leader of the vernacular tenants and professionals who increasingly clashed with the Urdu-speaking Muslim business and land-owning elite.

In April 1936, Haq founded the Krishak Praja Party (KPP). He was prime minister in a coalition government with the Muslim League from 1936 to December 1941. Following a bitter disagreement with Mohammad Ali Jinnah, he formed a second ministry initially allied with the Hindu Mahasabha and held office until March 1943.

In the 1946 provincial elections, the Muslim League decisively defeated the KPP. From 1947 Haq resumed his legal career as advocate general of East Bengal. In 1954 he returned to active politics as leader of the newly formed Krishak Sramik Party (KSP) that was victorious alongside the Awami League in the provincial elections of that year, but he lasted less than two months in office. Soon after the lifting of the Governor's Rule in June 1955, the KSP returned to form a coalition government, and Haq became governor of East Pakistan. Haq's efforts to replace the Awami League ministry in March 1958 with the KSP met with powerful opposition and culminated in his dismissal.

Haq retired and aged appreciably. He died in Dhaka's Medical College in April 1962. A populist controversialist for most of his life, his death prompted further controversy as to who should organize his posthumous commemorative meeting. About 2,000 people attended the government-sponsored meeting, and about 50,000 came to the unofficial one in Dhaka Stadium.

See also Awami League (AL); East Bengal; Jinnah, Mohammed Ali.

References

Talbot, I. *Pakistan: A Modern History.* New York: Hurst and Company, 1998

HINDU MAHASABHA

Hindu Mahasabha was a Hindu nationalist (or communalist, as it was initially called) movement founded in 1914 at Hardwar in reaction to the Muslim League that had been launched in 1906. In its early years it was overshadowed by the Indian National Congress (INC) Party that advocated secular politics while the Mahasabha was propagating a Hindu nationalism. The Lucknow Pact of 1916 and the ascendancy of the moderates in the Congress alienated many of the Mahasabha, which separated from the Congress and called to Hinduize all politics and militarize Hinduism. To circumvent the fragmentation of caste, language, and sect, the Mahasabha launched a movement for the consolidation of the Hindu *rashtra,* or Hindu Nation.

The movement sought to reclaim those who had left the ranks of Hindu and denounced the creation of Pakistan as the vivisection of Mother India. Since 1960 the Mahasabha has been in decline and no longer a significant force, having proved to be less potent than the Rashtriya Swayamsevak Sangh (RSS) the Association of National Volunteers.

See also Hindutva; Lucknow; Rashtriya Swayamsevak Sangh (RSS).

References
Anderson, Walter K., and Shridhar Damla. *The Brotherhood in Saffron: The Rashtriya Swayamsevak and Hindu Revivalism.* Boulder, CO: Westview Press, 1987
Hardgrave, R. L., and S. A. Kochanet. *India: Government and Politics in a Developing Nation,* 6th ed. Fort Worth, TX: Harcourt College Publishers, 2000
Jayaprasal, K. *RSS and Hindu Nationalism.* New Delhi: Deep and Deep Publications Pvt. Ltd., 1991
Khilnani, Sunil. *The Idea of India.* London: Hamish Hamilton, 1997

HINDUISM

Hinduism is a complex religion and a complicated system of arranging society for its votaries. Members of the highest caste of Hindus are called Brahmans (or Brahmins), and Brahmanism is the purest form of the Hindu faith. Brahmans usually are educated and cultural people. For them, the stories or myths on which the Hindu faith is founded have special meaning. They do not necessarily believe that these stories actually happened but rather that they reveal spiritual truths of importance. The lower castes of Hindus undoubtedly believe that these myths really happened and that they explain the world. About three-quarters of the population of India are made up of these lower Hindu castes.

All Hindus believe in transmigration, or constant rebirth, after death. If one's acts during life are good, then the person is reborn into a higher form. After millions of years of rebirth, a good person may reach Nirvana, which is not a heaven but a state of nothingness. Most Hindus also think that fate decides everything for them. They believe in the doctrine of Karma, that is, that human beings cannot escape their cycles of rebirth into the world.

One of the most confusing things about Hinduism is the character of its gods. A particular god may be gentle and helpful, but the same god is capable of the cruelest and bloodiest of actions. The god Vishnu, for instance, is considered the preserver and Siva is the destroyer, but both gods appear in many forms—sometimes noble and beautiful, sometimes terrifying.

See also Caste; Hindu Mahasaba; Hindutva.
References
Basham, A. L. *The Wonder That Was India.* New York: Macmillan, 1951
Hardgrave, R. L., and S. A. Kochanet. *India: Government and Politics in a Developing Nation,* 6th ed. Fort Worth, TX: Harcourt College Publishers, 2000
Pande, B. N. *Islam and Indian Culture.* Patna, Ind.: Khuda Bakhsh Oriental Public Library, 1987
Pandey, Gyanendra. *Hindus and Others.* New York: Viking Penguin, 1993
Radhakrishnan. *The Hindu View of Life.* New York: Oxford University Press, 1926
Varshney, A. *Ethnic Conflict and Civic Life: Hindus and Muslims in India.* New Haven, CT: Yale University Press, 2002

HINDUSTAN

"Hindustan" is a term used pejoratively mostly by Pakistanis to imply that, because India has a predominantly Hindu population, it should be called Hindustan. But a relatively few nationalistic Hindus would prefer that their country was named Hindustan. In 1947, Jawaharlal Nehru and his colleagues were adamant that their newly independent country was to be a secular, nonconfessional state. In effect this meant that the leaders of the new India regarded themselves in large part the successors of the British Raj and Pakistan's leaders as secessionists.

Bronze figure of the dancing Hindu god Shiva. Hinduism is a complex and variable religion with many gods. (Corel)

References
Hardgrave, R. L., and S. A. Kochanet. *India: Government and Politics in a Developing Nation,* 6th ed. Fort Worth, TX: Harcourt College Publishers, 2000

HINDUTVA

"Hindutva" is a term used by Hindu nationalists to define an India essence. Hindutva, meaning literally Hindu-ness, seeks to restore India to its civilization's greatness and to define in its own terms what it means to be a Hindu. Contemporary advocates of Hindutva in India sometimes refer to the pamphlet written by Vinayak Damodar Savarkar, entitled *Hindutva: Who Is a Hindu?* (first published in 1923). This pamphlet was thus a notable modern starting point for Hindu nationalist identity, relying heavily on stigmatization and suppression of "threatening others." It stresses the political, cultural, and religious supremacy of the Hindus, defined as those for whom India is at once a father- and motherland (i.e., the land of their ancestors) and the Holy Land (the birthplace of their religion). This notion tends to leave Muslims as the alien others, who must abide by the rules and respect the mores of the Hindu majority if they wish to remain in India. The ultimate aim of the Hindu right, advocating Hindutva, is the creation of a Hindu *rashtra* (Hindu nation).

References
Khilnani, Sunil. *The Idea of India.* London: Hamish Hamilton, 1997
Rinehart, R., ed. *Contemporary Hinduism: Ritual, Culture and Practice.* Santa Barbara, CA: ABC-CLIO, 2004
Tully, Mark. *India in Slow Motion.* New York: Penguin, 2002

HUMAN RIGHTS

Although present in the polemics of both India and Pakistan since 1947, accusations regarding violations of human rights have become a more prominent feature of their mutual altercations in recent years, especially regarding Kashmir, and in several respects this trend mirrors the greater salience paid to human rights internationally. The concept of human rights derives from the doctrine of natural rights, maintaining that individuals, by virtue of their humanity, possess fundamental rights beyond those prescribed in law. First formally incorporated into the U.S. Declaration of Independence (1776), human rights later became the basis for the Declaration of the Rights of Man and the Citizen that the French National Assembly adopted in 1789, and most written constitutions nowadays contain a bill of rights. Despite having no legal standing, the United Nations (UN) General Assembly adopted a Universal Declaration of Human Rights in 1948, listing individual and social rights and freedoms, followed in 1953 by the European Convention on Human Rights.

Human rights have thus traditionally been understood to be rights relating to life, liberty, equality, and dignity. In the Indian context, section 2(d) of the Protection of Human Rights Act 1993 defined human rights to mean those "rights relating to life, liberty, equality, and dignity of the individual guaranteed by the Constitution or embodied in the international covenants and enforceable by courts in India." Human rights in India have, over the course of more than fifty years, been given a strong constitutional foundation and have developed through recognized judicial interventions. The Pakistani record in this respect is patchier and less established.

Early in 2006 India was elected to the newly appointed UN Human Rights Council. Indian spokespeople said that this election was a recognition of its diplomatic standing in the comity of nations. India secured a total of 173 votes out of a maximum possible of 190. India received the most votes of any of the countries elected to the 47-member council. Following the elections, a draw was held to determine the length of each members' term on the council. India secured a one-year term, while China got three years and Pakistan two. All of the G4 group of the UN Security Council—India, Brazil, Germany, and Japan—were elected in 2006 to the newly constituted Human Rights Council.

References
Bose, Sumantra. *The Challenge in Kashmir: Democracy Self-Determination and a Just Peace.* Thousand Oaks, CA: Sage Publications, 1997

HURRIYAT CONFERENCE

The All-Parties Hurriyat (Freedom) Conference (APHC) was founded in 1990. This heterogeneous loose coalition of interests sought to have a decisive say in shaping Kashmir's future but notably has failed to produce a well-defined sustainable consensus since its launching. Its leadership mostly came from humble socioeconomic backgrounds and expressed considerable contempt for Farooq Abdullah and its National Conference Party, which it accuses of having no substantial constituency in the Kashmir Valley. Since the 1990s the APHC has tried, without notable success, to expand its appeals to the state's non-Muslim movement; however, the opening of an APHC branch in Jammu in the hope of recruiting Hindus has not been successful.

References
Bose, Sumantra. *The Challenge in Kashmir: Democracy, Self-Determination and a Just Peace.* Thousand Oaks, CA: Sage Publications, 1997

HYDERABAD

The most populous of the Princely States under the Raj with a Muslim ruler, the nizam, but a huge Hindu majority posed a major problem in 1947 as to its future. Although landlocked in the Deccan center of India, the nizam sought independence as a sovereign state and signed a one-year standstill agreement with India, pending a determination of the future direction. Soon, with mounting disorder in Hyderabad and the increasing influence of paramilitary Muslim extremists, the Indian government moved troops into the state in a so-called police action to restore law and order. Hyderabad then acceded to the Indian Union.

See also Princely States
References
Menon, V. P. *The Story of the Integration of the Indian States.* Mumbai: Orient Longmans, 1956
Ziegler, P. *Mountbatten: A Biography.* New York: Alfred A. Knopf, 1985

IDENTITIES

The rapid rise of identity politics in both India and Pakistan, especially from the late 20th century, has amply demonstrated the heterogeneity of these two ostensibly nation-states. Tensions within and between religions, caste, tribal, and ethnic communities have produced substantially more social conflict in political systems that apparently have less capability to manage such conflict, where political and other mobilizations threaten to outstrip and swamp institutionalization.

See also Caste; Communalism.

References

Hardgrave, R. L., and S. A. Kochanet. *India: Government and Politics in a Developing Nation,* 6th ed. Fort Worth, TX: Harcourt College Publishers, 2000

Huntington, S. *Political Order in Changing Societies.* New Haven, CT: Yale University Press, 1968

INDIAN NATIONAL CONGRESS (INC)

The Indian National Congress (INC) Party was founded in 1885 by anglophile Indians and some middle-class Britons to argue for constitutional development within India. By the 1920s the Congress, as it has come to be called, had been transformed into a mass movement with an organization stretching outward from New Delhi throughout each state and region. For more than three decades after independence, the Congress was the only genuinely all-India party not only because of its wide-ranging geographical distribution but in terms of its widespread electoral appeal, especially at general elections.

Indeed, the Indian National Congress (INC) Party has headed India's Union government for all but what amounts to a decade since independence, but its onetime hegemony's grip weakened appreciably since Nehru's death in 1964, especially in the 1990s. The imposition of Emergency rule in 1975–1977 by Nehru's daughter, Indira Gandhi, was seen by many as a betrayal of Congress's democratic credentials and led to the ouster of Congress from of-

fice in the 1977 elections by a loose coalition under Moraji Desai. Indira Gandhi regained office in 1980 but was murdered by her Sikh bodyguards in October 1984 to avenge the army's storming of the Sikh's Golden Temple in Amritsar during a battle against Sikh separatists.

Indira's older son, Rajiv Gandhi, succeeded her and was confirmed in a landslide election victory in December 1984. However, mounting scandals and the defection of some senior Congress figures, such as Vishwanath Pratap Singh, led to Rajiv Gandhi's defeat by an anti-Congress coalition in the November 1989 elections. Singh formed a National Front left coalition that included the agrarian socialists Janata-Dal, regional parties and leftists, with outside support from the Hindu revivalist Bharatiya Janata Party (BJP). This administration collapsed a year later, and a Janata Dal splinter group led by Chandra Shekhar formed a government with Congress support. Soon the collapse of this agreement in March 1991 preceded general elections in May–June of that year, and Rajiv Gandhi was assassinated in May during the election campaign. Congress emerged with the most parliamentary seats and, though still short of a majority, formed a government headed by Pamulaparti Venkata Narasimha Rao as prime minister.

Congress was defeated in the May 1996 elections, and a coalition government was inducted with Haradanahalli Dodde Gowda Deve Gowda as prime minister. This was replaced by a United Front coalition in April 1997, led by Inder Kumar Gujral, which collapsed in November 1997 and was replaced by a BJP-led coalition in March 1998, headed by Atal Bihari Vajpayee. The Vajpayee government fell in April 1999 after 13 months in office but was

Mohandas Gandhi, with All-India Congress's president Jawaharlal Nehru, at a meeting of the India Congress in Bombay in 1946. (Library of Congress)

reelected with a larger majority in October 1999. Contrary to the prediction of most political pundits in India, Congress won a majority of seats in 2004 and headed a new coalition, with the BJP becoming the major opposition party again. To the further surprise of many pundits, Sonia Gandhi refused to become prime minister, preferring a relatively small public role as leader of the Congress party. Dr. Manmohan Singh became prime minister.

See also Bharatiya Janata Party (BJP); Gandhi, Indira; Gandhi, Rajiv.

References

Ghose, S. *Indian National Congress, Its History and Heritage.* New Delhi: All India Congress Committee, 1975

Low, D. A., ed. *The Indian Congress Centenary. Hindsight.* New York: Oxford University Press, 1988

INDIAN POLITICAL SERVICE (IPS)

The Indian Political Service (IPS) was launched at the beginning of the 20th century during the viceroyalty of Lord George Curzon. An External Affairs department administered the North West Frontier Province and handled relations with Afghanistan, Tibet, Nepal, and the rulers of the Gulf states. A political department maintained contacts between the viceroy and the rulers of the Princely States. A third of the IPS was recruited from top members of the Indian Civil Service; two-thirds were senior army officers.

See also North West Frontier Province; Princely States.

References

Mason, Philip (pseudo. Woodruff). *The Men Who Ruled India: The Guardians.* London: Jonathan Cape, 1954

INDO-PAK JOINT COMMISSION

This Indo-Pakistan joint commission was set up in 1983 to provide further impetus to economic cooperation. Four subcommittees for trade, economics, information, and travel were set up under the aegis of this commission. It first met in January 1984, in Islamabad and New Delhi, and identified various areas in which both countries could cooperate to their mutual benefit. The subcommittee on trade identified a large number of items for commodity trade, including bulk trading. The joint commission ceased functioning in 1989, as Indo-Pakistan relations worsened, with deterioration being especially marked over Kashmir. During President Pervez Musharraf's visit to India on April 16–18, 2005, it was decided to reactivate the joint economic commission and the joint business council.

The two foreign ministers held the first of the revived joint commission meetings on October 4, 2005, expressed satisfaction at the revival of the joint commission, and hoped that it would contribute significantly in strengthening mutually beneficial relations and cooperation between the two countries. "The two sides decided to restructure and streamline the work of the joint commission in the light of developments that have been taken place since its last meeting in 1989," their statement said.

Elaborating, the statement added, "the understandings reached would form the guidelines for the future work plan for the joint commission." It said that the next meeting of the commission would be preceded by technical-level working groups on agriculture, health, science and technology, information, education, information technology and telecommunications, environment, and tourism. These were expressions of hope that the revival of the joint commission for the two countries could lead to the ironing out of differences in expanding the scope of trade and enhancing the quality of economic ties.

INDO-PAKISTAN RELATIONS AND THE UNITED NATIONS (UN)

The United Nations (UN) and its agencies have provided many forums for the conduct of Indo-Pakistan polemics and occasional agreements. India was a founding member of the UN in 1945, though this was two years before its independence, but India had been a member of the League of Nations (albeit under British suzerainty). Pakistan became a member of the UN in 1947, though it had to circumvent Afghanistan's opposition to its membership.

At India's behest and subsequent disappointment, the UN was requested to intervene in the dispute over Kashmir. India's request came before the Security Council on January 1, 1948, and a cease-fire was achieved by January 5, 1949. This cease-fire

was a notable achievement but less than the Indian government had initially hoped for or expected. However, the UN cannot claim all the credit for bringing about the cease-fire. An important contributory factor was that both the Indian and Pakistani armies were then still commanded by British generals, while many of the senior officers on both sides had served together before 1947 and had trained together at Britain's military colleges at Sandhurst (in the city of Camberley) or in India at Dehra Dun.

It was also the case that, toward the end of 1948, both sides saw that the chances of a quick settlement had passed and that there was a real danger of a full-scale war, which neither country desired. Nonetheless, UN mediation was probably decisive in tipping the scales in favor of a cease-fire, and subsequently its Military Observer Group helped to check incidents that might have led to another outbreak. Thus UN intervention was almost certainly instrumental in keeping alive the chances of a more permanent settlement and in preventing a full-scale war. Later, from the mid 1950s onward, India and Pakistani officers trained together in third-party military academies or served together in UN peacekeeping forces, enjoying apparently professional camaraderie even during times of Indo-Pakistan tension.

References

Ahmed, Mushtaq. *The United Nations and Pakistan.* Karachi, Pak.: Institute of International Affairs, 1955

Heimsath, Charles, and Surjit Mansinght. *A Diplomatic History of Modern India* New Delhi: Allied Publishers, Ltd., 1971

INDO-PAKISTAN WAR OF 1947–1948

The state of Jammu-Kashmir was one of over 550 Princely States that recognized the British paramountly. Immediately before the withdrawal of British troops and officials from India, the state came under pressure from India and Pakistan to join them. The maharaja of Kashmir, Hari Singh, vainly preferred to remain independent and tried to delay the issue. By the time of British withdrawal, however, the state was being invaded by so-called tribals from the North West Frontier Province (NWFP) and by regular professional Pakistani troops, and the Maharaja reluctantly decided to cede Kashmir to secular India. The government of India promptly airlifted Indian troops and weapons into Kashmir, and the first Indo-Pakistan War was underway. Then and subsequently, much controversy raged as to responsibility for the war. The Pakistani claim is that, since the majority of the Kashmir population was, and is, Muslim, the Princely State should have acceded to Pakistan. The Indian claim arose from both Maharaja Hari Singh's cession and the fact that considerable portions of Jammu-Kashmir were Sikh, Buddhist, and Hindu.

Azad Jammu-Kashmir (AJK) forces ("Azad" means liberated or free in Urdu) consisted of the local militia supported by tribals and Pakistan army units.

The AJK had several initial advantages, notably:

- Prior to the war, the Jammu-Kashmir state forces were spread around borders and so were badly deployed to counter large-scale activities.
- Some of the state forces joined AJK forces.
- The AJK were also helped by regular Pakistani soldiers, who acted as officers for some of the units, and the proportion of those soldiers was increasing.
- Some British officers may have helped the Pakistani with planning. British officers on the scene led the revolts by Islamic factions of Kashmir forces, who arrested and murdered Dogra officers, especially in the Gilgit region. They acted as advisers for the tribal militias and coordinated their attacks.

As a result of these advantages, the main invasion forces quickly brushed aside the Jammu-Kashmir state forces. The attackers; advantages were not pressed vigorously, however, and India forces soon halted the offensive by airlifting reinforcements. This was the swift follow-up to Kashmir's cession to India. The Pakistani AZK offensive petered out toward the end of 1947. The exception was in the high Himalayas sector, where the AZK were able to make marked gains until turned back at the outskirts of Leh in June 1948. Indeed, throughout 1948 many small-scale localized battles were fought. None of these gave a marked strategic advantage to either side, and the fronts gradually solidified. Support for the AZK forces by Pakistan's army gradually became more overt with regular Pakistani units in support.

By early November 1948, India's armed forces had started to gain ascendancy in all sectors. A formal cease-fire was declared on December 31, 1948.

Punch was finally freed after a siege of over a year. Pakistan's Gilgit forces in the high Himalayas, which had initially made considerable advances, were finally defeated. India's forces pursued Pakistan's as far as Kargil before being forced to halt because of supply problems. The Zoji-La Pass was prized open by using tanks (which up until then had not been thought possible at that altitude), and Dras was recaptured. The use of light tanks and armored cars was based on experience gained in Burma in 1945.

At this stage, Indian Prime Minister Jawaharlal Nehru appealed to ask the United Nations (UN) to intervene, and a UN cease-fire was arranged for December 31, 1948. A few days before the cease-fire was due to go into effect, the Pakistanis launched a counterattack that cut the road between Uri and Punch. Following protracted negotiations, both countries agreed to a formal cease-fire. The terms of the cease-fire were laid out in the United Nations Committee India and Pakistan (UNCIP) resolution of August 13, 1948, and were adopted by the UN on January 5, 1949. The terms required Pakistan to withdraw its forces, both regular and irregular, while allowing India to maintain minimum strength of its forces in the state to ensure regard for law and order. On compliance with these conditions, a plebiscite was to be held to determine the future of the territory. All in all about 1,500 soldiers were killed on each side during the war. Pakistan acquired roughly two-fifths of Kashmir, and India obtained the majority of Kashmir, including the valley—the economic and demographic heartland of the contested territory.

References

Chopra, V. D. *Genesis of Indo-Pakistan Conflict of Kashmir.* New Delhi: Patriot, 1990

Choudhry, G. W. *Pakistan's Relations with India 1947–1966.* London: Pall Mall Press, 1968

Das Gupta, J. B. *Indo-Pakistan Relations 1947–1955.* Amsterdam: Djambatan, 1958

Dixit, J. N. *Anatomy of a Flawed Inheritance: Indo-Pakistan Relations 1970–1994.* Delhi: Konark Publishers Ltd., 1995

Sisson, Richard, and Leo E. Rose. *War and Secession: Pakistan, India and the Creation of Bangladesh.* Berkeley: University of California Press, 1990

INDO-PAKISTAN WARS AND CONFLICT

Since their independence and bloody baptismal launchings in August 1947, there have been three major wars and one minor war between the succes-

Indian air marshal Arjan Singh and Army general J. N. Chaudhuri look at a map at defense headquarters in New Delhi on September 23, 1965, during the third conflict of the Indo-Pakistan wars. After Pakistani troops invaded Indian-controlled Kashmir on September 1, 1965, India retaliated by launching several attacks into Pakistan. (Hulton Archive/Getty Images)

sor states of India and Pakistan. At issue in each case was the ongoing dispute over Kashmir. Even in 1971, when the dispute primarily concerned East Pakistan, dispute over Kashmir exercised the armed forces of both countries.

The Wars in Chronological Order
- Indo-Pakistan War of 1947: Pakistan initially occupies one-third of Kashmir (India eventually occupies three-fifths).
- Indo-Pakistan War of 1965: India clashes with Pakistan on all fronts (after skirmishes in the Rann of Kutch) when Pakistan's troops attempt to seep into Indian-controlled Kashmir. This war results in a strategic stalemate and small tactical victories for India.
- Indo-Pakistan War of 1971: India defeats Pakistan decisively, and consequently an independent Bangladesh emerges, fashioned out of the East Pakistan of 1947–1971.
- Indo-Pakistan War of 1999, also known as the Kargil War: Kashmiri insurgents, backed by Pakistani troops, captures Indian army posts. The Indian army retaliates and recaptures the posts. International pressure—especially from the United States—forces Pakistan to back down. The war ends with India regaining its earlier hold on Kargil.

The Kashmir Factor
Disagreement over Kashmir has been at the root of most Indo-Pakistan conflict and has stemmed from the partition in 1947 and its aftermath. At the time, Kashmir was ruled by a Bogra maharajah, who dithered over his state's future. Immediately

following invasion of Kashmir by tribes from Pakistan, he acceded the land to India, though Pakistanis maintained that he did so under duress. Thus the first Kashmir War broke out with Indian and Pakistani troops contending to determine the future of this Princely State. This war lasted for more than a year, with each side at times making significant advances into the other's territory. The war was ended by a United Nations cease-fire. India managed to secure just under three-fifths of Kashmir, which included the fertile heartland of the Valley of Kashmir.

The second Kashmir War erupted in April 1965 (after armed skirmishes weeks earlier in the Rann of Kutch). Pakistani troops infiltrated Kashmir and sought to foment rebellion in Jammu-Kashmir under a plan code-named Operation Gibraltar. The outcome of this war was a military stalemate and a diplomatic settlement, brokered by the Soviet Union with American acquiescence, in Tashkent.

The third Indo-Pakistan War, in 1971, did not principally and directly involve the issue of Kashmir, but it was precipitated by mounting tension and clashes between West and East Pakistan. Thus a civil war was expanded into a 13-day Indo-Pakistan international war. After months of internal Pakistan tension and conflict, India decided to intervene in East Pakistan militarily. Within just a fortnight, Indian forces defeated Pakistan, with the aid of local so-called liberation contingents, and forced Pakistan to surrender.

The fourth armed Indo-Pakistan clash, in 1999, the Kargil War, was confined to a single Himalayan theater and was the first ground war between the two countries after they had developed nuclear weapons. This limited war nonetheless attracted considerable media and electronic coverage in both countries and in the wider world.

Other Conflicts

Apart from these specific wars, there have been several armed skirmishes between the neighboring countries from time to time. Some have seemed likely to erupt into all-out war; others have been limited in scope. The countries seemed likely, for example, to fight each other in 1955 after warlike posturing on both sides, though full-scale war did not occur. In 1984 there were armed clashes as both countries sought to control the Siachen Glacier border region in Kashmir. Further clashes erupted in this area in 1985, 1987, and 1995.

Between November 1986 and March 1987, India conducted a large-scale military exercise, code-named Operation Brasstacks. Tensions were high again in 1990 after militancy in Indian-administered Kashmir greatly increased. A terrorist attack on the Indian parliament in New Delhi in mid December 2001 was blamed by India on Pakistan-based terrorist organizations, Lashkar-e-Toiba and Jaish-e-Mohammed, prompting another Indo-Pakistan military standoff in 2001–2002.

INDUS CIVILIZATION

The Indus civilization, alternatively known as the Harappan civilization, is one of the earliest known civilizations (ca. 2600–1700 BCE) in northern Pakistan. Archaeological evidence first identified its early and substantive existence in the early 1920s at Harappa in the Sahiwal (Montgomery) district of the Punjab and then at Mohenjo-Daro near the Indus River in the Larkana district of Sindh—both locations in present-day Pakistan. Subsequent explorations have shown that the Harappan civilization was the most extensive of the world's three earliest civilizations, the other two being those of Mesopotamia and Egypt, both of which began before it. How and when the Harappan civilization came to an end remains uncertain pending much further excavation. But the attested facts that there was once a sophisticated and extensive civilization in what is now Pakistan serves as an inspiration to present-day Pakistanis and as evidence that their current incarnation is no mere novitiate or modern fabrication.

See also Indus River; Punjab.

References

Ahsan, Aitzaz. *The Indus Saga and the Making of Pakistan*. Lahore, Pak.: Nehr Ghar Publications, 1996

INDUS RIVER

The Indus is about 1,800 miles long with a name that has its origin in the Sanskrit word meaning ocean. It is one of the great rivers of Asia, and in its lower reaches has been the locale of an ancient Indus civilization, long before its present importance to Pakistan. The volume of water discharged varies considerably seasonally, and cultivation in the river's valley depends heavily on irrigation. To carry out a vast plan of irrigation, several huge barrages have been constructed.

The 5,000-year-old ruins of Mohenjo-Daro in present-day Pakistan. The city is carefully constructed in a grid pattern using bricks of uniform size. (Corel)

The Indus Waters Treaty of 1960 was an early substantive demonstration that the two successor states could reach and maintain an agreement. The Indus River rises in Tibet and flows through Pakistan into the Arabian Sea. Its source is within 100 miles of those of the Sutlej and the Brahmaputra, and the river is formed by the fusion of two mountain streams. In its upper course, it flows northwestward in the trough between the Kailas and the Ladakhi Ranges, then cuts across the Ladakh Range and continues its northwesterly course between it and the Zaskar (Zapskar) Range for about 300 miles. It is joined by the Zaskar River about 12 miles west of Leh, the capital of Ladakh (the chief town on the main central Asian trade route), recrosses the Ladakh Range near Kiris where it is joined by the Shyole and later by the Shigar near Skardu, the chief town of Baltistan. It flows another 100 miles under the shadow of the Himalayas receiving meltwater from the snowfields and glaciers of the Himalayas and the Hindu Kush, past Haramosh in a 10,000-foot gorge, but then it suddenly turns southwest where it is joined by the Gilgit River, having dropped to an altitude of 4,000 feet, and strikes across the Great Himalayas.

From Chilas it flows through the Kohistan highlands of Pakistan. On entering the Hazara district, 812 miles from its source, it is about 100 yards wide, navigable by rafts in August but of no great depth, and studded with sandbanks and islands. Near Attock (2,079 feet), it leaves the Himalayan region and is joined by the Kabul from Afghanistan. Below Attock the Indus flows along the western margin of the Potwar Plateau, to enter the Punjab plain near Kalabagh.

From Kalabagh to the sea, the Indus flows west of a flat plain formed by the river and its tributaries. Above Mithankot it receives the Panjnad (meaning five waters), carrying the waters of the Jhelum, Chenab, Ravi, Bear, and Sutlej. Throughout the Punjab the Indus is broken by islands and sandbanks. East of Kashmir and 64 miles downstream of Mithankot is the Gudu barrage, and further downstream is the Sukkur barrage (dating from 1932); 80 miles below Sukkur the river passes by Mohenjo-Daro (Moenjodaro, or mound of the dead, and the site of ancient Indus civilization), in Larkana district.

About 190 miles below Rohri is the Ghulam Mohammad (the lower Sind) barrage. In Sind the

Satellite photograph of the Indus River Valley in Pakistan and western India. (Corel)

Soon after the 1947 partitions, Pakistan accused India of deliberately cutting off supplies. India's supposed intention was to divert the waters of the three main eastern rivers into irrigation canals serving its own territory by 1962.

In accordance with World Bank suggestions, however, the two governments agreed in 1960 that feeder canals should be dug from the western rivers to supply the areas of Pakistan that had hitherto depended on the eastern rivers. Financial help was promised under the auspices of The World Bank.

As a result, Pakistan had the use of the western rivers and India that of the eastern. At the end of the 20th and the beginning of the 21st centuries, the Indus Waters Treaty is often cited as an example of what India and Pakistan can achieve together when they agree.

See also Indus River; Punjab; Sind.
References
Razvi, Mujtaba. *The Frontiers of Pakistan.* Karachi, Pak.: Dacca National Publishing House Ltd., 1971.
Spate, O. H. K. *India and Pakistan: A General and Regional Geography.* New York: Methuen, 1954

river's gradient is low and in some places carries down enough detritus to raise the riverbed above the level of the surrounding plains with the consequent threat of flooding.

As a protection against floods, the river is confined by bunds (levees). Near Tatta its distributaries begin to spread out on their way to the sea. This deltaic region is generally level but also infertile. The marshes make good pasturage, and rice grows abundantly where cultivation is possible.

See also Indus Civilization; Indus Waters Treaty (1960).
References
Ahsan, Aztzaz. *The Indus Saga and the Making of Pakistan.* Lahore, Pak.: Nehr Ghar Publications, 1996
Spate, O. H. K. *India and Pakistan: A General and Regional Geography.* New York: Methuen, 1954

INDUS WATERS TREATY (1960)

The partition of the subcontinent in 1947 not only divided territory, notably in Punjab and Bengal, but also left India in control of the headwaters of the rivers needed by both countries. The vast and complex Indus River system was supplemented by an extensive network of irrigation canals in the Punjab and the Sind.

INTER-SERVICES INTELLIGENCE (ISI)

Pakistan has two civilian intelligence agencies and two military intelligence services. The civilian Intelligence Bureau (IB) is responsible for national police affairs and counterintelligence. Along with the police's Special Branch, it reports to the interior minister and prime minister. Overshadowing them (in large part because the post of IB director is now filled by an army general) are the army's Directorate of Intelligence, responsible for military intelligence broadly defined and the increasingly influential Inter-Services Intelligence (ISI).

Army intelligence now has a Corps of Intelligence. The ISI's head is a lieutenant-general appointed by the army chief, but he reports to the prime minister. (When there is no prime minister, the ISI's director reported to General Pervez Musharraf in his capacity as chief executive.) About 80 percent of ISI is drawn from Pakistan's three military services and there is a small cadre of civilians. Most of ISI's officers are on deputation from the army. The ISI is primarily responsible for Pakistan's foreign intelligence. This means in effect a principal concentration on India but with some attention to Afghanistan, Sri Lanka, Nepal, Iran, and other neighboring states.

The year 1971 was significant for the ISI and led to a considerable expansion of its personnel and activities. Because it was believed that Bengali IB officers could not be trusted in East Pakistan, the ISI was heavily relied on and began to recruit Islamist groups, including students, for counterinsurgency operations. When Zulfikar Ali Bhutto came back to high office in 1972, he increased the budget of the ISI substantially and used the organization in Afghanistan to spy on domestic opponents. During the Soviet Union's occupation of Afghanistan (1979–1989), the ISI was expanded considerably with support coming from both Saudi Arabia and the United States. Its resources, influence, and foreign contacts swelled considerably as well. It also expanded its authority to include Pakistan's domestic arrangements, especially from 1999 under the direction of President Musharraf.

See also Afghanistan; Bhutto, Zulfikar Ali; Musharraf, Pervez; Research and Analysis Wing (RAW).

References

Cohen, S. P. *The Idea of Pakistan.* Washington, DC: Brookings Institution Press, 2004

Talbot, I. *Pakistan: A Modern History.* New York: Hurst and Company, 1998

IQBAL, MUHAMMAD (1873–1938)

Poet and putative father of Pakistan, Muhammad Iqbal is recognized as the national poet for the country that only came into being nearly a decade after his death. Born at Sialkot in Punjab to devout and pious Muslim parents who inculcated the teachings of Islam in him, he was educated at Government College, Lahore, where he graduated in 1899 and was appointed lecturer in philosophy. He then studied philosophy in Cambridge and also qualified as a barrister. He began practicing law in Lahore but soon gave it up to write full-time. Soon he was recognized as a thinker of importance and the most distinguished Urdu poet of his time. He was knighted in 1922 in recognition of his distinction as a poet.

Temperamentally he was unsuited to politics, and his only notable contribution in this respect was as president of the All India Muslim League in 1930 when he said:

> I would like to see the Punjab, North-West Frontier Province, Sind and Baluchistan amalgamated into a single state. Self-government within the British Empire or without the British Empire, the formation of a consolidated North-West Indian Muslim State appears to me the final destiny of the Muslims, at least of Northwest India.

This was the first time that the idea of a separate state for the Muslims had been put forward on the platform of a political party.

See also Baluchistan; Muslim League; Punjab; North West Frontier Province; Sind.

References

Bahadur, Lal. *The Muslim League: Its History, Activities and Achievements.* Lahore, Pak.: Book Traders, 1979

Cohen, S. "Nuclear Weapons and Nuclear War in South Asia: Unknowable Futures." In Ramesh Thakur and Oddny Wiggen, eds. *South Asia in the World: Problem Solving Perspectives on Security, Sustainable Development and Good Governance.* Tokyo: United Nations University Press, 2004

IRREDENTISM

"Irredentism" derives from Italian sources and means unredeemed, a claim to gain or regain territory. It thus posits a revisionist claim to territory usually on the ground that the claimant group or government believes it has a legitimate basis for its claim. In Indo-Pakistan relations, the best–known and most contested and substantial claim is that of Pakistan to the whole of Kashmir, principally on the ground of self-determination for the Muslim majority population of that state and on the supposition that, in the event of there being a free plebiscite, a majority of Muslims would vote to join Pakistan.

See also Azad Jammu-Kashmir (AJK); Kutch (Cutch), Rann of.

ISLAM

Islam is of great significance in South Asia's past and present. Today it is the state religion of Pakistan and of Bangladesh, and India has the second largest Muslim population in the world, after Indonesia.

Islam—"the inner peace that comes from submission to the will of Allah"—spread through Arabia in the last 10 years of the life of Mohammad (ca. 570–632) and was carried so rapidly eastward and westward that by the early 8th century, Muslim armies had entered Sind (now part of Pakistan) and taken Toledo in Spain. Islam thus became a complex ingredient within South Asia from the 8th century down to today.

While the Sunni majority of Muslims has always accepted the legitimate succession of Mohammed's first four caliphs, the influential Shia minority acknowledges the authority only of Mohammad's son-in-law, Ali, and his descendants. This sectarian division, the emergence of rival caliphates (in Baghdad, Cairo, and Cordoba), and a shift of political power through Syria to Iraq broke the early unity of Islam. Though receding in Europe by 800, Islam survived as a pervasive culture in substantial parts of Asia, west and south of China. Between ca.1000 and 1350, armies, traders, and proselytizers carried Islam widely into northern India.

Differences between the majority Sunni and minority Shia Muslims thus date back to the earliest days of Islam and are directly linked to the issue of succession following the death of the Prophet Muhammad. The Shia believe that, after Prophet Muhammad's death, his son-in-law, Ali, should have been given the reins of administration. They still regard him as the first iman, or spiritual leader. The Sunni, however, believe that the appointment of one of the Prophet's companions, Abu Bakr, as the first Caliph was correct.

The Sunnis also respect Ali as the fourth caliph of Islam. In 661 Ali was murdered, and his chief opponent, Muawiya, became caliph. It was the death of Ali that led to the great schism between Sunnis and Shias. Muawiya laid the foundation of family rule in Islam, and he was later succeeded by his son, Yazid. But Ali's son, Hussein, refused to accept his legitimacy, and fighting followed. Hussein and his followers were massacred in battle near Karbala in 680. The deaths of both Ali and Hussein gave rise to the Shia characteristics of martyrdom and sense of betrayal. Even in the early 21st century, Shia all over the world commemorate the killing of Hussein with processions of mourning, in Pakistan and other parts of the Muslim world.

Shia Islam has always been the faith of the poor and oppressed, of those waiting for deliverance. It is seen as a messianic faith awaiting the coming of the so-called hidden Iman, Allah's messenger who will reverse their fortunes and herald the reign of divine justice. Today, the Shia make up about 15 percent of the total worldwide Muslim population. In Pakistan, as in most Islamic countries, the differences between Sunni and Shia were initially confined to academic debate, and violent incidents were extremely rare. The relationships took a dramatic turn, however, in the 1940s and again since the early 1980s. Changes in the regional environment, in addition to the emergence of a much more politicized and at times violent aspects of Islam, introduced a new phenomenon of sectarianism to Pakistan.

The Soviet invasion of Afghanistan in late December 1977 brought funding from the United States and Saudi Arabia for (mostly Sunni) Islamic radical groups to fight against Kabul's pro-Soviet incumbents. The 1979 Islamic revolution that ended the monarchy in predominantly Shia Iran ushered in a new wave of Shia radicalism in the region. When the then Pakistani military ruler, General Zia-ul-Haq, tried to introduce his own concept of Sunni Islam, bloody conflict broke out. Radical groups such as Sipah-e-Sahaba and Tehreek-e-Jafria have their roots in the professions, policies, and clashes of those days. Many believe that during this period and afterward, Pakistan became the battleground for a proxy war, a stage on which different organizations and countries belonging to various schools of extremist Islam supported members of their faith and belief.

From the 1990s, the phenomenon of the Taliban (literally, students) also fueled this violence, as a number of Sunni extremist groups found both refuge and training grounds in Afghanistan. Violence continued sporadically in different forms even after the country's central government seemed to be in the saddle. In the early 21st century, new, more radical groups have emerged, and they target each other with venom. Between the incumbencies of General Zia and General Pervez Musharraf in Pakistan, successive military and/or political regimes have tried to tackle the problem but without notable successes, their disclaimers to the contrary notwithstanding.

The events of September 11, 2001, in the United States, wreaking great terrorist damage and destruction on American soil, produced dramatic changes in perceptions and policies around the world. In 2002 President Musharraf launched a major campaign against Islamic extremists, banning several groups. Within weeks, however, many had resurfaced with new names but the same old characteristics, and they were again outlawed by Pakistan's government in 2003. Yet recent history seems to suggest that declaring radical groups illegal and outlawed does little or nothing to solve the problem.

In fact some Sunni extremist groups based in Pakistan seem to have been redefining their agendas, joining up with suspected al-Qaeda groups in a so-called "global jihad." At least two groups, with bases in Pakistan, have been involved in attacks against other minorities, particularly Christians. Yet another group was found to be involved in the two attacks on President Musharraf's life in December 2003. The group's leader, Amjad Farooqui, was subsequently killed in a gun battle with security forces.

Senior Pakistani officials believe that the cycle of violence in 2004–2005 is partly sectarian and partly linked to the efforts by extremist groups to destabilize the government. Having been hit in Karachi and Quetta by government forces, it appears that terrorist groups then returned to the Punjab to carry out their activities. These same officials say that attacks on Sunni gatherings in Mutan in early 2005 suggest that, after a series of attacks against Shia mosques, a new group of extremists may have emerged to avenge the killings. After a brief respite in 2003, 2004 was a particularly bad year for internal violence in Pakistan. Between 1980 and 2005, more than 4,000 people have been killed in Shia–Sunni violence in Pakistan.

See also Afghanistan; al-Qaeda/al-Qa'ida; Taliban; Zia-ul-Haq, Muhammad.

References

Esposito J. L., ed. *The Oxford History of Islam.* New York: Oxford University Press, 1999

Maley, William, ed. *Fundamentalism Reborn? Afghanistan and the Taliban.* New York: Hurst and Company, 1998

Pande, B. N. *Islam and Indian Culture.* Patna: Khuda Bakhsh Oriental Public Library, 1987

Zahab, Abou M., and R. Olivier. *Islamic Networks:The Afghan-Pakistan Connection.* New York: Hurst and Company, 2004

ISMAY, BARON HASTINGS LIONEL
(1887–1965)

A distinguished British Army officer and public servant, Baron Hastings Lionel Ismay was born in India. He was chief of the viceroy's staff from the spring of 1947 until early 1948 and Lord Mountbatten's chief adviser and executor in the critical months that produced India and Pakistan as independent, mutually distrustful states.

Initially Ismay had hoped that partition could be avoided, but he came to accept its draconian necessity. After his extensive war efforts, Ismay was tired by the time he became Mountbatten's right-hand man in India. But his sense of duty was high and, as one of his biographers wrote

> [H]is performance as a catalyst, a tranquillizer, and a constructive negotiator was exemplary. Trusted by all parties, by his calmness and accumulated wisdom he balanced the mercurial energy of Mountbatten, who more than once despatched him to London to conduct critical negotiations. (Lewin 2004, 438–40)

Subsequent to his service alongside the last viceroy, Ismay was chair of the council for the Festival of Britain (held in 1951), secretary of state for Commonwealth Relations in Churchill's second administration, and then as the first secretary-general of NATO.

See also Mountbatten of Burma.

References

Lewin, Ronald. *Oxford Dictionary of National Biography.* New York: Oxford University Press, 2004

Wingate, Lord Ismay. *Memoirs.* London: Heinemann. 1960

Ziegler, P. *Mountbatten: A Biography.* New York: Alfred A. Knopf, 1985

JAMAAT-I-ISLAMI (JI)

This Islamic movement was founded in 1941 in opposition to the Muslim League–led Pakistan movement. Following the emergence of Pakistan, the JI moved its headquarters from East Punjab and worked for the Islamization of the state. Stringent membership requirements have limited the JI's impact, but its discipline and organization have been displayed in the many street rallies and agitations it has mobilized against what it has castigated as un-Islamic governments. The JI led the 1953 anti-Ahmadi agitation and opposed both Mohammed Ayub Khan and Zulfikar Ali Bhutto, though it eventually broke with Nawaz Sharif.

The JI came closest to influencing governmental policies during the early part of Zia's regime in the late 1970s. It eventually split from Zia because of its criticism of what it characterized as merely cosmetic state-sponsored Islamization and because of the restrictions imposed on its powerful student organization Jamiat-e-Tuleba-e-Pakistan in 1984. The JI closely supported Gulbudding Hekmatyar's fundamentalist Hezb-i-Islami during Afghanistan's turbulent civil war and Soviet occupation, and the support continued after the Soviet withdrawal. The JI has also supported Kashmiri militants and earlier aided opponents of East Pakistan's Awami League in 1970–1971.

Despite the JI's opposition to Anglo-American styles of democracy, it has contested national and provincial elections (with the exception of the February 1997 polls) including the 1985 partyless elections. It has met with little electoral success, however, because of its inability to expand beyond narrow lower-middle-class urban support. Informed commentators stress, however, that, despite its limited electoral impact, the JI can influence politics through both street agitation and formulating an Islamic agenda to which all parties have to respond.

See also Muslim League; Punjab.
References
Cohen, S. P. *The Idea of Pakistan.* Washington, DC: Brookings Institution Press, 2004

J

Talbot, I. *Pakistan: A Modern History.* New York: Hurst and Company, 1998

JAMMU-KASHMIR. *SEE* KASHMIR: ORIGIN OF INDO-PAKISTAN DISPUTE.

JANA SANGH

A Hindu-chauvinist party, Jana Sangh was formed in 1951 with its strength mainly in Hindi-speaking urban northern India. It merged with the Janata Party in 1977 and reemerged as the Bharatiya Janata Party (BJP) after 1980. Much of its political leadership was drawn from the Rashtriya Swayamsevak Sangh (RSS).

See also Bharatiya Janata Party (BJP); Janata Party; Rashtriya Swayamsevak Sangh (RSS).
References
Hardgrave, R. L., and S. A. Kochanet. *India: Government and Politics in a Developing Nation,* 6th ed. Fort Worth, TX: Harcourt College Publishers, 2000

JANATA DAL

A party formed from the Jan Morcha, the Janata Party faction of the Lok Dal and a Congress Party splinter known as the Congress (S). In 1989 it had 141 of the 144 seats held by the National Front in the parliament that formed the government led by Vishwanath Pratap Singh. After several splits and mergers, by 2002 it survived only in the state of Karnataka.

See also Janata Party; Jan Morcha.
References
Hardgrave, R. L., and S. A. Kochanet. *India: Government and Politics in a Developing Nation,* 6th ed. Fort Worth, TX: Harcourt College Publishers, 2000

JANATA PARTY

The Janata Party was created out of a wide variety of opposition parties to fight primarily against the Congress Party in the 1977 election, which was called immediately after the end of the Emergency (1975–1977). It formed Indira Gandhi's government in 1977–1979. It merged with the Jan Morcha and other parties to form the Janata Dal.

See also Emergency; Janata Dal; Jan Morcha.

References
Hardgrave, R. L., and S. A. Kochanet. *India: Government and Politics in a Developing Nation*, 6th ed. Fort Worth, TX: Harcourt College Publishers, 2000

JAN MORCHA

Jan Morcha, meaning People's Movement, was founded in October 1987 as a nonparty populist opposition group by Vishwanath Pratap Singh and others who had been expelled from Congress six months earlier. Later it merged with the Janata Dal. Its major leaders other than Singh left the party in April 1991. Singh, who had been finance and then defense minister under Rajiv Gandhi, became a controversial figure because of his efforts to tackle tax evaders and to eliminate corruption, especially from governmental arms deals. He was the principal architect of India's new liberal economic policy. He was ousted from Rajiv Gandhi's government in April 1987.

In the summer of 1988, the Jan Morcha merged with the Janata Party and the two Lok Dal factions to become the new Janata Dal. Also in the summer of 1988, Singh won a dramatic victory in a parliamentary by-election in Allahabad in his home state of Uttar Pradesh. Singh became India's prime minister from November 1989 to November 1990 and leader of the Janata Dal.

See also Janata Dal; Uttar Pradesh.

References
Hardgrave, R. L., and S. A. Kochanet. *India: Government and Politics in a Developing Nation*, 6th ed. Fort Worth, TX: Harcourt College Publishers, 2000

JHA, L. K. (1913–1988)

Lakshmi Kant Jha was one of India's most distinguished and versatile public servants. He was secretary to Prime Minister L. B. Shastri and then for Indira Gandhi. He was India's ambassador to the United States between 1970 and 1973. He built up a reputation as an economist of distinction, as a leader in the Indian Civil Service (ICS), and as chairman of the General Agreement on Tariffs and Trade (GATT) in the 1950s. He rendered signal services to the Reserve Bank of India (RBI). He was governor of Jammu-Kashmir (1973–1977).

Popularly known as LK, Jha was born in the Darbhanga district of Bihar. He graduated from Benares Hindu University and Trinity College, Cambridge, where he was a student of such renowned economists as Arthur Cecil Pigou, John Maynard Keynes, Sir Dennis Holme Robertson, and Joan Robinson. He joined the ICS in 1936. After serving in Bihar in the districts and in the provincial secretariat, he was seconded to the government in 1942. He worked successively as deputy secretary to the Chief Controller of Imports and Exports, joint secretary to the Ministry of Commerce and Industry, and secretary for the Ministry of Heavy Industry. He was India's principal representative in the General Agreement of Tariffs and Trade (GATT) and its chair (1957–1958). He was secretary of the Department of Economic Affairs in the Ministry of Finance in 1960 and was appointed to the newly created post of principal secretary to then Prime Minister Lal Bahadu Shastri in 1964 and then continued in the same capacity under Prime Minister Indira Gandhi.

From July 1967 to May 1970, Jha held the office of governor of the Reserve Bank of India when he stressed the importance of strengthening India's banking system, especially in contributing to economic growth. In May 1970 he became India's ambassador to the United States. When the Bangladesh War broke out in 1971, Jha was a principal and influential presenter of India's case.

From 1977 he was a member (and the deputy chairman) of the Brandt Commission, playing a major role in shaping its two main reports. Jha was a committed advocate of economic liberalization, a process that has gained much subsequent momentum in India. He argued that, although economic liberalization may temporarily bring in its wake adverse terms of trade, it would in the long run lead to increases in exports and greater competitiveness in the economy.

Jha died in Pune in mid January 1988, remaining fully committed to his work to the last. Indeed, at the time of his death he was a member of India's upper house of Parliament, the Rajya Sabha, and ,to perpetuate his memory, a lecture series (the L. K. Jha Memorial Lecturers) was instituted.

See also Azad Jammu-Kashmir (AJK); Bangladesh ; Gandhi, Indira; Shastri, Lal Bahadur.

JIHAD (JIHARDI)

Jihad is the term used in Islam for holy war, which derives from the Arabic for struggle. Hence a *jihardi* is someone who wages a holy war. Muslims are duty-bound to oppose those who reject Islam, by armed struggle if necessary. Historically, *jihad* has been invoked to justify both the expansion and the defense of Islam, though not necessarily by military attack. An associated polemical vocabulary relevant to Indo-Pakistan relations has acquired considerable usage, especially since the 1990s, relating to activities by groups variously called freedom fighters or terrorists, notably, for example, regarding Afghanistan, Kashmir, and Pakistan's North West Frontier region, such as Waziristan.

See also Islam.

References
Cohen, S. P. *The Idea of Pakistan*. Washington, DC: Brookings Institution Press, 2004

JINNAH, MOHAMMED ALI (1876–1948)

Ali Mohammed Jinnah, the first and foremost leader of Pakistan, was born in Karachi, the son of a wealthy merchant. He became principal begetter of an independent Pakistan and inherently suspicious of India and its probable policy. He studied in Bombay (later Mumbai) and Lincoln's Inn, London, and was called to the bar in 1897.

He soon built up a large and lucrative legal practice in Bombay. In 1910 he was elected to the viceroy's legislative council and, already a member of the Indian National Congress, in 1913 he joined the Indian Muslim League (ML). As its president in 1916 he brought about a peaceful coexistence agreement between the ML and the Indian National Congress Party through the Lucknow Pact. He resigned from the Indian National Congress in 1920, opposing its noncooperation policy against

An Afghan mujahedeen ("one engaged in struggle," or jihad*) demonstrates the positioning of a hand-held surface to air Stinger missile in 1988, when the mujahedeen were backed by the United States against the Soviets in control of Afghanistan. After the withdrawal of the Soviet Union from Afghanistan in 1989, the mujahedeen warlords fought a civil war against the royalists. When the Taliban came to power in 1994, former mujahedeen formed the opposition Northern Alliance, which still controls the area around Mazar-e Sharif. (Department of Defense)*

the Raj. He led the independents in the legislative assembly from 1923. Powerful in the Muslim League, he took the lead in seeking Hindu–Muslim unity. Much of Pakistan's history is closely associated with M. A. Jinnah, who came to personify Pakistan, especially from 1947 until his death from cancer. Jinnah was a—and perhaps the—dominant figure for South Asian Muslims from the 1920s onwards.

References

Jalal, Ayesha. *The Sole Spokesman: Jinnah, the Muslim League and the Demand for Pakistan.* Cambridge, UK: Cambridge University Press, 1985

Robinson, F. "Jinnah, Mohamed Ali. 1876–1948." *Oxford Dictionary of National Biography,* vol. 30. New York: Oxford University Press, 2004

Wolpert, S. *Jinnah of Pakistan.* New York: Oxford University Press, 1984

JOHNSON, LYNDON BAINES (1908–1973)

Lyndon Baines Johnson, popularly known as LBJ, was the 36th president of the United States (1963–1969), during which years he oversaw American relations with India and Pakistan. Born in Texas, he became a teacher and congressman's secretary before being elected a Democratic representative to the U.S. Congress in 1937. He became a senator in 1948 and then a skillful but ruthless leader of the Democratic majority in that house. Vice president under John F. Kennedy as of 1960, he became president immediately after Kennedy's assassination in November 1963. He was elected president in the 1964 elections by a huge majority.

By the time Johnson became president, Jawaharlal Nehru was ill and palpably aging. He had lost self-confidence after India's dramatic setbacks at the hands of China in October 1962. President Johnson had no special rapport with any of India's leaders, as was evident during the Indo-Pakistan armed clashes in 1965, and Washington concurred quietly with the peace talks being held in Tashkent in January 1966.

The escalation of the war in Vietnam led to mass protests within the United States and abroad and to personal attacks and abuse on Johnson personally. He was not notably a traveling president and never personally visited South Asia. After 1969, he retired from active politics.

See also Kennedy, John Fitzgerald; Nehru, Jawaharlal.

JOINT DEFENCE COUNCIL (OR COMMITTEE)

This was a project proposed by Mountbatten, Britain's last viceroy of India, that the two successor states should meet regularly and deal with joint security problems. In 1947, Britain still appeared likely to have a considerable military interest and presence in the subcontinent, and senior British officers were prominent in the training of both India's and Pakistan's armed forces.

Mountbatten initially believed that the continuing unity of the Indian armed forces, British-raised and mostly -officered, was essential. For a brief while—days rather than weeks—it seemed that Mohammad Ali Jinnah, as well as Jawaharlal Nehru, would support the idea of a Joint Defence Committee, and the committee met for a few times after August 1947. It soon became clear, however, that Indo-Pakistan relations were too tense and mutually suspicion-laden for the proposal to be permanent and practical.

See also Jinnah, Mohammed Ali; Mountbatten of Burma; Nehru, Jawaharlal.

References

Ziegler, P. *Mountbatten: A Biography.* New York: Alfred A. Knopf, 1985

JUNAGADH

In 1947, the Princely State of Junagadh had a Muslim nawab as head of state, who ruled over a predominantly Hindu population, in this respect being like the much larger state of Hyderabad, situated on the northwest coast of India with a population of about 700,000 inhabitants in 1947. Its boundaries were ill defined and intermingled with Hindu neighbors, making its future as part of India seem most likely—until Muslim League politicians took office in the state just before the mid August transfer of power. Encouraged by Mohammad Ali Jinnah, they procrastinated briefly, then at the last moment acceded to Pakistan. The Indian government soon became fearful that, if they acquiesced in the nawab's move , they would be in a weak position if the nizam (the sovereign) tried to follow the lead of his fellow Muslim leader and accede to Pakistan. On the other hand, if they intervened by force or by exerting economic pressure, they could be construed as encouraging similar action by Pakistan vis-à-vis Kashmir. Thus the question of what is to happen to Junagadh became a curtain raiser for the roughly analogous cases of Hyderabad and Kashmir

Faced with this small but exemplary Junagadh imbroglio, Lord Louis Mountbatten, Jawaharlal Nehru, and Vallabhbhai Patel, Jinnah, and Liaquat Ali Khan each sought to determine what they regarded as a rightful outcome. A provisional government of Junagadh was set up in Bombay (later Mumbai) that became a focus for revolt within the state. The nawab fled the country. The state council soon had second thoughts about accession to Pakistan. On November 8, 1947, the *dewan* (the ruler) appealed to India to take over the administration before it entirely collapsed. This invitation was accepted, and Indian troops moved swiftly into the state.

Pakistanis continued to maintain that Junagadh had legally acceded to their country and that India had committed aggression. A referendum of February 1948, under Indian auspices, produced a large majority in favor of accession to India.

See also Hyderabad; Princely States.
References
Ziegler, P. *Mountbatten: A Biography.* New York: Alfred A. Knopf, 1985

JUNEJO, MUHAMMAD KHAN (1932–1993)

Muhammad Khan Junejo was a Sindhi landlord and politician who became Pakistan's prime minister in 1985 following Zia-ul-Haq's lifting of martial law in December 1985. He had been active in politics since the 1960s and held minor offices. He was selected by Zia predominantly because of his Sindhi background and support.

Junejo attempted, with some mild-mannered courage, to be an active independent prime minister, but his efforts in this respect brought him to clash with Zia, who was not temperamentally inclined to share power. Relations between the two men deteriorated when Junejo pressed on with an investigation into the massive explosion at the Ojhri arms depot camp (situated in a heavily populated area between Islamabad and Rawalpindi), which threatened to embarrass the Inter-Services Intelligence (ISI) and perhaps Zia as well. When Zia summarily removed Junejo from office in May 1988, he cited ethnic violence in Karachi and the prime minister's inability to bring forward a Shariat bill. In reality Junejo's independent line on an Afghan settlement had been the major factor in Zia's annoyance with his prime minister.

The prime minister ensured Pakistan's signature on the Geneva Accord of April 1988, providing for the Soviet withdrawal from Afghanistan, but at the cost of losing office. Junejo then joined the Islamic Democratic Alliance (IDA), which entered the 1988 elections. Eventually, following his death, the Pakistan Muslim League split into Junejo and Nawaz Sharif factions.

See also Sharif, Nawaz; Zia-ul-Haq, Muhammad
References
Talbot, I. *Pakistan: A Modern History.* New York: Hurst and Company, 1998

KALAM, A. P. J. ABDUL (1931–)

Dr. Avul Pakir Jainulabdeen Abdul Kalam was president of India, and thus also the constitutional head of state, from 2002 to 2007. Born in October 1931 into a Muslim family, he was educated at the Madras Institute of Technology. He joined the R and D Organization Defence of the government of India in 1958 and then India's Space Research Organization in 1963. He held a number of scientific and space-related jobs and was principal scientific adviser to the Indian government from 1999 to 2001.

In 1982 he conceived India's Integrated Guided Missile Development Programme. He gained a number of national awards, including the Indira Gandhi Award for National Integration in 1997. In his first address to a joint sitting of both houses of Parliament after the election of a new Lok Sabha (lower house of India's Parliament) in 2004, President Kalam stressed that the new United Progressive Alliance government, led by the Indian National Congress (INC) Party and inducted into office on May 22, 2004, would be secular and pro-poor. He also made it clear that India was intent on pursuing an independent foreign policy that would stress the promotion of a multipolar world. The new government would give its highest priority to building closer political, economic, and other types of ties with its neighbors in South Asia and to strengthening South Asia's Association for Regional Cooperation (SAARC). "Dialogue with Pakistan on all outstanding issues will be pursued on a sustained basis within the framework of the Simla Agreement and all subsequent agreements between the two governments, including the Joint Statement of 6 January 2004," he said. These were declaratory aims mostly, for he could not actualize them decisively in a mere few years as president (2004–2007). On July 25, 2007, the 72-year-old former governor of Rajasthan, Pratibha Patil, was sworn in as India's president, the first woman to occupy that office, in succession to Abdul Kalam.

K

See also Nuclear Weapons; South Asian Association for Regional Cooperation.

References

Chandra, Ramesh. *Scientist to President: President A.P.J. Abdul Kalam.* New Delhi: Gyan, 2002

Pruthi, Raj. *President A.P.J. Abdul Kalam.* New Delhi: Anmol Publications, 2003

KARACHI

Karachi is the principal seaport, chief commercial and industrial center, and the most populous city of Pakistan. It lies on the Arabian Sea immediately to the northwest of the delta of the Indus River. The hinterland in the north is virtually desert. Formerly the capital of Sind province, Karachi is the headquarters of the district and division of Karachi. Karachi grew to its present size and eminence in a comparatively short time. When the British annexed Sind in the early 1840s, there was only a fishing village with a small fort and a ditch called Kalachi-jo-Kun with two gates: one called the Kharadar (the saltwater gate) facing the sea, and the other called Mithadar (the sweetwater gate) facing the Lyari River.

The greatest single stimulus to the growth of modern Karachi was the expansion of irrigation in Punjab and Sind, which gave it a great export trade, mainly in wheat and cotton. And the development of international air transport, especially after World War II, considerably increased Karachi's importance, as did the fact that it was designated the capital city of Pakistan upon independence in 1947. In 1957 the Karachi Development Authority was founded to plan the city's growth.

In October 1959 the capital was transferred to Islamabad, though many offices of the central government remained at Karachi. From August 1, 1960, the Federal Capital Area came to be known as the Federal Territory of Karachi. The Federal Territory was merged in the province of West Pakistan on July 1, 1961, as a division with a total area of 8.405 square miles and a population of 2.1 million in 1961 and about 10 million in 2005.

Today Karachi is the major airway, railway, road, and port center for linking with the rest of Pakistan and the rest of the world. After partition, there was a great influx of people from all over India. In the 1951 census, 58.7 percent of the city's inhabitants were refugees (Mohajirs), and this influx has posed long-term political problems for Pakistan, not least of which is the Mohajir-Sindhi conflict in Karachi.

Today Karachi provides major links in air communications with all parts of India, Australia, Malaysia, East Asia, Europe, and the Americas. Proximity to oil fuels, ample space at sea level, relative immunity from heavy rains and floods, and minimum frequency of low cloud cover all favor Karachi as an airport, and it is largely for climatic reasons that it has been preferred as a main communications and services base to Kolcatta or Mumbai.

See also Punjab; Sind.

References
Musharraf, P. *In the Line of Fire: A Memoir*. New York: The Free Press, 2006
Spate, O. H. K. *India and Pakistan: A General and Regional Geography,* 2nd ed. New York: Methuen, 1960

KARAKORAM NATURE PARK

The Karakoram Nature Park is the idea, formulated by the Kashmir Study Group in its report of 1997, proposing that a substantial part of Kashmir should be designated and maintained as a nature park under the joint auspices of India and Pakistan but without changing the question of political jurisdiction. The idea basically is that an Indo-Pakistan project could be brought into being, which would demonstrate practical cooperation between the two countries.

See also Azad Jammu-Kashmir (AJK).

References
Kashmir Study Group. *1947–1997: The Kashmir Dispute at Fifty: Charting Paths to Peace*. New York: Kashmir Study Group, 1997
Schaffer, Teresita C. *Kashmir: The Economics of Peace Building: A Report of the CSIS South Asia Program with the Kashmir Study Group*. Washington, DC: Center for Strategic and International Studies, 2005

KARGIL

Kargil is a district of Ladakh in Jammu-Kashmir where, from May to July 1999, India and Pakistan fought a war at an altitude of over 10,000 feet along a 200-kilometer (124-mile) trans-Himalayan front. This was no mere border skirmish, such as had occurred in the preceding 15 years across the 740-kilometer (459-mile) Line of Control (LoC) and 110-kilometer (68-mile) Actual Ground Position Line (AGPL). This fourth war of Kashmir was fought at formidable icy mountainous height, only months after the much publicized peace talks between India and Pakistan that were held principally in Lahore. This was India's first television war and fought only a year after both countries had conducted nuclear tests, thus broadcasting that both had nuclear weapons capabilities. Fortunately, they were not used by either country in Kargil in 1999.

In July of that year, the Indian government set up a committee of four members (chaired by a leading Indian strategist K. Subrahmanyam) to investigate and report on the Kargil War. The terms of reference were basically two:

> To review the events leading up to the Pakistani "aggression" in the Kargil District of Ladakh in Jammu and Kashmir, and
>   to recommend such measures as are considered necessary to safeguard national security against such armed intrusions.

The Kargil review committee report (also known as the Subrahmanyam Report) was released almost in its entirety to the public in December 1999. It ranged more widely than just analyzing the Kargil clashes of 1999 to place this episode in the context of India's policies vis-à-vis Pakistan since 1947, and it made extensive recommendations under 11 subheads, in Chapter 14, the penultimate chapter of the report. The subheads concerned:

1. National Security Council.
2. Intelligence.
3. Counter-Terrorist Operations.
4. Border Management.
5. Defence Budget and Modernisation.

6. National Security Management and Decision Making at the Apex.
7. India's Nuclear Policy.
8. Media Relations and Information.
9. Technology.
10. Civil Military Liaison.
11. Declaratory Policy for the LoC.

There was no similar Pakistan inquiry into Kargil that was published, though it may be that a government-sponsored investigation was held but its findings not publicly released

See also Ladakh; Lahore; Siachen Glacier.

References

"Kargil Review Committee Report." 1999. http://nuclearweaponarchive.org/India/KargilRCB.html

Musharraf, P. *In the Line of Fire: A Memoir.* New York: The Free Press, 2006

KASHMIR: ORIGINS OF THE INDO-PAKISTAN DISPUTE

In August 1947 as the Indian subcontinent was becoming independent from Britain, the rulers of the 565 Princely States, whose lands made up two-fifths of India and an aggregated population of about 99 million, were told by the departing imperial power to join either India or Pakistan. There was to be no third choice.

The present-day Indian state of Jammu-Kashmir became part of the Mogul empire under Akbar in 1586, having earlier been under Hindu rulers. After a period of Afghan rule from 1756, it was annexed by the Sikh rulers of the Punjab in 1819. In 1920 Ranjit Singh transferred the territory of Jammu to Gulab Singh by the Treaty of Amritsar. Soon British supremacy was imposed and recognized, until the Indian Independence Act of 1947. By this act the states were required to accede either to India or to Pakistan.

In 1947 the ruler of Jammu-Kashmir, Maharajah Hari Singh, whose state was contiguous to the two new countries, prevaricated and could not decide on which country to accede to, preferring the status quo or full independence, neither of which was practical at that time. He was a Hindu-Dogra, but the state's population was predominantly Muslim. He signed a standstill agreement with Pakistan so that services such as trade, travel, and communications would be uninterrupted. India did not sign a similar agreement.

In October 1947, Pushtu tribespeople from Pakistan's North West Frontier Province invaded Kashmir. Worried by increasing deterioration in law and order and mounting communal tensions, the Maharajah asked for armed assistance from India. The viceroy, Earl Louis Mountbatten, made clear to the Maharajah that military help could be forthcoming only if the state were to accede to India and that this would only be provisional pending a "referendum, plebiscite or election." According to the terms of Kashmir's accession, India's jurisdiction over the state was to extend to external affairs, defense, and communications. Exactly when Hari Singh signed the instrument of accession has been deeply controversial for over 50 years. According to official Indian accounts, Singh fled from Srinagar in the early hours of the morning of October 26, arriving in Jammu later in the day. There he was met by Rao Bahadar Pangunni ("VP") Menon, representative of Prime Minister Jawaharlal Nehru, and promptly signed the instrument of accession. On the morning of October 27, Indian troops were airlifted into Srinagar.

Recent research from British sources has indicated that Hari Singh did not reach Jammu until the evening of October 26 and that, due to poor flying conditions, Menon was unable to get to Jammu until the morning of October 27, by which time Indian troops were already arriving in Srinagar. To support the theory that the Maharajah acceded before Indian troops landed, Indian sources have now suggested that Hari Singh signed an instrument of accession before he left Srinagar but that it was not made public until later. This was because Hari Singh had not yet agreed to include the Kashmiri leader, Sheikh Abdullah, in his future government. To date no authentic original document has been made available.

Pakistan immediately contested the accession, suggesting that it was fraudulent, that the Maharajah acted under duress, and that he had no right to sign an agreement with India when the standstill agreement with Pakistan was still in force. Pakistanis also argued that, because Hari Singh fled from the Kashmir Valley, he was not in control of his state and therefore not in a position to make a decision on behalf of his people. Pakistanis claim, then and subsequently, that there is a dispute over the state and status of Jammu-Kashmir, and the accession issue forms a significant aspect of their

View of a mountain pass in Kashmir, the subject of bitter disputes between India and Pakistan for over half a century. (Corel)

argument. By stating that the instrument of accession was signed on October 26, when it clearly was not, Pakistanis believe that India has not shown good faith and consequently that this invalidates the instrument of accession. Indians argue, however, that, regardless of the discrepancies over timing, the maharajah chose to accede to India and he was not under duress. On the basis of Hari Singh's accession, India claims ownership of the entire state, including the approximately one-third of the territory currently administered by Pakistan. In 1949 Maharajah Hari Singh was obliged by the government of India to leave the state and hand over the government to Sheikh Abdullah. Hari Singh died in exile in Bombay (later Mumbai) in 1962.

There were about 35,000 deaths between the outbreak of the Kashmir insurgency in 1988 and 2005. Negotiations with Pakistan regarding the future of this disputed territory began in July 1999. Hopes of avoiding further violence were set back in December 2001 in an attack on the Indian parliament by suicide bombers; 13 people died. No group claimed responsibility, but Kashmiri separatists were blamed. Pakistani President Pervez Mushar-

raf's crackdown on militants helped to bring the two countries back from the brink of war.

Tension between India and Pakistan also increased following an attack on an Indian army base in Indian-occupied Kashmir on May 14, 2002. The attack, which killed 31 people, was attributed to Islamic terrorists infiltrating the Kashmir Valley from Pakistan. It led also to widespread criticism of President Musharraf for allegedly failing to combat terrorism in Kashmir.

In February 2002, 58 Hindu pilgrims returning from Ayodhya were killed when their train was set on fire following a confrontation with a Muslim crowd at Godhra in Gujarat. These clashes led to three months of intense intermittent communal rioting, during which at least 800 Muslims died from attacks by Hindus. Relations between India and Pakistan deteriorated following terrorist bombings in Bombay (Mumbai). Subsequently, however, Indo-Pakistan official relations improved with the two countries embarking on their most promising, if uncertain, attempts at peacemaking for years.

Elections of mayors, municipal corporations, councils, and committees were held from January 8 to February 17, 2005, in India's northern state of

Jammu-Kashmir, the first civic elections to be held in the state for 27 years. Despite calls from militant separatist groups, such as Lashkar-i-Tolba (LiT), for a boycott of the rolls and a campaign of intimidation and violence that killed at least four candidates and six activists, turnout averaged about 60 percent and in some districts was over 80 percent.

In the election for the Jammu municipal council, where for the first time some 100,000 Kashmiri Pandits were on the electoral polls, the Bharatiya Janata Party (BJP) was second only to the Indian National Congress Party in its tally of seats. Commentators reported the civic elections as strengthening local government institutions and tending to undermine the influence of separatist extremists.

See also Kashmir Study Group (KSG).

References
Bose, Sumantra. *The Challenge in Kashmir: Democracy, Self-Determination and a Just Peace.* Thousand Oaks, CA: Sage Publications, 1997
Brecher, Michael. *The Struggle for Kashmir.* New York: Oxford University Press, 1952
Chopra, V. D. *Genesis of Indo-Pakistan Conflict on Kashmir.* New Delhi: Patriot, 1990
Evans, A. 2005 "Kashmir: A Tale of Two Valleys— Kashmir Valley to the Neelum Valley." *Asian Affairs* (March 2005)
Lamb, A. *Kashmir: A Disputed Legacy, 1846–1990.* Hertingfordbury, UK: Roxford Books, 1991

KASHMIR STUDY GROUP (KSG)

The Kashmir Study Group (KSG) was first founded in 1996 by an American citizen and businessman who was born in Kashmir. In mid 2005, the KSG had 25 members, with diplomatic, academic, and political backgrounds. Most of the members are American, but two are from Britain and one from Germany. The members of KSG have conducted many meetings with interested parties, made studies of the region, and published reports of their findings.

In 1988 some members of KSG, in consultation with several Indians and Pakistanis, developed the *Livingston Proposal, Kashmir—A Way Forward.* This proposal was presented to government officials in India, Pakistan, and Kashmir. The reaction from many in South Asia, while guarded, was generally positive, and suggestions were made to develop the idea. Based on these suggestions, an extended set of proposals was put forward in February 2000. To aid the understanding of and publicity for the Livingston Proposal, a task force of the KSG studied and developed a report on the history, geography, and demographics of the Kashmir region.

See also Abdullah, Dr. Farooq; Abdullah, Sheikh Mohammad; Azad Jammu-Kashmir (AJK).

References
Kashmir Study Group. *1947–1997: The Kashmir Dispute at Fifty: Charting Paths to Peace.* Kashmir Study Group: New York, 1997
Schaffer, Teresita C. *Kashmir: The Economics of Peace Building: A Report of the CSIS South Asia Program with the Kashmir Study Group.* Washington, DC: Center for Strategic and International Studies, 2005

KASHMIRI PANDITS

These Brahmins from Kashmir, members of this distinct community, established themselves in northern India first at the Mughal courts and then, from the mid 19th century, in the service of the Dogra rulers of Kashmir. Jawaharlal Nehru's family were Pandits originally from the Vale of Kashmir, and India's first prime minister was generally known to the British as Pandit Nehru. The community developed and sustained a strong cohesion while adopting many aspects of Urdu and Persian court cultures. As a highly literate and socially elitist group, the Kashmiri Pandits were among the first to discuss and then implement social reform. As ethnic violence has increased in Kashmir since the late 1980s, Kashmiri Pandits have fled from the Vale to settle in Jammu, elsewhere in India, or overseas. However, Pandits are still influential in the bureaucracy and professions of India way beyond their numerical size.

See also Azad Jammu-Kashmir (AJK); Nehru, Jawaharlal.

References
Evans, A. 2005 "Kashmir: A Tale of Two Valleys— Kashmir Valley to the Neelum Valley." *Asian Affairs* (March 2005)
Malik, I.H. *Kashmir: Ethnic Conflict, International Dispute.* New York: Oxford University Press, 2003
Pant, Kusum. *The Kashmir: Pandits.* New Delhi: Allied Publishers Ltd., 1987
Sender, H. *The Kashmiri Pandits: A Study of Cultural Choice in North India.* New York: Oxford University Press, 1988

KENNEDY, JOHN FITZGERALD (1917–1963)

John Fitzgerald Kennedy, known as JFK, was the 35th president of the United States (1961–1963), the youngest president, and the first Roman Catholic to be elected to that office. As president, he had to assess the significance of the Sino-Indian border war in October 1962 while preoccupied with Soviet missiles being emplaced on Cuban soil and thereby posing the threat of direct attack on the American homeland. Kennedy sent John Kenneth Galbraith, the celebrated Harvard professor of economics, as U.S. ambassador to India, and Galbraith eventually published a substantial memoir of his time in New Delhi in this role.

For Kennedy and Nehru, their coincidental period of being at the pinnacle of political power in their respective countries was brief, being confined to Kennedy's presidency of two and three quarter years until his assassination in November 1963. However, they disagreed on Goa and the nuclear test ban treaty. Kennedy tried—unsuccessfully—to treat India as he did China, which had distinctly different policies toward the Soviet Union than did India, and he was impatient with what he took to be Nehru's intransigence over Kashmir. Nevertheless, Kennedy was more inclined than some of his foremost advisers to take India seriously, certainly more seriously than Pakistan, despite the latter's formal alignment and India's nonalignment.

See also Azad Jammu-Kashmir (AJK); Goa; Nehru, Jawaharlal.

References

Hilsman, R. *To Move a Nation: The Politics of Foreign Policy in the Administration of John F. Kennedy.* New York: Doubleday, 1967

Schlesinger, M. *A Thousand Days: John F. Kennedy in the White House.* Boston: Houghton-Miffflin, 1965

Sorensen, Theodore C. *Kennedy.* Boston: Hodder Headliner, 1965

KHAN, ABDUL GHAFFAR (1890–1988)

Abdul Ghaffar Khan was a leading Pushtun nationalist and advocate of Gandhian nonviolence who played significant roles in both Indian and Pakistani politics during his long life. Born in the village of Utmanzai in the Peshawar district of the North West Frontier Province (NWFP), he attended the Municipal Board High School in Peshawar and the Edwardes Memorial Mission School but left before completing his studies to obtain an army commission. Apparently he abandoned this career because he had witnessed a British subaltern insulting an Indian officer. He then spent a brief time in a school at Camp Upur and attended Aligarh Muslim University, a famous seminary for Muslims.

Despite his own patchy education A. G. Khan campaigned energetically from 1910 onward to popularize schooling among the illiterate Paktun tribespeople of the Frontier. He clashed with the British in April 1919, when he organized a public meeting to protest against the Rowlatt Act of that year. He was then arrested, for the first time, but released shortly afterward. Thereafter he embarked on a life that came to involve prolonged periods of imprisonment meted out by either British or Pakistani authorities. He resumed his educational activities in 1921, opening an Azad High School at Utmanzai and forming the Anjuman Islah-ul-Afghania (Society for the Reform of the Afghans) to carry on his work. By this date he had also been elected president of the provincial Khilafat Committee. His so-called anti-British activities culminated in his arrest of December 17, 1921. On his release, his followers honored him with the title Fakhr-i-Afghan (Pride of the Afghans), along with that of the Frontier Gandhi. The rest of his long life was punctuated by political activism and periods of imprisonment, including incarceration for most of World War II.

Abdul Ghaffar Khan was released from jail in January 1950 but banned from the Frontier. In 1955 he headed the campaign against the merging of the provinces of West Pakistan into one unit, soon leading to further controversy with the authorities. The campaign also led to a rift with his elder brother, Dr. Kahn Sahib, who in October 1955 became the chief minister of the newly integrated West Pakistan. After another brief spell in prison, Abdul Ghaffar Kahn joined Baluch and Sindhi nationalists and afterward joined Punjabi and Bengali politicians to form the Awami National Party (ANP) in 1957. It campaigned for the dissolution of the One Unit Scheme and demanded federal reorganization to give greater regional autonomy. Khan was arrested in October 1958, along with other opposition leaders. He was released the following April, avowedly on account of his "age and indifferent health," but he was disqualified from being a member of any elected body and placed under restrictive orders. He defied these to tour the Frontier and was subsequently rearrested on April 12, 1961. His health deteriorated rapidly because he was incarcerated in the by now familiar surroundings of Haripur prison. Shortly after his release in January 1964, he traveled to England for medical treatment. Abdul Ghaffar Khan embarked on a lengthy self-imposed exile in

Afghanistan in December 1964. He briefly visited India in November 1969 to receive the Nehru Peace Award. The formation of a NAP government in the Frontier in 1972 enabled him to return to Pakistan. A caravan of 6,000 vehicles escorted him from the Afghan border.

Within two months, however, the Zulfi Bhutto regime had dismissed the Frontier government and arrested Wali Khan and the other top NAP leaders for "anti-state activities." Abdul Ghaffar Khan was later arrested to prevent his return to Afghanistan. After the deposition of Zulfikar Ali Bhutto, General Zia-ul-Haq reversed the policy of repression. After some hesitation, Khan was allowed to return to Afghanistan, and for the next two years he shuttled between it and Pakistan. Soon, however, he was at loggerheads with the Pakistani authorities because he urged the refugees from the Soviet invasion of Afghanistan to return home, denying that the war in Afghanistan was a *jihad.* In December 1985, he attended the centenary celebrations of the National Congress in India, but he was by now increasingly frail. On May 15, 1987, he was admitted to the hospital in Bombay but was discharged a month later and traveled to Delhi, where he suffered a stroke on July 4, 1987. From then until his death, he never fully recovered consciousness. After an attack of pneumonia, he died in Peshawar on January 20, 1988.

In a rare demonstration of agreement, the governments of India, Pakistan, and Afghanistan each declared a period of official mourning. He was in a real sense a citizen of all three countries. An intensely religious man who lived an austere life, he nonetheless acted as a secular conscience in each of these three countries where he had spent most of his long life.

See also Afghanistan; Bhutto, Zulfikar Ali; North West Frontier Province; Rowlatt Acts; Zia-ul-Haq, Muhammad.

References

Korejo, M. S. *The Frontier Gandhi, His Place in History.* New York: Oxford University Press, 1993

Talbot, Ian. *Pakistan: A Modern History.* New York: Hurst and Company, 1998

Tendulkar, Dinanath Gopal. *Abdula Ghaffar Khan.* New Delhi: Gandhi Peace Foundation, 1967

KHAN, ABDUL QADEER "AQ" (1936–)

Dr. Abdul Qadeer Khan is widely considered to be the principal brain behind Pakistan's nuclear weapons program. Born in Bhopal, India, he migrated to Pakistan at the age of 16. Graduating from Karachi University, he went on to study metallurgical engineering at a number of European universities. He worked for four years at the Physical Dynamics Research Laboratory in Holland. He returned to Pakistan in 1975 and, for professional and patriotic reasons, offered his services to Zulfikar Ali Bhutto's nuclear program. Bhutto rather dramatically claimed in the early 1970s that he would encourage the Pakistani production of an Islamic bomb.

Khan built up a network of scientists and officials that allegedly supplied West German, Dutch, and British blueprints and suppliers' lists. Earlier Pakistani efforts had concentrated on the reprocessing route to nuclear weapons production. Dr. Khan sought an alternative that would be less vulnerable to international pressure through the enrichment of uranium at centrifuge plants at Sihala and Kahuta. During the 1980s components for the enrichment process were clandestinely acquired from high-technology Western firms.

In May 1998 Pakistan detonated some nuclear devices, a few days after India had conducted nuclear tests, both countries thereby advertising the fact (in the face of much criticism from other countries) that they had become nuclear-weapon capable. The network around Khan traded nuclear technology–related documents and materials with Iran, Libya, and North Korea and offered them to at least one other country: Iraq. The materials conveyed to other countries included centrifuges to enrich uranium and a document describing how to cast uranium to build a type of nuclear warhead. The International Atomic Energy Agency (IAEA) repeatedly has said, especially since 1998, that more information is needed on what the Pakistani network had provided to Iran and others. Dr. Khan effectively lives under house arrest in Islamabad , having been given immunity from prosecution by President Pervez Musharraf in 2004 after he publicly admitted his role in overseeing the nuclear network. Pakistan has taken no other action against members of Khan's group, about a dozen of whom were initially detained but subsequently released by the authorities.

See also Bhutto, Zulfikar Ali; Nuclear Weapons.

References

Musharraf, P. *In the Line of Fire: A Memoir.* New York: The Free Press, 2006

KHAN, ABDUL WALI (1917–2006)

Abdul Wali Khan, founder of Pakistan's Awami National Party (ANP), died in late January 2006 in Peshawar, aged 89. He was the political heir of his father, Khan Abdul Ghaffar Khan (1890–1988), who was known as the Frontier Gandhi for the way he championed a nonviolent struggle for an independent, united, secular India. Wali Khan began his political life in the Khudai Khidmatzar Party, founded by his father. He was successively president of the Awami National Party (ANP), the National Democratic Party (NDP), and the ANP, which he founded in 1986. He surprised many by his retirement from active politics in 1990 after an election defeat, but he remained the political mentor of the ANP and was widely regarded as the last leader who could unify the ethnic Pashtun people.

KHAN, AGHA MUHAMMAD YAHYA (1917–1980)

Agha Muhammad Yahya Khan was the Pakistani Army commander-in-chief and president who presided over the dissolution of Pakistan as a consequence of the 1971 Indo-Pakistan War, which culminated in the emergence of the newly independent state of Bangladesh.

Born at Chakwal in the Jhelum district of the Punjab, the son of a police superintendent, Yahya was commissioned into the army in 1938 after attending Punjab University and the Indian Military Academy, Dehra Dun. He served in Britain's Eighth Army in World War II. After independence he was promoted successively to become chief of the general staff in 1957. In 1966 he was promoted to commander-in-chief. When Mohammed Ayub Khan resigned on March 25, 1969, Yahya succeeded him as president.

The two and a half years in office proved to be disastrous for Pakistan. Ironically, this quintessential soldier sought, unsuccessfully, to be a political innovator. He dissolved the One Unit Scheme and, after the introduction of the Legal Framework Order, approved the holding of Pakistan's first national election under direct adult suffrage. But his expectation that the election would lead to stable, civilian-led government was not met. The parties supporting his plans performed locally. The People's Party of Pakistan (PPP) emerged as the dominant power in West Pakistan and the Awami League as overwhelmingly strong in the eastern wing. Postelection political negotiations were deadlocked and increasingly embittered. Yahya desperately ordered a military crackdown in East Pakistan on March 25, 1971, prompting the declaration of an independent Bangladesh and setting up his main conflict, which culminated in the defeat of the Pakistan army by Indian and local Bahini forces and the emergence of a substantially independent Bangladesh. The subsequent unconditional surrender on December 16, 1971, led to calls in West Pakistan that he be tried as a traitor. He resigned from office and was sentenced to five years' house arrest.

See also Awami League (AL); Ayub Khan, Mohammed; Bangladesh; Indo-Pakistan War of 1947–1948; Pakistan People's Party (Shaheed Bhutto) PPP (SB).

References

Choudhry, G. W. *The Last Days of United Pakistan.* Bloomington: Indiana University Press, 1974

Cohen, S. P. *The Idea of Pakistan.* Washington, DC: Brookings Institution Press, 2004

Talbot, I. *Pakistan: A Modern History.* New York: Hurst and Company, 1998

KHAN, IMRAN (1952–)

Pakistan's former cricket captain, Imran Khan, entered his country's national politics in 1966. He is a member of a famous cricket-playing Pushtun family who settled in Lahore. Imran was educated at the prestigious Aitchison College in Lahore and then at Keble College, Oxford. He entered professional cricket as an all-rounder. Soon his dashing style and considerable successes with both bat and ball made him hugely popular in both Pakistan and India, especially because television was converting cricket into an international spectator sport. Pakistan enjoyed its greatest ever international success during his time as captain from 1982 onward, the apex of which was victory in the 1992 World Cup.

In the early 1990s Imran Khan sought to present himself as a "born-again" Muslim and critic of the so-called brown sahib culture in which he had grown up. During the 1997 general election campaign, however, it was not always easy to escape this playboy past. His marriage to Jemima Goldsmith, from a rich Jewish family, whom he later divorced, also raised accusations of Jewish funding for his activities.

Imran first entered public life outside cricket as a fund-raiser for the Shaukat Khanum Memorial Cancer Hospital and as an outspoken critic of Pakistan's rampant corruption. He appeared to be supported by forces from the right of Pakistan politics who were looking for what they called a third option. His relations with Pakistan's other well-known celebrity in the western world, Benazir Bhutto, became increasingly fraught. By the time of the February 1996 opening ceremony of the Sixth Cricket World Cup, jointly hosted by India and Pakistan, Imran was persona non grata. After months of speculation and an unexplained bomb blast that destroyed the outpatient wing of the hospital, Imran finally founded his Tehrek-e-Insaaf (Truth Movement) Party on April 25, 1996. The February 1997 elections came too early for his fledgling party to become established. His party's failure to capture a single National Assembly or provincial assembly seat was nonetheless unexpected. Imran maintained that there had been electoral rigging and pledged to carry on his political career.

In 1997, Khan formed a party—Pakistan's Tehreek-e-Insaf (Movement for Justice) Party. Ten years later his party had only one seat (his own) in the national parliament. Although he is still regarded in some quarters as a national hero for leading Pakistan's cricket team to victory in the 1992 World Cup, and his popularity seems to have risen since he took a critical stand against General Pervez Musharraf, his critics and political opponents dismiss him as a political lightweight.

He was taken into custody and house arrest by General Musharraf in November 2007 but released only two weeks later to enable him possibly to run in the general elections scheduled for early January 2008.

See also Bhutto, Benazir; Cricket.

KHAN, LIAQUAT ALI (1895–1951)

Liaquat (or Liaqat) Ali Khan was a rich landowner in the United Provinces, a lawyer, a Muslim League leader, and the first prime minister of Pakistan. During the Muslim League Movement, he was general secretary of the party and acknowledged as Mohammed Ali Jinnah's right-hand man. He was finance member of the interim government in 1946. With the launching of Pakistan as an independent state, as of mid August 1947, he became simultaneously prime minister and minister of defense. Even as governor-general, Jinnah remained the leading political figure until his death in 1948. Liaqat encouraged the processes of centralization for Pak-

istan, and he publicly equated opposition to the Muslim League with hostility to Pakistan. The Objectives Resolution was passed while Liaqat was prime minister to provide an Islamic basis for future constitutions. By the time of his assassination, Liaqat appeared to be on the verge of both reactivating the Muslim League and steering Pakistan's foreign policy into a more Islamic direction.

He was gunned down by a hired assassin in Rawalpindi's army cantonment. Liaquat is still revered as the Quaid-I Millat political leader. During the 1980s, the Mohajir Qaumi Mahaz (MQM) encouraged his veneration as a specifically Mohajir figure. Liaquat married Irene Pant in 1933. After her conversion to Islam, Pant was known as Begun Raan'a Liaqat Ali Khan. She held a number of public appointments, including those of ambassador to Holland and Italy. She served briefly under Zulfikar Ali Bhutto as governor of Sind.

See also Bhutto, Zulfikar Ali; Jinnah, Mohammed Ali; Muslim League.

References

Talbot, I. *Pakistan: A Modern History.* New York: Hurst and Company, 1998

KHRUSHCHEV, NIKITA (1894–1971)

Nikita Khruschev was the first secretary of the Soviet Communist Party (1953–1964) and prime minister (1958–1964). He played the leading role in de-Stalinizing Soviet politics after Stalin's death in March 1953, and he pioneered good open relations with India, notably by undertaking visits to India, Burma, and Afghanistan between mid November and mid December 1955, during which he endorsed India's position on Kashmir and promised further aid and assistance to India. Born in the Ukraine, Khrushchev joined the Communist Party in 1918, fought in Russia's civil war, and rose rapidly in the party's hierarchy. In 1939 he became a full member of the Presidium of the Supreme Soviet. Within months of Stalin's death he became first secretary of the Communist Party of the Soviet Union (CPSU). At the 20th congress of the CPSO in 1956, he denounced Stalin and his cult of personality.

Among the notable events during his political preeminence were the Hungarian uprising of 1956, the Suez War of 1956, and the failed attempt to install missiles permanently on Cuban soil. Russia played a formally neutral but actually pro-Indian position regarding the Sino-Indian War of 1962.

Khrushchev was the first Soviet leader to engage in direct personal relations with some Western leaders.

A notably ebullient personality, he was deposed from office in 1964 and forced into retirement, being replaced by Brezhnev and Kosygin.

See also Afghanistan; Azad Jammu-Kashmir (AJK); Russia.

References

Khrushchev, N. *Khrushchev Remembers*. Boston: Little, Brown and Company, 1970

Lyon, P. *Neutralism*. Leicester, UK: Leicester University Press, 1963

Taubman, William. *Khrushchev: The Man and His Era*. New York: Simon & Schuster, 2004

KISSINGER, HENRY ALFRED (1923–)

American political scientist, diplomat, and public servant, Henry A. Kissinger skillfully used top-level links with Pakistan to inaugurate in the early 1970s a détente in his country's links with China and was thereby regarded with some suspicion by most Indian policy makers. Kissinger was President Richard M. Nixon's adviser on national security affairs in 1969 and became secretary of state under Presidents Nixon and Gerald Ford. Seemingly tireless when traveling and in intensive negotiation, he personified and popularized the notion of shuttle diplomacy.

He was born in Furth, Germany, but his family immigrated to the United States in 1938 to escape Nazi persecution of the Jews. He studied at Harvard and after war service worked for a number of public agencies before joining the Harvard faculty (1962–1971).

He was the main U.S. figure in the negotiations to end the Vietnam War (for which he shared the 1973 Nobel Peace Prize). He preferred relations with Pakistan rather than with India, especially in regard to China and the Vietnam War. After leaving public office in 1977, he returned to academe and to lucrative consultancies. Kissinger was an influential background figure during the administration of President Ronald Reagan, in which several of his protégés served.

See also Nixon, Richard Milhous.

References

Hersh, Seymour. *The Price of Power: Kissinger in the Nixon White House*. New York: Summit Books, 1984

Kissinger, H. *The White House Years*. London: Weidefeld & Nicolson and Michael Joseph, 1979

Henry Alfred Kissinger, U.S. national security adviser (1969–1975) and secretary of state (1973–1977). He utilized his connections with Pakistan to inaugurate an American-Chinese détente. (Library of Congress)

Kissinger, H. *Diplomacy*. New York: Simon & Schuster, 1994

KRISHAK PRAJA PARTY (KPP)

This radical Bengali party was founded by Fazlul Huq (Haq) in April 1936. It did well in East Bengal constituencies in the 1937 elections and formed a coalition government with the Muslim League from 1937 until December 1941. Following Huq's split with the Muslim League, it became a prominent part of the Progressive Coalition Assembly Party, which survived in office until March 1943, though by the time of the 1946 provincial elections it had lost a lot of its members to the Muslim League. After independence, KPP supporters formed the core of Fazlul Huq's Krishak Sramik Party, which played a prominent role in the United Front's crushing victory over the Muslim League in the spring 1954 provincial elections in East Pakistan.

See also Haq, Fazlul; Muslim League.

References
Talbot, I. *Pakistan: A Modern History.* New York: Hurst and Company, 1998

KUTCH (CUTCH), RANN OF

The Rann of Kutch is a territory contested by India and Pakistan, especially the western sector of the Great Rann known as Sir Creek, which is part of the Indus River's extensive delta and where the river's marshy distributaries tend to change courses with climatic variations.

The Rann is bounded on the north and northwest by Sind (Pakistan), on the east by two districts of India's Gujarat, on the south by the Gulf of Cutch and part of Gujarat, and on the west and southwest by the Arabian Sea. The Rann consists of the Great Rann on the north and the Little Rann to the southeast, consisting of about 18,129 square killometers (7,000 square miles) and nearly 5,180 square killometers (2,000 square miles), respectively. Overall, the Rann is believed to be a dry bed and arm of the sea, interspersed with marshes, wells, and springs. Those near the Rann are saline, and there is some salt production. Many local small hills and streams are almost dry except during the rainy season.

Cutch was under British rule from 1815 to 1947. In 1965 a much publicized dispute arose over the boundary line between India and Pakistan. Fighting broke out in April between the regular forces of both countries and stopped only when Great Britain intervened to secure a cease-fire. The dispute was referred by the United Nation's secretary-general to a tribunal, which in 1968 allotted about 10 percent of the border area to Pakistan and about 90 percent to India.

References
Razvi, Mujtaba. *The Frontiers of Pakistan.* Karachi, Pak.: Dacca National Publishing House Ltd., 1971
Spate, O. H. K. *India and Pakistan: A General and Regional Geography,* 2nd ed. New York: Methuen, 1960

LADAKH

Ladakh is a valley of the upper Indus River and a range at the northwestern section of the Himalayas, giving their name to the large eastern district of Kashmir, known to Indians at least since 1950 as the frontier district of Ladakh in the state of Jammu-Kashmir, as one of its *tehsils* (subdivisions). Before the cease-fire agreement between India and Pakistan, effective from January 1949, the district, then known as the Ladakh and Baltistan *wazarat,* included as its northwestern part Baltistan, or little Tibet, and had three *tehsils* (Ladakh, Kargil, and Skardu). The eastern end of the cease-fire line crossed the Ladakh Valley and bisected the Ladakh Range. This left Baltistan to the north and Leh, the district capital, with southern Ladakh including the whole of Leh *tehsil* and most of Kargil, on the Indian-controlled side.

With the partitions of the Indian subcontinent in August 1947, Ladakh as a district of Jammu-Kashmir became embroiled in the disputes between India and Pakistan. Both countries claimed that state as part of their territory. In October 1947 tribespeople from the North West Frontier of Pakistan invaded from the north, and Indian airborne troops were flown in to repel their advance. The same month the Hindu-Dogra ruler of Kashmir, Maharajah Hari Singh, announced that his state, although predominantly Muslim in population, would accede to the Indian union. India referred the dispute to the United Nations and a cease-fire came into operation in early January 1949.

The rival forces halted on a cease-fire line, which divided the state into two parts, the greater part of Ladakh district falling to India. Subsequently all efforts at a permanent settlement have failed, and there were armed clashes between Indian and Chinese troops in the Aksai Chin (northeast salient of Ladakh) and between Pakistan and India in Kargil across the Skardu-Leh road in 2002.

See also Kargil.

L

References

Spate, O. H. K. *India and Pakistan: A General and Regional Geography,* 2nd ed. New York: Methuen, 1960

Lamb, A. *Kashmir: A Disputed Legacy, 1846–1990.* Hertingfordbury, UK: Roxford Books, 1991

LAHORE

Pakistan's most populous and genuinely historical city, Lahore has been the venue for a number of Indo-Pakistan negotiations. Situated near Pakistan's Punjab boundary with India, Lahore is an important junction on Pakistan's western railway system with connections to Karachi, Peshawar, and Quetta and with India through Wagah. It is a leading commercial and banking city and the center of one of Pakistan's principal industrial regions, with many cotton, silk, shoes, rubber, iron, steel, and other mills. It is also notable for its gold and silver, lace, and ornaments. Lahore is the chief educational and cultural center of Pakistan. It is the seat of the University of the Punjab (founded in 1882), the oldest and largest in Pakistan, with numerous colleges and institutes.

The site of Lahore was occupied from early times. Much of it stands well above the surrounding country, raised on the remains of a succession of former buildings. The name "Lahore" appears under more than a dozen forms in its history, one of which, Lohawar, means the love of Loh. Hindu tradition traces the origin of Lahore to Loh, or Lava, son of Rama, hero of the epic Ramayana. It was under the Mogul empire that Lahore attained its greatest magnificence when it became a place of royal residence. The reigns of Humayum, Akbar, Jahangir, Shah Jahan, and Aurangzeb marked the golden period in the annals and architecture of the city.

From the accession of Bahadur Shah to the establishment of the rule of Raajib Singh in 1799, however, its history was one of successive invasions and conquests. The Sikhs ruled Lahore from 1765 to 1849 until at the end of the Second Sikh War, when it came under British domination with the rest of the Punjab.

Ranjit Singh made it the capital of his kingdom. Under British rule, it became the capital of the province of Punjab and remained so until the partition in 1947, when it became the capital of West Pakistan. From 1955 until 1959, it was the capital of the unified province of West Pakistan. According to the 1998 census, the population of Lahore was 5.06 million, making it by far Pakistan's second most populous city after Karachi (which was 9.2 million).

See also Karachi; Punjab.

LAHORE RESOLUTION (1940)

In the Lahore Resolution, the Muslim League first explicitly demanded the creation of Pakistan. The resolution was moved by a Bengali, Fazlul Huq (Haq). This foundational resolution foreshadowing Pakistan postulated a confederate state with the decentralization of power to federating units, though without specifying how much provincial autonomy or how much centralization—central issues for Pakistan's subsequent political history.

See also Muslim League.

LANGUAGE

India's constitution provides that the official language of the Union still be Hindi in the Devanagari script. Hindi is spoken by over 30 percent of the population. The constitution also originally provided that English should continue to be used for all official purposes until 1965 (15 years after the constitution came into force). But the Official Languages Act 1963, stipulated that, after the expiration of this period, English might continue to be used in addition to Hindi, for all official purposes of the Union for which it was being used immediately before that day and for the transaction of business in parliament.

Urdu is the national language and the lingua franca of Pakistan, though only spoken by about 10 percent of the population. English is used in diplomacy, higher education, and central government. About 60 percent of the population speak Punjabi.

Virtually all official intergovernmental discourses between India and Pakistan are conducted in the English language.

References

King, R. *Nehru and the Language of Politics of India.* New York: Oxford University Press, 1999

LASHKAR-E-TAIBA

Lashkar-e-Taiba (LeT) is an insurgent group active in Jammu-Kashmir since the mid 1990s. It was launched as a Pakistan-based movement professing an ultraorthodox version of Sunni Islam. Like Jaish-e-Mohammad, LeT is predominantly composed of Pakistani religious radicals. Its leader is Hafiz Mohammad Sayeed, a Pakistani academic turned fundamentalist activist. LeT cadres have been responsible for a large percentage of *fidayeen* attacks on IJK (India's Jammu and Kashmir) since 1992 and are the prime suspects regarding a number of massacres of non-Muslim civilians. LeT tend often to behead their victims. Along with Jamaat-I-Islami, LeT was formally banned in Pakistan in January 2002.

Challenging the shackles of official restraint, the LeT came out in early May 2004 in opposition to the Indo-Pakistan détente. In articles in its house publication, it called for an escalation of the *jihad* in Jammu-Kashmir. On May 2, Hafiz Mohammad Sayeed, head of the Lashkar's parent organization, the Jammat-ud-Dawa, called for Pakistan-administered Kashmir to be declared "as a base camp for Jihardis to launch attacks in occupied Kashmir."

Writing in *Ghazwa,* he also asserted that the *jihad* in Jammu-Kashmir would escalate after the ongoing Indian elections. The *Voice of Islam,* for its part, promised that the Lashkar would "continue to dispatch the dead bodies of Indian soldiers until Junagarh, Ahmedabad, Hyderabad, Deccan, Gurdaspur, Manwadar, and Kashmir become part of Pakistan."

The Lashkar seemed incensed by the quiet support that ordinary people in Pakistan had shown for the détente process with India. Discussing recent Indo-Pakistan cricket matches, the *Zarb-e-Taiba* asserted that "the sports of a *mujahid* are archery, horse-riding and swimming. Apart from these three sports, every other hobby is un-Islamic." Under the intoxication of cricket," it asserted, "Pakistanis have forgotten that these Hindu players come from the same nation that had raped our mothers, sisters, daughters, wives and daughters-in-law. These Hindus had desecrated our mosques and copies of the Holy Koran. They are the same Hindus who had dismembered Pakistan."

References
King, R. *Nehru and the Languages of Politics of India.* New York: Oxford University Press, 1999

LIAQUAT-NEHRU AGREEMENT (1950)
In April 1950, Jawaharlal Nehru made his first visit to Pakistan since independence (accompanied by his daughter Indira and son-in-law Feroze Gandhi). He was met at Karachi by Prime Minister Liaquat Ali Khan and his entire cabinet. Discussions revolved around issues relating to partition, but no specific agreement was reached on Kashmir or on other outstanding issues.

See also Khan, Liaquat Ali; Nehru, Jawaharlal.

LUCKNOW
Lucknow was the capital seat of the United Provinces of Agra and Oudh during British rule in India until 1947, and subsequently it has been the capital of Uttar Pradesh, the populous political heartland of the Indian Union. Situated in north central India 410 kilometers (225 miles) southeast of Delhi and 330 kilometers (200 miles) northwest of Benares (Varanasi) on the river Gomali (or Gumbi), a major tributary of the Ganges.

Lucknow has played a role in a number of historical events. A British garrison was besieged for five months during the Indian Mutiny of 1857 in one of the most publicized episodes of the mutiny. The Lucknow Pact of 1916 was concluded at a joint session of the Congress, and the Muslim League called for self-government from British rule. Subsequently, Lucknow became a focal point of the movement for an independent Pakistan. Lucknow is a center of Indian and Islamic culture, as well as an industrial and commercial city, with many magnificent buildings, schools, and government offices.

See also Indian National Congress; Muslim League; Uttar Pradesh.

MACMILLAN, HAROLD (1894–1986)

Harold Macmillan was a British politician and prime minister (1957–1963) who supported Britain's highly controversial Government of India Act of 1935 and who in 1958 was the first serving British prime minister to visit India and Pakistan. He was born in London, the grandson of the publisher Daniel Macmillan. After war service, he studied at Oxford and became a Conservative minister to Parliament in 1924. Then for 20 years he was a member of the left reformist wing of the party. Eventually he became minister of housing (1951–1954), minister of defense (1954–1955), foreign secretary (1955, during which time he was not notably interested in South Asian matters), and chancellor of the exchequer (1955–1957).

A strong advocate of military intervention against Nasser's regime in Egypt in 1956, he was among the first in the British cabinet to urge withdrawal when he saw the consequences of the economic and diplomatic opposition wielded by the Dwight D. Eisenhower administration. Macmillan succeeded Anthony Eden as prime minister in January 1957.

Macmillan worked closely with President John F. Kennedy, especially regarding relations with the Soviet Union, China, and India, and on nuclear matters. Kennedy in particular consulted with Macmillan during the 1962 Sino-Indian War, which was simultaneous with the Cuban missile crisis. In January 1958, Macmillan set off on a six-week-long Commonwealth tour, of some 35,000 miles and 34 different overnight stops, principally endeavoring to repair the damage inflicted by the Suez War misadventure.

After some initial iciness, Macmillan was greeted and flattered by Jawaharlal Nehru. Macmillan was welcomed in Pakistan, though he had some foreboding at the state of Pakistan and the bitterness of Indo-Pakistani relations. In 1963, Macmillan resigned from the prime ministership due to ill health and left the House of Commons in 1964. He became chancellor of Oxford University in 1960 and was made an earl on his 90th birthday in 1984.

See also Eisenhower, Dwight David; Kennedy, John Fitzgerald; Nehru, Jawaharlal.

References
Horne, A. *Harold Macmillan: The Official Biography.* Vol. I, 1894–1956; Vol. II, 1957–1986. New York: Macmillan, 1989

M

MAHABHARATA

Mahabharata is the major Sanskrit epic of Hindu culture and history and a holy book. Dating from the first millennium BCE, its 110,000 couplets make it the longest epic in the world. It was orally transmitted and later became literature, printed in Sanskrit and in other languages. Various editions were brought together and published in the 10th century as the *Mahabharata*. The central plot concerns the conflict between two related families, the Kurus (spirits of evil) and Pandus (spirits of good). Woven around this story are myths, legends, folk tales, and metaphysical pieces. For contemporary Indians, some of the *Mahabharata* provides rich metaphors or analogies for Indo-Pakistan relations.

References
Baxter, Craig. *The Jana Sangh: A Biography of an Indian Political Party.* New York: Oxford University Press, 1971
Sen, Amartya. *The Argumentative Indian: Writings on Indian Culture, History and Identity.* London: Penguin, 2005
Thapar, Romila. *Cultural Transactions and Early India: Tradition and Patronage.* New York: Oxford University Press, 1987

MAHAJAN, PRAMOD (1949–2006)

Pramod Mahajan was sometimes described as India's first modern spin doctor, whose organizational and tactical skills helped to transform the Bharatiya Janata Party (BJP) from a sometimes extremist Hindu organization into a mainstream political force, especially as demonstrated in the years 1998–2006. Before his murder by a jealous younger brother, Mahajan was widely regarded as the forthcoming leader and fund-raiser for the BJP and likely to induct, by his skills and example, a new generation of leaders into his party.

Mahajan was born into a lower-middle-class Hindu family in the south of Andhra Pradesh state. He soon migrated with his family to a small town in western Maharashtra, of which the great port city of Bombay (Mumbai) is the capital. He graduated with a degree in physics, a postgraduate degree in political science, and a diploma in journalism. In the mid 1970s he joined the magazine of the Rashtriya Swayamsevak Sangh (RSS), *Tarun Bharat,* as a subeditor.

At the time of his assassination, Mahajan was emerging as the most likely political leader of the BJP. He stood as part of a young, eloquent, media-conscious second generation of parliamentarians and their backers and supporters who were waiting to succeed the aged old guard, most notably Atal Bihari Vajpayee and Lal Krishna Advani, who had risen to political prominence propounding a Hindu nationalism. Mahajan was general secretary of the BJP's parliamentary board and its central election committee, the party's two highest policy-making bodies. He was also a minister to parliament and a captivating orator in Telegu and English. Although an accomplished political strategist, Mahajan rarely contested or won elections himself, entering parliament mostly through the Rajya Sabha, the indirectly elected upper house. Even those, however, who had reservations about his political integrity did not doubt his political acumen and determined commitment to Hindu hegemony.

Mahajan's reputation rose rapidly after the 2003 regional elections in three important states, in which the BJP snatched unexpected victories, but India's political ground was beginning to move. The Hindutva Movement, the BJP's guiding philosophy, had been discredited by anti-Muslim riots, especially in Gujarat where many Muslims were slaughtered during communal clashes. As the most articulate and media-friendly of the BJP's leaders, Mahajan was often on television—an aspect of popular media of increasing importance because even the poorest villages were coming to own at least one communal television set.

Mahajan's general record of success was punctuated with a severe setback in 2004. He concocted the slogan "India's Shining" for the 2004 general election in which the BJP claimed credit for India's economic revival and rising international reputation, but for some of the middle classes and villages the slogan had no positive resonance. At the polls in 2004 the BJP was defeated after six years at the head of a coalition government. Mahajan took the blame for this debacle, but his own political standing soon generally recovered and he resumed prominence.

See also Advani, Lal Krishna; Bharatiya Janata Party (BJP); Hindutva; Rashtriya Swayamsevak Sangh (RSS); Vajpayee, Atal Bihari.

MANILA TREATY (1954). *SEE* SOUTH EAST ASIA TREATY ORGANIZATION.

MASS MIGRATION. *SEE* DIASPORAS.

MCMAHON LINE

The McMahon Line is the northeastern border of India with China, charted by British officials at the time of World War I but unmarked. It is recognized by India as the legitimate border with China. But China rejected India's claim and overran this terrain in the October 1962 Sino-Indian War.

References

Lamb, Alastair. *The China-India Border.* New York: Oxford University Press, 1964

Maxwell, Neville. *India's China War.* London: Jonathan Cape, 1970

MENON, RAO BAHADAR VAPAL PANGUNNI ("V. P.") (1894–1966)

V. P. Menon began service as a clerk in the Home Department of the government of India in 1914. From 1917 until the transfer of power in August 1947, he was in continuous association with the various stages of constitutional reform in India. He was promoted by successive stages to the position in 1942 of constitutional adviser to the governor-general. This important position he held until August 1947. He held other posts, including that of secretary to the cabinet. In 1947 he was specially selected for the post of secretary to the newly created

Ministry of States. In this capacity he worked directly under Sardar Vallabhbhai Patel, the deputy prime minister of India. By the time the new constitution came into force on January 26, 1950, the 565 Princely States had been integrated into the pattern of the republic.

After his retirement from the states ministry in 1951, he was for some time the acting governor of Orissa. Menon, having acted as constitutional adviser to the governor-general and later as secretary to the newly created Ministry of States, then played a major part in creating the new Indian order. In 1956 Menon published an authoritative historical account of the events in which he was closely involved, which he entitled *The Story of the Integration of the Indian States* and dedicated to Sardar Vallabhbhai Patel.

See also Mountbatten of Burma; Patel, Vallabhbhai; Princely States.

References

Menon, V. P. *The Story of the Integration of the Indian States.* New Delhi: Orient Longmans, 1956

Schofield, V. *Wavell: Soldier and Statesman.* London: John Murray, 2006

MENON, V. K. KRISHNA (1897–1974)

Vengalil Krishnan Krishna Menon was an Indian diplomat, minister of defense, and outspoken critic of the United States and of Pakistan, especially at the United Nations (UN) in 1950s. He was born into a large and wealthy family and studied at the University of Madras and the London School of Economics, at which time he also qualified as a barrister. During his years in London he became friendly with India's future prime minister, Jawaharlal Nehru. With India's independence in 1947, Nehru appointed Menon as high commissioner in London, an office he held for five years.

On several occasions he headed India's delegation at the UN, playing a publicly prominent role in articulating and formulating India's nonaligned foreign policy, with Nehru preferring the description an independent foreign power. Menon was elected to the lower house of the Indian parliament in 1957 and again in 1962. From 1956 to 1957, he was a minister without portfolio in Nehru's cabinet, and from 1957 to 1962 he was minister of defense, a period that ended in personal ignominy and the end of Nehru's support for him.

Chinese foreign minister Chen Yi, left, toasts Indian defense minister V. K. Krishna Menon, right, in Geneva, Switzerland, at a time when their two countries were at peace. Soviet foreign minister Andrei Gromyko, center, looks on. (Library of Congress)

Menon's overall record as minister of defense was a sad one; the Indian public and some members of the Congress attributed the debacle in the 1962 war to his neglect of military preparedness vis-à-vis China. On one occasion when he was minister of defense, all the service chiefs tendered their resignations in protest against the minister's policy of neglecting India's military preparedness, especially along the northern border.

Menon largely escaped censure on this occasion because of Nehru's support and protection. But immediately following China's successful three-pronged assault on India in October 1962, Menon tendered his resignation in the face of widespread criticism and calls for him to step down. Nehru was reluctantly compelled to see Menon leave office. Thereafter Menon's political fortunes plummeted. He virtually left the Congress and allied himself with the leftist block, outside parliament, though he remained an idiosyncratic independent.

See also Nehru, Jawaharlal.

References

Brecher, M. *Nehru: A Political Biography.* New York: Oxford University Press, 1959

George, T. J. S. *Krishna Menon: A Biography.* London: Jonathan Cape, 1964

MIRZA, ISKANDER (1899–1969)

Iskander Mirza was governor-general and president of Pakistan (1956–1958). Born in Bombay into a Shia family from West Bengal during the Raj, he served in the Indian Political Service while retaining his military commission (he was the first Indian from Sandhurst to be commissioned). He became Pakistan's defense secretary in 1949 and governor of East Pakistan in 1954, both posts in which he was a prime spokesperson for Pakistan's relations with India.

He was interior minister in Bogra's cabinet of talents, which followed Muhammad Ghulam's dismissal of the Constituent Assembly, and the following year he succeeded the ailing Ghulam as governor-general. By this time political power had slipped from the hands of true politicians to those of the bureaucrats and their military allies. In this situation Mirza encouraged the formation of the Republican Party. After the promulgation of the 1956 constitution, Mirza took the post of president.

After a succession of weak prime ministers had come and gone, Mirza dissolved the National Assembly on October 10, 1958, and proclaimed martial law. This move was considered by many at the time as a preemptive strike to prevent elections, which might have curtailed the Pakistan establishment's foreign policy interests. As early as May 1958, Mirza had confided to the U.S. ambassador to Pakistan that "only a dictatorship would work in Pakistan." Mirza briefly shared power with Mohammed Ayub Khan following the coup, but within three weeks he was out of office and in exile in London. He died in 1969 and was buried in Teheran

See also Ali Choudhry Muhammad; Ayub Khan, Mohammed; Bogra.

References

Ayub Khan. *Friends Not Masters: A Political Autobiography.* New York: Oxford University Press, 1967

Gauhar, Altaf. *Ayub Khan: Pakistan's First Military Ruler.* Lahore, Pak.: Sang-e-Meel Publications, 1993

Talbot, Ian. *Pakistan: A Modern History.* New York: Hurst and Company, 1998

MOHAJIR QAUMI MAHAZ (MQM)

The Mohajir Qaumi Mahaz (MQM) party was founded in March 1984 by Altaf Hussain and other members of the All-Pakistan Mohajir Students Organisation (APMSO). The MQM represents the Urdu-speaking Mohajir population who migrated from India at the time of the creation of Pakistan, including General Pervez Musharraf's family. In the beginning, it appealed especially to lower-middle-class Mohajirs who felt discriminated against by the state's preferential politics regarding employment and admission to educational institutions. It also fed on the tensions stemming from rapid socioeconomic change in such cities of Mohajir settlement as Karachi and Hyderabad. The MQM also reflected the increasing ethnicization of Pakistani politics.

The MQM rapid rise to prominence and then to power in Karachi was primarily at the expense of the Jamaat-I-Islami (JI). The MQM was propagated and propelled by the spread of ethnic riots between the Mohajirs and Pushtuns from the mid 1980s onward. Altaf Hussain's leadership and claim to be launching what he called a Mohajir nationality accompanied the MQM's growing prominence in local bodies. The party governs Karachi and other cities in Sindh province. The movement soon acquired a reputation not only for violence and the intimidation of opponents, but also for promoting local public benefits.

Following its winning of 13 National Assembly seats in the 1988 elections, the MQM acquired considerable political leverage. It became part of the Pakistan People's Party (PPP) coalition both nationally and in Sindh. Relations with Benazir Bhutto's government became acrimonious over such matters as Mohajir accusations of police wrongdoings and the contentious issue of the repatriation of Biharis from camps in Bangladesh. The MQM's decision to support Nawaz Sharif's September 1989 no-confidence motion against the PPP government took the incumbency by surprise.

Thereafter law and order declined rapidly in both urban and rural Sindh, culminating in a notorious day in Hyderabad on May 27, 1990, when the police opened fire in a Mohajir locale. The ensuing violence led to the end of Benazir Bhutto's first administration within three months. In the 1990 elections the MQM redemonstrated its political power, ruling in Sindh for the next 19 months. The violence arising from disagreements between supporters of Altaf Hussain [MQM(A)] and the Haqiqi faction [MQM(H)] was part of the background to the so-called Operation Clean-Up of May 1992. Army raids uncovered torture chambers and arms caches in areas of Karachi previously controlled by the MQM(A), but army support for the rival MQM(H) did not result in long-term electoral benefits.

Despite Altaf Hussain's continued exile in London, the MQM(A) won decisively in the 1993 provincial elections following the dismissal of Nawaz Sharif, although it boycotted the national polls. After a brief period of reconciliation the MQM(A) resumed street fighting with the PPP following the controversial decision to form a new Malir district of Karachi in March 1994. The withdrawal of the army in December 1994 led to gun battles between the rival factions of the MQM coinciding with increasing sectarian clashes and Mohajir-Sindhi violence.

In May–June 1995 armed clashes broke out in Karachi between the MQM(A) and the police and rangers. Talks between the PPP and MQM(A) failed to bring about peace. Ruthless counterinsurgency measures did, however, bring some calm to Karachi by the spring of 1996. Charges of killings were later used by President Farooq Leghari against Benazir Bhutto's administration. MQM supporters celebrated the dismissal of the government on November 5, although they were less pleased with the appointment of the Sindhi nationalist, Mumbaz Ali Bhutto, as caretaker chief minister. The MQM(A) won 28 Sindhi assembly seats and 12 National Assembly seats in the February 1997 elections, once again beating the MQM(A).

In late May 2007, the Muttehida Qaumi Movement (MQM, formerly known as the Mohajir Qaumi Mahaz) threatened to withdraw its support from the federal and Sindhi provincial governments after criticism that it provoked clashes that left more than 40 people dead in Karachi, Pakistan's largest city.

MQM's founder, Altaf Hussain, is a firebrand speaker who is based in Edgware, northwest London, England. He fled Pakistan in 1992 after the army crackdown on his party, alleging that it was involved in terrorist activities.

Hussain, by profession a pharmacist, was convicted and sentenced to 25 years in prison in absentia by an antiterrorism court for kidnapping and torturing an army officer. He was also accused and sought for several cases of murder, though he denies all the charges.

Hussain directs his followers in Karachi by addressing them regularly by telephone. Despite its ethnic-based politics, the MQM claims to be the only significant political force in Pakistan to stand up openly for secular values. Hussain became a British citizen during Tony Blair's Labour government.

Critics of Hussain—among them Imran Khan, the former cricket captain of Pakistan who became an active politician—have repeatedly demanded that Hussain be expelled from Britain. Khan has said that he will discuss the issue with British authorities whom he accuses of giving sanctuary to Hussain.

See also Bhutto, Benazir; Ershad, Hossain Muhammad; Jamaat-I-Islami (JI); Pakistan People's Party (Shaheed Bhutto) PPP (SB); Sharif, Nawaz.

References

Hardgrave, R. L., and S. A. Kochanet. *India: Government and Politics in a Developing Nation,* 6th ed. Fort Worth, TX: Harcourt College Publishers, 2000

MOHAJIRS

The Mohajirs are predominantly Urdu-speaking migrants, originally from the United Provinces in 1947—and were named after the migrating companions of the Prophet Mohammad. Facing the acute problems of migration and resettlement in 1947, they included some of the best educated and most pro-Pakistan of all Indian Muslims. Many Indian Muslim families, having decided to opt for the new state of Pakistan, had to choose between going to the east or the west wing. Some families found themselves divided and scattered into both wings. The Mohajirs were part of Pakistan's initial ruling elite but became marginalized in the 1970s. In Pakistan's first 25 years, they operated at the national (not provincial) level, though located largely in the Sindh. They constituted only 3 percent of the population but held 21 percent of government jobs. They were prominent in the army (two army chiefs were Mohajirs, including President Pervez Musharraf). Seven of the twelve biggest businesses were controlled by Gujarati-speaking Mohajirs.

See also Mohajir Qaumi Mahaz (MQM); Sind.

References

Cohen, S. P. *The Idea of Pakistan*. Washington, DC: Brookings Institution Press, 2004

MOUNTBATTEN OF BURMA (1900–1979)

Admiral of the Fleet Earl Mountbatten had a distinguished career as a sailor and statesman, including a brief but meteoric impact in 1946–1947 as Britain's last viceroy of India and as the first governor-general of independent India.

He was a great-grandson of Queen Victoria, cousin of Queen Elizabeth II, and uncle of Prince Philip Mountbatten. He was known to all the British Royal family as Uncle Dickie. His father, Prince Louis of Battenberg, was first sea lord in 1914. Renouncing his foreign titles, his father was created Marquis of Milford Haven in 1917, and in consequence for much of his life Earl Mountbatten was known as Lord Louis.

His career of public service had three peaks: as supreme commander, South East Asia Command

Lord Louis Mountbatten hands over power to Quaid-i-Azam Mahomed Ali Jinnah on August 14, 1947, the official date of Pakistan's formation. (Library of Congress)

(SEAC, 1943–1945); as last British viceroy and first governor-general of India; and then as head of the British Navy and chairman of Britain's chiefs of staff. As head of SEAC, he initially led a defensive but then a triumphantly victorious campaign in northeast India and Burma; in September 1945 he presided over the surrender of the southern Japanese armies in Singapore.

Late in 1945, Clement R. Attlee, Britain's prime minister, chose Mountbatten to succeed Archibald Percival Wavell as viceroy of India with instructions to transfer power either to a united India or to more than one successor state by June 1948. Faced with a deteriorating situation of political division and mass migrations and violence, by June 1947, Mountbatten gained acceptance of a plan both from the leaders of the Indian National Congress and of the Muslim League and from the British government. The plan called for the transfer of power to two dominions, India and Pakistan, on August 15, 1947. Mountbatten remained as governor-general of independent India until June 1948.

Unlike Wavell, his immediate predecessor as viceroy, Mountbatten had great support and discretionary authority from the British government. He was instrumental in shortening the timetable for the British withdrawal to the two successor governments of India and Pakistan, and he infused the whole complex process of the transfer of power with energy and purposefulness, especially in regard to the integration of the Princely States.

Mountbatten believed and openly advocated that there should be joint détente arrangements for the two successor states and that he would be the governor-general for both countries. These latter ambitions were thwarted by Mohammed Ali Jinnah's determination to be the first governor-general of Pakistan. Mountbatten and his wife, Edwina, had exceedingly close relations with Jawaharlal Nehru. Mountbatten was murdered by Irish terrorists while on a sailing holiday off the northwest coast of Ireland in late August 1979.

See also Ali, Choudhury Muhammad; Attlee, Clement Richard; Jinnah, Mohammed Ali; Nehru, Jawaharlal; Wavell, Archibald Percival, First Earl Wavell.

References
Ziegler, P. *Mountbatten: A Biography.* New York: Alfred A. Knopf, 1985

MUHAMMAD, GHULAM (1895–1956)

Muhammad Ghulam was a civil servant who became governor-general of Pakistan from October 1951 to August 1955. A Pushtu from Julhundur, he built up a reputation as a financial expert under British rule, both in the Indian Audit and Accounts Service and in administrative posts in Hyderabad and Bhopal. He became the first finance minister upon the independence of Pakistan. After Ali Khan Liaquat's death he became Pakistan's third governor-general.

Muhammad Ghulam was a tough, ambitious, and rather authoritarian figure who arguably hastened the undermining of parliamentary democracy in Pakistan by his dismissal of Khwaja Nazimuddin from the office of prime minister in April 1953 and also the Constituent Assembly (the lower house of parliament). He relied heavily on the support of Mohammed Ayub Khan and the military. Plagued with ill health, he resigned as governor-general in 1955 and died soon after. Iskander Mirza succeeded him.

See also Ayub Khan, Mohammed; Mirza, Iskander.
References
Talbot, I. *Pakistan: A Modern History.* New York: Hurst and Company, 1998

MUMBAI

Mumbai is the official name, since 1995, of Bombay, India's most populous city and the only natural deepwater harbor on the western coast of the subcontinent. It is built on a group of islands linked by causeways.

Bombay was ceded to Portugal in 1534 and then to Britain in 1661. It was the headquarters of the East India Company in the subcontinent from 1685 to 1708. It is a major airport and railway terminus, has two prestigious universities (founded in 1916 and 1957), and is well-known for its textile, carpet, machines, chemicals, oil products, and exports. There's a nuclear reactor at nearby Trombay.

The city was damaged by a series of terrorist bomb attacks in 2003. It is a celebrated center for India's film industry (and is colloquially known as Bollywood), as well as a center for making Hindi and Marathi language films. Presently and prospectively, Mumbai is a principal nodal city for India's air and naval contacts and for trade with Pakistan, particularly with Karachi.

References
Srinivasan, T. N. *Eight Lectures on India's Economic Reforms*. New York: Oxford University Press, 2000

MUSHARRAF, PERVEZ (1943–)

Pakistani military leader and president (1999–), born in New Delhi, Pervez Musharraf is the second of three sons whose father was in public service since 1947 specializing in financial matters within Pakistan's foreign policy. Musharraf immigrated with his family to Karachi, Pakistan, in 1947, joined the army, and was a career soldier for 35 years. He fought in the 1965 and 1971 wars against India. He rose through the ranks and in 1998 was appointed army chief by Nawaz Sharif. He supported and may have helped plan Pakistan's invasion of Indian-held territory in the Kargil sector of Kashmir in 1999.

Angered by Nawaz Sharif's decision, under American pressure, to withdraw from the Kargil territory and upon learning that he had been sacked as army chief, Musharraf seized power in 1999 in what was in effect a countercoup. He became head of a military-dominated government, dissolved parliament, suspended the constitution, and reestablished a National Security Council.

In 2001, he assumed a major role, especially in conjunction with the United States, in international efforts against terrorism, particularly those focused on Afghanistan. In April 2002, he received apparently overwhelming support in a controversial nationwide referendum to extend his term of office for another five years. Also in late 2002, he was once more at the center of international attention during the confrontation between Pakistan and India over Kashmir. He survived assassination attempts by Islamic extremists in 2002 and again in December 2003.

In the eight years since he first seized power in 1999 from the civilian government of Prime Minister Nawaz Sharif, General Musharraf has repeatedly promised that his country would become a full-fledged democracy, and he has repeatedly failed to make it so. Instead, he has allowed the military to entrench itself more in business, reinforcing its role as a state within the state; he has allowed fundamentalist groups to flourish, partly as a counterweight to the established political parties he mistrusted; and he has presided over a pronounced decline in the power and authority of the central government and a rise in demands for greater au-

Pervez Musharraf was head of Pakistan's armed forces from 1999 to 2007 and president from 1999 to 2008. His military and political power was in steep decline from 2007 to 2008. (Pakistan Mission to the UN)

tonomy from regions such as Baluchistan and the North West Frontier Province.

On the positive side, General Musharraf has tried to make progress in talks with the government of India, notably over the future of Kashmir, but at the same time he has allowed militant groups to continue their attacks on Indian forces in that territory. Musharraf also has presided over an economic program of privatization, helping to attract a notable increase in foreign aid and investment. However, the benefits of that growth have failed to filter through to the bulk of the Pakistani population and have done little or nothing to stabilize the political situation.

When he came to power in 1999, Musharraf was widely regarded as a potential savior of the country from the corruptions of civilian rule and a staunch opponent of Muslim fundamentalism. As a boy he had lived in Turkey with his family for some years, and by 1999 he was said to have modeled himself on Kemal Ataturk, the founder of the modern Turkish state, who established a secular democratic constitution while maintaining a military order.

By 2007 General Musharraf had failed on two fronts. He had allowed some of his generals to support Jihadism, greatly increasing its influence in public life. He also had repeatedly balked at reintroducing genuine free and fair democratic elections.

The former civilian governments of both Nawaz Sharif and Benazir Bhutto were riddled with corruption, and the international community was inclined to give General Musharraf the benefit of the doubt in 1999, while ironically going through the motions of condemning the overthrow of democracy.

In October 2007, by launching a second coup d'état (this time an incumbency coup, called by its perpetrators a state of emergency, accompanied by the imposition of martial law), Musharraf acutely embarrassed the United States and other allies, including the United Kingdom. The evidence suggests that Musharraf's second coup was not so much against fundamentalist groups as against the judges of the Supreme Court. It seems that they might not have confirmed his eligibility to stand for election as president before he had given up his military uniform and retired from the army; so he dismissed his high-level judicial critics.

There are no easy solutions to Pakistan's instability, and few believe that democratic elections alone will bring about a fundamental transformation and lasting order and peace. Furthermore, no stability is possible without the close involvement of the military and security establishments. But the experience of 1999–2007 suggests that weak and indecisive military rule provides no solution either.

Siding with America in its war with the Taliban and al-Qaeda has not notably helped General Pervez Musharraf to recruit friends and allies at home. Domestic opposition to his pro-American stance stiffened in 2007 following some of the most intensive fighting since Pakistan's army entered the lawless tribal belt bordering Afghanistan at America's behest in 2001.

Pakistan's army has received drubbings from militants with links to the Taliban and al-Qaeda. On October 6, 2007, while General Musharraf was being reelected as Pakistan's president, militants attacked a truck full of paramilitary troops with a roadside bomb in North Waziristan. An army convoy that rumbled to the scene was ambushed by 300 militants, who killed 22 soldiers and wounded 11. Pakistan's army struck back with days of so-called punitive action in the Mir Ali district (where northern Waziristan meets the southern section of the North West Frontier Province), where General Musharraf had said that al-Qaeda had taken refuge. Thousands of people fled air strikes against villages. The bodies of dozens of Pakistani soldiers, many with their throats slit, were recovered. According to official figures, 200 militants and 50 soldiers were killed. An unknown number of civilians also died. Subsequently, commentators reported mounting concern within the army over killing fellow citizens. Between July and early October 2007, Pakistan's security forces lost more than 250 men, many in suicide bombings. More than 200 soldiers taken captive in southern Waziristan in August 2007 were freed three months later.

General Pervez Musharraf was reelected for another five-year term as Pakistan's president on October 6, 2007, but his victory was overshadowed by a court case that could yet strip him of power. Pakistan's Supreme Court ruled on October 5, 2007, that, while the election could go ahead, the results could not be officially announced until it was decided whether Musharraf was eligible to be a candidate. Under Pakistan's constitution, military personnel cannot stand until two years after retirement. The verdict was released on October 17, 2007. The poll was skewed by abstentions that gave Musharraf 99.3 percent of the vote in the four provincial assemblies, the National Assembly, and Senate. In several assemblies his opponent received no votes. The court disqualified Musharraf, and Musharraf responded by "disqualifying" the court.

See also Afghanistan; Bhutto, Benazir; Karachi; Sharif, Nawaz.

References

Ahmad, Ishtiaq, and A. Bashir. *India and Pakistan: Charting a Path to Peace.* Pakistan: Islamabad Society for Tolerance and Education, 2004

Musharraf, Pervez. *In the Line of Fire: A Memoir.* New York: The Free Press, 2006

MUSLIM LEAGUE

The Muslim League was formed in Dhaka (1906) as the All India Muslim League, a religious organization to safeguard and promote Islamic worship in British India. The League became a political movement in 1935 under the leadership of Mohammed

Ali Jinnah as Muslims left the India National Congress Party ostensibly because it had become predominantly Hindu in policy and aspirations. The breach widened with congressional state electoral victories in 1937. The Muslim League supported India's full participation in World War II, but it intensified its demand for Muslim autonomy and, from 1942 onward, advocated a separate Muslim Pakistan. The League's uncompromising policies led to partition, and by 1946–1947 there was no doubt that Jinnah and the League had overwhelming support from India's extensive Muslim population.

After Jinnah's death in 1948, the League never again found a leader of comparable stature. New parties emerged in Pakistan, and in the general election of 1955 the League lost the absolute majority it had enjoyed since the launching of the state. The formation of the Republican Party in 1956 was a further blow to the League and led to the emergence of a national non-Muslim League leadership. The Muslim League was dissolved along with other parties in the Mohammed Ayub Khan martial law period, but in 1962 the Convention and Council Muslim League came into existence. This started a trend for the proliferation of mostly personality-based Muslim Leagues, all of which have attempted to claim the historic mantle of the founders of Pakistan, especially that of Jinnah. The neofundamentalism of the 1980s thus led to a revival for the League, which won 17 of 73 seats for the National Assembly in 1984 and supported the ruling Islamic Democratic Alliance (1990–1993).

In India, too, a vestigial Muslim League survives. A number of scholars have commented on the League's weak institutionalization and faction-ridden provincial branches even in the heydays of the late 1940s and early 1950s. After Zia-ul-Haq's lifting of martial law in 1985, Muhammad Khan Junejo formed a Pakistan Muslim League (OML). After his death and during the constitutional crisis of 1993, it split into PML(N) and PML(J) factions. The latter sided with the Pakistan People's Party (PPP) in both the 1993 and the 1997 polls. Its relationship with the Punjab branch of the PPP was uneasy during Benazir Bhutto's second administration (October 1993–November 1996).

See also Bhutto, Benazir; Jinnah, Mohammed Ali; Zia-ul-Haq, Muhammad.

References
Jalal, Ayesha. *The Sole Spokesman, Jinnah, the Muslim League and the Demand for Pakistan.* New York: Cambridge University Press, 1985; Lahore, Pak.: Sang-e-Meel Publications, 1999
Jalal, Ayesha. *Democracy and Authoritarianism in South Asia. A Comparative and Historical Perspective.* New York: Cambridge University Press, 1995
Talbot, Ian. *Pakistan: A Modern History.* New York: Hurst and Company, 1998

MYANMAR

Myanmar is bounded on its eastern flanks by China, Laos, and Thailand and to its west by the Indian Ocean, Bangladesh, and India. From 1947 to 1971, when what was then East Pakistan, Myanmar was intimately affected by Indo-Pakistan relations but less since 1958 when soldiers took over government in Rangoon (the same year as Mohammed Ayub Khan's coup in Pakistan) and thereafter basically followed an isolationist and certainly a markedly unilateralist foreign policy. On June 9, 1989, the government changed the name of the country in English from Burma to the Union of Myanmar.

Myanmar is inhabited by many ethnic nationalities. There are over 135 national groups with the Bamars (Burmen) comprising just under 70 percent of the population, forming the largest group. In the 18th and early 19th centuries, the Burmese kingdom was militaristic and fought against Thailand (formerly Siam), sacking its capital on at least two occasions. After Burma's invasion of the kingdom of Assam, the British East India Company retaliated in defense of its Indian interests and in 1826 drove the Burmese out of India. Territory was annexed in South Burma, but the kingdom of Upper Burma, ruling from Mandalay, remained independent. A second war with Britain in 1852 ended with the British annexation of the Irrawaddy Delta. In 1885 the British invaded and occupied Upper Burma. In 1886 all Burma became a province of Britain's Indian Empire. There were violent uprisings and much pronationalist activity, especially among the University of Rangoon's student body in the 1930s. In 1937 Burma was administratively separated from India by the British and permitted some degree of self-government, and independence was achieved in January 1948. In 1958 there was an army coup, and another in 1962, led by General Ne Win, who installed a revolutionary council and dissolved parliament.

The council ruled until March 1974 when the country became a self-proclaimed one-party socialist republic. On September 18, 1988, the armed forces seized power again and set up the State Law and Order Restoration Council (SLORC). The military junta did not accept the outcome of the 1990 general election, and the leader of the party that won the elections, Aung San Suu Kyi (who was awarded the Nobel Peace Prize), was put under house arrest.

NARAYANAN, KOCHERIL RAMAN (1920–2005)
Indian diplomat and statesman, Kocheril Raman Narayanan was his country's vice president (1992–1997) and president (1997–2002). Narayanan was the first Dalit (formerly known as an untouchable) to attain high office. He was born in a thatched hut at the village of Uzhavoor in Kottayam district, Kerala, on October 27, 1920. He was the fourth of seven children of a physician who practiced herbal medicine. He gained a degree in English literature at the University of Travancore and then became a temporary lecturer at University College, Trivandrum, in 1943. Narayanan then spent a year working as a journalist, but in 1945 he went to England where he studied political science under Harold Laski and worked as the London correspondent of the *Social Welfare Weekly* (edited from Bombay) and *The Hindu*. He was also active in Vengalil Krishnan Krishna Menon's India League.

Laski recommended Narayanan to Jawaharlal Nehru, who arranged for the young man to join India's Foreign Service in 1949. He served with missions in Rangoon, Tokyo, London, Islamabad, Canberra, and Hanoi, as well as holding various posts at the Ministry of External Affairs, including headship of the Policy Planning division. He was India's ambassador to Thailand (1967–1969), to Turkey (1973–1975), and to China (1976–1978). He spoke Chinese and was the first Indian ambassador in Beijing for 15 years. After retiring from the Foreign Service in 1978, Narayanan became vice chancellor of Jawaharlal Nehru University, but 18 months later he was appointed by Indira Gandhi as India's ambassador to the United States, where he served until 1984.

Narayanan was elected to the Lok Sabha for three successive terms in 1984, 1989, and 1991, representing Ottapalam in Kerala; he was minister for planning (1985), for external affairs (1985–1986), and then for science and technology for three years. He was a member of the Indian delegation to the United Nations' General Assembly in 1979. During his presidential term (1997–2002), Narayanan twice dissolved the Lok Sabha after determining that no one was in a position to secure the confidence of the house.

See also Dixit, J. N.; Menon, V. K. Krishna; Nehru, Jawaharlal.
References
The Times (London) (November 11, 2005)

NATIONALISM. *SEE* TWO-NATIONS THEORY.

NEHRU, BRAJ KUMAR (1909–2001)
Widely known as BK, Braj Kumar Nehru was one of India's most prominent and long serving public servants and diplomats. A cousin of Jawaharlal, he represented India at reparations talks after World War II and in the important sterling balance negotiations with Britain. He served as India's high commissioner in Britain and later as ambassador to the United States. For 14 years he was chairman of the investment committee of the United Nations, until his retirement in 1991.

Nehru was educated at Allahabad University, the London School of Economics, and Balliot College, Oxford. He qualified as a lawyer and in 1934 joined the Indian Civil Service (ICS). Within the ICS he became prominent among those who helped India to navigate in the challenging years following independence. He was generally suspicious of Pakistan's policies via-à-vis India.

His many posts included the governorships of Assam, Kashmir, and Gujerat. In 1997 he published his memoirs, *Nice Guys Finish Second*, which covered several decades of his and India's vicissitudes. He was supportive of his niece, Indira Gandhi, during her declared Emergency.

References

Nehru, Brajkumar. *Nice Guys Finish Second*. New York: Viking, 1997

NEHRU, JAWAHARLAL (1889–1964)

Indian statesman and long-time prime minister and foreign minister concurrently (1947–1964), Jawaharlal Nehru was born in Allahabad into a family with Kashmiri roots, his father, Motilal, a prosperous lawyer. Jawaharlal was educated in England at Harrow School (Winston Churchill's school) and Trinity College, Cambridge, and then was admitted to the English bar. He returned to the family home and practiced in the High Court of Allahabad. In February 1916 he was married in Delhi to a young, 17-year-old, Kashmiri girl, Kamala, née Kaul, by whom he had a daughter Indira in November 1917. During the summer of his wedding, Nehru spent several weeks wandering in Kashmir's mountains leaving his family in the valley. Kamala soon became a victim of tuberculosis and spent the last 10 years of her short life in Switzerland and other sanatoria, vainly seeking a cure. She died late in February 1936.

Nehru held an adult vision of himself as an Indian Garibaldi, working for independence. His father's influence and later that of Mahatma Gandhi encouraged him to enter and to persist actively in politics, as a member of the Indian Congress from 1918 onward. He was imprisoned by the British in 1921 and spent 18 of the next 25 years in jail. In 1928 he was elected president of the Indian National Congress, an office he often held afterward. He was the leader of the Congress's Socialist wing until 1947. Despite being sympathetic to the allied cause in World War II and opposed to the various forms of fascism, in 1942 he, in common with other Indian National Congress Party leaders, turned down the British government's offer, brokered by Sir Stafford Cripps, of dominion status for India. The principal architect and formulator of India's foreign policy, Nehru distrusted most Pakistani leaders believing that their foreign policies were animated by deep antipathy toward India and a fixation on Kashmir. Nehru never really established rapport with Jinnah and probably had less genuine dialogue with this preeminent Pakistani leader than did Mohandas Gandhi.

In the early years after independence, Nehru met with Liaquat Ali Khan to deal with matters consequent on partition and the formation of the two

Jawaharlal Nehru, who held office from 1947 to 1964, was the first prime minister and foreign minister of independent India until his death. (Library of Congress)

successors' states to the Raj. In the months before his death, moves were afoot, initiated by Sheikh Mohammed Abdullah, to promote talks between Mohammed Ayub Khan and Nehru, but these did not materialize. In fact, during his 17 years as India's prime minister and foreign minister, Nehru had remarkably few bilateral meetings with his Pakistani counterparts. An intellectually self-reliant, rather solitary man with few close friends (the Mountbattens and Vengalil Krishnan Krishna Menon being the only notable rare exceptions after 1947), Nehru had the ability to make crowd-pleasing and memorable speeches. In the 1930s and 1940s, he published several eminently readable books. His political career in India was probably at its height between 1950 and 1957, but his last two years were of illness and decline.

The heyday of Nehru's international reputation and influence came in the 1950s when he was widely regarded as a principal spokesperson for nonalignment [in contrast to a Pakistan that relied on formal alliances such as the Southeast Asia Treaty Organization (SEATO) and the Baghdad Pact] and a promoter of international settlements despite the Cold War.

See also Gandhi, Indira; Gandhi Mohandas
   Karamchand; Jinnah, Mohammed Ali; Mountbatten
   of Burma.

References

Akbar, M. J. *Nehru: The Making of India.* New York:
   Viking, 1989

Desai Sar, R. D., and Anand Mohan, eds. *The Legacy of
   Nehru: A Centennial Assessment.* Springfield, VA:
   Nataraj Books, 1992

Gopal, S., P. Kalhan, and S. Wolpert. *Nehru: A Tryst
   with Destiny.* New York: Oxford University Press,
   1996

NEHRU, KAMALA (1899–1936)

Nehru Kamala, née Kaul, came from a well-to-do
Delhi family of Kashmir's immigrants. She married
Jawaharlal Nehru in 1916. Becoming active in con-
gressional politics, she was imprisoned by the
British. She died of tuberculosis in Switzerland.

NEHRU, MOTILAL (1861–1931)

An extremely wealthy and successful Allahabad
lawyer of Kashmiri Brahmin origin, Motilal Nehru
was the father of Jawaharlal. Initially a supporter of
the British Empire, he came to be much influenced
politically by his son Jawaharlal and gradually became a congressional nationalist. He was president
of the All India National Congress in 1928.

NIXON, RICHARD MILHOUS (1913–1994)

Richard Milhous Nixon was the 37th president of
the United States (1968–August 1974) when he resigned, the first U.S. president to do so, after being
found guilty of being involved in the Watergate
scandal. In the offices of vice president and president, he had a lot to do in relations with India and
Pakistan. Richard Nixon was born in Yorba Linda,
California, into a lower-middle class Quaker family
of Irish descent. He attended Whittier College and
Duke University. After five years' practice as a
lawyer, he served in the U.S. navy (1942–1946),
then ran for Congress as a Republican in California
in 1947. He defeated his Democratic Party opponent by accusing him of being a communist sym-
pathizer, a tactic he used often in his career. His
outspokenness and tactical skills enabled him to
rise swiftly and high in political circles. After serving in the U.S. Senate (1951–1953), he became
vice president under Dwight D. Eisenhower in 1953
and was reelected in 1956. In 1959 on an official
visit to Moscow, Nixon achieved much notice for
his outspoken exchange with Nikita Khrushchev.
As the Republican presidential candidate in 1960,
he lost the election narrowly to John F. Kennedy.
Standing for the governorship of California in
1962, he was again defeated.

Despite declaring that he was retiring from politics, he ran in and won the presidential election of
1968 by a small margin and was re-elected in 1972
by a large majority. The foreign policy of his presidency (1969–1974)—in many respects a Kissinger–
Nixon foreign policy—was notable principally for
the continuing controversy, at home and abroad,
over the Vietnam War, especially the invasion of
Cambodia in 1970 and the heavy U.S. bombing of
North Vietnam, which ended with the eventual
signing of a cease-fire in 1973. Other notable foreign
policy matters were Nixon's initiation of a strategic
arms limitation treaty with the Soviet Union, his reopening of U.S. relations with the People's Republic
of China in 1972, and his visit there in 1972, the first
by a U.S. president.

In his long and tumultuous political career,
Nixon paid three contrasting visits to the subcontinent. The first was in 1953, when he was Eisenhower's vice president. In Pakistan he met Mohammed Ayub Khan for the first time and
established rapport with him. Nixon noted that at
that period of his career Ayub was strongly pro-
American and advocated that Pakistan should be allies and friends with the United States. Regarding
others that Nixon met on this diplomatic safari, he
recorded much later in his memoirs, published in
1978, that the "least friendly leader I met on this trip
was Nehru." In 1964, when Nixon visited Pakistan,
but not India, he was a lawyer/businessman and
spoke warmly of meeting "his old friend, President
Ayub Khan" again. In 1969, Nixon visited Pakistan
and India perfunctorily on the first leg of a presidential around-the-world trip, which subsequently
got only a passing mention in his memoirs, though
his partiality for Pakistan in Indo-Pakistan relations
was evident to observers.

In 1970–1971 Nixon deliberately sought to tilt in
favor of Pakistan and against India, arguing that
India was now close to the Soviet Union despite its
avowed nonalignment. Nixon also claimed that, in
1971–1972, Indira Gandhi was hypocritical and du-
plicitous regarding the use of force and was planning to dismember Pakistan, possibly including
West Pakistan.

See also Ayub Khan, Mohammed; Eisenhower, Dwight
  David; Gandhi, Indira; Nehru, Jawaharlal.
References
Ambrose, Stephen E. *Nixon: The Triumph of a Politician.*
  New York: Simon & Schuster, 1987
Black, Conrad. *Richard Milhous Nixon: The Invincible
  Quest.* London: Quercus Publishing, 2007
Gopal, S. *Jawaharlal Nehru.* New York: Harvard
  University Press, 1976–1984
Hersh, Seymour. *The Price of Power: Kissinger in the
  Nixon White House.* New York: Summit Books, 1984
Nadel, Laurie. *The Biography of Richard Nixon.* New
  York: Macmillan, 1991

NONALIGNMENT

"Nonalignment" is a term that first acquired a prodigious popular currency in the 1950s to signify dissociation from the Cold War. There is some controversy as to who first coined the term, but it is very likely that it was first used by Indian spokespersons to convey the idea that their country was genuinely independent and nonpartisan in relation to the Cold War and would eschew membership in military alliances.

The term "Non-Aligned Movement" (NAM) was coined in the early 1970s and was straightaway invested with a pedigree that traced its origins back to a meeting of Jawaharlal Nehru, Gamal Abdel Nasser, and Josip Broz Tito at the latter's holiday resort island of Brioni off the Adriatic coast and even more decisively to a meeting in Belgrade of 25 states in September 1961. From 1970 the movement has sought to meet regularly at the summit level every three years and also for its member states to rally and campaign together on common causes. India was from the start a prominent and influential member. Pakistan joined the NAM only in 1979. Originally the NAM sought to promote decolonization and to avoid what was regarded as domination by either the Western industrialized world or the communist bloc. Since the early 1970s it has sought also to provide a significant forum to set the political and economic priorities of developing countries and especially since the end of the Cold War to resist the domination of the United Nations system by the United States.

Soon after becoming India's new minister for external affairs, in May 2004 Kunwar Natwar Singh gave an interview in which he insisted that the NAM and nonalignment are not synonymous. "We were non-aligned before NAM was born," he said.

Non-alignment means you have to have an independent foreign policy. And you take steps to safeguard your vital interest without injuring the interests of other people. This needs a great deal of skills. Natwar Singh also said the "NAM needs reform and change." The international agenda of the 1940s was different from the 1960s and 1970s. Forty years ago the great questions were apartheid, colonialism and imperialism. You have a new agenda now. These are financial, terrorism, ecology, AIDS population. Nonaligned countries should get together and assert their view in the UN etc.

See also Nehru, Jawaharlal; Singh, Karan.
References
Lyon, P.. *Neutralism.* Leicester, UK: Leicester University
  Press, 1963
Singham, A. W., and Shirley Hume. *Non Alignment in an
  Age of Alignments.* London: Zed Books, 1986
Willetts, Peter. "The Non-Aligned Movement and
  Developing Countries, in 2004." Prepared for the
  Annual Register. www.staff.city.ac.uk/p.willetts
  /PUBS/AR00-NAM.DOC

NORTH WEST FRONTIER PROVINCE

The North West Frontier Province (NWFP) is the area of mountainous country constituting a frontier and strategic buffer in northwestern Pakistan, east of Afghanistan. These border lands, known as the frontier region or more commonly as the tribal areas, are now called special, and they extend in the north to Chitral as far as the Hindu Kush Range and in the south as far as Baluchistan. In 1901 the frontier region, with six settled districts (Peshawar, Mardan, Kohat, Banu, Dera Ismail Khan, and Hazara), was constituted into a separate province under a chief commissioner. In July 1947, upon the partition of the Punjab, a referendum was held in the NWFP, and the people of the province, including those of the tribal belt, voted overwhelmingly to join Pakistan.

After Pakistan became independent, propaganda was carried on in the frontier areas by Afghanistan for an independent Pathan state, variously to be called Pakhtunistan or Pathanistan, which would comprise the whole of the old NWFP including the settled districts. In July 1949 the Afghan national assembly repudiated its treaties with Britain regarding the tribal territories, specifically disavowing the Durand line as the agreed-on international boundary. Afghanistan's attempts to promote Pathan separatism were renewed and intensified in 1955 when the NWFP was integrated with West Pakistan (from December 1971, Pakistan), leading to an armed incursion of the tribes on the other side of the Durand line in September 1960 and again in March 1961 and intermittently from the 1980s onward.

See also Afghanistan; Durand Line; Punjab.

References

Barton, Sir William. *India's North-West Frontier.* London: John Murray, 1939

Shah, Mehtab Ali. *The Foreign Policy of Pakistan. Ethnic Impacts on Diplomacy 1971–1994.* London: I. B. Tauris, 1997.

Wolpert, Stanley. *Jinnah of Pakistan.* New York: Oxford University Press, 1984

NUCLEAR WEAPONS

Questions regarding the possession and utilization of nuclear weapons have bedeviled Indo-Pakistan relations since the 1960s, because both countries refuse to become parties to the Non-proliferation Treaty (NPT) and its consequent requirements.

The United States, Russia, Britain, and France, in that order, tested nuclear weapons and then possessed them, becoming at first unitlaterally and then jointly committed to confining the possession of nuclear weapons to themselves. Despite their efforts, China tested a nuclear device in October 1964 (only two years after the Sino-Indian War) to the immediate alarm of India much more than of Pakistan. India tested its first nuclear device in October 1974 in the face of protest from Pakistan, though both India and Pakistan continued to stay outside the NPT system.

Toward the end of 2006, it became apparent that India and Pakistan were ready to sign a major agreement on nuclear risk reduction. The two countries managed to overcome serious differences on this issue in six years of hard negotiations, bringing them to the point where an agreement might be given mutually acceptable shape in the third round of the so-called composite dialogue. Such an agreement was given a preliminary initialing by the respective foreign secretaries when they met in New Delhi in November 2006. At the same time, the foreign secretaries indicated that, in addition to nuclear risk, both sides had successfully concluded agreements on the streamlining of visa regimes, on the expansion of the 1974 bilateral protocol relating to the number of shrines open to visitors, and the signing of the revised protocol on shipping services. Sir Creek and Siachen remained under negotiation (for more information, see the entries on these locations).

The United States put considerable pressure on India and Pakistan to work out a nuclear risk reduction agreement. The May 1998 tests and subsequent confrontations between the two nuclear neighbors since then had set alarm bells ringing across the world. The Lahore Declaration of 1999, signed by former prime ministers Atal Bihari Vajpayee and Nawaz Sharif, began the process of moving toward agreement when the two parties agreed to "take immediate steps for reducing the risk of accidental or unauthorized use of nuclear weapons and discuss concepts and doctrines with a view to elaborating measures for confidence-building in the nuclear and conventional fields, aimed at prevention of conflict." Foreign secretaries Shivshankar Menon and Riaz Mohammad Khan were finally disposed by late 2006 to initial an agreement on "reducing the risk from accidents relating to nuclear weapons."

The 1999 Lahore agreement borrowed language from a similar agreement made between the United States and the former Soviet Union, which said, "Each party undertakes to maintain . . . its existing organization and technical agreement to guard against the accidental or unauthorized used of nuclear weapons under its control." Furthermore, the parties undertook "to notify each other immediately in the event of an accidental, unauthorized or any other unexplained incident involving a possible detonation of a nuclear weapon, which could create a risk of outbreak of nuclear war." Such an agreement had been projected as a possible model for India and Pakistan by several U.S.-based think tanks over the years.

Nuclear confidence-building measures (CBMs) under discussion between India and Pakistan include the setting up of hotlines at the command and control levels. By 2005, dedicated communication links existed between the director-generals of military operations, but there have been discussions also on the possibility of opening hotlines between the two heads of government. Again borrowing from the U.S.–USSR example, India and Pakistan have discussed the setting up of nuclear risk reduction centers to facilitate quick and accurate official communication. The earlier no-first-use treaty offer by

India was also a proposal suggested by U.S. think tanks, but Pakistan rejected it immediately.

A draft nuclear risk reduction agreement was eventually hammered out through the composite dialogue to the satisfaction of the governments of India and Pakistan by 2006, and it indicated a major breakthrough for both sides. The absence of communication between New Delhi and Islamabad had been a source of major worry for strategic experts on both sides, also emphasizing the need for transparency and communication to reduce the nuclear risk for both countries. For much the same reason, proposals to open several hotlines have been rejected so far because, experts say, many channels of communication could spread confusion and actually add to nuclear risk

See also Ramanna, Dr. Raja

References

Cohen, Stephen P. *The Idea of Pakistan*. Washington, DC: Brookings Institution Press, 2004

Subrahmanyam, K. "Prospects for Security and Stability in South Asia." In Stephen P. Cohen, ed. *The Security of South Asia: American and Asian Perspectives*. Urbana: University of Illinois Press, 1987

Synnott, Hilary. *The Causes and Consequences of South Asia's Nuclear Tests*. International Institute for Strategic Studies (IISS) Adelphi Paper No 332. New York: Oxford University Press, 1999

OBJECTIVES RESOLUTION

The Objectives Resolution was introduced by Liaquat Ali Khan and accepted by Pakistan's Constituent Assembly in March 1949. It was a first main step in preparing a constitution for Pakistan and was written in Islamic terms, a feature that aroused the resentment of Hindus who moved a series of amendments, none of which led to changes.

When Liaquat Ali Khan, Pakistan's first prime minister, moved the Objectives Resolution in the Constituent Assembly in March 1949, he suggested that Islam had "a distinct contribution to make" because its concept of social justice "meant neither charity [n]or regimentation."

The purpose of the resolution was to provide a declaration of national objectives, but some aspects of the form of the new state were outlined in its provision. The state was to be democratic, with guarantees of fundamental rights and social justice to all, and a federation of autonomous units. On the day the Objectives Resolution was adopted, the Assembly established a Basic Principles Commission to consider the appropriate steps for inducting the constitution. Soon the detailed work of the Basic Principles Commission was devolved on to subcommittees.

See also Khan, Liaquat Ali; Lahore Resolution (1940).
References
Callard, K. 1957. *Pakistan: A Political Study*. London: Allen & Unwin, 1957
Sayeed, Khalil B. *The Political System of Pakistan*. Boston: Houghton-Mifflin, 1967

ONE UNIT SCHEME

The One Unit Scheme was the idea, ascendant briefly in the mid 1950s, that the provinces of the North West Frontier, the Punjab, Sind, Baluchistan, and the Princely States and Frontier regions should be brought together into a united province of West Pakistan. It was an idea that not only sought to reduce provincial rivalries within West Pakistan but also to protect and maintain the center's ascen-

dancy from East Pakistani—and hence Bengali—challenges.

See also Baluchistan; North West Frontier Province; Punjab; Sind.
References
Ayub Khan. *Friends Not Masters: A Political Autobiography*. New York: Oxford University Press, 1967
Gauhar, Altaf. *Ayub Khan: Pakistan's First Military Ruler*. Lahore, Pak.: Sang-e-Meel Publications, 1993
Talbot, I. *Pakistan: A Modern History*. New York: Hurst and Company, 1998

OPERATION BRASSTACKS

This was India's code-name for massive military maneuvers near Pakistan's border from November 1986 to January 1987. The scale of the maneuvers and Pakistan's response in deploying its troops near the border raised the specter of war in both countries.

References
Ayub, Mohammed. "South-West Asia after the Taliban." In Ramesh Thakur and Oddny Wiggen, eds. *South Asia in the World: Problem Solving Perspectives on Security. Sustainable Development, and Good Governance*. Tokyo: United Nations University Press, 2004
Turner, Barry, ed. *Statesman's Yearbook*. Santa Barbara, CA: ABC-CLIO, 1987
Ward, Inna, ed. *Whitaker's Almanac*. 1987

OPERATION GIBRALTAR

Operation Gibraltar is the code name for Pakistan's planned operation against India, formulated first by the foreign office but then taken up by Mohammed Ayub Khan. The plan was based on self-preening and optimistic "lessons" from the Rann of Kutch conflict and from limited Indo-Pakistani skirmishes fought earlier in the year. In early May 1965, Ayub Khan decided that a second phase of his invasion plan involving a massive invasion of Kashmir across the Line of Control by disguised men, armed for guerrilla and sabotage activities, should be unleashed. Thus, 30,000 men comprising the so-called Gibraltar Forces were assembled in Murree, just north of Islamabad and Rawalpindi. General Musa Khan, commander-in-chief of the Pakistan army, was initially critical of the plan masterminded by Zulfikar Ali Bhutto and Aziz Ahmad. Musa was soon distressed to find that, despite his objections, Ayub soon decided to go ahead with the plan and to carry out raids. The final go-ahead was given when he visited Murree during the second week of July 1965 to address a special conference of the force commanders of Operation Gibraltar. The operation actually began on August 5, 1965, and ended in an apparent military stalemate that was more disastrous for Pakistan than it was for India.

See also Ayub Khan, Mohammed; Azad Jammu-Kashmir (AJK); Bhutto, Zulfikar Ali.

References

Ayub Khan. *Friends Not Masters: A Political Autobiography.* New York: Oxford University Press, 1967
Gauhar, A. *Ayub Khan: Pakistan's First Military Ruler.* Lahore, Pak.: Sang-e-Meel Publications, 1993
Srivastava, C. R. "Lal Bahadur Shastri: Prime Minister of India, June 1964–1966. A Life of Truth in Politics." In *A Dictionary of World History.* New York: Oxford University Press, 1995

ORGANISATION OF THE ISLAMIC CONFERENCE (OIC)

The Organisation of the Islamic Conference (OIC) was founded in 1969 with the objectives of promoting Islamic solidarity among member states, safeguarding Muslim holy places, and promoting the rights of all Muslim peoples. It had a membership of 57 members at the end of 2005.

Early in 1974, Zulfikar Ali Bhutto was markedly reluctant to agree to Bangladesh's representation at that year's annual summit conference of OIC, to be held in Lahore, at a time when his government had not recognized East Pakistan's legitimate successor state, Bangladesh. Prevailing opinion among the members of the OIC caused Bhutto to accept Bangladesh's attendance—in a delegation headed by Mujib-Ur Rahman. Although India today has over 100 million Moslems, it has not sought to become a member of the OIC. Among India's neighboring states, Afghanistan, Azerbaijan, Bangladesh, Kyrgyzstan, Maldives, Oman, Pakistan, Tajikistan, Turkmenistan, and Uzbekistan are members.

See also Afghanistan; Bangladesh; Islam; Lahore.

PAKISTAN MUSLIM LEAGUE–NAWAZ (PML–N). *SEE* SHARIF, NAWAZ.

PAKISTAN NATIONAL ALLIANCE (PNA)

The Pakistan National Alliance (PNA), a multiparty coalition, was launched in January 1977 to oppose the Pakistan's People Party (PPP) in national elections held that year. It included the Jamaat-I-Islami (JI), Muslim League, Tehrik-I-Istiqlal (TI), and others. Despite drawing large crowds, the PNA performed badly in the election, winning only 36 seats to the PPP's 155. This led to allegations of ballot rigging. The PNA mounted street agitations in an attempt to force the PPP to hold fresh elections. The military was used to restore order in Lahore and in some other cities.

Following negotiations between Zulfiqar Ali Bhutto and the PNA, General Zia-ul-Haq initiated what he called Operation Fair Play in early July 1977, and soon the PNA split over the issue of political cooperation with Zia's martial law regime. Some of its members went into opposition, whereas the JI forged close links with Zia's regime in its early days.

See also Jamaat-I-Islami (JI); Pakistan People's Party (Shaheed Bhutto) PPP (SB); Tehrik-I-Istiqlal (TI).
References
Talbot, I. *Pakistan: A Modern History.* New York: Hurst and Company, 1998

PAKISTAN PEOPLE'S PARTY (SHAHEED BHUTTO) PPP (SB)

This faction of the PPP was founded by Mir Murtaza Bhutto, a brother of Benazir Bhutto, early in 1996, soon after his return to Pakistan after 16 years of exile. He was elected to the Sindh provincial assembly in 1993. The PPP (SB) clamored for a return to the radical ideals of Z. A. Bhutto and the early PPP. It was critical both of Benazir Bhutto's leadership and of her husband Asif Ali Zardari's influence within the PPP.

After Mir Murtaza Bhutto's death during an encounter with police, his widow, Ghinwa Bhutto,

P

took over as leader of the party. The PPP (SB) fielded 35 National Assembly candidates and competed for 55 Sindh provincial seats at the 1997 elections. Despite some pockets of sympathy for Ghinwa in the interior of Sindh, she was defeated by Begum Bhutto (Z. A. Bhutto's widow and Benazir's mother) in the Larkana constituency. The PPP (SB) emerged with only one National Assembly seat and two seats in the Sindh assembly.

See also Bhutto, Benazir; Bhutto, Zulfikar Ali; Sind.
References
Feldman, Herbert. *The End and the Beginning: Pakistan 1969–1971.* New York: Oxford University Press, 1975
Talbot, I. *Pakistan: A Modern History.* New York: Hurst and Company, 1998

PAKTUNS. *SEE* PATHANS.

PATEL, VALLABHBHAI (1875–1950)

This Indian lawyer and politician was also popularly known as Sardar (leader). In 1947 Patel was second only to Jawaharlal Nehru as a towering figure in congressional and national politics, though he lacked Nehru's international linkages and interests. Patel was a staunch Hindu, conservative and broadly identified with the business community. In 1947 he was inclined to be tough in dealings with Pakistan, but Mohandas Gandhi persuaded him to be more conciliatory and to work closely with Nehru, which he did as deputy prime minister and as the home minister in the Indian cabinet.

He was a lawyer by training and began his political career in local government in Ahmedabad from 1917. He joined the Gujarat sabha, a political body of great assistance to Mohandas Gandhi during his political campaigns. He played a leading role in the

Kheda peasants' Satyagraha (the struggle for independence by nonviolent noncooperative means) in 1918 and in the Bardoli Satyagraha of 1928, both launched in opposition to the colonial government's attempts to raise the land tax on peasant farmers. For his participation, Ghandi gave him the honorific title of Sardar (wise leader). He joined the Salt Satyagraha of 1930, the individual civil disobedience movement of 1940–1941 and the Quit India Movement of 1942, following each of which he spent long periods in prison.

He was, with Jawaharlal Nehru, a key negotiator on behalf of the Indian National Congress during the talks leading to the transfer of power from the British in 1947. As deputy prime minister in newly independent India, he played a leading role in ensuring the integration of most of the Princely States within the Indian Union, and he strongly adhered to the view that Kashmir should not be conceded to Pakistan.

References

Gandhi, Rajmohan. *Patel: A Life*. Ahmedabad, Ind.: Navjivan Press, 1991

Guha, Ramachandra. *India after Gandhi: The History of the World's Largest Democracy*. New York: Macmillan, 2007

Ziegler, Philip. *Mountbatten: A Biography*. New York, Alfred A. Knopf, 1985

PATHANS

Pathans are the Pashto-speaking tribes of southeastern Afghanistan and northwestern Pakistan. Pashto, an eastern Iranian language, has two dialects: The soft, called Pashto (or Pushto), is spoken by the tribes of Afghanistan and those of Pakistan south of the towns of Kohal and Thal. The hard, called Pakhto (or Pukhto), is spoken by the tribes of Pakistan north of those towns. The word "Pathan" is a Hindi variant of the Pakhto word "Pakhtana," which means "speaks of Pakhto," and it commonly refers to speakers of both dialects. Pathans generally are farmers, herders, and warriors.

According to their own histories, the Pathans originated in Afghanistan and are descended from a common ancestor. Several tribes are known to have moved from Afghanistan to present-day Pakistan between the 13th and 16th centuries. In Afghanistan, Pathans are the predominant ethnic group, and the main tribes are the Durranis, south of Kabul, and the Ghilzais, east of Kabul. In Pakistan,

Pathans predominate north of Quetta between the Sulaiman Mountains and the Indus River. A tribal border separates the so-called tribal areas from the settled areas. Hill tribes ostensibly are governed by their own chiefs but subject also to the Pakistan government through political agents. Control over the tribal areas has frequently been thwarted by the refusal of tribespeople to obey their chiefs and by Afghanistan's recent and continuing involvement in international and civil war.

See also Afghanistan; North West Frontier Province; Taliban.

Reference

Caroe, O. *The Pathans*. New York: Oxford University Press, 1958

Spain, James W. *The Way of the Pathans*. New York: Oxford University Press, 1962

Spain, James W. *Pathans of the Latter Day*. New York: Oxford University Press, 1995

PLEBISCITE

A plebiscite is a direct vote by the whole body of citizens in a state on a particular question or questions. The term is synonymous with referendum, meaning an expression of opinion by a whole community, as distinct from a general election, which means voting for a government on a whole range of issues. In Indo-Pakistan relations, especially in the late 1940s, plebiscite was spoken of, but not acted on, as a device to determine Kashmir people's wishes about the future of their state.

PRINCELY STATES

In 1947 there were 565 separate princely states, or native states, which were principalities ranging in size from Hyderabad or Kashmir to petty principalities, the smallest of which were only a few acres of territory. Two main attitudes to their future prevailed in 1947. One was that the rights and responsibilities of Britain, hitherto the paramount power, would lapse as soon as British rule came to an end. The states would then become fully independent and would be free to negotiate new agreements if they thought it desirable to do so. Against this view were those, mostly in the ranks of the Congress, who suspected that the British were bent on weakening the new state of India at birth by abetting balkanization and perhaps in the future practicing further acts of divide and rule. What actually happened was a tremendous amount of tension and conflict, either with Pakistan or, as in the majority of states, with India. (Most princes were given and guaranteed pensions, until much later Indira Gandhi repudiated these arrangements.) Junagadh, Hyderabad, and Kashmir proved to be the most contentious cases.

See also Azad Jammu-Kashmir (AJK); Hyderabad; Junagadh.

References
Callard, K. *Pakistan: A Political Study.* London: Allen & Unwin, 1957
Menon, V. P. *The Story of the Integration of the Indian States.* New Delhi: Orient Longmans, 1956

PUNJAB

"Punjab" is a much used traditional, but variable name for a large region in the northwest of the South Asian subcontinent. For decades prior to 1947, Punjab was a province of British India. The word itself literally signifies five waters or five rivers, referring to the Jhelum, Chenab, Ravi, Beas, and Sutlej rivers, which, taken together, form the Panjnad (Panchnad), which in turn joins the great river Indus.

The name was applied primarily to the triangle of mostly alluvial plains between the Indus and the Sutlej, stretching northward to the foothills of the Himalayas. Dominant British influence in the Punjab was established in the early 19th century. From 1849 to August 1947, the Punjab formed a major province of British India, the boundaries of which were frequently changed before and after 1947. The Punjab was constituted an autonomous province of British India in 1937. In 1947, the province was partitioned between India and Pakistan into East and West Punjab, respectively.

The name of "East Punjab" was changed to "Punjab (India)" under the constitution of India, in effect as of 1950. On November 1, 1956, the former states of Punjab and Patiala, along with the East Punjab States Union, were integrated to form the State of Punjab within the Union Republic of India. On November 1, 1966, under the Punjab Reorganization Act of 1966, the state was reconstituted as a Punjabi State.

The new Punjab state became a predominantly Punjabi-speaking Sikh area and Hariana a predominantly Hindi-speaking area. Henceforth, the name "Punjab" became something of a misnomer. Only the Beas (Bias) is wholly in the state, together with the upper Sutlej.

References
Singh Gopal, ed. *Punjab Today.* New Delhi: South Asian Publishers, 1994
Spate, O.H.K. *India and Pakistan: A General and Regional Geography,* 2nd ed. New York: Methuen, 1960

PUNJAB BOUNDARY FORCE (PBF)

Set up in 1947 to help implement the partition process, the Punjab Boundary Force (PBF) was soon virtually overwhelmed by the enormity of its task and was soon disbanded. The PBF consisted of 55,000 troops, mainly British-officered (commanded by a British major general) and included detachments of Gurkhas, who were presumed to be outside the main communal pulls of Muslim, Hindu, and Sikh identities. The force's directive was to diminish communal violence and to help with the restoration of order. By the last week of August, however, the leaders of India and Pakistan had each decided that the PBF favored the other side and was too weak to alter the course of events constructively. On August 29, 1947, a Joint Defence Committee meeting in Lahore decided that the force should be disbanded. The PBF had been well nigh overwhelmed by the scale of violence and its tasks.

See also Lahore.

References
Ziegler, P. *Mountbatten: A Biography.* New York: Alfred A. Knopf, 1985

PUTIN, VLADIMIR (VLADIMIROVICH) (1952–)

A leading Russian politician and president (1999–), Vladimir Putin was born in Leningrad (now St. Petersburg). He graduated from Leningrad's State University in 1975 and began his career in the KGB as an intelligence officer, stationed mainly in East Germany (1975–1989). Following the collapse of the Soviet Union in 1991, he retired from the KGB (Committee for State Security) and became first deputy mayor of Leningrad in 1994, moving to Moscow in 1996.

In 1998 he was appointed deputy head of management in Boris Yeltsin's presidential administration. He then became head of Federal Security and of Yeltsin's Security Council. He was promoted to be Russia's prime minister in August 1999. In December 1999 Yeltsin resigned as president, appointing Putin as acting president until official elections were held in early 2000. Putin was reelected Russia's president in 2004. Active in the Group of Eight (the world's most economically important powers) and determined to show that Russia is a great power, especially in relation to world energy resources, Putin has paid official visits to India (like most of his immediate predecessors) but has not shown the degree of personal interest in that country that Khrushchev and Gorbachev had displayed. Putin has, however, gone on record as advocating permanent membership of India on the United Nations Security Council.

R

RADCLIFFE, SIR CYRIL (1899–1977)

Viscount Radcliffe was a British lawyer, public servant, and chair of many commissions, not the least of which were the two boundary commissions set up with the passing of the Indian Independence Act in 1947. Radcliffe was born in Llanychan, Denbigshire, Scotland, the third of the four children (all sons) of a soldier. His mother was the daughter of a London solicitor who was president of the Law Society in 1890–1891. Radcliffe was at school at Haileybury, notable for its Indian connections and especially for sending recruits to the Indian Civil Service. He entered New College, Oxford, and soon had a markedly meteoric career as an academic and lawyer. In World War II, he served in Britain's Ministry of Information, becoming its director-general in 1941. In 1945 he resumed his lucrative practice at the bar. In 1949 he was the first man in over 60 years to be appointed to the House of Lords direct from the bar. Because of mutual suspicion and distrust between the Indian National Congress Party and the All India Muslim League, Radcliffe was principally responsible for the character and controversial details of the partitions of the Punjab and Bengal. Although Radcliffe lectured and published extensively in his later life, he was remarkably and notably reluctant to speak or write about his role as the leading putative partitioner in 1947, though there was no doubting his lifelong interest in India and intense admiration for the achievements of the Raj (his elder brother died in India while serving in the army).

See also Abell, Sir George Edmond Brackenbury; Beaumont, Christopher; Menon, V. K. Krishna; Raj, the.

References
Armstrong, Robert. In Smith, George Lord Blake and C. S. Nicholls, eds. *Dictionary of National Biography 1971–1980.* New York: Oxford University Press, 2002
The Times (London) (April 4, 1977)

RADHAKRISHNAN, SARVEPALLI (1888–1975)

Academic, scholar, and public servant who was president of India, 1962–1967. Born in Tiruttani, Madras, he was educated at Madras Christian College. He soon acquired an international reputation as a scholar and was often invited to deliver lectures in distinguished series and to represent his university at home and abroad.

He became professor successively at the universities of Mysore, Calcutta, and then Oxford. In 1927, he represented Calcutta University at the Congress of Universities of the British Empire in London and delivered the Upton Lectures on Hindu Philosophy. Going to the United States, he delivered the Haskell Lectures at Chicago and attended the International Congress of Philosophy at Harvard, where he spoke on the role of philosophy in the history of civilization.

From 1936 to 1939, he was the Spalding Professor of Eastern Religions at Oxford. He delivered the British Academy's Master Mind Lecture on Buddha in 1937. With his return to India at the outbreak of World War II, he was appointed vice chancellor of Benares University. After India became independent, he was appointed to a number of prestigious positions. He prepared a report on India's universities as chairman of the Universities Commission. In 1949 he became ambassador to the Soviet Union in what proved to be the twilight of Stalin's autocratic rule and a time when Soviet–Indian relations were correct but not cordial.

He was elected vice president of India in 1952 when Rajendra Prasad was president. His years in office as president encompassed the military setback at the hands of China in 1962 and the wars with Pakistan in 1965. Radhakrishnan's mastery of

English made him an internationally reputed and influential interpreter of philosophy, Eastern religions, and Western thought. His son, Dr. Sarvepalli Gopal, became a distinguished historian in his own right and chief historical adviser to India's Foreign Service. He wrote, inter alia, a full and dispassionate biography of his father.

References
Gopal, Sarvepalli. *Radhakrishnan: A Biography.* New York: Oxford University Press, 1989

RAHMAN, SHEIKH MUJIB-UR (1920–1975)
The foremost founding father of independent Bangladesh and intimately involved with India and Pakistan in 1971–1975, Mujib was born into a family of landowners at Tongipara, East Bengal. He studied law at the universities of Calcutta and Dacca (later Dhaka) and was active in student politics. He was a founding member of the Awami League in 1949, campaigning in favor of autonomy for East Pakistan, and from 1954 until his death he was accepted as leader of the league. He was arrested on several occasions during Mohammed Ayub Khan's regime. Despite the overwhelming victory of the Awami League in East Pakistan in 1970, the Pakistani government refused to make any concessions to demands for greater autonomy. In April 1971 Mujib was charged with treason and imprisoned. Military intervention by India in East Pakistan in December 1971 produced an independent Bangladesh and secured Mujib's release. He declined to accept the post of president of the new country but agreed to become prime minister in January 1972.

He tried hard to establish a parliamentary democratic socialist administration in the face of corruption and the hostility of powerful landowners. In February 1974, Zulfikar Ali Bhutto finally recognized Bangladesh, under pressure from other Islamic states, and Mujib was thereby able to attend a meeting of the Organisation of Islamic Conferences (OIC) in Lahore. Mujib's assumption of autocratic powers in January 1975 intensified opposition to his rule and precipitated military conspiracies. The following August he, his wife, and most of his family—except his daughter Sheikh Hasina—were murdered in an army coup.

See also Awami League (AL); Ayub Khan, Mohammed; Bangladesh.

References
Rahman, M. *Emergence of a New Nation in a Multi-Polar World: Bangladesh.* Dhaka, Bangladesh: University Press Ltd., 1979

RAJ, THE
Literally meaning rule, the Raj was a widely used semicolloquial term to designate Britain's Indian Empire within the overall sprawling British Empire. The Raj was, to a considerable extent, the successor and expansion of Britain's East India Company (John Company), which ceased to exist after 1858.

The Raj was a complex patchwork of protectorates and of territories directly administered by the British Crown. The protectorates or Princely States accounted for about half of the subcontinent's land area and a third of its population (by about 1900). Many were tiny pockets of territory, but some, such as Hyderabad and Mysore in the south and Kashmir in the north, covered large areas.

The various princely rulers were each nominally independent but actually were subject to British control through a system of subsidiary treaties. The remainder of the subcontinent and the majority of its population comprised the so-called British India proper. British India was apportioned into provinces, such as Bengal and the Punjab. Routine responsibility for the system fell primarily and substantively to the viceroy, at the apex of the hierarchal structure. Authority was exercised through governors in each of British India's provinces and through political agents in Princely States. The viceroy's government of India enjoyed wide discretion under the suzerainty of the British government in London from 1858 until 1947 when the Raj was superseded by independent India and Pakistan.

See also Azad Jammu-Kashmir (AJK); Bengal; Punjab.
References
Tully, M., and Z. Masani. *From Raj to Rajiv: 40 years of Indian Independence.* New York: BBC Books, 1988

RAMANNA, DR. RAJA (1925–2004)
Dr. Raja Ramanna was an eminent Indian nuclear scientist and the leading architect of the nuclear programs that culminated in India's testing of a nuclear device in the western desert of Rajasthan in May 1974. Four years later he was approached by Saddam Hussein to institute a similar program in Iraq. Dr. Ramanna treated the proposal summarily with scorn.

Raj Ramanna was born in Tumjur in the southern state of Karnataka. After graduating from Madras Christian College, he went to London University for higher studies, completing his doctorate in 1949.

In 1972 Indira Gandhi, the prime minister, ordered scientists at the Bhabha Atomic Research Centre (BARC) in Bombay to develop a nuclear device, and Ramanna was appointed to lead the project. Named the Peaceful Nuclear Explosion (PNE), the program was kept highly secret. Apart from the scientists closely involved, only Gandhi and one of her advisers knew of it. Ramanna assembled a team of some of India's most promising scientists, among them P. K Iyengar, Rajagopala Chidambaram, and N. S. Venkatesan, and the group made possible the PNE within two years. India tested a nuclear device in May 1974 in Pokharan, Rajasthan. Later, angry that Western critics had labeled him an Indian Dr. Strangelove, Ramanna wrote that the test had been "in the spirit of keeping in touch with the science and technology of neutron-multiplying systems." This test was conducted, Ramanna said, "at a time when the so-called superpowers were publicising their greatness in the use of nuclear explosions for peaceful purposes. All the technical papers coming in on the subject of peaceful nuclear explosions suddenly stopped after 1974 and after that it became a crime against humanity to conduct a nuclear test for any reason." India did not perform a nuclear test again for more than 20 years.

At the invitation of Dr. Homi Bhabha, India's then leading scientist and the scientist adviser to the prime minister, Jawaharlal Nehru, Ramanna joined the Tata Institute of Fundamental Research. In 1972 he became head of BARC, and in 1974 he was finally able to transmit the coded message to Indira Gandhi that signaled a successful nuclear detonation: "The Buddha is smiling." After the test Ramanna's reputation was high, and, due to his distinguished position in India's defense establishment, he became the head of the Indian Army defense, research, and development organization and was later the head of the national atomic energy commission.

In 1981, when Indira Gandhi became prime minister again, she reappointed him head of BARC, and he began work on more test projects, which were never completed. In 1990 he was elected to India's Upper House of parliament and immediately afterward Prime Minister Vishwanath Pratap Singh appointed him the minister of state for defense.

Though the Indian government persisted for years in proclaiming that the device was never intended to intimidate, Ramanna eventually admitted that he had never been under any illusions about its purpose. "An explosion is an explosion, like a gun is a gun, whether you shoot somebody or shoot at the ground," he said. Ramanna spoke frequently in favor of India's nuclear advancement, believing that such a defense was essential to national security. As defense minister, he declared that the country would never strike first in a nuclear conflict, and he was pleased at the resumption of nuclear testing in India in 1998.

See also Gandhi, Indira; Nehru, Jawaharlal; Singh, V. P.

References

Jaswant, Singh. *Defending India.* New York: Macmillan, 1999

Lyon, P. "Strategy and South Asia: Twenty-five Years On." *International Journal* Toronto: Canadian Institute of International Affairs, 1972

RAMAYANA

The *Ramayana* is one of the two great Sanskrit epics of ancient India. It tells the story of Rama, his wife Sita, and the evil forces ranged against them. Though ascribed to the sage Valmiki, it derives from oral tradition. Its 24,000 couplets make it one quarter the length of the *Mahabharata.*

References

Sankalia, H. D. *Ramayana, Myth or Reality?* New Delhi: People's Publishing House, 1991

Thapar, Romila. *Cultural Transactions and Early India: Tradition and Patronage.* New York: Oxford University Press, 1987.

RAO, P. V. NARASIMHA (1921–2004)

Prime minister of India from 1991 to 1996, twice foreign minister, and the head of other ministries, Pamulaparti Venkata ("P. V.") Narasimha Rao played a significant part in conducting his country's relations with Pakistan as well as a major role in opening up his nation to the global economy.

Rao was born on June 28, 1921, at Karimnagar to Andhra Pradesh, into a Brahmin farming family. He gained degrees in science and law from Osmania and Nagpur Universities and then found employment with a weekly newspaper as a reporter. In 1957

P. V. Narasimha Rao served as India's ninth prime minister from 1991 to 1996. Rao enacted sweeping free-market economic reforms, a surprising departure from the policies of the Gandhi family that he had loyally served. (UN Photo/Evan Schneider)

Rao was elected to the Andhra Pradesh legislative assembly, where he retained his seat for the next 20 years.

In 1962, he became a minister in the state government and in 1971 was made chief minister. In this post he put limits on the size of agricultural holdings, alienating large landowners in the process, even though he himself gave up all but 120 acres of his 1,200 acres.

In 1974, he was appointed general secretary of the Indian National Congress Party's national governing committee, and in 1977 he was elected to the Lok Sabha (the lower house of India's parliament). Throughout his career, Rao was a loyal supporter of Indira Gandhi, supporting her when the Congress Party split into rival factions in 1969 and also when she imposed what became a two-year state of emergency in 1975. When Gandhi returned to power in 1980, she made Rao her foreign minister. Although he professed to a dislike of traveling, he was well suited to the job in other respects. In addition to several Indian languages, he spoke English, French, Arabic, Spanish, and Farsi.

As India's foreign minister, Rao faced the taxing job of maintaining a close relationship with the Soviet Union, a close associate since the mid 1950s, while also expressing strong disapproval of the Russian invasion of Afghanistan from 1989. There was also the fallout from the Iranian revolution, which ushered in the age of the ayatollahs and a long and bloody Iranian–Iraq war.

In Pakistan from 1977, General Zia-ul-Haq had started the process of Islamization, which led to a fundamentalist-wracked country and the emergence of the Taliban in Afghanistan. Nonetheless Rao maintained open channels of communication with Pakistan by visiting that country several times and meeting its leaders.

In July 1984, Rao became home minister responsible for the police and internal security. Three months later, Mrs. Gandhi was shot by her own Sikh bodyguards over the Indian army's military action at the Golden Temple in Amritsar, and Rajiv succeeded his mother. He moved Rao to the defense ministry and then to the ministry of human resource development, where his responsibilities included education. In July 1986, he was given the additional portfolio of health and family welfare before, in early 1988, Rajiv Gandhi invited him to return to foreign affairs; he remained at that post until December 1989.

After Rajiv Gandhi was assassinated on May 21, 1991, for India's alleged interference in Sri Lanka, the Congress Party tried to persuade his widow, Sonia, to become its president. When she refused, Rao was offered the job; he was seen as a compromise that could unite the party during the national election campaign that had been interrupted by Gandhi's murder. But after the election Rao emerged as a serious candidate for party leader and thus prime minister.

With the country in turmoil and real worries that Indian democracy might be derailed, Rao took over as India's ninth prime minister on June 21, 1991, a week before his 70th birthday. He took over at a time when India was facing its worst economic crisis since independence from Britain in 1947: Inflation was turning at 17 percent, and the country had some £50 billion of foreign debt. But having won the election, Rao chose to stay on in high office and proved to be the leader who dragged the Indian economy out of its financial slough.

To deal with the economic crisis, Rao immediately advocated austere measures. "We cannot tolerate waste, inefficiency and indifference to quality, in the public sector or any other sector," he said. He raised interest rates and devalued the rupee, cut farm subsidies, jettisoned regulatory controls, cut defense spending, and privatized half of India's public sector, including the banks. All his reforms, he said, were "part of a long process of liberalization, bringing India into time with the changes, the opening up, in the rest of the world around us."

In 1996, Rao was defeated in the general election largely because of persisting allegations of corruption in his government. He was forced to resign as party president, and in December he was also compelled to stand down as the Congress Party's parliamentary leader because of the corruption scandal. In 1998, the Congress Party refused even to select him as a candidate in national elections because of his failure to stop the razing of the Babri mosque by Hindu zealots in 1992. In 2000 came the bribery case, which undermined his reputation. He was accused of paying bribes totaling $800,000 (£545,000) to four ministers to parliament (MPs) to support his

Congress Party government in a crucial vote of no-confidence in July 1993. The MPs, who belonged to regional parties, had hidden the money in personal and party bank accounts, it was claimed. A case was lodged against Rao when one of the MPs decided to give evidence in return for immunity from prosecution. The former prime minister was briefly put under house arrest before he was eventually cleared.

See also Afghanistan; Gandhi, Indira; Gandhi, Rajiv.

References

Godbole, Madhav. *Unfinished Innings: Recollections and Reflections of a Civil Servant.* Mumbai: Orient Longman, 2003

Kidwai, Rasheed. *Sonia: A Biography.* New York: Viking Penguin, 2003

Rao, Narasimha P. V. *Ayodhya: 6 December 1992.* New York: Viking, 2006

RASHTRIYA SWAYAMSEVAK SANGH (RSS)

Founded in 1925, the Rashtriya Swayamsevak Sangh (RSS) transcribes as the National Association of Volunteers in English and is widely regarded as the ideological and organizational core of Hindu communalism and chauvinism. The RSS is a large, sprawling, amorphous organization claiming 7–8 million activists in India.

About 4 million attend daily *shakhas*—early morning parades where, in khaki uniforms, they engage in physical exercises, sports, and what is called ideological discourse. In 2005 the RSS ran 22,000 schools, had 45,000 units working in slums, and was active in over 10,000 of the villages where India's tribal minorities live.

Adherents of the organization aim to promote the ideology of Hindutva (Hindu-ness), and portray Hindutva as necessitating an end to special arrangements for non-Hindus such as the family-law system currently enjoyed by India's 150 million Muslims. The Muslims fear that Hindutva's aim is to promote Hinduism over Islam. Besides the Bharatiya Janata Party (BJP), the "family" associated with the RSS includes the Vishwa Hindu Parishad (VHP), or World Hindu Council, which avows to establish "a Hindu state and Hindu glory."

See also Bharatiya Janata Party (BJP); Communalism; Vishwa Hindu Parishad (VHP).

References

Hardgrave, R. L., and S. A. Kochanet. *India: Government and Politics in a Developing Nation,* 6th ed. Fort Worth, TX: Harcourt College Publishers, 2000

RELIGION

India is a secular state. Any worship is permitted, and the state itself endorses no religion. In 1997, the principal religions were Hindus (77 million), Sunni Muslims (80 million), Shia Muslims (27 million), Sikhs (19 million), Protestants (18 million), Roman Catholics (16 million), Buddhists (7 million), Jains (5 million), and other (19 million).

Pakistan was founded as a Muslim state. The Muslims are mainly Sunni with a mixture of 15–20 percent Shia. Other religious groups are Muslims (97 percent); Christian (2 percent); Hindus, Parseens Buddhists, Andianis (i.e., aboriginal or autochthonous peoples); and others. There is a Minorities Wing in the Religious Affairs Ministry to safeguard the constitutional rights of religious minorities.

See also Hinduism; Islam.

References

Chaudhri, Nirad C. *The Continent of Circe: Being an Essay on the Peoples of India.* London: Chatto and Windus, 1965

Deol, Harnik. *Religion and Nationalism in India: The Case of the Punjab.* New York: Routledge, 2000

Oberoi, Harjot. *The Construction of Religion Boundaries: Culture, Identity and Diversity in the Sikh Tradition.* Chicago: University of Chicago Press, 1994

Pande, B. N. *Islam and Indian Culture.* Patna, Ind.: Khuda Bakhsh Oriental Public Library, 1987

Van Der Veer, Peter. *Religious Nationalism: Hindus and Muslims in India.* Berkeley: University of California Press, 1994

RESEARCH AND ANALYSIS WING (RAW)

RAW is a well-known acronym in India for an organization whose detailed character and activities are not well-known. RAW stands for the Research and Analysis Wing either of India's prime minister's department or the cabinet's secretariat, which was established in 1968 to handle internal intelligence. RAW performed with a high level of accuracy during the 1971 Indo-Pakistan War, when few in India even knew of its existence. Thereafter its personnel and activities were much expanded. During Indira Gandhi's premiership, RAW reported directly to the prime minister, and, during her Emergency (June 1975–March 77), it was, with her political household, a principal source of intelligence and policy advice. Subsequently, it is widely believed in India, and even more so in Pakistan, that RAW is well endowed with resources for the conduct of its predominantly clandestine opera-

tions. A tip-off by RAW in the first week of February 2004 helped to foil a third assassination attempt on Pakistan's President Pervez Musharraf, according to *The Times* of India. RAW alerted Pakistan's Inter-Services Intelligence (ISI) with intelligence information based on what it called communication intercepts among militant groups opposed to Musharraf. Over the decades, India has frequently accused the ISI of fomenting terrorism through its operatives, particularly of training militant groups to be active in Indian Kashmir, especially since 1989 as armed revolt sporadically has raged against New Delhi's rule.

See also Gandhi, Indira; Inter-Services Intelligence (ISI).

References

Cohen, S. *The Idea of Pakistan.* Washington, DC: Brookings Institution Press, 2004

ROWLATT ACTS

Sir Sidney Rowlatt (1862–1945), a judge in the United Kingdom from 1912 onward, was appointed chair of the Indian Sedition Committee in 1917–1918. He was vested with the authority to decide the nature of the special powers sought by the British government in India to combat subversion, in the wake of the Russian Revolution.

Rowlatt's recommendations were enacted in 1918 and gave the government arbitrary rights of arrest and detention. Their promulgation was used by Mohandas Gandhi as a rallying point for his call to the Indian National Congress for noncooperation and was opposed by a great variety of Indian politicians, including Abdul Ghaffar Khan. But a nationwide strike (a *hartal*) that was called by Congress for April 6, 1919 lacked the self-discipline on which Gandhi relied. Attacks on Europeans were followed by arson. The violence provoked reaction, most tragically at Amritsar. The Rowlatt Acts remained, however, a symbol of persecution rather than a comprehensive practice. Indeed, they were never in themselves put into practice.

See also Amritsar; Gandhi, Mohandas Karamchand; Indian National Congress; Khan, Abdul Ghaffar.

References

Spear, P. *India: A Modern History.* Ann Arbor: University of Michigan Press, 1961

RUSSIA

Indo-Russian relations in the early 21st century have been characterized and in large part defined by frequent high-level visits by the leaders of one country to the other. For example, Putin visited India on December 3–5, 2004, for the fifth Indo-Russian summit, and Manmohan Singh visited Moscow in May 2005 to participate in Russia's celebrations marking the 60th anniversary of the end of World War II. He visited Moscow again on December 4–7, 2005, for the annual India–Russia bilateral summit.

Several agreements on a variety of subjects, including intellectual property rights for defense hardware and development of a satellite-based communication system, were signed. At a press conference in Moscow, Indian Foreign Secretary Shyam Saran said, "an area that is an important item at the talks is energy partnership." Saran also said that "India's relations with Russia in defense had grown over the years from a vendor-client association to one of partnership." He added that "we are looking at taking this new kind of relationship into newer areas" (*India Weekly* 2005).

He said that the pact on intellectual property—that will last until 2010—will help the two countries jointly to develop advanced defense equipment, such as the BrahMos supersonic cruise missile. Regarding trade, the foreign secretary said that this had stagnated lately at around US$1.8 billion a year, and fresh proposals would be discussed to make it more dynamic, as was the case of India's relations with the United States and the Economic Union.

References

Cameron, James. *Point of Departure.* London: Arthur Barker, 1967

Guha, Ramachandra. *India after Gandhi. The History of the World's Largest Democracy.* New York: Macmillan, 2007

Mehrotra, Santosh. *India and the Soviet Union: Trade and Technology Transfer.* Soviet and East European Studies 73. New York: Cambridge University Press, 1990

India Weekly (December 6, 2005): 11.

Menon, K. P. *The Flying Troika.* New York: Oxford University Press, 1963

S

SAARC. *SEE* SOUTH ASIA (AND SAARC).

SAPRU, SIR TEJ BAHADUR (1875–1949)

Sir Tej Bahadur Sapru was a Kashmiri Brahmin, lawyer, scholar, and moderate Indian politician. After distinctions as a student, he became a barrister and started his practice at the Allahabad High Court as a colleague of such legal luminaries as Motilal Nehru, father of Jawaharlal. In 1921, at the age of 46, he became law member of Lord Reading's executive office. But the exit of Montagu from the India office and Mohandas Gandhi's imprisonment caused him to resign his membership of the Executive Council, switching thereby from serving the Raj to endorsing moderate Indian nationalism.

He joined the National Convention of Annie Besant, the theosophist, which had the support of many parties except the Congress, and he was elected its president in 1923. At the Round Table Conference in London in 1930, he articulated the demand for provincial autonomy and responsibility to the legislature. He was made a member of the Privy Council in 1934 and was in favor of a new constitution under the Government of India Act in 1935.

In 1944 he was called by Gandhi for consultations with regard to a compromise agreement with Jinnah, but he warned that this would ultimately lead to the partition of India. He was the first president of the Indian Council of World Affairs (ICWA) from 1943 until his death. Sapru House in New Delhi is now the headquarters of the ICWA and was earlier also the home of the Indian School of International Studies before it became part of the Jawaharlal Nehru University. This Persian and Urdu scholar was widely respected for his integrity and moderation.

See also Gandhi, Mohandas Karamchand; Jinnah, Mohammed Ali; Raj, the.

References

Low, D. A. *The Indian National Congress.* Centenary Hindsights. New York: Oxford University Press, 1988

SAVARKAR, VINAYAK DAMODAR (1883–1966)

A Brahmin, like G. K. Gokhale and Bal Gangadhar Tilak, who became a leading Hindu communalist, Vinayak Damodar Savarkar was the second son of a landowner. At the age of 10, learning of bloody Hindu–Muslim riots in the United Provinces, he led a gang of his schoolmates in a stone-throwing attack on the village mosque. At 16, his anger at the hanging of two Maharastrian terrorists caused him to devote his life to driving the British out of India. In 1905 he arranged for a huge bonfire of foreign cloth and persuaded Tilak to speak to the crowd that had gathered to witness the event. As a result he was expelled from the Fergusson College Poona, where he was studying, but, with Tilak's help, he obtained a scholarship to study in London (1902–1910) from a supporter there.

In London he organized the New India group, which learned the art of bomb making from a Russian revolutionary. One member of the group (Madanlal Dingra) shot and killed an important official of Britain's India Office and was hanged for this crime. Savarkar himself was arrested a few months later. By this time he had already published his nationalistic interpretation of the 1857–1858 mutiny and called it *The First Indian War of Independence.* When the ship carrying him back to India stopped at Marseilles, Savarkar swam ashore and claimed asylum on French soil, but he was recaptured by the British. The Hague International Tribunal ultimately judged his recapture by the British irregular but justifiable. In 1911, Savarkar was transported to the Andaman Islands. He was released in 1924, but his movements were restricted and until 1947 he was forbidden to take part in politics.

Later he was elected leader of the Hindu Mahasabha. He stood trial in 1948 along with Nathuram Godse (the assassin of Mahatma Gandhi), who was known as a devoted lieutenant of Savarkar. He was acquitted for lack of evidence linking him to the crime itself.

SHARIF, NAWAZ (1949–)

Prime minister of Pakistan (1990–1993 and 1997–1999), Nawaz Sharif was born in the Punjab in 1949, educated at St. Anthony School, Lahore. He was finance minister, government of Punjab (1981–1985), chief minister of the Punjab (1985–1990), and leader of the opposition in the National Assembly of Pakistan (1993–1997).

General Pervez Musharraf, chief of the army staff, assumed the responsibilities of the chief executive of the country immediately following the removal of Prime Minister Nawaz Sharif on October 12, 1999. Sharif was at first imprisoned and then exiled by Musharraf's regime with the condition that he would not be allowed back into Pakistan or to engage in politics. Sharif's political heartland is the Punjab, more than 60 percent of the country by wealth and population and the most solidly functioning part, as well as the base of Pakistan's army. It has always been hard to run Pakistan without a base in Punjab.

Returning to Pakistan in November 2007 after eight years of living in exile abroad, Sharif's future critically depends on his standing in Punjab. Thus in late 2007 Sharif began to look like a plausible challenger to the Musharraf–Benazir Bhutto tandem that the United States and Britain had hoped would wobble its way through elections to produce a secular, liberal-tinged leadership, backed by a solid block in parliament.

See also Lahore; Musharraf, Pervez.
References
Cohen, S. P. *The Idea of Pakistan.* Washington, DC: Brookings Institution Press, 2004
Talbot, Ian. *Pakistan: A Modern History.* New York: Hurst and Company, 1998

SHASTRI, LAL BAHADUR (1904–1966)

Lal Bahadur Shastri was independent India's second prime minister and Jawaharlal Nehru's immediate successor. Although Shastri's tenure as prime minister lasted only 19 months, it was a period of high ex-

Nawaz Sharif was the prime minister of Pakistan from 1990 to 1993 and from 1997 to 1999, when he was ousted in a bloodless military coup led by Gen. Pervez Musharraf. After years of exile, he returned to Pakistan in 2007 and campaigned in the 2007 elections. (Reuters/Corbis)

citement. Initially, within months of succeeding Nehru as prime minister, Shastri stopped off in Karachi and met with Mohammed Ayub Khan in what was for both parties a probing exercise. But within months, tension and conflict became uppermost in Indo-Pakistan relations. Two major armed clashes with Pakistan came in 1965, the second being much more severe than the first. Under Shastri's leadership, India conducted a standoff campaign, Operation Desert Hawk (January–May 1965) in the Rann of Kutch and Operation Grand Slam in September 1965, which involved both country's army and air forces along Pakistan's eastern borders and India's western borderlands from Kashmir to the Arabian Sea.

Under Shastri's astute leadership, India fought skirmishes and then a stalemate war with Pakistan. These two engagements soon came to be a considerable boost to Indian morale after the debacle of China's three-pronged attack along her northern territories three years earlier. The Indo-Pakistan War of September 1965 was followed by peace negotiations between the two countries, brokered directly by the Soviet Union and indirectly by the United States, and signed at Tashkent on Soviet soil. At Tashkent, with the signatures scarcely dry on the agreed documents, Shastri died of a heart attack on January 11, 1966—a modest man of considerable mettle who died leaving no house, no land, and no money.

Lal Bahudur Shastri was born on October 20, 1904, close to the holy Indian city of Benares (now Varannsi). His was a lower-middle-class family whose members were mostly schoolteachers, sub-postmasters, or workers in similar positions. He was a student at the Kastri Vidya Peeth (inaugurated as a national institution of higher education by Mohandas Gandhi in February 1921 in a rented building in Benares) where, after four years' study, he was awarded the equivalent of a bachelor of arts degree. In the 1920s as an Indian National Congress Party volunteer, Shastri was first a village-level worker and then a provincial leader. In the 1920s he joined the Servants of the People Society and was in 1930 confirmed as a life member of the society. From August 1942 until August 1945, he was imprisoned by the British for his political activities. Thereafter, he was close to Nehru and to the upper echelons of the Congress Party.

Several social and political issues of national importance and international interest emerged or found successful resolution during the time that Shastri held political power in Nehru's cabinet, as well as when he took over the premiership to become the Attlee of India: the Kamara's plan to revitalize the Congress in government; the question of Nehru's successor; the English-Hindi national language controversy; problems of food scarcity and food grain imports; the Hazratbal episode of the stolen sacred relic from its shrine in Kashmir; the complicated diplomatic negotiations over Kashmir in the United Nations; the tangled web of tightrope relations with China; the United States and the USSR; some controversy and suspicion over the circumstances of Shastri's sudden death while abroad; and, finally, Shastri's considerable and sustained posthumous acclaim.

See also Azad Jammu-Kashmir (AJK); Operation
    Gibraltar.

References
Srivastava, C. P. *Lal Bahadur Shastri: Prime Minister of India, June 1964–January 1966. A Life of Truth in Politics.* New York: Oxford University Press, 1995

SIACHEN GLACIER

The Siachen glacier is located north of the Line of Control (LoC), which divides Indian and Pakistani Kashmir and is therefore not clearly delineated as being under the possession of either country. India and Pakistan have fought since 1984 over this glacier, the world's highest battleground. India controls most of it. Both India and Pakistan have stationed a considerable number of troops on the glacier and spend large sums to maintain them. The principal purpose of India's military occupation of the glacier in 1984 was to prevent Pakistan from gaining control of an undelineated area of Jammu-Kashmir beyond NJ 9842, the last defined point on the Line of Control established in 1972.

Once the cease-fire line reached that point in the Karakorum Mountains, the cartographers, in light of the terrain, specified that it continued "thence north to the glaciers." This proved to be a costly piece of cartographic optimism. Pakistan interpreted the line to proceed northeast to the Karakoram Pass on the Chinese border, while India took it to run along the Saltoro Range and Siachen glacier northwest to the Chinese border.

In early June 2005, Manmohan Singh became the first Indian prime minister to visit Indian troops camped in igloos on the Siachen glacier. Dr. Singh flew in a military helicopter to meet Indian troops on the 6,300-meter (20,669-foot) high glacier, more of whom have died from frostbite and hypothermia than from enemy fire, since this coldest of limited wars erupted in 1984.

On his arrival, Singh told the troops, "The time has come that we make efforts that this battlefield is converted into a peace mountain." He added, however, there could be "no redrawing of boundaries for reasons of security and prestige." The 72-year-old Dr. Singh was winding up a three-day visit to Kashmir, and he was required to undergo a health check before traveling into the challenging climatic conditions prevailing on the glacier.

See also Azad Jammu-Kashmir (AJK); Kargil; Singh,
    (Maharaja) Sir Hari.

References
Musharraf, P. *In the Line of Fire: A Memoir.* New York: The Free Press, 2006

SIKHISM

Sikhism is the faith of about 20 million people worldwide. Nearly all Sikhs are, however, of Punjabi

Sikh children wearing traditional costumes pose for the camera in India. (Corel)

ancestry. Following the partition of the British Raj in India in 1947, some 80 percent of Sikhs live in the Indian State of Punjab, formerly East Punjab.

The most widely accepted definition of Sikhism was enunciated in 1945 by the Sikhs' most authoritative elected committee, the Shiromani Gurdwara Parbandhak Committee. The opening statement of the *Rahit Maryada* (*A Guide to the Sikh Way of Life*) goes:

> A Sikh is any man or woman whose faith consists of belief in one *Akal Purakh* (immortal God), in the ten Gurus, and in the teachings of the Guru Granth Sahib (the Sikh Scriptures) and of the ten Gurus, and who has faith in the *amrit* (initiation by water) of the tenth Guru and who professes no other religion.

One of the main grievances behind the recent and still sporadically recurring unrest in the Punjab is the refusal of the Indian Union government to grant Sikhism recognition as a separate religion under the constitution of India. Most Sikhs reject the assertion that they are a Hindu sect. Sikh teach-

ing about God is monotheistic and was defined authoritatively by Guru Nanak (1469–1539).

In the Sikh tradition a guru is more than a teacher, but rather one who reveals knowledge of the divine and who dispels the darkness of spiritual ignorance. The Supreme Guru, God, is often referred to as *Satguru* (true Guru) and *Vahiguru* (wonderful Guru). According to Sikh doctrine, there have been only 10 human gurus, their lives spanning the years from 1469 (the birth year of Nanak) to 1707 (the death of Guru Gobind Singh). They are believed to be one in spirit, a favorite analogy being the lighting of wicks from a single flame. Any apparent inconsistencies in teaching, such as Guru Nanak's peaceful approach and the sixth and the tenth gurus' call to take up arms, is attributed to the demands of changing contexts, not to a fundamental difference in message.

The last guru, Gobind Singh, did not appoint a successor but indicated that the scriptures, hereafter to be referred to as *Guru Granth Sahib,* were to be regarded as taking his place. Sikhism is thus in an emphatic sense a "religion of the book," since the scriptures are regarded as the gurus' body made manifest. This belief entails having the *Guru Granth Sahib* present, consulting it at all ceremonies, and installing it with appropriate symbols of authority: a canopy, a special stand, and a fan made of white yak hair.

Guru Gobind Singh also passed authority on to the *panth* (the Sikh community). In 1699 he dramatically actualized the concept of *Khalsa,* which means both pure and owing allegiance to no intermediaries and which therefore refers to Sikhs who observe the Sikh *dharma* strictly. He called for volunteers who would be ready to lay down their lives.

Five of his followers who accepted the challenge became the nucleus of the *khalsa,* a community of men and women formally initiated with *amrit* (sweetened water stirred with a two-edged sword). They eschew caste divisions, observe a strict diet (often vegetarian), and maintain the five signs of their commitment at all times: uncut hair, a comb, and cotton shorts to signify cleanliness and restraint, and a steel waistband and sword. They also commit themselves to keep four cardinal rules of conduct: (1) not to cut hair anywhere on the body, (2) to refrain from tobacco and other intoxicants, (3) to not eat meat, and (4) to not commit adultery.

Essential to the understanding of *khalsa* is the concept of *sant-sipahi* (the saint-soldier). The Sikh is to protect the defenseless and, if necessary, fight for right to prevail. Yet it is right to draw the sword only when all efforts to restore peace prove useless. Guru Nanak taught paradoxically that "highest is truth, but higher still is truthful action." Human life must demonstrate the quality of truth in action. The gurus took for granted the Hindu concepts of *karma* and successive rebirths as well as liberation from this system, or *molasha.* One barrier to this freedom is believed to be *maya,* ignorance of one's true nature and a false, materialistic view of the world. Through the guru's grace one can perceive the truth and live accordingly.

Sikhism acknowledges no priestly caste, and women, like men, can and do carry out the tasks required in the Gurdwara, reading the scriptures, singing, distributing the sweet mixture called *karah prashad,* and preparing and serving the corporate meal. In practice fewer women than men serve on Gurdwara managerial committees, and women cook more often than men. Women never act as *panj piare,* the five Sikhs respected for their strict adherence to *khalsa* discipline, who train candidates for the *amrit* initiation ceremony.

See also Punjab; Raj the.

References
Tatla, Singh Darshan. *The Sikh Diaspora: The Search for Statehood.* Seattle: University of Washington Press, 1999

SIMLA (SHIMLA)

Now the state capital of India's Himachal Pradesh was developed in the 19th century by the British as a relatively cool hill station retreat from the scorching summer heat of the Indo-Gangetic plains. It is situated 230 kilometers (143 miles) north of Delhi, on a series of ridges 2,134 meters (7,000 feet) above sea level.

The first governor-general to retreat from the heat of Calcutta to Simla was Lord William Pitt Amherst (1773–1857) in 1827. By the mid 1860s it was accepted that the viceroy and his entourage should evacuate Calcutta in late March and remain in Simla until October or November, an annual migration that continued until World War II. Before 1903, when the railway reached Simla, the journey was exhausting and hazardous, the distance about equal to that between London and Warsaw.

The change of capital of the Raj from Calcutta to New Delhi in 1912 lessened the disruption of government. Most homes at Simla were white bungalows, although a viceroy's lodge was built in 1888, and these were official residences for the governor of the Punjab and the commander-in-chief of the army. Since 1947, the Indian government has utilized Simla for major conferences, notably in 1972 for Indo-Pakistan negotiations, which marked the diplomatic aftermath of their 1971 war.

References
Spate, O. H. K. *India and Pakistan: A General and Regional Geography,* 2nd ed. New York: Methuen, 1960

SIMLA AGREEMENT (1972)

The Simla Agreement of July 1972 formally concluded the 1971 Indo-Pakistan War. The opening of peace negotiations between India and Pakistan at the highest level had been delayed for some months, partly because of Pakistan's refusal to recognize Bangladesh and partly because the leaders of both countries made a number of foreign visits in the first half of 1972 to obtain support for their respective positions.

After talks had been held at the official level on April 26–29, President Zulfikar Ali Bhutto and Indira

Gandhi met in Simla from June 28 to July 3 and signed an agreement providing that India and Pakistan should resolve their differences through bilateral negotiations or other peaceful means; that their forces should be withdrawn from territories occupied during the war of December 1971; and that both should respect the Line of Control (LoC) in Kashmir resulting from the cease-fire of December 17, 1971. Following ratification by both parties, the agreement came into effect on August 6. Considering that India won the December 1971 war decisively and Pakistan lost, President Bhutto played his weak hand adroitly and with every appearance of confidence.

The Simla Agreement was welcomed by all the major Indian parties except the Jana Sangh whose president, Atal Bihari Vajpayee alleged on July 7 that Gandhi had entered into a secret agreement with Bhutto to waive India's claim on Azad Jammu-Kashmir and to hand over some areas of the Kashmir Valley to Pakistan in the name of rationalization of the existing frontiers.

A delegation of Jana Sangh members of parliament urged President Shri Varahagiri Venkata Giri on July 16 not to ratify the Simla Agreement until it had been submitted to a referendum. At a press conference on July 12, Gandhi completely denied there had been any secret understanding between Bhutto and herself. On August 3, an overwhelming majority of the Lok Sabha (lower house of India's parliament) approved the agreement by voice vote on August 3; it was also approved the same day by the Rajya Sabha (upper house of India's parliament). It came into effect on August 4 with the delivery to Pakistan of India's instrument of ratification.

See also Azad Jammu-Kashmir (AJK); Bangladesh; Bhutto, Zulfikar Ali; Gandhi, Indira; Simla (Shimla); Vajpayee, Atal Bihari.

References

Bhutto, Benazir. *Daughter of the East: An Autobiography.* London: Hamish Hamilton, 1988

Wolpert, S. *Zulfi Bhutto of Pakistan: His Life and Times.* New York: Oxford University Press, 1993

SIND

Sind is the most southerly province of Pakistan with a considerable frontage on the Arabian Sea, which includes the great port city of Karachi, its country's most populous city, and a new naval base west of Karachi. Sind was a tributary state of the Moghul

Empire from 1592, maintaining some independence until it was conquered by Sir Charles Napier's army in 1843. It became a province of British India and then (with Punjab, North West Frontier Province, and Baluchistan) one of the four provinces of Pakistan from 1947. Irrigation, notably the Lloyd Barrage and use of the Indus River waters, enabled otherwise arid plains to produce wheat, rice, and cotton. Sind is the home province of the Bhutto family, whose estates are around Hyderabad and Larkana. From the 1960s to the 1980s, Sind provided the main political support base for the Bhutto-led People's Progressive Party (PPP).

See also Bhutto, Zulfikar Ali; Karachi.

References

Spate, O. H. K. *India and Pakistan: A General and Regional Geography,* 2nd ed. New York: Methuen, 1960

SINGH, JASWANT (1938–)

Born in what is now Pakistan, Jaswant Singh is a former cavalry officer who resigned his commission in the late 1960s to enter public life. Now in his seventh parliamentary term, Singh is a leading member of the Bharatiya Janata Party (BJP) of India. Minister of External Affairs in the BJP government since late 1999, he also had authority in India's Ministry of Defence from 2001. He also served earlier as minister of finance and deputy chairman of the Planning Commission. He was one of Prime Minister Atal Bihari Vajpayee's closest advisers and the author of the BJP's first extensive study of strategy, *Defending India* (1999).

See also Bharatiya Janata Party (BJP); Vajpayee, Atal Bihari.

References

Singh, Jaswant. *Defending India.* New York: Macmillan, 1999

Who's Who 2005. New York: Palgrave Macmillan, 2005

SINGH, K. NATWAR (1931–)

Kunwar Natwar Singh, a very literate professional diplomat for most of his life, became India's foreign minister in the Congress-led government of Dr. Manmohan Singh, which came into office in May 2004. Thus he again became centrally concerned not only with India's foreign policy but with Indo-Pakistan relations in particular. Natwar was educated at St. Stephen's College, Delhi University, from which he graduated with first-class honors in history in 1951, and from Corpus Christ College, Cambridge (1952–1954).

He joined India's Foreign Service in 1953, and over several decades he acquired considerable experience in affairs related to the United Nations (UN), the Commonwealth, nonalignment, Pakistan, and China, as well as the affairs of the home base of the Indian foreign ministry in New Delhi. He soon became close to Indira Gandhi when she became prime minister of India early in 1966. He was deputy secretary to the prime minister (1966–1967), director of her secretariat in New Delhi (1967–1970), and then joint secretary (1970–1971). He was deputy high commissioner in London (1973–1977) and ambassador to Pakistan (1980–1982). He was active on India's behalf in UN assemblies and conferences and in Commonwealth and nonaligned meetings [including the summit meeting of the Non Aligned Movement (NAM) in New Delhi in 1983]. After Indira's death, he was close first to Rajiv Gandhi and, after his death, to Sonia Gandhi. With a wide range of interests and hobbies, he has written a number of books and articles as well as reviewed books for a variety of publications.

On November 7, 2005, Natwar Singh was removed from the office of foreign minister (but initially remained a minister without portfolio), following a report on the UN oil-for-food program, written by former U.S. Federal Reserve Chairman Paul Volcker, which seemed to implicate Singh and the Indian National Congress Party. Prime Minister Manmohan Singh took over the foreign minister's portfolio and ordered an inquiry by Supreme Court judge R. S. Pathak. Natwar Singh said that the charges against him and the Congress were baseless.

See also Gandhi, Indira; Gandhi, Rajiv; Gandhi, Sonia; Singh, Manmohan Dr.

SINGH, KARAN (1931–)

Dr. Karan Singh is the son and heir of the last maharaja of Jammu-Kashmir and Maharani Tara Devi, born in Cannes, France. Educated at Delhi University, he earned an MA and PhD. He has been regent of Jammu-Kashmir (1949–1952) and governor (1965–1967), and he holds the honorary rank of major general in the Indian army and honorary colonel of its Jammu-Kashmir regiment. Singh has authored several books on political science, philosophical essays, travelogs, translations of Dogra Pahar, folk songs, and original poems in English.

See also Singh, (Maharaja) Sir Hari.
References
Who's Who 2005. New York: Palgrave Macmillan, 2005

SINGH, MANMOHAN (1932–)

Dr. Manmohan Singh became India's 14th prime minister in May 2004, having previously been well-known as a distinguished economist and finance minister (1991–1996) and close to the Gandhi family (to Indira Gandhi, Rajiv Gandhi, and Sonia Gandhi).

Manmohan Singh was born into a poor Sikh family on September 28, 1932, in the village of Gah in the then Punjab province of undivided India. Gah today is a rural backwater about 80 kilometers (50 miles) southwest of Islamabad in Pakistan's Punjab province, where he completed his primary school education in the 1930s. Dr. Singh's father moved his family from Gah a few years before partition. Manmohan Singh completed his matriculation examinations at the Punjab University in 1948. His academic career took him from Punjab to the University of Cambridge, where he gained a first-class honors degree in economics in 1957. Dr. Singh followed this with a PhD in economics from Nuffield College at Oxford University in 1962. His book, *India's Export Trends and Prospects for Self-Sustained Growth,* was an early critique of India's inward-oriented trade policy. Serving on the academic staff of Punjab University and then of the prestigious Delhi School of Economics, he had a brief stint at the United Nations Conference on Trade and Development (UNCTAD) secretariat as well during these years. He was secretary-general of the South Commission in Geneva between 1987 and 1990.

Dr. Singh spent five years (1991–1996) as India's finance minister, ushering in a comprehensive policy of economic reforms widely recognized as beginning the liberalization of the Indian economy. He has represented India at many international conferences and in several international organizations. For example, he led the Indian delegation to the Commonwealth Heads of Government Meeting in Cyprus in 1993 and to the World Conference on Human Rights in Vienna in 1993.

As soon as he became prime minister, Manmohan Singh made clear that he wanted to continue the dialogues with Pakistan initiated by his predecessor, Atal Bihari Vajpayee, and to sustain, if possible, a process or processes of improvement in relations with India's contiguous western neighbors. On August 5, 2004, the Pakistan government announced that it will turn the birthplace of India's newly installed prime minister, Dr. Manmohan Singh, into a model village as a gesture of goodwill to strengthen the ongoing peace process. Pakistan's new prime minister, Chaudry Shujaat Hussain, directed the provincial government to declare Gah a model village and to name the school Manmohan Singh Government Boys Primary School, a statement from the Pakistan prime minister's office said.

See also Gandhi, Sonia; Singh, K. Natwar.

References

Guha, Ramachandra. *India after Gandhi. The History of the World's Largest Democracy.* New York: Macmillan, 2007

Panagriya, Arvind. "Growth and Reforms During 1980s and 1990s." *Economic and Political Weekly* (Bombay) (June 19, 2004)

Singh, Manohan. *India's Export Trends and Prospects for Self-Sustained Growth.* Oxford, UK: Clarendon Press, Oxford, 1964

SINGH, RAJENDRA (1922–2003)

Rajendra Singh was a right-wing political activist in India and leader of Rashtriya Swayamsevak Sangh [RSS, or National Volunteer Corps (1994–2000], which was the parent ideological body of India's Hindu nationalistic Bharatiya Jananta Party (BJP). Singh was born into an agriculturalist Rajpat family in northern Uttar Pradesh. A very successful student who initially majored in physics, Singh was highly regarded by his tutors and soon taught spectroscopy at the prestigious Allahabad University, known in the 1930s as the Oxford of the East.

Attracted by the ideology of the RSS at the time of independence in 1947, Singh formally joined this Hindu revivalist movement, with its criticisms of Pakistan and of Muslims in the subcontinent. He became a *pracharak* (full-time member) in the early 1960s, exchanging his relatively comfortable lifestyle for the discipline and asceticism the RSS imposes on its cadres. Until the late 1980s, the RSS was at the margins of Indian politics. In the mid 1980s Singh became the general secretary of the RSS, which allied with other extremist Hindu organizations to build up an increasing vote bank.

In 1994, Singh became the first non-Brahmin head of the RSS and set about reducing the secre-

tiveness of the movement and turning it into a serious electoral force. Four years later the BJP emerged as the largest single political party following general elections. Though it was unable to sustain itself in office, as the core of a coalition government, the BJP reemerged to form the government in 1998 and remained in power until the general elections of 2004. Singh gave up the leadership of the RSS in 2000, amid tributes to his skills.

Singh was unusual among RSS leaders in being interested and well-informed about world affairs generally. He showed marked skills in utilizing the media, and he kept up with his university contemporaries, two of whom became prime ministers for brief periods. Though soft-spoken, he was widely regarded as a master tactician who could be forthright, aggressive, and outspoken when necessary.

See also Bharatiya Janata Party (BJP); Hindutva; Rashtriya Swayamsevak Sangh (RSS); Uttar Pradesh.

SINGH, (MAHARAJA) SIR HARI (1895–1961)

Lieutenant General Sir Hari Singh was the last ruling maharaja of Jammu-Kashmir. He dithered in August 1947 as to whether his country should try for independence but then appealed for help, in the face of armed raiders invading the Vale of Kashmir from Pakistan. Singh then accepted help from the Indian army and signed an accession to India.

Sir Hari Singh succeeded his uncle Sir Pratab Singh, as ruler of Kashmir in October 1925. During negotiations with Britain in the early 1930s, he was one of the leading delegates of the Chamber of Princes to the 1930 Round Table Conference in London. In 1944 he was appointed one of the two Indian representatives in the War Cabinet in London. He disregarded popular demands for greater democratic powers in his state, and disturbances occurred on several occasions.

In 1948, Maharaja Hari Singh abdicated in favor of his son, Yuraj Karan Singh, who was appointed regent in 1949 and in 1952 was elected head of state, retaining the title of Maharaja and a diminished share of the privy purse. Hari Singh died in Bombay on April 26, 1961, aged 65. It was announced in New Delhi in July 1961 that the government of India had recognized Yuraj Karan Singh as maharaja of Jammu-Kashmir in succession to his father but that he had voluntarily decided not to use the title of maharaja as long as he was the elected head of state.

Karan Singh would also inherit the property that his father had owned in his capacity as maharaja, and there would be no reduction in his privy purse.

See also Azad Jammu-Kashmir (AJK); Singh, Karan
References
Keesing's Contemporary Archives: Record of World Events.
    London: Cartermill International, August–
    September 1961
Singh, Karan. *Heir Apparent: An Autobiography.* New
    York: Oxford University Press, 1982

SINGH, V. P. (1931–)

A leading politician and prime minister of India for a few months in 1999, Vishwanath Pratap "V. P." Singh, was born in Allahabad, Uttar Pradesh, the son of an influential local raja. He was educated at Poona and Allahabad universities. In 1971 he was elected to the Lok Sabha (India's lower house of parliament) as a representative of the Indian National Congress Party—often called the Congress (I) Party. During the administrations of Indira Gandhi and Rajiv Gandhi, he served as minister of commerce (1976–1977) and again in 1983 as chief minister of Uttar Pradesh (1980–1982), Union minister of finance (1984–1986), and minister of defense (1986–1987). He instigated zealous anticorruption campaigns while minister in these two latter posts. In 1987 he was dropped from the government and the Congress (I) Party when he exposed the Bofors Scandal, which involved payments for arms deals concluded by senior officials closely connected with Rajiv Gandhi.

Widely respected for his probity and sense of principle as head of the broad-based Janata Dal coalition, V. P. Singh emerged for a few years as the most regarded opposition politician in India. He was elected prime minister early in 1990, but in November he was defeated on a vote of confidence and superseded by Chandra Shekhar.

References
Hardgrave, R. L., and S. A. Kochanet. *India: Government
    and Politics in a Developing Nation,* 6th ed. Fort
    Worth, TX: Harcourt College Publishers, 2000

SIPAH-I-SAHABA-I-PAKISTAN (SSP)

A militant Sunni organization, Sipah-i-Sahaba-i-Pakistan (SSP) has been involved in violent clashes with Shia activists, and a number of its leaders have been assassinated. The organization's strength lies in its Jhang heartland in the Punjab.

Portrait of V. P. Singh, who served as prime minister of India for a few months in 1999. (Reuters/Bettmann/Corbis)

References
Talbot, I. *Pakistan: A Modern History.* New York: Hurst
    and Company, 1998

SIR CREEK. *SEE* KUTCH (CUTCH), RANN OF.

SOVIET UNION. *SEE* RUSSIA.

SOUTH ASIA (AND SAARC)

South Asia is, in some significant sense, a world of its own and yet indubitably a substantial part of the wider world, the planet Earth. South Asia is widely viewed, especially by interested outsiders, as one of the most fractious and vulnerable regions in today's world, not the least because of its dense and complex record of past and persisting conflicts within and between states.

The end of the Cold War, the collapse of the Soviet Union, and transforming technology certainly have widened and complicated the scope for fresh thinking on approaches to security and to development in and for South Asia, as for elsewhere in the world. Today's emphasis is often on nonconventional, or at least less traditional, aspects of strategy, including economic strength and the interdependencies of states (ostensibly nation-states, especially those cocooned together in a common regional framework). By contrast with narrow or traditional forms of analysis, heavily based on military power, a full appreciation today requires a look at the wider agendas that are actually part of professed policies and practices—agendas that include environmental, resource, and ethnic factors. Liberalizing their economies, foreign trade, and attracting investment are the goals of all South Asia's present-day incumbent governments, which seem to proclaim, perhaps prematurely or too emphatically, that the age of *dirigisme* is now entirely superseded.

Regionalizing with South Asian Association for Regional Cooperation (SAARC)

There have been many attempts at defining South Asia as a region and its distinctive characteristics over the years. There have been a few notable efforts by geographers, political scientists, strategists, and even, occasionally, students of international relations. Perhaps there will be many more. Institutionally, however, the only actual embodiment that is self-consciously South Asian and that takes the region for its perimeters and parameters began about 20 years ago with the South Asian Association for Regional Cooperation (SAARC), with its seven founder members: India, Pakistan, Bangladesh, Nepal, Bhutan, Sri Lanka, and the Maldives.

Even today the South Asian Association for Regional Cooperation is the only multipurpose regional organization for and coextensive with South Asia, and it is notable for providing arenas for regular discussions among its seven member countries, even though officially bilateral and contentious issues, such as Kashmir and Indo-Pakistan relations, were at the start excluded from deliberations. Gradually and tentatively, SAARC meetings have in fact provided occasional opportunities for bilateral meetings at the highest political level to take place, even if formally outside the official business of the SAARC meeting.

The highest authority of the association rests with the heads of state or government, who meet annually at the summit level. The Council of Foreign Ministers, which meets twice a year, is responsible for formulating policy, reviewing progress, and deciding on new areas of cooperation and the mechanism deemed necessary for them. The Council is supported by a Standing Committee of Foreign

Secretaries (i.e., the highest bureaucratic rank for diplomats) and by the Programming Committee and 11 technical committees. There is a secretariat in Kathmandu, capital of Nepal, headed by a secretary-general nominated by member states for a period of three years, which may in special circumstances be extended. Decisions at all levels are taken on the basis of unanimity. The foreign ministers of the seven member countries met for the first time in New Delhi in August 1983 and adopted the Declaration on South Asian Regional Cooperation whereby an Integrated Programme of Action (IPA) was launched. The charter establishing SAARC was adopted at the first summit meeting in Dhaka (previously Dacca) in December 1985.

SAARC, the product mostly of Zia Rahman's high political effort, as well as Sri Lankan and Bangladeshi bureaucratic inputs, has remained a rather weak body since its launching. Its secretariat in Kathmandu is tiny and far from replete with resources. Its weaknesses derive primarily, but not exclusively, from the persisting mutual suspicions between India and Pakistan (though a few relatively short-lived episodes of détente have been tried but unsustained for long). SAARC's scheduled annual summit has been postponed on at least three occasions. And India's initial and occasionally repeated insistence that strictly bilateral problems should not be discussed within SAARC, although it has not entirely hobbled all such negotiations, has certainly limited and circumscribed them.

SAARC so far has suffered in the eyes of its critics, both from within and outside South Asia, by comparison with the Association of Southeast Asian Nations (ASEAN). But ASEAN was weak at its outset, confining itself to rather low-level cultural and other matters, and it did not meet at summit level until the mid 1970s, several years after its launching in 1967, which then symbolized in part a new Indonesian–Malaysian détente and embryonic partnership. Then the challenge of Vietnam, especially in 1975, led to ASEAN summits in Bangkok in 1976 and in Kuala Lumpur in 1977, which invigorated the association and led to the ratcheting up of its political concerns and quickly to the emergence of a fairly formidable instrument for the multilateral diplomacy of its member states. There can be no doubt that ASEAN, especially since it has acquired close links with Asia-Pacific Economic Cooperation (APEC), has acted in ways that some SAARC members have regarded enviously. Both India and Pakistan have in the early 21st century sought, with some success, to regularize their relations with ASEAN.

ASEAN's increasing membership and even more its dialogue practices with external powers and mounting common security concerns and concerted policies are all of interest, by analogy at least to SAARC. As a promoter and advocate of regional solidarity and community building, ASEAN now holds as many as 200 variegated annual meetings—each holding aloft the label of ASEAN. Very slowly, SAARC is moving comparably but nervously in the same direction.

India's efforts to recruit (Babrak Karmal's) Afghanistan into SAARC in the 1990s and again in 2005 were abortive and advanced rather maladroitly, as was Premadasa's (of Sri Lanka) individualistic overture to ASEAN for his country's membership in that body. Conceivably either Afghanistan and/or Mynamar might join SAARC in the future, though neither eventuality seems immediate, but the addition of either would only add enormously to the association's problems. Indeed, post-Taliban Afghanistan today is so plagued with problems that it is still virtually a state without a statewide apparatus. The withdrawal of Soviet troops in February 1989 and the subsequent collapse of the Soviet Union (with the consequent emergence of several new successor states as Afghanistan's and South Asia's neighbors) have in effect magnified rather than lessened Afghanistan's problems. Myanmar still suffers from the oppressively arbitrary and crude misrule of the State Law and Order Restoration Council (SLORC), comprising 21 leading military commanders, formally above the government. Geographically the hinge between South and Southeast Asia, Myanmar recently has obtained membership and concluded links with ASEAN, though not without some difficulties and costs, rather than with SAARC.

The member states of SAARC agreed in principle at their summit in New Delhi, in early May 1995, to move toward the creation of an eventual free trade area. This was intended to boost intraregional trade, which in 2000 stood at about US$3 billion (£1.8 billion). To move toward this goal, it was agreed to prepare a charter for action toward a South Asian Preferential Trade Area (SAPTA). The member states agreed to initiate a series of tariff concessions under a series of SAARC Preferential Trading Arrangements, which the leaders indicated that they expected to ratify jointly by December 1995. Two hundred and twenty-two items were identified to be considered for reciprocal concessional import duties as part of a high SAPTA round. Ministers expressed a willingness to reveal which items were involved, but only after the summit ended. Six of the seven member states backed plans to approach an eventual free trade area, with Pakistan abstaining on the issue during the foreign minister–level talks.

Indian commentators greeted SAARC's cautious immediate agenda with some skepticism in the light of the regional grouping's modest achievements since its creation in 1985. SAARC, wrote the daily *Hindustan Times*, "is trying to step out of its perambulator. Not having done so earlier was not a sign of good health for a 10-year-old." Several commentators have remarked that progress in welding SAARC into a more effective political and economic bloc has traditionally been impeded by political suspicion and distrust among members, most notably between India and Pakistan, SAARC's largest and most powerful members.

In Asia, as elsewhere, some people regard the global economy as an American plot. They speak as if humanity could all get back to a more humane and friendly world if only the United States would desist from imposing its brutal and self-seeking free market ideology on everyone else in the wake of its Cold War victory. By way of contrast, ironically enough, in the United States many people see the advent of the borderless global economy as a threat, if not a conspiracy, that will erode America's national sovereignty and transfer its best jobs abroad—all for the benefit of a greedy unpatriotic business elite.

Such beliefs have fueled fierce opposition to free trade and fostered some crude economic isolation, as if economic globalization could somehow be stopped. This cannot be done. No one country can stop or evade globalization—not even the United States or Japan, still less the South Asian countries. The emerging countries that have chosen free market ecnomomies (because they believe them to work) contribute to the growth of a global economy as much as the United States. The clock cannot be turned back irreversibly on technological advances, on the huge increases in international trade and capital flows, and on the worldwide spread of education and science that are globalization's driving forces.

Whether propelled by television (mostly CNN, BBC, or Sky) or by radio (and the transistor has penetrated most South Asian villages by now), or by World Bank exhortations, no one can entirely escape the insistent choruses of current orthodoxies.

References

Chaturvedi, S. K., S. K. Sharma, and Kumar
Madhrendra. *Encyclopaedia of SAARC.* New Delhi: Pragun Publications, 2006

SOUTHEAST ASIA TREATY ORGANIZATION (SEATO)

The Southeast Asia Treaty Organization (SEATO) was launched by American policy (dominated by J. F. Dulles) in September 1954 to underpin what was regarded as the inherently weak Geneva settlement on Indo-China that same year. Curiously enough, given its geopolitical position, Pakistan was a founding member of SEATO from its inception until it gradually faded away between the early 1970s and early 1990s. Only East Pakistan could accurately be described as geographically part of Southeast Asia.

Although SEATO was an American-devised and -led alliance, for Pakistan it was primarily seen as a set of linkages, which might help vis-à-vis India. India regarded SEATO as an unwelcome intrusion, bringing and settling Cold War rivalries into South Asia.

See also Alliances and Alignment; Dulles, John Foster.
References

Kux, Dennis. *India and the United States, 1941–1991: Estranged Democracies.* Washington, DC: National Defense University Press, 1993

Talbot, Ian. *Pakistan: A Modern History.* New York: Hurst and Company, 1998

SUHRAWARDY, HUSEYN SHAHEED (1892–1963)

Huseyn Shaheed Suhrawardy was a leading Bengali politician and briefly, for just over a year (September 1956–October 1957), prime minister of Pakistan and thus active and influential in both Bengali and all Pakistan politics. Born in Midnapore, West Bengal, the son of a Calcutta High Court judge, he was educated at St. Xavier's College, Calcutta (later Kolcatta), and Oxford University. He came into politics

through the Calcutta Corporation and was deputy mayor in 1923. He built up a power base in the Bengal National Chamber. From 1936 on, he was active in Muslim League politics. He was a minister between 1937 and 1941 and 1943 and 1945, becoming increasingly at odds with the Dhaka Muslim League old guard and managed by the time of the 1946 elections to become prime minister of Bengal. His actions at the time of the August 16, 1946, Great Calcutta Communal killing were highly controversial. Just before partition he campaigned hard but unsuccessfully for a sovereign United Bengal State. He stayed in West Bengal after the launching of Pakistan in mid August 1947 and worked with Mohandas Gandhi to try to defuse communal violence.

In February 1950, he founded the Pakistan Awami League. To enter the 1954 East Bengal legislative assembly elections, he joined with Fazlul Haq's KSP in the United Front to advance the demand for provincial autonomy. The United Front dealt a devastating blow to the Muslim League. Haq became chief minister, and Suhrawardy entered the central cabinet. The governor-general dismissed the United Front government after less than two months in office. Suhrawardy led the campaign against the insertion of a number of so-called Islamic provisions in the debates on Pakistan's constitution. With the formation of the Republican Party, he tried to forge a national coalition that would keep the Muslim League out of office. Governor-General Iskander Mirza at first put obstacles in the way of the Republican Party, but, after the resignation of Chaudri Muhammed Ali in September 1956, Mirza allowed an Awami League–Republican coalition to take office with Suhrawardy as prime minister.

Suhrawardy's Muslim League opponents were prepared to compromise their principles over the One Unit Scheme in order to undermine his ministry. Mirza soon used the growing rift between the Republicans and Suharwardy to present him with an ultimatum to resign or face dismissal. Suhrawardy was a redoubtable opponent of the Mohammed Ayub Khan regime. He was arrested in Karachi in January 1962 under the Security of Pakistan Act; his arrest sparked off widespread student disturbances in East Pakistan.

Following his release, he led in October 1962 a broad-based National Democratic Front directed against the Ayub regime, but following a heart attack in January 1963 he had in effect to retire from active politics. He went to Beirut a couple of months later and was about to travel for medical treatment in Switzerland when he died.

See also Ayub Khan, Mohammed; Haq, Fazlul; Mirza, Iskander; Muslim League.

References
James, Sir Morrice. *Pakistan Chronicle.* New York: Hurst and Company, 1993
Noorani, A. G., ed. *The Muslims in India: A Documentary Record.* New York: Oxford University Press, 2003

TALBOTT, NELSON "STROBE" (1946–)

Nelson "Strobe" Talbot served as U.S. deputy secretary of state from 1994 to 2001, especially in the years 1998–2001. He was a principal adviser to President Bill Clinton on relations with Pakistan and India. For 21 years prior to his service in government, he was a correspondent and columnist for *Time* magazine. After leaving government service, he became president of the Brookings Institution.

On May 11, 1998, three nuclear devices were exploded at Pokran under the Thar, or Great Indian Desert, shaking the surrounding villages and eliciting much wider reactions. One immediate effect was to plunge United States–India relations, already troubled by decades of tension and controversy, into a new and acrimonious standoff. The situation deteriorated further when Pakistan responded with tests of its own two weeks later. From June 1998 through September 2000, in the most extensive engagement ever between the United States and India, Deputy Secretary of State Strobe Talbott and Indian Minister of External Affairs Jaswant Singh met 14 times in seven countries on three continents. They grappled with urgent issues of arms control and nuclear nonproliferation, but they also discussed their visions for the United States–India relationship, the potential for economic and strategic cooperation between the two countries, and the implications of Hindu nationalism for the evolution of Indian society, politics, and security. Talbott later claimed that their personal rapport helped raise the level of trust between the two governments. As a result, the United States was able to play a crucial role in defusing the crisis between India and Pakistan, thus perhaps averting a war that could have escalated to nuclear conflagration.

See also Clinton, William Jefferson.

References

Talbott, S. *Engaging India: Diplomacy, Democracy and the Bomb.* Washington, DC: Brookings Institution Press, 2004

T

TALIBAN

The term "Taliban," or "Taleban," derives from Persian and means students of religion. It is the name adopted by an Islamic revolutionary movement active in Afghanistan, which was founded in 1995 by a group of young men of fundamentalist views who emerged from religious schools (*madrassas*) and who initially concentrated their attention in conflict against the Soviet occupiers (1979–1989). They organized themselves as an unofficial army. During the civil war that followed the Soviet withdrawal from Afghanistan, the Taliban captured Kabul in 1996 and took control of most of the country. Employing harsh measures, they installed a strictly conservative Islamic government, which they sought to maintain by means of an uncompromising observance of Muslim Shariah (law). Men were ordered to grow beards and wear black clothes; women were forbidden to work outside the home or receive education and were made to wear heavy veiling (*burqa*).

In October 2001 the Taliban refused to give up Osama bin Laden, following his boasted claim to have been the instigator of the terrorist acts in the United States the previous month. Subsequently, heavy attacks led by the United States on Afghanistan resulted in the overthrow of the Taliban regime, though remnants—and possibly new recruits—continue to be disruptive forces, especially in Afghanistan and Pakistan.

Active revival of the Taliban insurgency in 2005–2006 led to increased killings, with most of the casualties being inflicted in the south of Afghanistan, the heartland of the Taliban. With their al-Qaeda allies, they found refuge in the neighboring provinces and tribal areas of Pakistan. Commentators critical

Taliban "ambassador" to Pakistan Abdul Salem Zaeef (foreground, center) gestures during a news conference in Islamabad, Pakistan, on September 21, 2001. Afghanistan's Taliban rulers refused to hand over terrorist leader Osama bin Laden, warning that U.S. attempts to apprehend him by force could plunge the whole region into crisis. The United States entered into a war with the Taliban in October 2001 for its role in harboring terrorists believed responsible for the September 11 attack on the World Trade Center and the Pentagon. (AP/Wide World Photos)

of President Pervez Musharraf are inclined to say that it is imperative that more pressure be put on the government of Pakistan to seal their too porous northern borders. Of chief concern are the North West Frontier Province, the tribal area of Waziristan, and the province of Baluchistan.

See also al-Qaeda/al-Qa'ida; Terrorism.
References
Adamec, L. W., and F. A. Clements. *Conflict in Afghanistan: An Encyclopaedia. Roots of Modern Conflict.* Santa Barbara, CA: ABC-CLIO, 2003
Musharraf, P. *In the Line of Fire: A Memoir.* New York: The Free Press, 2006

TASHKENT CONFERENCE (1966)
In 1966, the president of Pakistan, Mohammed Ayub Khan, and the prime minister of India, Lal Bahadur Shastri, met in Tashkent, capital of the Soviet Central Asian republic of Uzbekistan in the Soviet Union and negotiated for seven days (January 4–10), following the Soviet government's offer of its good offices in helping to resolve the Indo-Pakistan dispute, after the warfare between them the previous year. The Soviet Prime Minister Alexei Kosygin was in Tashkent throughout the seven days' negotiations, and contemporaries generally agree that he played a vital part in their eventual successful termination, after it had seemed at one time that they would end in deadlock. The Indian delegation led by Shastri, including Sardar Swaran Singh (foreign minister), Y. B. Chavan (defense minister), and C. S. Jha (foreign secretary). The Pakistan delegation included Zulfikar Ali Bhutto (foreign minister) and their ministers of Information and Commerce.

This summit meeting ended on January 10 with the signing by Khan and Shastri of a nine-point declaration, known officially as the Tashkent Declaration, under which India and Pakistan, pledged themselves, inter alia, to restore

> normal and peaceful relations between the two countries: to withdraw their armed forces, not later than 25 February 1966 to the positions they held before 5 August 1965 (the outbreak of Indo-Pakistan hostilities); to repatriate captured prisoners of war; to restore diplomatic relations between the two countries, as well as economic and trade relations, communications, and cultural exchanges; to end hostile propaganda; and to deal with the question of refugees and illegal immigrants.

Within a few hours of the signing of the Indo-Pakistan Declaration, Shastri, who was 61, suffered a heart attack in the early the morning of January 11 in his villa in Tashkent and died.

See also Ayub Khan, Mohammed; Bhutto, Zulfikar Ali; Shastri, Lal Bahadur.
References
Guha, R. *India after Gandhi. The History of the World's Largest Democracy.* New York: Macmillan, 2007
Keesing's Contemporary Archives: Record of World Events. London: Cartermill International, Archives January 22–29, 1966

TEHRIK-I-ISTIQLAL (TI)
Tehrik-I-Istiqlal (TI) is a party founded in 1969 by the retired Air Marshal Asghar Khan, a leading po-

litical opponent of Mohammed Ayub Khan. Its political appeal was basically limited to a small, urban middle-class following. Asghar Khan was defeated by Khurshid Hasan Mir of the Pakistan People's Party (PPP) in the 1970 elections, together with all the other TI candidates. Asghar Khan stayed among the opposition during Zulfikar Ali Bhutto's governance but returned to public prominence again during the Pakistan National Alliance (PNA) agitation in 1977, though his party had again emerged seatless in the preceding elections.

From the outset of the Zia regime in July 1977, the Tehrik distanced itself from the incumbent government and joined the Movement for the Restoration of Democracy (MRD) in 1981. Asghar Khan found working within the PPP- led alliance difficult, and he left the MRD in 1986. The next year he met with members of Kabul's communist regime, and this led to a number of Frontier and Balochistan leaders leaving the Tehrik, which failed to win a single seat at either the provincial or National Assembly elections in 1988. The polemical circumstances accompanying the dismissal of Benazir Bhutto's first administration in August 1990 led Asghar Khan to link his party with the PPP in the PDA in 1993. The TI once more moved into opposition.

See also Ayub Khan, Mohammed; Bhutto, Zulfikar Ali; Bhutto, Benazir; Jamaat-I-Islami (JI); Tehrik-I-Istiqlal (TI).

References

Talbot, I. *Pakistan: A Modern History.* New York: Hurst and Company, 1998

TEHRIK NIFAZ SHARIA-I-MUHAMMED (TNSM)

This movement for the introduction and implementation of the Shia code was founded in 1979 in response to Zia-ul-Haq's state-sponsored Islamization in Sunni terms. The movement was registered as a political party in 1987. Three years later it joined the Pakistan Democratic Alliance (PDA) in opposition to the Islami Jamhoori Ittehad Party (IJI). By the time of the 1993 general elections, it had split to form the Pakistan People's Party (PPP), for which Shias nonetheless continued to vote. Its influence was further diminished, however, because of factional divisions and disagreements. TNSM has been involved in violent clashes with the Sipah-i-Sahaba-i-Pakistan (SSP), both in Karachi and in a number of Punjabi cities.

See also Pakistan People's Party (Shaheed Bhutto) PPP (SB); Sipah-i-Sahaba-i-Pakistan (SSP).

References

Talbot, I. *Pakistan: A Modern History.* New York: Hurst and Company, 1998

TEN POSSIBLE OPTIONS FOR KASHMIR

Ever since the Kashmir issue became actively contentious between India and Pakistan in 1947–1948, many so-called solutions have been proposed, either multilaterally or bilaterally, utilizing the United Nations' (UN's) good offices or by specific arrangements. What follows is an indication of 10 major proposals made for Kashmir in recent years.

Asia Society Proposal

According to a report by the U.S.-based Asia Society, India and Pakistan should jointly control both parts of Kashmir, and the LoC (Line of Control) should be converted into an international boundary (IB).

Dixon Proposal

The Australian jurist, Sir Owen Dixon, proposed to trifurcate the state in 1950. He suggested that the disputed territory be divided into three zones and plebiscites be conducted separately for the three zones. The three zones were to be (1) the Kashmir Valley plus the Muslim areas of Jammu-Poonch, Rajori, and Doda (with Kargil forming part of the valley); (2) Jammu with the remaining district of Ladakh; (3) Pakistan-occupied Kashmir (POK) plus the northern areas.

Trieste Formula

Under an agreement signed between Italy and the Slovenian Republic of former Yugoslavia in 1954, the disputed city of Trieste (disputed since World War II) was divided between the two countries along the existing demarcation line with some minor changes. The city's inhabitants were given free access to both sides of the partition line. Going analogically by this model, India would end up keeping Ladakh, Jammu, and other parts of Kashmir, except for the valley, which would go to Pakistan. With this transfer, Pakistan would have almost half the total area of Jammu-Kashmir because it already had POK. By this proposal, residents on both sides would have access to both sides of the dividing line.

Jagat Mehta's Proposal

Former Indian Foreign Secretary Jagat Mehta proposed the following steps to solve the Kashmir issue:

1. Pacification of the Kashmir Valley.
2. Restoration of an autonomous Kashmiriyat.
3. Conversion of the Line of Control (LoC) into a soft border, permitting free movement and facilitating economic exchanges.
4. Immediate demilitarization of the LoC to a depth of 5 to 10 miles with agreed-on methods of verifying compliance.
5. Conduct parallel democratic elections in both parts of Kashmir. The governments elected therein may facilitate more and more exchanges.
6. Final suspension of the dispute between the two countries for an agreed-on period.
7. Pending final settlement, no internationalization of the Kashmir issues or pressure for a plebiscite.

Andorra Solution

Andorra is a Princely State located on the border between France and Spain, and it was claimed by both Spain and France. In 1993, the two countries reached an agreement and gave Andorra an independent constitution and gave them autonomy bordering on complete freedom. Andorra adopted parliamentary democracy but retained the titular heads of state nominated by France and Spain.

Under an Andorra-style proposal, the Kashmir Valley would become a principality with foreign policy, defense, and financial support shared by India and Pakistan. The Andorra proposal would result in the Kashmir Valley—including Pakistan-occupied Kashmir—dominated by Muslims, being carved out into a principality with its own parliament. However, India and Pakistan would have nominated representatives. The state would have open borders. The solution requires also the tripartite partition of Jammu-Kashmir.

According to some experts, such an agreement was almost finalized in 1963–1964 negotiations between President Mohammed Ayub Khan and Prime Minister Jawaharlal Nehru.

Kashmir Study Group (KSG) Proposal–1 (1998)

The KSG proposal in its original version envisaged partition of Kashmir in three parts: one comprising the northern areas and Pakistani Kashmir to stay with Pakistan and the other consisting of Jammu and Ladakh remaining within India, whereas the Valley of Kashmir would be reconstituted, through a plebiscite, as a sovereign entity (but one without an international personality).

This proposal came under severe criticism in India. The KSG then came forward with a modified version recommending that

a portion of the prince state of Jammu and Kashmir be reconstituted as a sovereign entity (but one without an international personality) . . . through an internationally supervised ascertainment of the wishes of the Kashmiri people on either side of the Line of Control.

This ascertainment would follow agreement among India, Pakistan, and representatives of the Kashmiri people to move forward with this proposal. The sovereignty of the new entity would be guaranteed by India, Pakistan, and appropriate international bodies.

The new entity would have its own secular, democratic constitution, as well as its own citizenship, flag, and legislature, which would legislate on all matters other than defense and foreign affairs.

India and Pakistan would be responsible for the defense of the Kashmiri entity, which would itself maintain police and gendarme forces for internal law and order purposes. India and Pakistan would be expected to work out financial arrangements for the Kashmiri entity, which could include a currency of its own.

The borders of Kashmir with India and Pakistan would remain open for the free transit of people, goods, and services in accordance with arrangements to be worked out between India, Pakistan, and the Kashmiri entity.

Although the present Line of Control would remain in place until such time as both India and Pakistan decided to alter it in their mutual interest, both India and Pakistan would demilitarize the area included in the Kashmir entity, except to the extent necessary to maintain logistic support for forces outside the state that could not otherwise be effectively supplied. Neither India nor Pakistan could place troops on the other side of the Line of Control without the permission of the other state.

Kashmir Study Group (KSG) II (February 2005)
KSG recommended that portions of the former Princely State of Jammu-Kashmir be reconstituted into self-governing entities enjoying free access to one another and to and from both India and Pakistan.

1. Three self-governing entities—Kashmir, Jammu, and Ladakh—would be established within the portion of the pre-1947 state now administered by India. These three self-governing entities would take part in a body that would coordinate issues of interest to all of them, such as internal trade and transportation.
2. Two entities—Azad Jammu-Kashmir and the Northern Areas—would be established on the side now administered by Pakistan. Like the entities on the Indian side, they would each be represented in a coordinating body that would consider issues in which they both had an interest.
3. An all-Kashmir body would be set up to coordinate areas of broader interest, such as regional trade, tourism, environment, and water resources. This body would include representatives from each of the five entities as well as from India and Pakistan.

Each of the new entities would have its own democratic constitution, as well as its own citizenship, flag, and legislature, which would legislate on all matters other than defense and foreign affairs. India and Pakistan would be responsible for the defense of the entities, and the entities would maintain police forces to maintain internal law and order. India and Pakistan would then be expected to work out financial arrangements for the entities.

Citizenship of the entities would also entitle individuals to acquire Indian or Pakistani passports (depending on which side of the Line of Control they live on). Alternatively, they could use entity passports subject to endorsements by India or Pakistan as appropriate.

The borders of the entities with India and Pakistan would remain open for the free transit of people, goods, and services in accordance with arrangements to be worked out among India, Pakistan, and the entities.

Although the present Line of Control would remain in place until such time as both India and Pakistan decided to alter it in their mutual interest, both countries would demilitarize the area included in the entities. Neither India nor Pakistan could place troops on the other side of the Line of Control without the permission of the other state.

All displaced persons who left any portion of the entities would have the right to return to their home localities.

Musharraf Formula (October 2004)
Musharraf suggested in October 2004 that India and Pakistan could consider identifying seven regions of Jammu-Kashmir on both sides of the Line of Control, demilitarize them, and grant them independence or joint control or govern them under the aegis of the United Nations (i.e., change their status).

Chenab Formula
The Chenab formula was proposed in the early 21st century by Niaz Naik, a senior Pakistani foreign office official. The plan seeks to divide the Indian state of Jammu-Kashmir on communal lines along the Chenab River and to cede the western side to Pakistan. Under this proposal, India would retain Hindu- and Buddhist-majority areas of Jammu and Ladakh, respectively, while the northern areas of Pakistan-occupied Kashmir (POK), the Kashmir Valley, and districts with Muslim majorities in Jammu and Kargil regions would join Pakistan.

Jammu-Kashmir Liberation Front (JKLF) Proposal
The JKLF proposed the formation of an 11-member International Kashmir Committee (IKC) consisting of one representative, each from the UN, the United States, Russia, France, Britain, China, Germany, Japan, and the Organization of Islamic Conference, and two representatives from the Non Aligned Movement (NAM). This committee would oversee a Kashmir settlement in five phases, beginning with (1) the formulation of an agreement; (2) the withdrawal of Indian, Pakistani, and foreign militant forces from the entire state; (3) the demilitarization of all Kashmiri militants; (4) the opening of all roads between the two halves of Kashmir, followed by a secular democratic constitution with representation

from Kashmir, Jammu, Ladakh, Pakistani Kashmir, and the northern territories; and (5) a UN-supervised referendum 15 years later by which the residents of the state would decide on whether to join India, Pakistan, or remain independent.

The proposal was clearly loaded in favor of the independence option.

References

Abdullah, Sheikh Mohammad. *Flames of the Chinar: An Autobiography.* Translated by Khuswant Singh. New York: Viking, 1993

Guha, Ramachandra. *India after Gandhi. The History of the World's Largest Democracy.* New York: Macmillan, 2007

Lyngdoh, James M. *Chronicle of an Impossible Election: The Election Commission and the 2002 Jammu-Kashmir Assembly Elections.* London: Penguin, 2004

Thomas, Raju. *Perspective on Kashmir: The Roots of Conflict in South Asia.* Boulder, CO: Westview Press, 1992

TERRORISM

Terrorism is a means used to coerce with threats of violence and/or by inculcating extreme fear. The term took on a particular and general relevance in European history from the so-called Reign of Terror, the bloodiest period of the French Revolution (April 1793–July 1794). "Terrorism" literally means the ideology or doctrine advocating and commending the use of terror for political ends.

India and Pakistan have both experienced terrorism on their soil, especially in the past decade or so and especially as perpetrated by the Taliban and al-Qaeda. India accuses Pakistan of encouraging terrorists to infiltrate their territory, especially in Kashmir, and Pakistan, though less regularly and emphatically, accuses India of terrorism. The governments of both countries are officially committed to extensive counterterrorist preparations and operations.

A report by the U.S. Congressional Research Service (CRS) in mid October 2004 on nuclear terrorism said, inter alia:

> The fear regarding Pakistan is that some members of the armed forces might covertly give weapons to terrorists or that; if President Musharraf were overthrown, and Islamic fundamentalist government on a state of chaos in Pakistan might enable terrorists to obtain a weapon.

> Terrorists or rogue states might acquire a nuclear weapon in several ways. The nations of greatest concern, as potential sources of weapons or missile materials, are widely thought to be Russia and Pakistan.

Pakistan, a close ally of the United States in the task of combating terrorism, especially since September 11, 2001, has often been described by South Asian experts as a "potential source" of radicalism, weapons proliferation, terrorism, and even nuclear war. The CRS report said that, although it would be difficult for the terrorists to launch a nuclear attack on any U.S. city, such an attack is plausible and would have catastrophic consequences, in one scenario killing over half a million people and causing damage of over US$1 trillion.

Russia, the report noted, has many tactical nuclear weapons, as well as much highly enriched uranium (HEU) and weapons-grade plutonium, which do not have adequate safeguards. The report concludes: "If terrorists acquired a nuclear weapon, they could use many means in an attempt to bring it into the United States, which has many thousands of land and sea borders as well as dozens of ports of entry."

See also al-Qaeda/al-Qa'ida; Assassinations and Attempted Assassinations; Nuclear Weapons; Taliban.

References

Cohen, S. P. "Nuclear Weapons and Nuclear War in South Asia: Unknowable Futures." In Ramesh Thakur and Oddny Wiggen, eds. *South Asia in the World: Problem-Solving Perspectives on Security, Sustainable Development, and Good Governance.* Tokyo: United Nations University Press, 2004

Dershowitz, Alan M. *Why Terrorism Works: Understanding the Threat. Responding to the Challenge.* New Haven, CT: Yale University Press, 2002

Laqueur, Walter. *The Terrorism Readers: A Historical Anthology.* London: Wildwood House, 1979

Laqueur, Walter. *Terrorism.* New York: Praeger, 1997

Laqueur, Walter. *No End to War: Terrorism in the Twenty-First Century.* New York: Continuum International Publishing Group, 2003

THIMAYYA, KODANDERA SUBAYYA, GENERAL (1906–1965)

General Kodandera Subayya Thimayya was trained at the Royal Indian Military College and at Britain's

Royal Military College, Sandhurst, from which he was commissioned in 1926. Before World War II, he served in Britain's Indian Army in Iraq and on the Northwest Frontier.

In 1944, he was appointed commander of a brigade of the 25th Indian Infantry Division, the first Indian to lead a brigade in action. He then fought with distinction in Arakan (Burma), being awarded a Distinguished Service Order (DSO). After representing the Indian Army at the surrender of the Japanese at Singapore and serving briefly with the occupation forces in Japan, he returned to India in 1946. In 1948 he assumed command of the Indian Army fighting Pakistani forces in Kashmir. Later he was commandant of the National Defence Academy in 1950–1951 and quartermaster general in 1951–1953.

In 1953 General Thimayya was appointed chairman of the Neutral Nations Repatriation Committee in Korea. On his return to India, he served successively as general officer commander-in-chief of various Indian commands and in 1957 became chief of the army staff and commander-in-chief of the army.

In 1959, following reported differences with Krishna Menon, then minister of defense, he tendered his resignation, but at Jawarharlal Nehru's request he agreed to withdraw it. Retiring from the Indian Army in 1961, he took over as commander of the United Nations forces in Cyprus (UNFICYP) in June 1964, playing a key part in restoring order on a number of occasions.

See also Azad Jammu-Kashmir (AJK); Menon, V. K. Krishna; Nehru, Jawaharlal.

References

Maxwell, N. *India's China War.* London: Jonathan Cape, 1970; New York: Penguin, 1992

TILAK, BAL GANGADHAR (1856–1920)

Bal Gangadhar Tilak was Indian political leader, scholar, and national activist, called by Indians *Lokamanya* (honored by the people). He was born at Ratnagiri, Maharashtra, into a Maratha family of Chitpavan Brahman caste. Educated at the Deccan College, Poona, he studied mathematics and then law before turning to journalism.

He became the owner and editor of two weekly newspapers, the *Mahratta* and the *Kesari Lion,* in the Marathi and English languages, respectively. His use of Marathi was particularly influential, and in vil-

Bal Gangadhar Tilak was one of the founders of India's independence movement. He founded the Indian Home Rule League and worked within the Indian National Congress for a short time, leaving to be part of the more radical New Party movement that sought more direct action toward the independence of India. (Athalye, D. V., The Life of Lokamanya Tilak, 1921)

lages people would gather together to have the *Kesari* read to them. He thus became widely known for his bitter criticisms of British rule and also of those moderate nationalists who advocated social reform on Western lines as well as political reform on constitutional lines. He believed that social reform would divert energy from politics, and he derided the reliance of the moderates on speeches and petitions as "political mendicancy." He strove to widen the popularity of the nationalist movement (which at that time was largely confined to the upper classes) by introducing Hindu religious symbolism and by invoking popular traditions of the Maratha struggle against Muslim rule, creating an annual festival honoring Sivaji, the 17th-century Maratha hero and bitter enemy of the Moghul government. Though this furthered the Indian nationalist movement, it also made it more communal and alarmed the Muslims.

When the Indian National Congress met at Surat in 1907, Tilak unsuccessfully challenged the moderates for the leadership, after which he led his extremist group out of the party, not to return until 1916. What was considered to be the inflammatory character of his language led to his conviction for sedition twice: once in 1897 after two British officials had been assassinated in Poona and again in 1908. He spent six years in prison after the second conviction, making use of the time to write his commentary on the *Bhagavad Gita,* in which he emphasized the value of selfless activity rather than withdrawal from the world. Tilak was one of the first to maintain that Indians should cease to cooperate with foreign rule, but he always denied that he had ever encouraged the use of violence. In 1919 he unsuccessfully sued the British journalist, Sir Valentine Chirol, for libel arising out of statements to that effect in the latter's book *Indian Unrest* (1910).

By this time he had mellowed sufficiently to oppose Mohandas Gandhi's policy of boycotting the elections to the legislative councils, established as part of Britain's Montagu-Chelmsford reforms, advocating instead "responsive cooperation." He died in Bombay on August 1, 1920.

See also Gokhale, Gopal Krishna; Savarkar, Vinayak Damodar; Tilak, Bal Gangadhar.

References
Wolpert, S. *Tilak Bal Gangadhar.* Berkeley: University of California Press, 1962

TRUMAN, HARRY S. (1884–1972)

Truman was president of the United Sates from 1945 to 1953. Together with Secretary of State Dean Acheson, he had a somewhat uneasy set of relations with India and particularly with Jawaharlal Nehru at a time when the United States was disposed to regard South Asia as a region, which was primarily a British rather than an American sphere of interest.

Truman was born in Lamar, Missouri, and served as a captain in the U.S. forces in France during World War I. Both before and after the war Truman tried various businesses—all unsuccessfully.

He entered local politics in 1922 and eventually won a seat in the U.S. Senate in 1934. He was President Franklin D. Roosevelt's somewhat surprising choice for vice president in 1944. When Roosevelt died in April 1945, Truman became president and then went on to be elected in his own right in 1948.

Truman had somewhat tepid but mercurial relations with India. Though warmly welcoming India's independence in 1947, the Truman administration was critical of India's circumspect attitude to the Korean War and its interpretation of communist China's policies and attitudes. Jawaharlal Nehru made an official visit to the United States in October 1949 (at a time when his sister, Lakshmi, was India's ambassador in Washington), but, despite official cordialities and much media attention, nothing of substance resulted. Nehru resented and rejected repeated calls by Truman and by Dean Acheson to accept third-party arbitration over Kashmir. Neither during his presidency nor subsequently or posthumously did Indians or Pakistanis regard Truman as a major significant figure for them.

References
Gopal, S. *Jawaharlal Nehru.* 3 vols. London: Jonathan Cape, 1975–1983

TWO-NATIONS THEORY

The idea that the Muslims and Hindus of the South Asian subcontinent are or should comprise two nations based on religion, not on geography, goes back to the 19th century. The two-nation theory was advanced by Muslims in the subcontinent as justification for the partition of India and for the creation of a state made up of geographically contiguous units where the Muslims were numerically in a majority. Once that state was created, the two-nation theory lost its force even for the Muslims.

References
Callard, K. *Pakistan: A Political Study.* London: Allen & Unwin, 1957

UNITED KINGDOM (BRITAIN) AND INDO-PAKISTAN RELATIONS

For historical and contemporary reasons, Britain has been a considerable, perhaps declining, but certainly changing influence in Indo-Pakistan relations.

The conquest of the vast and populous Indian subcontinent by the small West European archipelago of Britain, thousand of miles distant, was a remarkable phenomenon. Gaining decisive victories at Plassey and Buxar in northern India in the mid 18th century, Britain gradually spread its control, either direct or indirect, throughout the subcontinent. The Princely States were not, for the most part, of any great antiquity. Most of them arose on the ruins of the Mogul Empire in the 18th century. However, the full extension of British rule was not completed until the 19th century.

In 1858, after the so-called Mutiny of the previous year had been suppressed, British India formally came under direct Crown control. With the exception of the annexation of upper Burma in 1886, the period of British territorial expansion in South Asia was over. Arrangements were made with the rulers of hundreds of Princely States, large and small, leaving them dependent but in control of more than a third of the subcontinent. Even so, in 1912 Delhi superseded Calcutta (now Kolcatta) as the political capital of the British Raj and from 1947 of independent India.

During World War II, the peoples of South Asia displayed markedly different allegiances and activities. Most of the leaders of the Indian National Congress Party were arrested and imprisoned after commencing a Quit India campaign against British rule, while Mohammad Ali Jinnah and the Muslim League were cobelligerents with the British. About two million Indians (meaning Hindus, Muslims, Sikhs, and others) fought in many theaters as forces within the British Army. And Subhas Chandra Bose and his self-proclaimed Indian National Army fought and obtained Japanese aid against Britain

U

and its allies, until the fortunes of war swung against Japan.

In the seminal year of 1947, Britain sought, rather desperately, to manage the partition of Punjab and Bengal provinces and to supervise the emergence of the two newly independent states of India and Pakistan and the integration therein of the Princely States. The future of Kashmir became an unresolved source of disagreement, and violence between India and Pakistan, which Britain was not able to abate significantly.

In the years immediately after 1947, British governments tried to be evenhanded and nonpartisan, even though there were outspoken individuals and groups of Britons who were openly partisan in favor of either India or Pakistan. Meanwhile, the British government maintained intermittently close liaison with the United States on the Kashmir issue, though the Americans tended for the most part to defer to British expertise. In the late 1940s and early 1950s, Britain was still arguably the most important single country for both India and Pakistan; for each of them it was their principal trader, investor, and supplier of weaponry.

In these years British politicians and officials generally assumed that Britain had, if not a special *locus standi* on Kashmir, then at least experience and relevant knowledge likely to ease and facilitate a solution (or solutions). Such attitudes persisted prominently for 10 to 15 years beyond 1947 in the official British mind. They were qualified, however, by two sharp considerations more sensitive to Indian than to Pakistani sensibilities. From 1949 onward, it was patently clear that India objected to any further consideration of the Kashmir case in the United Nations (UN), believing itself badly served and let down by that organization. Furthermore, the Indian government, with British concurrence, consistently refused to allow formal discussion of the Kashmir question at Commonwealth prime ministers' meetings. For India, this was a domestic issue or one that should only be resolved bilaterally with Pakistan. For Britain, conscious of the acutely controversial nature of the Kashmir issue, there was a reluctance to expose the relatively fragile and untried postwar consultative Commonwealth to such a potentially disruptive matter.

In January 1957, the Kashmir dispute was brought back to the UN Security Council by Pakistan. Soon Indo-British relations became openly strained again because of what many Indians considered to be Britain's anti-India posture in the ensuing Security Council proceedings. The Pakistan move back to the UN (following a period of direct occasional intermittent negotiations between India and Pakistan, which had ended in failure) ostensibly was because of a declaration by the Indian government that a new constitution adopted by the Constituent Assembly of Jammu-Kashmir would come into force as of January 26, 1957—exactly seven years after the adoption of India's republican constitution.

In the Security Council, Britain, together with the United States, sponsored a resolution affirming that decisions regarding the disposition of the State of Jammu-Kashmir could legitimately be affected only by means of a free and impartial plebiscite held under UN auspices. Britain also supported Pakistan's proposal for the introduction of a temporary UN force in Kashmir to facilitate demilitarization. It thus became virtually an article of faith in official Washington and Whitehall that only if the Kashmir dispute could be resolved would a lasting improvement in Anglo-American relations with South Asia become possible. Accordingly, successive British governments and American administrations acted on the somewhat tenuous belief that they would be more successful if they concerted their efforts than if each of them operated alone.

India's many disputes with Pakistan, but especially the one over Kashmir, and British attitudes to these disputes considerably affected both official Indo-British and British-Pakistani relations between 1947 and 1971–1972, and they were much influenced by the vicissitudes of the Cold War. India's decisive victory over Pakistan in the 1971 war dramatically transformed the power balance of South Asia in India's favor. For about 15 years, following the Simla Accord between India and Pakistan in 1972, Britain generally was inclined to be very wary of seeming to intervene in any subsequent eruptions of Indo-Pakistan troubles, at least not over Kashmir.

In the 1970s and the 1980s, as more Kashmiris came to settle in Britain as immigrants, the issue of Kashmir became to some extent more complex and entwined in British politics. Whereas in the 1940s and 1950s British members of Parliament referring to Kashmir in their speeches were likely to have served either in a military or an administrative capacity in the subcontinent earlier in their careers, in the 1980s–1990s and thereafter, they were much more likely to be influenced by the fact that a substantial number of constituents of South Asian origin lived in their constituency. The fact that in any British parliamentary session nowadays there are liable to be a number of mentions made of Kashmir or questions asked relating to Kashmir is in large part explainable in these terms.

Successive Indian governments since the 1980s and the early 1990s repeatedly have made it crystal clear that they are opposed to mediation efforts on Kashmir, whether by the United Nations, the Organization of Islamic Conferences (OIC), the Non Aligned Movement, or the Commonwealth. Attempts to claim, or even to imply, that any of these organizations might help are quickly brushed aside, and India's standard response is to insist that the only continuingly relevant document is the Simla Agreement of 1972, concluded immediately after the Indo-Pakistan War of 1971, which prescribes bilateral dealings between the two principals only. Granted acute Indian (just as Pakistani) sensitivities concerning Kashmir, any suggestions by British politicians or those in the media proposing mediation or good offices are likely to be resented, rebutted, and even dubbed partisan on the side of Pakistan.

Since the 1990s and earlier, the British government has stressed that its "longstanding position" remains that the dispute over the status of Kashmir can be settled only by peaceful agreement between India and Pakistan, and that this is—and should—be entirely in keeping with the terms of the 1972 Simla Agreement. The official British position now states that it has been made repeatedly clear to both sides that it is hoped that they will be able to reach a peaceful settlement of the issues involved and that Britain is ready to help resolve the dispute but preferably only if both sides are willing to accept British mediation. Meanwhile, the British government maintains a regular dialogue with both the Indian and Pakistani governments and continues to express concern about the violence in Kashmir, especially condemning those who use violence for political ends.

Today, then, the British government is not directly involved in the Kashmir dispute. Even so, it recurrently finds it difficult to formulate a policy that satisfies both India and Pakistan simultaneously. What spokespersons in Islamabad and New Delhi usually want (even if they no longer expect) is not neutrality, still less indifference or passivity, by outside powers, but partisanship—on their side. Today, and for the foreseeable future, Britain, now inextricably a part of the European Community, would like to see the Kashmir dispute resolved peaceably and permanently. All present indications, however, are that such a consummation is far from imminent.

See also Attlee, Clement Richard; Churchill, Sir Winston L. Spencer; Mountbatten of Burma; Wavell Archibald Percival, First Earl Wavell.

References

Ahmad, Ishtiaq, and A. Bashir. *India and Pakistan: Charting a Path to Peace.* Islamabad, Pakistan: Islamabad Society for Tolerance and Education, 2004

Bajpai, K. Shankar. "Untangling India and Pakistan." *Foreign Affairs* (May–June 2003)

Deshpande, Ahirudh. *British Military Policy in India 1900–1945: Colonial Constraints and Declining Power.* New Delhi: Manohar, 2003

Lipton, M., and J. Firn. *The Erosion of a Relationship: India and Britain Since 1960.* Royal Institute of International Affairs. New York: Oxford University Press, 1975

Lyon, P. "The First Great Post-colonial State: India's Tryst with Destiny." In James Mayall and Anthony Payne, eds. *The Fallacies of Hope: The Post-colonial Record of the Commonwealth Third World.* Manchester, UK: Manchester University Press, 1991

Lyon, P. "Britain and the Kashmir Issue." In Raju G. C. Thomas, ed. *Perspectives on Kashmir: The Roots of Conflict in South Asia.* Boulder, CO: Westview Press, 1992

Malik, K. N., and P. Robb, eds. *India and Britain: Recent Past and Present Challenges.* New Delhi: Allied Publishers Ltd., 1994

UNITED STATES AND INDO-PAKISTAN RELATIONS

The United States has been an intrusive and often substantial influence in Indo-Pakistan relations since the early 1950s. Even during the early 1940s and President Franklin Delano Roosevelt's fourth term of office, American pressure was put on Britain to facilitate the emergence of an independent India (and eventually of Pakistan). American interests and activities have thus colored Indo-Pakistan relations for most of its history, though the specifics of this factor can best be seen (as in this book) in terms of individual presidencies and their changing contexts.

Throughout the long years, 1947–late 1980s of the Soviet–American Cold War, Pakistan was formally aligned with the United States, both bilaterally and through membership of the Baghdad Pact [later the Central Treaty Organization (CENTO)], and the Southeast Asia Treaty Organization (SEATO), whereas India was a leading member of the Non-Aligned Movement (NAM). As self-appointed champion and custodian of the Nuclear Non-proliferation Treaty (NPT), the United States was critical of India and Pakistan's nuclear ambitions, especially in the late 1990s as both India and Pakistan test-fired nuclear devices.

The al-Qaeda attacks on New York and Washington, D.C., on September 11, 2001 led, inter alia, to President Pervez Musharraf's lining up with the United States in counterterrorist activities, especially vis-à-vis Iraq and Afghanistan.

As a consequence of shared hostility toward India, Pakistan was in close cordial relations with China since the late 1950s and especially from early 1963 when they signed a boundary treaty. During the 1970s Pakistan developed close relations with the United States, providing support for the U.S.-backed Afghan rebels opposed to the Soviet Union. Pakistan joined the NAM in 1979 and drew closer to the Islamic states of western Asia and Africa, while insisting that India, despite its millions of Muslims, was not to be regarded as an Islamic state.

During the Persian Gulf crises and the ensuing Iran–Iraq war of 1990–1991, Pakistan sent 11,000 troops to Saudi Arabia to guard Islamic shrines, but there was considerable anti-Americanism among Pakistanis and some expressions of popular support for Saddam Hussein. Under pressure from the United States and Britain, General Musharraf had, by 2007, deployed about 90,000 Pakistani troops along the border with Afghanistan. About 1,000 had been killed between 2003 and 2007.

In 2007 Musharraf was seeking to be reelected as president and then to step down as head of the army before being sworn in for another term. But he lost the support of many Islamist and moderate Pakistanis, apparently since trying to dismiss the chief justice in March 2007. He thus faced several possible legal challenges to his reelection plans. Analysts say he might impose a state of emergency if the court blocks his bid for reelection. A senior Pakistan security official (as reported in *The Times* [(London) (September 21, 2007)] claimed that many Pakistanis objected to General Musharraf's ties with the United States but said that Osama bin Laden's repeated calls on Pakistani Muslims to wage a holy war could herald a new wave of violence in Pakistan. Many Pakistanis regard Musharraf's regime as an incompetent American puppet lacking democratic legitimacy.

In a video publicly released by al-Qaeda on September 21, 2007, Ayman al-Zawahiri, bin Laden's Egyptian-born deputy, also said that General Musharraf would be punished for desecrating Islamabad's Red Mosque in July 2007 and called for Muslims to fight the United States and its allies. The same video included footage of al-Qaeda's leader in Afghanistan, Mustafa Abu al-Yazeed, meeting a senior Taliban commander. The videos were among several issued by al-Qaeda to coincide with the anniversary of the attacks on American homeland centers in 9/11. The United States gave Pakistan at least US$10 billion in mainly military aid over the five years of 2002–2007, while also repeatedly demanding that General Musharraf do more in campaigns against terrorists.

American policies in South Asia in the early 21st century have been substantially shaped and influenced by events in Afghanistan, events in Iraq, and Iran's awkward assertive unilateralism, even more than by Indo-Pakistan relations, although Pakistan is much more directly affected and involved by the conflict in Afghanistan and Iraq than is India.

In March 2007, on the fourth anniversary of the Anglo-American intervention in Iraq, the United States principally and Britain were struggling to impose law and order in this war-torn state. A possible worsening scenario would be the collapse of Iraq into outright full-scale civil war. Many outsiders already took the view that civil war had engulfed Iraq. Arguably, however, this is not strictly the case as a civil war is definable as a struggle to take over control of a country's government. Despite Western efforts, however, to establish a stable government in Iraq, that has yet to happen.

The principal factions in Iraq are the Shia majority and the Sunni minority, the ruling group, which exercised draconian rule under Saddam Hussein, himself a Sunni. A major element in his rule, besides the armed forces and police, was the Ba'ath Party, nominally pan-Arabic in its ideology. These elements of Saddam Hussein's rule were dissolved and disbanded by American forces in 2004, but the Saddamites, who resent their fall from power, continue to play a major role in Iraqi affairs through the activities of militias locked in fierce and violent struggle with their Shia counterparts.

Shia–Sunni antipathies plague Pakistan's politics too. The militias have between them created major patches of disorder, especially marked in urban centers, which Western military forces identify as insurgencies. Intertwined with these insurgencies, in Baghdad and Basra for instance, there are vicious outbursts of terrorism (suicidal acts, the deliberate killing of civilians and children as well as soldiers, and the like), largely conducted by Islamic militants, mainly anti-Western in motivation. Much of the weaponry used by the militants comes from Iran.

It is widely accepted in Western circles that the key to rescuing Iraq from its current turmoil, if at all, is to defeat both insurgents and terrorists. Anglo-American sources hope that it will be possible to do so by enhancing the efficiency and reliability of the nascent post-Saddam Iraqi army, with which the elected Iraqi government is struggling, with American and British assistance to recruit, train, and equip. Western forces involved in Iraq agree that, if the Iraqi army can be brought to a reasonable level of effectiveness, it offers the best hope of inducting a new order and securing respect for governmental authority ambitions for Iraq held by incumbent governments in Pakistan and in India too.

See also Bush, George Walker.

References

Barnds, William J. "The United States and South Asia: Policy and Process." In Stephen P. Cohen, ed. *The Security of South Asia: American and Asian*

Perspectives. Urbana: University of Illinois Press, 1987

Buzan, Barry. "A Framework for Regional Security Analysis." In Barry Buzan and Gowher Rizvi, eds. *South Asian Insecurity and the Great Powers.* New York: St. Martin's Press, 1986

Heimsath, Charles, and Surjit Mansing. *A Diplomatic History of Modern India.* New Delhi: Allied Publishers Ltd., 1971

Kux, Dennis. *India and the United States: Estranged Democracies, 1941–1991.* Washington, DC: National Defense University Press, 1992

Kux, Dennis. *The United States and Pakistan, 1947–2000: Disenchanted Allies.* Washington, DC: Woodrow Wilson Center Press; Baltimore, MD: Johns Hopkins University Press, 2001

UTTAR PRADESH

Uttar Pradesh is the most populous state of the Indian Union and consequently an important political heartland. Located in north India, it is bounded on the north by Himachal Pradesh, Tibet, and Nepal; on the east by Bihar; on the south by Madhya Pradesh; and on the west by Rajasthan, Haryana, and Delhi. The capital is Lucknow, and the sole official language has been Hindi since April 1990.

The area now known colloquially and officially as UP has undergone several different definitions and demarcations since the early 19th century. In 1833 the then Bengal Presidency was divided into two parts, one of which became the Presidency of Agra. In 1836 the Agra area was named the North West Province and placed under a lieutenant governor. In 1877 the two provinces of Agra and Oudh were placed under one administrator, who was called Lieutenant-Governor of the North West Province and Chief Commissioner of Oudh. In 1902 the name was changed to United Provinces of Agra and Oudh, and the lieutenant governorship was altered to a governorship in 1921. In 1935 the name was shortened to United Provinces. On independence in 1947, the states of Rampur, Banaras, and Tehri-Garwal were merged into the United Provinces. In 1950 the name of the United Provinces was changed to Uttar Pradesh.

See also Lucknow; North West Frontier Province.

References

Guha, Ramachandra. *India after Gandhi. The History of the World's Largest Democracy.* New York: Macmillan, 2007

Thakur, Janardhan. *All the Prime Minister's Men.* New Delhi: Vikas Publishing House, 1977

VAJPAYEE, ATAL BIHARI (1926–)

Atal Bihari Vajpayee is an Indian politician and the longest serving prime minister, aside from the once dominant Congress party. He is an advocate of improved relations with Pakistan in his later career. A high caste Brahmin, he was born in Gwalior in the central state of Madhya Pradesh. He was educated at Victoria (now Laximbai) College, Gawalior, and at the DAV College, Kanpur. In his late teens he was jailed briefly for opposing British colonial rule, but he played no major part in the freedom movement. He flirted with communism before choosing to support the Hindu nationalist Rashtriya Swamyamsevak Sangh (RSS), and he became a founding member of the Jana Sangh in 1951—both right-wing organizations that later developed close links with the Bharatiya Jana Sangh (BJS).

He served as president of the BJS (1968–1973) and (after a further period in detention) as leader of the Jana Sangh Parliamentary Party (1957–1977). He was external affairs minister in 1977–1980 and again in 1988, and in 1980 he helped found the Bharatiya Janata Party (BJP), serving as its president (1980–1986) and as leader of the opposition in India's parliament (1993–1998). He served briefly as prime minister of India in 1996 and again from 1998 to 2004, but he resigned as head of BJP after its electoral defeat in May 2004. Increasingly throughout his ministerial career, he sought to effect a détente, even an entente, with Pakistan. His first major effort ended in an unproductive Indo-Pakistan summit in 2001. However, his subsequent effort while prime minister bore more fruit and established a peace process continued by the Congress Party–led government, which took office as of May 2004, despite continuing differences over Kashmir.

An orator of high repute, Vajpayee later transcended his political roots in the RSS to emerge as the moderate voice of the BJP and someone who developed a much wider popular appeal than his more hard-line colleagues. Indeed, the BJP's Hindu revivalism has antagonized many of India's huge

Muslim population, as well as other minorities and many moderate Hindus. Vajpayee has, at times, tried to appeal to Muslims and other minority groups, and he has been a reassuring figure for India's mainly secular establishment. His personal integrity has never been seriously questioned, but arms bribery scandals exposed corruption in his government and at times cast doubt on his judgment. A lifelong bachelor, he lists cooking as one of his hobbies and writes intellectual poetry in his spare time.

See also Advani, Lal Krishna; Jana Sangh; Rashtriya Swayamsevak Sangh (RSS).

References

Hardgrave, R. L., and S. A. Kochanet. *India: Government and Politics in a Developing Nation*, 6th ed. Fort Worth, TX: Harcourt College Publishers, 2000

Vajpayee, A. B. *Speeches on Ayodhya Issue*. New Delhi: Bharatiya Janata Party, 1992

VISHWA HINDU PARISHAD (VHP)

The Vishwa Hindu Parishad (VHP) (World Hindu Council) is the most publicly extreme of India's sectarian Hindu groups and propagates a violently anti-Muslim agenda. It is a far-right communal pressure group in Indian politics, has enthusiastically active cadres, and raises money from its network of overseas supporters, especially from the United States. An umbrella movement founded in 1964 aiming at the reinvigoration of Hinduism, it plays an active part as an expression of Hindu sentiment and organizer of action. The leaders of the VHP are almost all Rashtriya Swayamsevak Sangh (RSS) members, but the majority of its members in about 3,500 branches are not RSS cadre. Supported by the RSS, however, the VHP has developed its own range or "family" (a favorite metaphor) of organizations involved in social welfare work among untouchables, tribals, and the rural poor—to those most susceptible to religious conversion.

The VHP operates medical missions, orphanages, student hostels, vocational schools, and temples. It has gained prominence through its campaigns to strengthen Hindu identity and solidarity, dramatically symbolized by its role in the Ayodhya temple controversy and conflict. The VHP is widely believed by its critics to have played a major part in the demolition of the Babri mosque in early December 1992, which led to widespread rioting—though exact evidence of VHP involvement is obscure.

See also Ayodhya; Rashtriya Swayamsevak Sangh (RSS).
References

Hardgrave, R. L., and S. A. Kochanet. *India: Government and Politics in a Developing Nation,* 6th ed. Fort Worth, TX: Harcourt College Publishers, 2000

WAKHAN CORRIDOR

This so-called corridor salient, or panhandle, is a thin finger-like strip of Afghan territory separating Russia (formerly the Soviet Union) from India and Pakistan in the Pamir region of central south Asia. The Wakhan Corridor is approximately 240 kilometers (150 miles) long and 80 kilometers (50 miles) wide. The far eastern end of the Wakhan shares a 65-kilometer (40-mile) border with China. To the north lies Russia and to the south the northernmost extension of the Indian–Pakistan subcontinent. There are few inhabitants in this inhospitably desolate terrain. The corridor was mapped and demarcated as part of Afghanistan by the British and Russians in the second half of the 19th century, and it was intended to produce a wedge of territory to separate competing nearby jurisdictions, as it does today. The Wakhan was annexed by the USSR in 1980 to halt alleged arms supplies to Afghan guerrillas from Pakistan and China, an annexation that ended with the withdrawal of Soviet troops from Afghanistan in 1989.

See also The Great Game.

References

Brobst, Peter J. *The Future of the Great Game: Sir Olaf Caroe, India's Independence and the Defence of Asia.* Akron, OH: University of Akron Press, 2005

WAVELL, ARCHIBALD PERCIVAL, FIRST EARL WAVELL (1883–1950)

Archibald Percival Wavell was a scholarly career soldier who reached the highest of ranks in the British army and who, toward the end of his life, played an important but ultimately frustrating role as Britain's penultimate viceroy of India. Wavell was educated at Winchester College and passed into the Royal Military College, Sandhurst, in 1900. Thereafter he had a varied career as a professional soldier. From 1903 he spent a number of years in India, where his early childhood had been spent.

In July 1941, Wavell was appointed commander-in-chief in India. At first the South Asian theater

seemed quiet compared with the Middle East from whence Wavell had just come. But then, in December 1941, Japan came into the war. Wavell, whose reputation then stood high in the United States, was nominated supreme commander of the ill-fated command of the Southwest Pacific. But his small and ill equipped forces were soon swept aside by advancing Japanese troops. Wavell was criticized for the loss of Singapore, though the British 18th division was landed only two days before the capitulation. However, Wavell still had the confidence of his troops, and his resilience as a commander was exemplified by the fact that he gave orders for the eventual recapture of Burma to be studied by his planning staff before their evacuation from Burma.

Policy priorities dictated that the war against Germany had to be won before that with the Japanese. But Wavell had to fight the Burma war with little help from home, and he had little success. In June 1943 Wavell was appointed viceroy of India in succession to the Marquis of Linlithgow. In July he was raised to the peerage as Viscount Wavell, of Cyrenaica and of Winchester. He had been promoted to field marshal in January of that year. Hindus and Moslems were at loggerheads when Wavell arrived as viceroy and had somehow to be mutually involved in an agreement before British India, the Raj, might be granted self-government. Wavell's first significant act was administrative and characteristic. Bengal was in the grip of severe famine, and the new viceroy relieved a critical situation by an immediate personal reconnaissance followed by extensive military aid. Thereafter he was immersed in politics.

In the summer of 1945 he took the initiative by releasing the Indian National Congress Party leaders who had been in jail since 1942. He then set to work with considerable and characteristic patience to seek some agreement on the future of India. When the first series of talks broke down in July 1945, he issued a public statement assuming the blame personally. His task was not made easier by the fact that, after the general election of 1945, the Labour government, although desiring to endow India with self-government, did not lay down a clear-cut policy.

A delegation of three UK cabinet ministers conferred with the viceroy and with the party leaders for months in Delhi during 1946, but the parties could not agree. Wavell repeatedly urged the British government to reach a decision as to what it would do in the absence of an all-India agreement. A definite statement was not made until February 1947, when Wavell's replacement by Lord Louis Mountbatten of Burma was simultaneously announced with some abruptness. Thereafter Wavell returned to London (on what turned out to be the last three years of his life), untrammeled by heavy responsibility for the first time for 10 years.

See also Mountbatten of Burma; Raj, the.
References
Schofield, Victoria. *Wavell: Soldier and Statesman.*
London: John Murray, 2006

WAZIRISTAN

Waziristan is a region in the northwest of the Republic of Pakistan, lying between the Kurram and Gumal rivers. It is bounded to the east by Dera Ismail Khan, Bannu, and Kohat district and to the west by the Durand line, which forms the boundary with Afghanistan. The region is administered as two agencies, North and South Waziristan, by political agents responsible to the commissioner of Dera Ismail Khan Division.

Waziristan is mountainous with mostly barren and treeless hills and drainage from the west toward the Indus. The rivers are the main corridors to the interior. The topography of Waziristan is a mass of rocks and stones, intermixed with a poor growth of grass and thinly sprinkled with dark evergreen bushes. Precipices and steep stony ascents, broken ground, and ravines all make precautions against attack difficult and crime easy. Local peoples are notorious as border raiders and robbers. The blood feud is a local institution. Much violence has punctuated the history of Waziristan and its peoples. As Pashto-speaking Pathans, the Waziris have close racial and linguistic affinities with the adjacent Afghan population. Their territory, moreover, lies midway between the Khyber and Bolan Passes, and it remained outside the chief campaigns fought on the North West Frontier in the days of the British Raj. Furthermore, it had never been subjected to regular administration either by the Mughals (also known as the Moguls) or by the British government in India.

The region has a history of Muslim clerics encouraging tribespeople to fight the so-called occupying forces, a cry that still resonates today. During the 1930s and 1940s, the Faqir of Ipi, now legendary as a freedom fighter, waged a highly effective guerrilla campaign against the British until their departure in 1947.

The Waziris are divided into two principal groups, the Darwest Khel, generally referred to as Waziris, and the Mahsuds. The Darwest Khel is the more settled and sophisticated of the two and comprises the main tribe of North Waziristan. They live in the lower hills bordering on the Kohat and Bannu districts and the territory lying on both sides of the Kurram River. They comprise two chief sections, the Utmanzai and Ahmadzai, of which there are numerous subdivisions. The Mahsuds, who are the dominant tribe in southern Waziristan, live in the tract of country lying between the Tochi Valley on the north and the Gumal River on the south.

Waziristan, which has been a notoriously turbulent frontier region for centuries, has been deeply embroiled in Pakistan–Afghan relations since 1947. Despite Afghanistan's general questioning of Pakistan's legitimacy, and specifically of the Durand line legitimacy, in the late 1940s (with some Afghans proposing that there should be an independent Pakhtunistan), Waziristan was relatively peaceful from the 1950s until the Soviet invasion of Afghanistan in December 1979, leading to a conflict that lasted almost a decade. Pakistan's military operations in the front line of the so-called U.S.-led war on terror since 9/11 have only caused, ironically, the further Talibanization of the border tribal regions in 2005 and early 2006, spreading to areas traditionally under only light government control, if any. In 2003, an 80,000-strong Pakistani force was deployed to flush out forces loyal to the Taliban and al-Qaeda, perhaps to the satisfaction of some elements in New Delhi who were glad to see so much of Pakistan's army tied down in this other frontier region. But more than three years after Pakistani soldiers first entered the tribal area of South Waziristan, many politicians from the tribal area, media commentators, and retired soldiers expressed the view that the operation has produced few positive results. Instead, there is said to be an encroaching Taliban-style influence. Shopkeepers have been told not to sell music or films, barbers are instructed not to shave beards, and women have been told not to go to the market. More than 100 progovernment elders and politicians were reported to have been killed in the second half of 2005.

Since 2005, when a shaky agreement was signed between the army and militants in South Waziristan, an uneasy peace (at best) has prevailed. The local administration has to try to conduct matters with an alliance of mainly antigovernment tribal elders and pro-Taliban clerics. The effect is a clear rise in Taliban influence.

See also Afghanistan; North West Frontier Province.
References
Caroe, O. "The Geography and Ethnics of India's Northern Frontiers." *The Geographical Journal* (1960)

WEST BENGAL

West Bengal is a state of the Union of India and is situated in the northeast of the subcontinent. It is bounded on the north by Sikkim and Bhutan, on the east by Assam and Bangladesh (from 1947–1971, East Pakistan), on the south by the Bay of Bengal, on the southwest by Orissa, on the west by Bihar, and on the northwest by Nepal. The state of West Bengal, mostly coterminous territorially with its present shape and size, came into existence as a consequence of the Indian Independence Act 1947, and in that year many thousands of non-Moslem Bengalis immigrated into West from East Bengal, while Moslem Bengalis moved from East to West Bengal. The territory of Cooch-Behar State was merged with West Bengal on January 1, 1950, and the former French possession of Chandernagore became part of the state on October 2, 1954. Under India's States Reorganization Act of 1956, certain portions of Bihar State (an area of 8,176 square kilometers [3,157 square miles] with a population of 1,446,385) were transferred to West Bengal. At the 1991 census, Hindus numbered almost 51 million, Moslems 16 million, Christians 384,000, Buddhists 204,000, Sikhs 55,000, and Jains 34,000.

References
Hardgrave, R. L., and S. A. Kochanet. *India: Government and Politics in a Developing Nation,* 6th ed. Fort Worth, TX: Harcourt College Publishers, 2000
Morris-Jones, W. H. *The Government and Politics of India.* London: Hutchinson & Co, 1964

WILSON, HAROLD (1916–1995)

Harold Wilson was a British Labour politician and two-time prime minister (1964–1970 and 1974–1976). During his prime ministerships, especially the first, together with his relevant ministerial colleagues and officials, he expended much effort, mostly behind the scenes, to end the fighting between India and Pakistan in 1965: first over the Rann of Kutch and later in the year regarding the wider Indo-Pakistan war. His efforts bore some fruit over Kutch but he had virtually exhausted his diplomatic capital and had to concede primary mediatorial roles to the Soviet Union and the United States regarding the wider war, which was terminated diplomatically in January 1966 at Tashkent in what was still then part of the Soviet Union. Throughout most of his political career, Wilson showed much

Harold Wilson sought, without much success, to promote Indo-Pakistan détente. (Hulton\Archive by Getty Images)

interest in India and concern for the state of Indo-Pakistan relations, especially while he was Britain's prime minister, but he never personally visited South Asia. He published his memoirs in 1986. He was knighted in 1976 and created a life peer in 1983.

See also Cripps Mission; Kutch (Cutch), Rann of.

References

Pimlott, Ben. *Harold Wilson.* New York: HarperCollins, 1992

Ziegler, Philip. *Wilson, the Authorised Life.* London: Weidenfeld and Nicolson, 1993

WULLAR BARRAGE

Wullar Barrage is the name of one of India's water control systems, a navigation project, at the mouth of Wuller Lake in Jammu-Kashmir. It was started by India to make the river Jhelum navigable during the summer. Pakistan, however, claims that it is a violation of the 1960 Indus Waters Treaty on the sharing of the six rivers that run between India and Pakistan.

A 10-member delegation led by India's secretary for Water Resources, left Delhi on July 3, 2005, for two days of talks in Islamabad, where the contentious issues regarding the barrage were discussed by the two governments for the first time since 1998, covering all the technical aspects of the project. A spokesperson for the Pakistan foreign office said that, under the Indus Waters Treaty, only 10,000 acre-feet of water storage was allowed, while the project envisaged storage of 324,000 acre-feet, which was 32 times what the treaty allowed. Furthermore, the self-same Pakistan source said that the Indian design contemplated construction over the Jhelum River, while the treaty stated that no human-made structure was allowed over it.

See also Indus Waters Treaty (1960).

References

Dawn (July 5, 2005)

ZAMINDAR SYSTEM

Zamindar, or zemindar, is the owner of an agricultural estate. The word derives (via Hindi) from Persian: *zamin* means land and *dar,* holder. During the Raj, zamindars were landowners whose proprietary rights were assigned by the British. They often possessed large estates and paid revenue to the Raj. Many of the zamindars supported and profited from British rule before 1947, and they are still important in the economic and political life of Pakistan.

ZIA-UL-HAQ, MUHAMMAD (1924–1988)

Muhammad Zia-ul-Haq was a Pakistani military leader and president (1978–1988). He was born near Jallandhar, Punjab, northern India. He served in Burma, Malaya, and Indonesia in World War II and in the wars with India (1965 and 1971), rising rapidly to become general and army chief of staff (1976).

He planned and carried out a bloodless coup in 1977, deposing Z. A. Bhutto's government. Zia imposed martial law, banned political activity and introduced an Islamic code of law. Despite considerable international protest, he sanctioned the hanging of Zulfikar Ali Bhutto in 1979 on a charge of complicity in murder. Zia was killed in a plane crash near Bahawalpur, though it was not clear whether this was an accident or sabotage.

See also Bhutto, Zulfikar Ali.
References
Guha, R. *India after Gandhi: The History of the World's Largest Democracy.* New York: Macmillan, 2007

ZIAUR, RAHMAN (1936–1981)

General Rahman Ziaur was chief martial law administrator of Bangladesh (1976–1977) and president from April 1977 to his death in an insurrection and would-be coup d'état, which turned out to be an aborted army mutiny. Previously, after the murder of Sheikh Mujib-Ur Rahman in August 1975, he

had wielded effective supremacy as chief of army staff in the military government.

His assumption of the presidency was ratified by a referendum and confirmed by an election in June 1978. In 1979, parliamentary elections gave his Bangladesh National Party (BNP) an overwhelming majority. Civilian parliamentary government was restored and President Ziaur retired from the army.

Muhammad Zia ul-Haq, president of Pakistan (1978–1988), with Secretary of State George Schultz during a visit to the United States in December 1982. Although generally considered a ruthless dictator, Zia was nevertheless popular among the lower classes in Pakistan. (Department of Defense)

Holding the rank of major when East Pakistan revolted in 1971, he played a key part in the operations against West Pakistani forces. In office he pursued a policy of nonalignment and détente with Pakistan, and he attempted important economic and social reforms. Following his murder in Chittagong on May 30, 1991, his widow, Begum Zia Khaleda, eventually assumed the leadership of the BNP and became prime minister of Bangladesh.

In the early 21st century and beyond, even more than in the immediately preceding decades, it will be necessary to know about regions and localities, as well as personalities and policies, to understand the tones and textures of nationalism within and between India and Pakistan, these ostensibly nation-state societies.

Locality, intra-, and extrastate policies have to be seen and related to the whole nation-state policy in which they are encapsulated. Political economy and sociology, as well as traditional and postmodern strategic studies, need to be utilized if comprehensive understanding of what is occurring is the aim.

Indeed, at no previous period in their long and complicated histories have such diverse regions and vast populaces found themselves drawn so irresistibly into new orbits of political influence, and by national, economic, and social ideologies that widen the expectations and ambitions of some but leave many others bewildered, confused, and uncertain. Neither in the past nor in the present is it likely in the immediate future that Indo-Pakistan relations will be other than ambiguous, complex, and important for the extensive populations of these two powers.

There are at least three interrelated serious problems that Pakistan will have to resolve if it is to make and maintain cordial constructive relations with India—or even to continue as a coherent state at all. The major problem is that the country has no genuinely embedded democracy and is plagued by many burgeoning *jihardi* and Islamic groups. For several decades the military and in particular Pakistan's powerful Inter-Services Intelligence (ISI) have been the clandestine supporters of myriad mujahedeen groups. Intended for selective deployment first in Kashmir and then in Afghanistan, where they were designed to fight proxy wars for the army, at low cost and low risk, these projects have turned out to be disastrous: spawning thousands of armed but intermittently employed *jhardis*, millions of modern weapons, and proliferating mili-

Epilogue

tant groups. The military and intelligence community in Pakistan may have once believed that it could use *jhardis* for its own ends, but the Islamists have followed their own agenda and have at times brought their struggle onto the street and into the confusion of the country's politics.

Secondly, there is undoubtedly a fundamental flaw in Pakistan's political system. Democracy has never thrived within it, at least in part because landowning remains almost the only social base from which responsible and representative politicians can emerge. In general Pakistan's educated middle class—which in India seized office in 1947 and emasculated the power of its landowners—has been largely excluded in Pakistan from the mostly febrile political process. As a result, in many of the backward parts of Pakistan the local feudal zamindars can expect their people to vote for their chosen candidates. Such allegiance can be enforced. Many of Pakistan's biggest zamindars have private prisons and even private armies.

In such an environment, politicians tend to come to power more through deals done within Pakistan's small elite than through the will of the people. Behind Pakistan's swings between military government and corrupt electoral democracy lies a remarkable continuity of interests. To some considerable extent the military, industrial, landowning, and bureaucratic elites are interrelated and support one another.

A third and fundamental issue facing Pakistan and limiting its resilience is its desperate education crisis, the abject failure of the government to educate more than a fraction of its own people. The educational gap is a most striking illustration of how Pakistan is lagging behind India. In India about 65 percent of the population is literate, and the number rises every year, but in Pakistan the literacy figure is under half and falling. Out of 162 million Pakistanis in 2007, 84 million adults of 15 years and above are illiterate. Among women the problem is worse still: 65 percent of all female adults are illiterate. As the population increases, the problem worsens.

The virtual collapse of Pakistan's government schooling has meant that many of the country's poorest people have no option but to place their children in the *madrassas* (Islamic religion schools) system, where they are provided an ultraconservative but free education, often subsidized by religious endowments provided by the Wahhabi Saudis or other benefactors.

Altogether there are now an estimated 800,000 to one million students enrolled in Pakistan's *madrassas*. Though the links between the *madrassas* and al-Qaeda are often exaggerated, it is true that *madrassas* students have been closely involved in the rise of the Taliban and the growth of sectarian violence. It is also true that the education provided by many *madrassas* is often wholly inadequate to equip children for modern life in a civil society.

Today in the world's media, never has the contrast between the two countries seemed so stark. India is widely portrayed as a coming superpower, singularly close in potential to China; Pakistan is often characterized as a failed state, a world center of Islamic radicalism, of *madrassas*, and massacres; the hiding place of Osama bin Laden; and the only U.S. ally that Washington seems ready to bomb. Furthermore, from Pakistan in 2007 has come the noise of automatic weapons storming the Red Mosque in central Islamabad and the creaking of unsustainable would-be authoritarian regimes or undisguised army rule.

Yet overall the contrasts are complex but not so stark. First-time visitors to Pakistan are often surprised by Pakistan's pockets of visible prosperity. There is far less obtrusively visible poverty in Pakistan than in India, relatively fewer beggars, and perhaps less pervasive criminalized politics. In many respects the infrastructure of Pakistan is much more advanced and better maintained. There are better roads and airports, as well as more reliable electricity supplies. No wonder Indo-Pakistan relations are complex.

The sheer persistence of a particular government or regime in power, army-led or otherwise, does not necessarily or even usually of itself produce legitimacy. And although longevity does not of itself bestow legitimacy, mere durability can inculcate over time a kind of prescriptive title bred of familiarity and public acquiescence. Even so, the maximum political life cycle of such a system tends to be well-nigh coterminous with the career of its dominant ruling figure (Mohammad Ayub or Zia-ul-Huq, for instance). Once the autocrat dies or is assassinated or deposed, then his eponymous system tends to crumble fast and to be reconstituted or replaced.

The critical factor is, however, not the dominance of a particular personality or set of oligarchs (for no one ultimately can escape the inexorable, irreversible ticking of their biological clock) but whether or not they have established and worked institutions that can survive and be used after their progenitors have left the scene (as the Fifth Republic in France outlived the passing of de Gaulle). What is certain, however, is that the nondurability of regimes, absolutely and well-nigh by definition, precludes institutionalization.

Pakistan's complex relations with its colossal eastern neighbor India are, in the early 21st century, mixed and volatile, capable very suddenly of showing apparent improvements or swift deterioration. In the early 21st century, too, Pakistanis from time to time accuse Indians of helping to foment unrest in Sindh and elsewhere in their country, while repudiating Indian charges that the government of Pakistan stirs up unrest in Gujerat, Punjab, and Kashmir. Such accusations of conducting indirect or proxy wars are frequently bandied about.

The most continuing abrasive issues between the two countries concerns their nuclear policies, whether they will become parties to an American-sponsored proposal for a South Asia nuclear-free zone or will come fully within the scope of the nuclear non-proliferation regime in the immediate future.

India and Pakistan celebrated 60 years of independence in mid August 2007 in rather different styles and tones. Pakistan was partially reeling from a series of political and other crises; so responses to the 60th anniversary of independence were muted with fireworks banned and public gatherings discouraged. In marked contrast, India, enjoying an economic boom and political stability, marked the anniversary with a series of parades, speeches, and gun salutes. Indo-Pakistan relations in this 60th postindependence year were low key and officially rather cordial. There were even attempts to resolve the 60-year dispute over Kashmir.

The chronology for this book is quite extensive because the items in it cover a wide range of Indo-Pakistan encounters, with a strong stress on bilateral relations. However, the entries and analysis in this book also have to take some account of conflict within neighboring countries such as Afghanistan, Iraq, or the member countries of SAARC, but these events are not recorded at all fully in this chronology.

Historical accounts of conflict between countries generally tend to record the interplay between leaders, but encounters range wider than this to embrace religious, ethnic, and other groupings. In other words, history is mostly written "from above," that is, it stresses the roles of governments and elites. But this study has sought also to take some account of "history from below," from grassroots (or rice roots) level, to indicate not only the significance of particular events but also to explain, where appropriate and possible, the changing causes of conflict.

A major working assumption in this study is that the causes of war and conflict are specific rather than generic, in other words, that history never exactly repeats itself. That is a plausible reason for the fairly detailed attention to particulars in this chronology and more generally throughout the study.

Chronology

30 January	Mahatma Gandhi is assassinated by a Hindu fanatic.
March	India's communists begin campaign to overthrow the state by violence. Campaign lasts for three and a half years. Issue of the accession of Kashmir and Jammu is brought before the UNSC by India.
June	Earl Louis Mountbatten, the first Indian-born governor-general, leaves India.
July	Indo-Pakistan agreement on the size of sterling balances is reached.

1947

British Raj in India ends. Punjab and Bengal partitioned. Integration of Princely States. Naga secessionist movement begins.

15 August — India and Pakistan become independent. Pandit Nehru is confirmed as India's prime minister, M. A. Jinnah as Pakistan's governor-general.

October — Kashmir crisis cause by the first Indo-Pakistan War.

1948

1 January — India lodges a complaint in the United Nations Security Council (UNSC) against Pakistan, accusing the latter of supporting tribal attacks into Kashmir.

13 August — The United Nations Commission for India and Pakistan (UNCIP) passes a resolution providing for:
1. Cease-fire.
2. Withdrawal of Pakistan's troops and tribals, followed by Indian withdrawal.
3. Plebiscite.

September — Indian troops are sent into Hyderabad; the nizam accedes to the Indian Union, with much criticism from Pakistan. Jinnah dies.

December — Indo-Pakistan judicial tribunal is set up to resolve boundary disputes between East and West Bengal and between East Bengal and Assam.

1949

April — India decides to remain in the British Commonwealth while becoming a republic and adopts a constitution as a federal republic. Nehru visits Washington, D.C., and addresses a joint session of Congress.

Britain devalues the pound sterling vis-à-vis the U.S. dollar, from $4.03 to $2.80; most Commonwealth countries (including India but not Pakistan) follow.

9 June   Under the auspices of UNCIP, a cease-fire line agreement is signed in Karachi by military representatives of Pakistan and India, along with representatives of UNCIP.

17 August   After the Karachi Agreement on Kashmir, UNCIP proposes a tripartite meeting at political level on August 17 to conclude a truce agreement stipulating a program of withdrawal of forces. The meeting is cancelled in view of persisting differences between the two sides.

17 October   Article 370 is inserted into the Indian Constitution giving Kashmir certain special rights not given to other states of India.

17 December   Following UNCIP's final report the UN Security Council requested its president, General A. G. L. McNaughton (Canada), to mediate between the parties and find a "mutually satisfactory basis for dealing with the Kashmir problem."

1950

January   In January General McNaughton begins mediation efforts but finds the positions of the two parties wide apart.

26 January   The republic of India is inaugurated.

April   Nehru makes his first visit to Pakistan (accompanied by his daughter, Indira, and son-in-law, Feroze Gandhi). He is met at Karachi by Prime Minister Liaquat Ali Khan and his cabinet. The Liaquat–Nehru Pact is signed.

12 April   The UNSC appoints Sir Owen Dixon, eminent jurist from Australia, as UN representative on Kashmir. The appointment is accepted by both India and Pakistan.

June–July   Owen Dixon conducts intensive negotiations with governments of Pakistan and India and also meets Shaikh Abdullah in Srinagar and Ghulam Abbas in Muzaffarabad.

July   The possibility of partition-cum-plebiscite is raised at the Liaquat–Nehru meeting in New Delhi in July 1950, during which both sides seem ready to explore ideas beyond their original positions.

September   The Dixon Plan, proposed by Sir Owen Dixon, UN representative for India and Pakistan on Kashmir, is submitted to the Security Council. It proposes assigning Ladakh to India and the Northern Areas and Pakistan-occupied Kashmir (POK) to Pakistan, to split Jammu between the two, and to hold a plebiscite in the Kashmir Valley.

December   Sardar Vallabhbhai Patel, a strong man in India's relations with Pakistan, dies.

1951

16 January   Nehru and Liaquat hold a meeting in London during the Commonwealth Prime Minister's Conference. The prime ministers of Australia, the UK, Canada, New Zealand, and Ceylon (as of 1972, Sri Lanka) are present.

An Australian suggestion about posting a Commonwealth brigade in Kashmir and holding a limited plebiscite is not acceptable to either country, with Pakistan insisting on a plebiscite for the entire state and India unwilling to countenance the stationing of "foreign troops on Indian soil."

28 January	The president of the UN Security Council states that:
	(a) The question of accession should be decided by plebiscite,
	(b) The plebiscite is to be conducted under conditions ensuring complete impartiality, and
	(c) hence to be held under the aegis of United Nations; "these matters are not disputed between the parties."
July	India's first Five-Year Plan published.
September	India's President Rajendra Prasad threatens to resign over the Hindu Code Bill.
7 September	The UN Security Council's representative Frank Graham presents 12 proposals to India and Pakistan. While some are acceptable to both, disagreement persists on the quantum and disposition of troops and on the induction into office of a plebiscite administrator. Meetings to resolve the differences, held in New York and Geneva, fail to achieve results.
October	Liaquat Ali Khan is assassinated, gunned down by a hired assassin in Rawalpindi's army cantonment.
	Dr. S. P. Mookerjee, former president of the Hindu Mahasabha, launches the Jana Sangh, a communalist party.
1952 March	India's first general elections are held: Congress wins large majority, thereby maintaining and legitimizing one-party dominance.
	Language riots break out in East Pakistan; Bengalis are critical of Punjabis.
16 July	In his revised proposals, Graham tries to narrow down the differences on the size and disposition of troops but does not succeed. Negotiations continue and an agreement is reached on all points

except the size of Pakistani Kashmir and of Indian and Kashmir state forces to be retained on the eve of the plebiscite and the timing of the plebiscite administrator's appointment.

1953	Further negotiations at UN and in Geneva do not reduce the March 27 differences on these basic points. Finally, Graham reports the failure of his mission to the Security Council on March 27, 1953.
	Agreement is reached by the prime ministers of India and Pakistan, meeting in Delhi regarding the settlement of Bengal boundary disputes.
25–27 July	Pakistani and Indian prime ministers meet in Karachi and agree that a resolution of their disputes is "essential to progress in both countries."
August	Sheikh Abdullah's government in Kashmir is dismissed by J. Nehru; Abdullah is arrested.
17–20 August	Pakistan's Prime Minister Mohammed Ali visits New Delhi. A communiqué issued at the end of meetings says that the issue of Kashmir "should be settled in accordance with the wishes of the people of that State with a view to promoting their well-being and causing the least disturbance to the life of the people of the State." Both countries agree on the appointment of a plebiscite administrator by the end of April 1954.
October	Formation of Andhra Pradesh, India's first linguistic state.
	Akali Dal begins demand for a Punjab Subha.
1954 April	A Sino-Indian agreement is reached on Tibet, whereby India recognizes Tibet as part of China.

June	Zhou Enlai (Chou En-lai) visits Delhi. Joint statements are released on Panch Sheel; principles of peace are issued.	Naga insurgency begins in northeast India.

Pakistan signs a mutual defense agreement with the United States.

Pakistan's constitution introduces the One Unit Scheme and presidential system.

September   SEATO, the Southeast Asian Treaty Organization, is launched from Manila, with Pakistan as a member and India opposed.

1957

20 January   India's first atomic reactor, at Trombay near Bombay (Mumbai), is inaugurated by Nehru; it started operation in August 1956.

The Muslim League is defeated by the United Front in East Pakistan elections.

22 January   India and Pakistan sign a new trade agreement

24–26 January   Zhou Enlai visits Delhi for talks with Nehru.

1955

January   Congress declares that a "socialistic pattern of society" is the objective of planning.

26 January   Kashmir's constitution providing for incorporation of the territory into India comes into force. Anti-Indian protest demonstrations occur in Karachi, Lahore, Hyderabad, and Dacca (later Dhaka).

February   Soviet economic assistance to India is inaugurated, with the announcement of the building of a steel mill.

April   Bandung conference takes place, with Indian and Pakistan's participation.

Throughout the year India has to wage an almost ceaseless polemical battle in the UN over Kashmir.

Pakistan adheres to the Iraq-Turkey Treaty and the Baghdad Pact.

30 January   Control over movements of Commonwealth nationals in India (in effect of Pakistani and South African nationals) are made similar to control over movements of foreigners.

December   Soviet leaders Bulganin and Krushchev visit India and announce support for India's stand on Kashmir and are critical of Pakistan's membership of SEATO and the Baghdad Pact.

New Delhi announces that, following the resignation of the minister of defense, the portfolio has been taken over by Nehru.

1956

July   The three nonallied triumvirs—Tito, Nasser, and Nehru—meet on Tito's Adriatic holiday island, Brioni.

25 March   Elections to Jammu-Kashmir state assembly, held on March 25 and 30 respectively, resulted in a majority for the ruling National Conference Party.

October   Nehru condemns Anglo-French and Israeli action in Suez but not the Soviet suppression of the Hungarian uprising. Pakistan is critical of Soviet suppression in Hungary but equivocal about the Suez War.

5 April   India's second general election results show Indian National Congress Party (Congress) majority in the Lok Sabha and in 11 of the 13 state assemblies. Congress also wins the outstanding four seats in Himachal Pradesh.

November   India's States Reorganisation Bill is passed; the militant phase of the

13 April	Sardar Mohammad Ibrahim Khan, president of the All-Jammu-Kashmir Moslem Conference, takes office as president of the Azad Jammu-Kashmir government [i.e., of Pakistan-controlled Kashmir (POK)].
14 April	Nehru, in a speech in New Delhi, makes a further appeal to the great powers to stop tests of nuclear bombs.
17 April	Nehru forms a new Indian Congress-led government.
	Krishna Menon becomes minister of defense.
17 May	Nehru visits Ceylon at the invitation of Bandaranaike (May 17–20) to participate in 2,500th anniversary celebrations of the birth of the Buddha.
25 May	India and Communist China renew their two-year trade agreement of October 14, 1954, from 1956 to December 31, 1958, by an exchange of letters.
3 June	Baghdad Pact's Permanent Council holds its third annual meeting in Karachi (June 3–6).
	Nehru makes extensive tour of several Scandinavian countries.
23 June	Pakistan and Afghanistan sign an air agreement and exchange ratifications on December 12.
26 June	Commonwealth Prime Minister Conference held in London (June 26–July 5). India is represented by Nehru and Pakistan by H. S. Suhrawardy.
10 July	Pakistan's Prime Minister H. S. Suhrawardy visits the United States (July 19–26) and has talks with President Dwight D. Eisenhower and John Foster Dulles (July 10–12).
4 November	Dr. Karan Singh, son of the former Maharaja, is reelected Kashmir's head of state for the next five years by the Kashmir state assembly without opposition.
9 November	India and Soviet Union sign an agreement in New Delhi implementing details of credit agreement of May 21, 1956.
27 November	Nehru publicly issues a renewed appeal to the United States and the Soviet Union to end nuclear weapon tests and to bring about effective disarmament.
6 December	Indian government announces agreement with British-owned Burmah Oil Company on formation of joint rupee company to exploit new oil resources in northeastern Assam; agreement establishes Oil India Private, Ltd., signed January 14, 1958.
11 December	Pakistan's Prime Minister I. I. Chundrigar resigns.
16 December	New Pakistan cabinet under Malik Feroze Noon is sworn in.
1958	President Mirza abrogates Pakistan's constitution and dismisses the central and provincial governments.
	Ayub Khan becomes Pakistan's head of government and chief martial law administrator in a peaceful coup.
October	India protests to China over Aksai Chin Road.
1959	
January	I. Gandhi is elected president of the Congress Party. Zhou Enlai lays claim to large areas of India's territory. President Eisenhower visits India as part of an extensive foreign tour.
March	Dalai Lama flees from Tibet into India. China reacts critically.

July	Kerala's communist-led state government is dismissed.
15 September	Pakistan's President Ayub Khan meets with Jawaharlal Nehru at Delhi airport, and they speak of settling Kashmir.

1960

May	President Ayub and Nehru meet in London at Commonwealth Prime Ministers' Conference and discuss Kashmir but without making progress toward settlement.
July	India adopts a Forward Policy in border areas. Khrushchev visits India.
September	Indus Waters Treaty between India and Pakistan is signed.
	Feroze Gandhi, Indira's husband, dies.
	Nehru visits Karachi and Rawalpindi. Kashmir forms one of main topics of discussion with Ayub but without results.

1961

	Queen Elizabeth II visits India and Pakistan as part of an extensive Commonwealth tour.
November	During Nehru's visit to the United States, President John F. Kennedy asks him to solve the Kashmir issue (at the insistence of Ayub Khan). Nehru rules out any solution other than the one based on the cease-fire line.
December	Indian forces invade and annex the Portuguese colony of Goa, stirring up much foreign criticism, especially from Pakistan.

1962

January	India's third general elections are held.
20 October	Chinese offensive is launched across India's borders.

7 November	Nehru accepts Defense Minister Krishna Menon's resignation from the cabinet.
21 November	China announces unilateral cease-fire.
26 December	India, under pressure from the United States and Britain, engages in six rounds of secret talks with Pakistan on Kashmir and other related issues. Pakistani Foreign Minister Zulfikar Ali Bhutto and Indian External Affairs Minister Sardar Swaran Singh participate in the talks.
	First round at Rawalpindi (December 26–29, 1962) is confined to preliminaries, historical aspects, and respective stands.
	India seems ready to accept the partition of Kashmir while urging that the division should take into account geographic, administrative, and other considerations and that the settlement should involve the least possible disturbance to the life and welfare of the people.
1963	Second round of Pakistan–India talks held in Delhi (January 16–20, 1963) and a third in Karachi (April 21–25), with Pakistan calling for a plebiscite and India opposing it. At the fourth round in Calcutta (March 12–14), India suggests an adjustment of the cease-fire line to settle the dispute, which Pakistan rejects, while a fifth round in Karachi (April 21–25) is taken up with India's protest at the recently signed Pakistan–China boundary agreement under which some part of the former State is ceded to China. At a sixth and final round at Delhi (May 14–16), Pakistan proposes a plebiscite confined to the Kashmir Valley, which it further suggests should be placed under international control for 12 to15 months prior to the holding of elections.

If the plebiscite is not acceptable, then the people's wishes should be ascertained by some other form and the dispute settled. India rejects both proposals. During these talks India offers Pakistan some strips of territory to the west and north of the valley but will concede no part of the valley itself.

March

Sino-Pakistan border and territorial agreement is vehemently criticized by the Indian government for purporting to deal with territory that India regards as its own.

August

Many of Nehru's senior cabinet colleagues, including Moraji Desai, resign under the Kamaraj Plan to work for the party.

Indian government creates the State of Nagaland in the extreme northeast.

1964
March

Anti-Muslim violence breaks out in India.

24 May

Nehru invites Sheikh Abdullah to Delhi, and the two have cordial discussions. Abdullah travels to Pakistan and also to Pakistani Kashmir, where he confers with President K. H. Khurshid. Some say that Nehru has a change of heart on Kashmir, though others deny it.

Ayub later records that Abdullah proposes confederal arrangements among Pakistan, India, and Kashmir, which he rejects. Mirza Afzal Beg, who accompanies Abdullah to Pakistan, later tells Indian author P. L. Lakhanpal, "various solutions of the dispute were talked about in general terms but no preferences for any particular solutions were indicated."

27 May

Nehru dies at age 74 and is succeeded as India's prime minister by L. B. Shastri. I. Gandhi becomes minister of information and broadcasting.

Nehru's sudden death in New Delhi aborts Abdullah's mission. Abdullah returns to India.

August

Indira Gandhi is elected to parliament (Rajya Sabha, or upper house) for the first time.

12 October

Ayub and Shastri meet in Karachi for several hours of conversation about world affairs and Indo-Pakistan relations, but no dramatic announcements are made, nor is there any expression of mutual goodwill. However, it is agreed that the next main contact will be at ministerial level.

October–November

The Communist Party of India splits.

20 December

Five hundred are arrested in India, suspected of being Chinese spies.

The Vishwa Hindu Parishad (VHP) is founded by Swami Chinmayananda.

1965
9 April

Indian and Pakistani soldiers clash in the border region of the Rann of Kutch, northwest India, and southeast corner of Pakistan.

30 June

India and Pakistan sign a cease-fire regarding Rann of Kutch.

September

The war between India and Pakistan along Pakistan's eastern borders from Kashmir to the Arabian Sea lasts five weeks.

October–December

Much active diplomacy takes place, especially involving Britain, the United States, and the Soviet Union to settle the outstanding disputes of the Indo-Pakistan war diplomatically.

1966

Prime Minister Lal Bahadur Shastri and President Ayub Khan sign the Tashkent Agreement on January 10, 1966, formally ending the five weeks of war between Pakistan and India of August–September 1965.

10 January	Shastri dies after signing the Indo-Pakistan Tashkent Agreement.
24 January	Indira Gandhi is sworn in as prime minister.
6 June	The Indian rupee is devalued by 35.5 percent under World Bank pressure.

1967

February	The Mizo insurgency escalates.
	India holds its fourth general elections. Indira Gandhi is forced to accept Moraji Desai as deputy prime minister.
12 March	Indira Gandhi is reelected prime minister of India, marking the end of dominance by the Congress throughout India.
May	Indira Gandhi announces 10-point program, including bank nationalization and abolition of Maharajas' privy purses and privileges.
	The Pakistan People's Party (PPP) is founded, with Z. A. Bhutto as its head.
1968	After the third general election in India in 1967, there are ministries formed in several states made up of coalitions of parties, other than in the Congress, which result in 1968 being a year of marked political instability for India. Coalitions fall apart consequent to the inability of any single party to form a stable government, and president's rule has to be imposed with the promise of fresh elections in the near future. This occurs first in Haryana toward the end of 1967and is followed in 1968 by West Bengal in February, Uttar Pradesh in April, Bihar in June, and the Punjab in August. This political fluidity impairs the continuity of administration, which is all the more essential because of the increase in various forms of public turmoil and agitation.

1968	Communal disturbances are also more frequent than in 1967, particularly in the states of Assam, West Bengal, Bihar, Uttar Pradesh, Kerala, and Mysore. An ominous aspect of this increase in communal rancor is its eruption in parts of southern India.
2 January	The Indian government releases Sheikh Abdullah. During the rest of the year he proposes various solutions, none of which seem generally acceptable within India. Indo-Pakistan discussions, mainly of a technical nature, are resumed regarding eastern rivers, especially the Farraka Barrage and the threatened loss of irrigation water in East Pakistan, but little progress is made.
February	The Rann of Kutch Tribunal issues its findings, awarding a portion of the territory in dispute to Pakistan [about 777 square kilometers (300 square miles) of its claim] and by April the two sides begin the work of border demarcation.
19 June	India protests to China, alleging Chinese complicity in training subversives in Nagaland.
1 July	Nuclear Non-proliferation Treaty is signed by the UK, the United States, USSR, and several other states, but not by India or Pakistan.
8 July	India's president Zakir Husain arrives in Moscow on a 10-day visit.
13 November	In Pakistan, PPP leader Z. A. Bhutto is arrested following disorders in West Pakistan.

1969

January	The centenary of the birth of Mahatma Gandhi is celebrated throughout India and many places overseas.
30 January	Indian prime minister Indira Gandhi, prays at the spot near the

River Jumna where the Mahatma was assassinated 21 years before.

February
President Ayub Khan of Pakistan proposes discussions with opposition leaders for constitutional reform (February 26–March 13); he holds a conference of political leaders in Rawalpindi.

25 March
President Ayub Khan resigns; General Yahya Khan, commander-in-chief of the army, on March 31 assumes office as president. Communal violence afflicts parts of India.

Gujerat goes through an orgy of violence—Hindu-Muslim riots, the like of which India has not experienced since partition in 1947—engulfs several parts of the state; nearly 1,000 people are killed. The course of Pakistan's or India's foreign relations is little affected by their internal turmoil.

The Rann of Kutch dispute, which has brought about Indo-Pakistan armed clashes early in 1965, is formally concluded in June. Following demarcation of the boundary and exchange of maps, each party withdraws from the territory it is no longer entitled to hold.

March
A series of discussions on the Farraka Barrage covers technical aspects of the problem but fails to reach an agreement on how the Ganges water is to be allocated when the barrage is completed. Throughout the year, a stalemate over Kashmir continues to impede a general rapprochement.

1970
February
Indo-Pakistan talks on Ganga waters begin in Islamabad.

March
Joint communiqué is issued at the end of talks on Farraka Barrage in Islamabad.

Indus Waters Treaty between India and Pakistan, signed in 1960, expires.

President Yahya Khan announces the legal framework order laying down rules for transferring power back to civilian authorities.

April
Field Marshal Ayub Khan, Pakistan's president (1958–1969), dies of a heart attack in Islamabad.

13 May
Pakistan lodges a protest against the communal riots that broke out in Bhiwandi (Bombay) and urges the Indian government to protect the Muslim minority.

21 July
India and Pakistan agree in a joint communiqué that Farraka should be the point of delivery of Ganges waters to Pakistan, at the end of meeting July 16–21 in New Delhi.

October
India sends a note to Pakistan on Kashmir.

November
East Pakistan's coastal districts are hit by a cyclone in which more than a million die.

December
Pakistan's National Assembly elections are held—166 of the 300 seats in the Assembly are won by the Awami League, while 81 seats are won by the Pakistan People's Party, displaying a pattern of marked regionalization of political preferences.

Gandhi dissolves parliament and calls for midterm parliamentary elections.

1971
March
Gandhi wins a two-thirds majority in the Lok Sabha (the lower house of parliament).

25 March
Pakistan's army begins military crackdown in East Pakistan; Mujib-ur Rahman is arrested in Dhaka by the army and imprisoned.

Refugees from East Pakistan, especially Hindus, start fleeing across the border into Assam and West Bengal.

July   By July it is estimated that at least 7 million people have fled across the border into India and that refugees are still arriving at the rate of about 50,000 a day. Many of the refugees are living in the open or in makeshift camps, facing starvation and cholera as the monsoon season begins.

August   Indira Gandhi signs the Treaty of Peace, Friendship and Co-operation with the Soviet Union.

3 December   Pakistan Air Force attacks Indian air bases; the third open Indo-Pakistan War begins. Pakistan makes a formal declaration of war on India.

4 December   In the eastern section, Indian troops, in concert with the Mukti Bahini (local freedom fighters), move into East Pakistan at several points.

6 December   India accords recognition to Bangladesh, and Pakistan breaks off diplomatic relations with India.

8 December   General Sam Manekshaw, India's chief of the Army staff, calls on Pakistani "occupation" forces in Bangladesh to surrender immediately to the Indian army.

9 December   In a statement in parliament, India's defense minister announces that Pakistan's largest submarine, the U.S.-built *Ghazi,* was sunk off Vishakhapatnan on the night of December 3–4.

10 December   India guarantees safe conduct for planes from several countries to evacuate foreign nationals from Karachi, Islamabad, and Dacca.

14 December   At the UN, the Soviet Union uses its veto for the third time to block a U.S. resolution calling for an immediate

Indo-Pakistan cease-fire and troop withdrawal.

16 December   Pakistan's army commander surrenders in Dhaka; Bangladesh emerges de facto as an independent state.

17 December   India orders a unilateral cease-fire on the western front. President Yahya Khan accepts the cease-fire.

20 December   Z. A. Bhutto succeeds Yahya Khan as head of government in Pakistan.

22 December   The UN Security Council Resolution on a cease-fire demands that a durable cessation of hostilities be observed and remain in effect until withdrawals take place, and it calls for international relief assistance and the rehabilitation of refugees.

1972

3 January   At a public meeting in Karachi, Z. A. Bhutto receives approval to release Sheikh Mujib-Ur Rahman from jail.

12 January   Sheikh Mujib-Ur Rahman is sworn in as prime minister of Bangladesh.

30 January   Pakistan quits the Commonwealth over Bangladesh.

Pakistan's third constitution is introduced; riots break out following the tabling of the Sindhi language bill.

4 February   Britain recognizes Bangladesh.

9 February   Accord is issued in Calcutta, after talks between Indira Gandhi and Sheikh Mujib-Ur Rahman, promising the withdrawal of India's armed forces from Bangladesh by March 25.

14 February   India, in a letter to the UN secretary-general, offers to hold direct talks with Pakistan "at any time, at any level and without precondition."

3 March   Pakistan's Lieutenant General Gul Hasan, chief of staff of the Army, and

Air Marshal Rahim Khan, Air Force chief, are replaced by General Tikka Khan and Air Marshal Zafar Choudhry, respectively.

12 March

India's armed forces withdraw from Bangladesh at a ceremonial parade in Dacca.

4 April

The National Assembly convenes in Islamabad to frame a new constitution for Pakistan.

25 April

India's chairman of the Policy Planning Committee of the Ministry of External Affairs D. P. Dhar, a Kashmiri, leaves for Islamabad for talks with Bhutto's emissary.

30 April

India and Pakistan agree to a summit meeting between Indira Gandhi and Z. A. Bhutto at the end of May or beginning of June, according to a communiqué released after the meetings of the special emissaries of the president of Pakistan and the prime minister of India at Muree and Rawalpindi.

28 June

Zulfikar Ali Bhutto and Indira Gandhi meet in Simla, India, to deal with consequences of the 1971 war. On July 2, the two leaders reach an accord and sign the Simla Agreement.

June–July

On Jammu-Kashmir, the accord renames the cease-fire line as the line of actual control to reflect some minor adjustments that are mutually agreed on, and it pledges both sides to respect the new line. A proviso is added at Bhutto's insistence saying that this would be "without prejudice to the recognized position of either side." It also commits both countries to "further undertake to refrain from the threat of use of force in violation of this line."

15 July

Pakistan's National Assembly ratifies the Simla Agreement.

25 July

India's Union Cabinet approves the Simla Agreement.

10 August

Simla Agreement is formally ratified by the Indian parliament.

Representatives of India and Pakistan's Army chief reach an agreement on procedure for the delineation of the line of control in Jammu-Kashmir in light of the cease-fire of December 17, 1971.

28 November

First meeting of the Army chiefs of India and Pakistan (December 1), with Generals Manekshaw and Tikka Khan, is held in Lahore; they issue a joint statement.

11 December

Agreement on the delineation of LoC in Jammu-Kashmir is reached in accordance with the Simla Agreement of the previous June–July. Maps are initialed by representatives of the two armies.

12 December

India's Foreign Minister, Sardar Siwaran Singh, makes a statement in parliament that India has informed Pakistan of its withdrawal of the claim on two villages (Dhum and Chilkot).

1973
20 February

Two 18-year-old Pakistanis, Basharat Hussain and Mohammad Hussain, are shot dead by the police when they attempt an armed raid on the Indian High Commission in London.

A 15-year-old Pakistani boy involved in this attempt is later sentenced by the Juvenile Court. Newspaper reports say that the raid was organized by the Black December group.

April

Gandhi breaks the tradition of appointing the chief justice on the basis of seniority.

Indian troops annex Sikkim.

Tribal insurgency breaks out in Baluchistan.

12 April	Pakistan's new constitution is authenticated by President Bhutto.		5–9. After discussion on the various issues mentioned in the Delhi Agreement of August 28, 1973, they sign a tripartite agreement regarding repatriation of prisoners held in these countries.

12 April — Pakistan's new constitution is authenticated by President Bhutto.

10 July — The National Assembly of Pakistan passes a resolution authorizing the government to recognize Bangladesh.

24–31 July — The Special Representative of the Prime Minister of India P. N. Haksar, a Kashmiri, and the Pakistan Minister of State for Defence and Foreign Affairs Aziz Ahmed hold talks in Rawalpindi to try to solve the humanitarian problems set out in the Indo-Bangladesh Declaration of April 17, 1973.

14 August — Pakistan's third constitution is promulgated, Z. A. Bhutto becomes prime minister, and Fazal Ilahi Chaudhry becomes president.

28 August — P. N. Haksar and Aziz Ahmed sign an agreement in Delhi to solve the humanitarian problems that resulted from the August 28 conflict of 1971. This agreement provides for the repatriation of prisoners who are nationals of India, Pakistan, and Bangladesh to their respective countries. The government of Bangladesh concurs in this agreement.

19 September — The repatriation of Muslim Bengalis from Pakistan and of the non-Bengalis from Bangladesh begins.

1974

February — Pakistan recognizes Bangladesh, which is admitted to the Organisation of the Islamic Conference (OIC), founded in1969, for its summit meeting in Lahore.

March — J. P. (Jaya Prakash) Movement starts in Bihar.

9 April — Dr. Kamal Hossain, foreign minister of Bangladesh, Sardar Swaran Singh, minister of external affairs, India, and Aziz Ahmed, minister of state for defense and foreign affairs of Pakistan, meet in New Delhi April

5–9. After discussion on the various issues mentioned in the Delhi Agreement of August 28, 1973, they sign a tripartite agreement regarding repatriation of prisoners held in these countries.

Swaran Singh and Aziz Ahmed sign an agreement on the release and repatriation of persons detained in either country prior to the conflict of 1971.

May — Railway strike occurs in India.

18 May — India tests a so-called peaceful nuclear explosion (PNE).

19 May — At a press conference in Lahore, Prime Minister Bhutto demands what he calls a nuclear umbrella to protect Pakistan from nuclear blackmail after India carries out a successful peaceful nuclear explosion on May 18.

31 May — Reacting to the nuclear explosion by India, Pakistan calls for the postponement of the talks on restoration of postal telecommunication and travel facilities planned for June 10 until "a more favourable atmosphere is created."

25 July — In response to a request from members of the Pakistan National Assembly that the government of Pakistan should take up with the government of India the question of Sadar Bazar riots of April–May 1974 in Delhi, Aziz Ahamed says:

(i) in the past, Pakistan used to take up such cases with India under Nehru–Liaquat pact; (ii) the pact was primarily about East Pakistan and adjoining Indian provinces and with East Pakistan gone, no useful purpose would be served by lodging a protest with New Delhi and (iii) under the Simla Agreement, it would be treated as an internal matter.

27 July	Under Parliamentary pressure however, the government of Pakistan handed over an aide-memoire to the government of India expressing concern over the Sadar Bazar riots.
16 August	The government of India, through an aide-memoire, replies to the government of Pakistan's aide-memoire on the Sadar Bazar riots, saying it is unable to agree that Pakistan had any right to raise officially a matter that falls entirely within India's domestic jurisdiction.
11 September	The National Assembly of Pakistan declares the Ahmadiyas sect non-Muslim.
14 September	Kewal Singh, foreign secretary of India, and Agha Shahi, secretary of foreign affairs of Pakistan, sign the following agreements in Islamabad: (i) Agreement relating to the exchange of postal articles. (ii) Agreement regarding establishment of telecommunication services like telephone, telex, and telegrams. (iii) Visa agreement to provide travel facilities to nationals of either country desiring to visit the other. This agreement defined the types of visas, the check posts at the registration formalities. (iv) Protocol on visit of pilgrims from either country to the religious shrines situated in the other. Agha Shahi hands over a letter of understanding for the cessation of hostile propaganda by the radio broadcasting stations of both countries. At the conclusion of the meeting held at Islamabad on September 12–14, a joint communiqué is issued covering the progress made during these talks.
21 October	Kewal Singh replies to the letter from Agha Shahi, and the agreement for cessation of hostile propaganda by

the radio broadcasting stations of both countries comes into force.

22 November	At the conclusion of the talks in Islamabad between the Indian delegation led by Narottam Sehgal, secretary, ministry of tourism and civil aviation, and the Pakistan delegation led by Major General Fazal Maqeem Khan, secretary, defense and aviation, a joint communiqué is issued regarding progress of civil aviation matters between the two countries, and they decide to continue the dialogue in New Delhi. No agreement is reached.
30 November	Y. T. Shah, secretary to the government of India, ministry of commerce, and Ejaz Ahmed Naik, secretary, government of Pakistan, ministry of commerce, hold talks in New Delhi on November 26–30, 1974, and sign a protocol on the resumption of trade. This protocol provided for a trade agreement to be signed in the near future.

1975

15 January	Indian delegation, led by Ramakrishnaya, secretary government of India, ministry of shipping and transport, holds meetings with the Pakistan delegation led by T. Kidwai, secretary, government of Pakistan, ministry of communications at New Delhi on January 11–15, 1975, and signs a protocol on the resumption of shipping services.
23 January	Pursuant to the protocol signed on November 30, 1974, on the resumption of trade, Y. T. Shah and Ejaz Ahmed Naik meet at Islamabad and sign a trade agreement.
31 January	The Cotton Corporation of India and the Pakistan Cotton Export Corporation sign an agreement in Bombay under which India is to import raw cotton valued at 250 million rupees from Pakistan.

Prime Minister Bhutto declares that he will call for a *hartal* in Jammu-Kashmir as well as in Pakistan and Pakistan-occupied Kashmir to protest against the projected agreement between the government of India and Sheikh Mohammad Abdullah. India points out that this utterance is against the meeting in Peshawar.

8 February   Hayat Mohammad Khan Sherpao, chief minister of the Northwest Frontier Province, is assassinated while addressing a public meeting in Peshawar.

12 February   The United States lifts its arms embargo on Pakistan imposed during the 1965 Indo-Pakistan War.

15 February   Kewal Singh sends a protest letter to Agha Shahi criticizing Pakistan radio reports about "bloody clashes" in Kashmir over the agreement between Gandhi and Sheikh Abdullah.

June   Gandhi is found guilty of corrupt electoral practices by Allahabad High Court.

25–26 June   The Emergency is imposed by Indira Gandhi. It lasts 21 months.

15 August   Sheikh Mujib-Ur Rahman, president of Bangladesh is assassinated.

November   Chinese troops ambush an Indian security patrol along India's northern border, killing four men in the first flare-up between the two countries in eight years.

1976
22 March   Lieutenant General Mohammad Zia-ul Haq is appointed as the next chief of Army staff in Pakistan.

12 May   Pursuant to the letters exchanged between Prime Minister Indira Gandhi and Prime Minister Bhutto on March 27, 1976, April 11, 1976, and April 18, 1976, delegations from India and Pakistan, led by the

respective Foreign Secretaries Jagat Mehta and Agha Shahi, meet in Islamabad with the objective of resuming normalization of relations. The joint statement issued after the talks announces agreement on the following:

(i) Withdrawal of complaints from ICAO and the restoration of air links and over flights.
(ii) Resumption of goods and passenger traffic by rail via Wagah-Attari border check post.
(iii) The re-establishment of diplomatic relations at ambassadorial level.
(iv) Private sector participation in bilateral trade.
(v) Repatriation of detainees from both countries.

21 June   K. S. Bajpai is announced as India's ambassador-designate to Pakistan.

28 June   The agreement for resumption of railway traffic between the two countries is signed.

16 July   The agreement for resumption of air services between the two countries is signed.

21 July   Air services between India and Pakistan resume. Ambassadors-designate to both countries reach their respective capitals by the first flights.

22 July   After a lapse of 11 years, the rail link between Amritsar and Lahore is reestablished.

24 July   Diplomatic relations, suspended in 1971, are formally reestablished when Ambassadors K. S. Bajpai and Syed Fida Hussain present their credentials.

10 September An Indian aircraft flying from Delhi to Bombay is hijacked by six armed men. On January 5, 1977, the government of Pakistan releases the hijackers, which the Indian

spokesperson describes as "highly regrettable."

1977

11 January — The Pakistan National Alliance is formed from nine political parties.

10 February — Indian Ambassador K. S. Bajpai orally conveys to Agha Shahi the Indian government's objection to the publication of a white paper on Kashmir.

Director General of the Foreign Office Mehdi represents Pakistan for the funeral of President Fakhruddeen Ali Ahmad.

March — Messages of felicitations are sent by Prime Minister Indira Gandhi and Acting President Jatti to Prime Minister Bhutto and the Pakistan president, respectively, on PPP's success in Pakistan's elections. Following the elections in India, Prime Minister Bhutto sends messages of congratulations to Prime Minister Moraji Desai on the occasion of the election of the first non-Congress government in India.

7 March — General elections are held for the National Assembly in Pakistan.

10 March — Elections are held for the four provincial assemblies in Pakistan.

8 April — Moraji Desai replies to Z. A. Bhutto's letter on April 8. Bhutto has stated that a no-war pact with India can be considered only if the Kashmir issue is resolved or if a self-executing or monitoring machinery is provided for the settlement of their dispute.

11–14 April — Indo-Pakistan trade talks at the secretary level are held in New Delhi April 11–14, 1977, to review the 1975 Trade Agreement between the two countries. It is decided to extend the validity of the agreement to January 22, 1978.

5 July — General Zia-ul-Haq removes Prime Minister Bhutto from office, declares martial law, and appoints himself the chief martial law administrator.

3 September — Z. A. Bhutto is accused of conspiracy to murder.

16 September — Z. A. Bhutto is arrested in Larkana.

10 November — The Supreme Court issues its verdict on *Begum Nusrat Bhutto vs. Chief of the Army Staff and Federation of Pakistan,* validating the extraconstitutional measures in a state of emergency "in the interest of the State and for the welfare of the people, as also the fact that the Constitution was not abrogated, but merely held in abeyance."

1978

4 January — India and Pakistan exchange detainees still held in each other's countries following the 1971 conflict.

6–8 February — Indian Foreign Minister Atal Bihari Vajpayee pays a goodwill visit to Pakistan.

9–19 February — Four hockey matches between India and Pakistan—two in India and two in Pakistan—are played for the first time in a decade.

20 February — Dr. Amir Mohammad, adviser to Pakistan's chief martial law administrator, visits India at the invitation of S. S. Barnala, minister for agriculture and irrigation.

18 March — Bhutto is sentenced to death in a unanimous decision by Lahore High Court.

14 April — India and Pakistan sign a bilateral agreement on the Salal Dam in India. Agha Shahi, adviser to General Zia on foreign affairs, visits India in this connection.

6–8 May — The Commerce Secretaries of the two countries meet in Islamabad to review trade connections.

Karakoram highway is opened to traffic in the presence of M. Keng Piao, vice premier of People's Republic of China.

19 August	Agha Shahi, in his speech at the Pakistan Association of World Federalists in Karachi, says that, with regard to conventional armaments, Pakistan is awaiting response from India to Pakistan's proposals, first made in 1974, to negotiate a mutual and balanced reduction of force.
31 August	Meeting between India's Prime Minister Desai and General Zia in Nairobi at the funeral of President Kenyatta.
1 September	The government of Pakistan is permitted in principle to allow an Indian consulate to open in Karachi in return for a Pakistani consulate to be opened in Bombay.
2–4 September	Pakistan Minister for Food and Agriculture Khwaja Mohammad Safdar visits India from September 2–4 in connection with purchase of wheat seeds. An agreement is reached for the sale of wheat seeds by India to Pakistan. Two planeloads carrying tents, milk powder, medicines, and cotton sheets are sent by Pakistan to India for the flood-affected areas.
16 September	General Zia is sworn in as president, replacing Fazal Elahi Chaudhry, who retires upon completion of his term.
22 September	An Indian cricket team arrives in Karachi on September 25 on an eight-week tour of Pakistan.
25–29 September	A four-member delegation from India goes to Pakistan to discuss locust control.
3–5 October	General Zia visits Hunza and Karakoram highways on October 3–5. He is accompanied by 15

ambassadors; India's ambassador declines the invitation. Agha Shahi, speaking in the UN General Assembly, calls for a just and honorable solution of Jammu-Kashmir issue in the spirit of the Simla Agreement.

7–9 October	Another round of trade talks between India and Pakistan is held in Islamabad. There is not much progress.
29 October	President Zia tells a press conference that there is no question of abolishing the visa system between India and Pakistan. Pakistan returns a portion of wheat seeds purchased from India on the grounds that the seeds are infested with weevil. India and Pakistan agree to streamline and speed up railway traffic between the two countries during the two-day talks between the officials held in New Delhi.
18–19 November	L. K. Advani, minister for information and broadcasting, goes to Pakistan on an official visit. Pakistan's minister for information raises the subject of disturbances in Aligarh in his discussions with Advani. Advani meets President Zia briefly at the venue of a cricket match. A group of Sikh pilgrims visits Nankana Sahib on the occasion of the birth anniversary of Guru Nanak.
7 December	Pakistan's Foreign Office issues a strongly worded statement regarding the tone and content of India's foreign minister's speech in India's Parliament while replying to a motion on December 6 regarding a study conducted by the UN Subcommission on Protection of Discrimination and Protection of Minorities that listed Jammu-Kashmir among the problems still awaiting settlement. On the same

day, the Indian ambassador is summoned by the Pakistan foreign secretary in this connection.

1979

17 January — Ganga Singh Dhillon, a representative of the Nankan Shaib Foundation, visits Pakistan and meets General Zia.

21 January — General Zia, at a banquet for China's visiting Vice Premier Li, says that the Kashmir problem is the greatest hurdle in the process of the normalization of Indo-Pakistan relations.

17–22 January — The permanent Indus Commission, constituted under the Indus Waters Treaty in 1960, undertakes its 60th tour of inspection in Pakistan.

3 February — A four-member public sector delegation of Pakistan, led by Farooq, managing director, heavy mechanical complex, Taxila, visits India.

10 February — Shariat benches composed of three Muslim judges (*qazis*) are established in the high courts in Pakistan.

March — General Zia, in an interview, says that the Kashmir question is the only hindrance in the process of normalization and that India should honor the UN resolution.

12 March — Pakistan announces its decision to withdraw from CENTO.

10–19 March — Indian journalists Kuldip Nayar and Khushwant Singh visit Pakistan.

31 March — Pakistan Foreign Office, in an official statement, mentions that President Zia has proposed in his reply to India's Prime Minister that Pakistan, India, and other states in South Asia should issue a joint declaration renouncing the manufacture or acquisition of nuclear weapons.

4 April — Bhutto is executed in Rawalpindi's central jail and buried near Larkana, his family home.

21 April — Zia, in a press conference talking about the Jamshedpur riots, says that he is grateful to Moraji Desai and the Indian government for not having said a word about Pakistan's internal affairs.

About 1,000 Sikh pilgrims, led by Sardar Jeevan Singh Umranangal, visit Panja Sahib.

28–31 May — S. Shah Nawaz, foreign secretary of Pakistan, visits India and holds discussions with India's foreign secretary on bilateral and other matters of mutual interest.

At the Islamic Foreign Minister's meeting in Fez, Agha Shahi, Pakistan's adviser on foreign affairs, says that the people of Jammu-Kashmir, whose destiny is of continued concern to the Islamic world, deserve support for the realization of their right to self-determination, recognized by the resolutions of the UN Security Council.

The Indus Commission holds its 40th session in Islamabad.

Nine hundred and twenty Sikh pilgrims visit Lahore to attend ceremonies in connection with the martyrdom of Guru Arjun Dev.

25–29 June — Benazir Bhutto, at a press conference in Karachi, asks why the government of Pakistan has not protested to India against anti-Muslim riots in several parts of India. She accuses the government of Pakistan of being silent when Muslims are being slaughtered in India.

About 500 Sikh pilgrims visit Lahore in connection with the anniversary of Ranjit Singh's death.

25 July — The 100,000th visa of 1979 is given by the Indian Ambassador to Syed Roshen. The Indian Airlines manager offers a free return ticket to Syed Roshen.

August	Agha Shahi, in a speech at the UN Committee for Elimination of Racial Discrimination, urges Indian government to take steps for the preservation of autonomy of educational institutions for minority communities, particularly the Muslims.
1–6 September	General Zia, at the Nonaligned Conference in Havana, says that Pakistan is determined to seek the resolution of Jammu and Kashmir problem in accordance with the relevant UN resolutions and the spirit of Simla Agreement.
	India's Foreign Minister S. N. Mishra meets Agha Shahi in Havana and later General Zia. Bilateral relations are reviewed.
16–18 September	Indo-Pakistan technical trade talks are held in Islamabad. Pakistan's delegation does not show any inclination to have a meaningful trade in the private sector after which the talks are adjourned.
30 September	A group of 76 Hindu followers of Sant Shadaramji visit Pakistan.
1 October	A delegation of Sikhs from different countries is led by American Sikh, Ganga Singh Dhillon, who is visiting Pakistan. They are feted by General Zia.
1–18 October	Agha Shahi makes a reference to Kashmir in a speech before the UN's General Assembly. Later Pakistan's Ambassador to the UN speaks in response to India's reply.
	Manzur Ilahi, a senior member of Pakistan's Civil Service Commission, visits India and holds discussions with members of the UPSC.
	Islamization measures are announced by President Zia, who also announces a decision to postpone indefinitely the elections scheduled for November 17.

15 November	General Zia visits Azad Jammu-Kashmir (POK) and declares that Pakistan will continue to support the Kashmiri people's right to self-determination and that his government has made India recognize the existence of the Kashmir dispute.
	Over a thousand Sikh pilgrims visit Nankana Sahib on the occasion of Guru Nanak's birthday. American Sikh Ganga Singh again visits Pakistan as a guest of General Zia.
	Prime Minister Charan Singh sends a message of sympathy on the death of 165 people in a PLA crash in Saudi Arabia.
17 November	Maulana Maududi, founder of Jammat-i-Islami, dies in Lahore.
21 November	The United States embassy in Islamabad is ransacked and burned by a mob. Two U.S. embassy officials die in the fire.
5 December	A staff member of the Indian embassy, on the way to his residence, is waylaid by Pakistan intelligence agents and taken into custody, where he is beaten up and interrogated. A strong protest is made to Pakistani Foreign Office by charge d'affaires S. K. Lambah.

1980

1 January	India's Ambassador K. S. Bajpai is called to Pakistan's Foreign Office and his attention is drawn to Prime Minister Charan Singh's statement on December 31, 1979, expressing concern over the U.S. decision to lift the arms embargo against Pakistan.
	K. S. Bajpai is reminded of Pakistan's long-standing offer to enter into negotiations with India for a mutually balanced reduction of forces.
	General Zia, in his inaugural speech at the Islamic Foreign Ministers'

	Conference, makes a deliberate and provocative reference to Kashmir.
4–7 February	India's foreign secretary R. D. Sathe visits Pakistan on February 4–7. He meets the president, his adviser on foreign affairs, and the finance minister. There are two rounds of discussions between the two delegations.
	A letter from India's prime minister is handed over to General Zia.
	The foreign secretary discusses the situation in the region arising from the induction of Soviet military troops into Afghanistan and tries to allay Pakistan's misgivings about the Indian stand with respect to developments in Afghanistan.
9 March	The Pakistan Cabinet authorizes Pakistan Steel to go ahead with negotiations with India for the purchase of 300,000 tons of iron ore.
14 March	The Zakat and Ushr Ordinance (No. XVII of 1980) is promulgated in Pakistan.
10–14 April	Sardar Swaran Singh, special emissary of Prime Minister Indira Gandhi, visits Pakistan. He meets General Zia and has two sessions with Agha Shahi. The discussions include the situation in Afghanistan. Singh tries to allay Pakistan's apprehensions regarding India's stand on Afghanistan. Pakistan revives the earlier proposal of military balance.
18 April	Prime Minister Indira Gandhi meets General Zia in Salisbury, Rhodesia (later Zimbabwe).
7 May	Hashim Qureshi, who along with five others had hijacked the IAC plane *Ganga* to Lahore in 1971 and had been sentenced to 14 years of imprisonment by the Special Court, is released by the Supreme Court.

14 May	K. S. Bajpai, on completion of his tenure, leaves Pakistan. K. Natwar Singh, the new ambassador, reaches Islamabad and presents his credentials on May 28.
21 May	A Pakistani delegation visits India for talks on the import of iron ore from India.
3 June	General Zia, in a television speech says that consequent upon the signing of an agreement between India and the Soviet Union for the purchase of arms worth 16,000 million rupees, "We are taking necessary steps to safeguard our sovereignty and national defence."
13–17 June	Two Sikh Jathas visit Pakistan to take part in the Gor Mela.
22 June	Tribal violence in Tripura, India, claims 1,000 lives.
25–27 June	Discussions between civil aviation authorities of the two countries are held in New Delhi.
15–17 July	Agha Shahi visits India. He meets Prime Minister Indira Gandhi twice and has two rounds of discussions. Afghanistan and bilateral relations are discussed.
16 August	The government of Pakistan issues a statement expressing "serious concern" at the widespread incidence of anti-Muslim violence in Moradabad and in other parts of India.
20 August	India's Ambassador K. Natwar Singh protests to General Zia for having issued a critical statement and says that it amounted to interference in the internal affairs of India.
21 August	K. Natwar Singh visits Karachi and meets Begum Nusrat Bhutto and Benazir Bhutto. He delivers to Begum Bhutto a letter from Prime Minister Indira Gandhi in which she thanks her for the message of

condolence on the death of Sanjay Gandhi.

4 September   An official of the Indian embassy in Islamabad is kidnapped, assaulted, and robbed, allegedly by Pakistani intelligence officers. He is questioned about the functioning of the embassy. A protest is lodged with the Pakistan foreign secretary by S. K. Lambah as well as with the Pakistan embassy at Delhi.

The Pakistan government in an official note discourages their nationals from visiting India.

22–26 September   Ram Jethmalani, member of parliament, and Acharya Vedalankar of the Friends of Afghanistan Organization visit Pakistan.

11–13 November   Another round of Indo-Pakistan technical level trade talks is held in Islamabad.

18 November   Pakistani Ambassador Abdus Sattar meets India's Prime Minister Indira Gandhi and gives her a message from General Zia.

K. Natwar Singh has three meetings with General Zia during the month at which bilateral relations are discussed.

A record number of 3,500 Sikh pilgrims visit Nankana Sahib on the occasion of the birth anniversary of Guru Nanak.

1 December   General Zia makes a statement reassuring the people of Pakistan that there is no threat to Pakistan from India. This statement comes after an intense anti-India propaganda in the Pakistani media on the occasion of Soviet President Brezhnev's visit to India.

25 December   Agha Shahi, speaking at the banquet given during his visit to Beijing, refers to Kashmir and says that Pakistan has been endeavoring to

evolve jointly with India a mutually acceptable solution of the Jammu-Kashmir dispute.

1981

10–12 January   K. Natwar Singh delivers a letter from Indira Gandhi to General Zia.

Pakistan releases 14 crew members of *Saraswati* and five other prisoners.

N. Krishnan, additional secretary (UN), Ministry of External Affaires (MEA), visits Pakistan and has discussions with Dr. Bhatti, additional secretary (UN) in the Pakistan Foreign Office, on the draft declaration for the forthcoming Non-aligned Foreign Minister's Conference.

26 January   K. Natwar Singh speaks on Pakistan television (for the first time) on India's Republic Day.

27 January   Sarod concert is held at the Indian Embassy in Islamabad on the occasion of India's Republic Day.

February   Agha Shahi leads a delegation held in New Delhi to the Non-aligned Foreign Ministers' Conference.

A special meeting of the Indo-Pakistan Indus Water Commission is held in Islamabad to discuss arrangements for the inspection of water works on the Ravi and Sutlej.

Nobel Laureate Professor Abdul Salaam visits India.

12 April   The Consul General of India, Mani Shankar Aiyer in Karachi, walk out of a meeting organized by the Institute of Foreign Relations in protest against the Institute Chairman's reference to the Kashmir issue in the context of racial discrimination in South Africa.

13 April   A 2,000-strong Sikh *Jatha,* led by Sardar Santokh Singh, visits Punja

Sahib. President Zia receives some members of the delegation.

8 June
Foreign Minister P. V. Narasimha Rao arrives in Pakistan. He meets General Zia and holds detailed talks with Foreign Minister Agha Shahi.

10 June
Joint press statement issued in Islamabad after discussions between P. V. Narasimha Rao and Agha Shahi. Results of visit are the diffusion of tensions, clarification on contentious issues including Afghanistan, increasing the number of cities in visas, from three to four, and Pakistan's decision to participate in trade fairs in India.

11 June
Narasimha Rao addresses the Pakistan Institute of International Affairs, Karachi.

30 June
K. Natwar Singh meets General Zia prior to going to Delhi for consultations.

July
A group of 400 Sikh pilgrims visits Pakistan on the occasion of death anniversary of Maharaja Ranjit Singh.

20 July
The Pakistan government announces a grant of loans to the chiefs of the erstwhile states of Kathiawar and Junagadh.

15 August
Ustad Asad Ali Khan, a Rudraveena player, performs in Karachi.

18 August
Pakistan Foreign Office spokesperson says that the alleged anti-India campaign is baseless and without any foundation. He is commenting on Indira Gandhi's remark in Nairobi expressing concern over the anti-India campaign mounted by Pakistan.

1–2 September
Pakistan Foreign Office spokesperson expresses "concern" over what he describes as "a recent ploy of false and fabricated news items that had appeared in some Indian newspapers." Lambath gives a protest note to Bhatti, additional secretary in the Pakistan Foreign Office.

15 September
The official spokesperson of the government of Pakistan issues a long statement announcing the formal acceptance by Pakistan of the package proposal for the supply and sale of U.S. arms to Pakistan.

The concluding portion of the statement is a paragraph suggesting Pakistan's readiness "to enter into immediate consultations with India for the purpose of exchanging mutual guarantees of non-aggression and non-use of force in the spirit of the pro-Simla Agreement." Even the government newspaper, the *Pakistan Times*, reports the principal thrust of this statement through its headlines: "Positive Turn in Dialogue with US." It is thus clear that this is the context in which Pakistan has made this suggestion. Copy of the Pakistan official spokesperson's statement is given to India's Ambassador in Islamabad the same evening.

29 September
An Indian Airlines Boeing, on a scheduled flight Delhi-Amritsar-Srinagar, is hijacked by five persons and forced to land at Lahore Airport.

Agha Shahi, commenting on Indira Gandhi's interview with *Le Figaro*, expresses surprise and disappointment at having chosen to question Pakistan's bona fides about the settlement of Afghan issue.

30 September
Hijackers leave the plane.

2 October
In a speech at the UN General Assembly, Agha Shahi refers to Kashmir and says, "the only outstanding dispute pertains to J and K [Jammu-Kashmir] which should be resolved in the spirit of the Simla Agreement and in the light of relevant UN agreements."

4 October	A group of students from St. Stephen's College, Delhi, visits Pakistan as guests of President Zia.
31 October	Pakistan's foreign secretary Piracha transits through Delhi, en route to Kathmandu.
November	An official Pakistani delegation to India's Trade Fair is led by President's Adviser Hamid D. Habib.
5 November	Pakistan Foreign Office spokesperson, through a handout, states that the Pakistani proposal for a Non-Aggression Pact has been given to Natwar Singh by Secretary-General Shah Nawaz on September 14.
16 November	A 3,000-strong Sikh *Jatha*, led by Prakash Majitha, visits Pakistan on the occasion of the birth anniversary of Guru Nanak.
20 November	Pakistan Commerce Secretary Izharul Haq visits India and holds talks with Indian Commerce secretary.
22 November	Pakistan government confirmed their offer of no-war pact in an official note communicated by them in Islamabad.
	Indo-Pakistan Hockey series is held.
6 December	India's Embassy sent a note to the Pakistan Foreign Office seeking permission for Natwar Singh and S. K. Lambah, along with their wives, to visit Charsadda (in NWFD) on 15 December to have lunch with Abdul Wali Khan. Permission is not given.
24 December	A seven-point aide-memoire given to the Pakistan Foreign Office in Islamabad by Natwar Singh stating the elements of an agreement on nonaggression and nonuse of force.

1982

3–31 January	Indira Gandhi suggests a friendship treaty with Pakistan in her meeting with Pakistani journalists. The matter also comes up for discussion during Agha Shahi's call on her.
12 January	An aide-memoire is handed over to Foreign Minister Narasimha Rao by Pakistan's Ambassador Abdus Sattar in response to the Indian aide-memoire of December 24, 1981, mentioning eight elements for a no-war pact.
17 January	Karan Singh, one of the Embassy chauffeurs, is waylaid by Pakistani intelligence personnel and beaten. A protest note is delivered by S. K. Lambah to the Pakistan government.
29 January	Agha Shahi visits India. Pakistan welcomes Indian prime minister's proposal to establish a joint commission.
1 February	Joint press statement, issued at the end of the visit of Agha Shahi, states that officials of the two countries will meet in Islamabad before the end of February 1982 to continue their exchange of views on the contents of the proposed agreements.
17–19 February	A reference to Kashmir is made by Agha Hilaly, leader of the Pakistan delegation to the Human Rights Commission in Geneva Replies are given by the leader of the Indian delegation B. R. Bhagat, MP.
19 February	P. V. Narasimha Rao, minister for external affairs, makes a statement in the Rajya Sabha on the recent visit to India of the Foreign Minister of Pakistan.
22 February	Forty-four developing countries belonging to the Group of 77, including Pakistan, participate in a conference in New Delhi. The Pakistani delegation is led by Niaz Naik, Pakistan's permanent representative to the UN in New York.

24 February As a result of the statement made by Agha Hilaly in Geneva, it is conveyed to the Pakistani Ambassador in New Delhi, that the Foreign secretary level talks for the no-war pact had to be postponed for the time being.

25 February P. V. Narasimha Rao makes a statement in the Lok Sabha in response to a Calling Attention Motion regarding the reported statement of the head of the Pakistani delegation Agha Hilaly, raising the issue of Kashmir at the meeting of the UN Human Rights Commission at Geneva and the reaction of the government.

A press release is issued by the government of Pakistan in Islamabad regretting the postponement by government of India of the visit of Foreign Secretary Sathe to Islamabad, which was to have taken place from March 1 to 4.

24 March P. V. Narasimha Rao makes a statement in the Rajya Sabha, calling attention to the situation arising out of the indefinite postponement of the official level talks on the no-war pact.

29 March Natwar Singh leaves Islamabad for New Delhi.

1 April In an interview given to Kuldip Nayar, General Zia says Gilgit, Hunza Skardu of the Northern Areas are not part of the "disputed territory."

3 April Lambat expressed concern to the Additional secretary, Pakistan Foreign Office, on the appointment (for the first time) of three observers from Northern Areas to the Pakistan Federal Council, the announcement of which is made by General Zia a few hours earlier on the same day.

Three thousand pilgrims visit Pakistan to celebrate Baisakhi Mela.

Pakistan's finance minister informs the Majlis-e-Shoora (Parliament) that, during 1980–1981, goods worth US$97,203,000 were exported to India while Pakistan's imports from India were worth US$2,207,000.

31 May Natwar Singh meets President Zia in Islamabad and hands over the Indian prime minister's letter to him. In his letter the prime minister reiterates his firm desire for friendship with Pakistan and calls for perseverance by both countries in an effort to restart the process of negotiations and as a first step proposes a meeting of the Joint Commission that could pave the way for discussions of friendship treaty and no-war pact.

One thousand Sikh *yatris* participate in the death anniversary celebrations of Guru Arjun Dev.

1 June Following Natwar Singh's meeting with General Zia, secretary-general in the Pakistan Foreign Office, S. Shah Nawaz, hands over to the Indian mission in Islamabad a draft of an "Agreement on Non-aggression, Renunciation of Force and Promotion of Good Neighbourly Relations."

26 June India's draft of the proposal for an Indo-Pak Joint Commission is handed over to the Pakistan CDA in New Delhi by Foreign Secretary M. Rasgotra.

2 July Both India and Pakistan issue statements on the 10th anniversary of the Simla Agreement.

3 July President Zia receives a 10-member delegation of Sikh *yatris*.

24 July President Zia sent felicitations and best wishes to Zail Singh on his election as president of India.

31 July A draft protocol on exchange of information, consular access, and modalities of rules and repatriation of prisoners/detainees of one country in the other is handed to the Pakistan embassy in New Delhi.

K. D. Sharma, the new Indian ambassador, arrives in Islamabad.

4 August An Indian Airlines plane is hijacked by a Dal Khalsa activist while on a regular flight from Delhi to Srinagar via Amritsar. The plane is refused permission to land at Lahore by the Pakistani government and lands instead at Amritsar.

K. D. Sharma presents his credentials to President Zia.

11 August A draft of a treaty of peace, friendship, and cooperation is given by M. Rasgotra in Islamabad to Pakistan's foreign secretary Niaz Naik.

15 August Bharati Shivaji, the Mohini Attam dancer, is denied permission to perform at the celebrations conducted for Independence Day.

22 August Pakistan and China sign a protocol on the opening of the Khunjerab border pass between POK and China's Sinkiang province.

Pradesh Congress President Murli Deora visits Pakistan.

27 August Sheikh Ishart Ali, President Zia's adviser on business coordination and internal trade, visits India.

7 September Tripartite coordination meeting on the implementation of Lahore–Amritsar coaxial cable link as part of the Asian Telecommunication Union is held in Lahore.

A group of Sikh pilgrims, mostly women, visits Pakistan.

October J. R. D. Tata commemorates 50 years of civil aviation in the subcontinent by piloting a Leopard Moth from Bombay to Karachi and back.

Two unofficial and one 3,000-strong official Sikh *jathas* visit Pakistan.

1 November Indira Gandhi receives Zia-ul Haq in New Delhi. During their meeting they authorize their foreign ministers and foreign secretaries to proceed with talks leading to the establishment of the South Asian Association for Regional Cooperation. It is also agreed to consider the Pakistani draft of a nonaggression pact and the Indian draft of a treaty of peace, friendship, and cooperation.

2 November India and Pakistan sign a protocol on the exchange of information and consular access to nationals of either country imprisoned or detained in the other.

For the first time in many years, a few Hindu pilgrims visit the Katas Raj temple in Pakistan.

A delegation of the Punjab, Haryana, and Delhi chambers of commerce, led by Veerendra Punj, visits Pakistan.

Professor Jabi, health adviser to the Pakistan president, visits India to attend the 7th International Conference on E and T Surgeons held in Surat.

December Pakistan Industries Minister Soomro visits Delhi to attend the closing ceremony of Asiad.

22–24 December Niaz Naik, Pakistan's foreign secretary, visits Delhi. There are discussions on a no-war pact and friendship treaty proposals. Differences continue on basic aspects.

Draft of the Joint Commission Agreement is initialed.

1983

17 January Foreign Secretary Natwar Singh visits Pakistan for consultations prior to the 7th Non-aligned Summit in New Delhi.

25 January The Pakistan government establishes an ombudsman's office, the Wafaqi Mohtasib.

18 February A trade and industry delegation of FICCI visits Pakistan.

10 March Joint Commission Agreement is signed by the two foreign secretaries in the presence of Indira Gandhi and General Zia during the Seventh Conference of Heads of State and Government of Non-aligned countries held in New Delhi.

April A 35-member Pakistani delegation of businesspeople and industrialists attend a seminar organized by the Federation of Indian Export Organisation in New Delhi.

A 3,000-strong Sikh *Jatha* visits Pakistan.

30 May An advance party of seven Indian officials, led by Natwar Singh, goes to Islamabad to hold an informal preparatory meeting.

4 June Foreign Minister Narasimha Rao visits Pakistan in connection with the first meeting of the Indo-Pak Joint Commission.

Its report is signed by the two foreign ministers in Islamabad.

The ministers reiterate the commitments of their governments to hold further discussions, at an early date, on Pakistan's proposal for an agreement on nonaggression and nonuse of force and on India's proposal for a treaty of peace, friendship, and cooperation.

July An Indian delegation visits Pakistan to hold discussions on the avoidance of double taxation between the two countries in the field of aircraft profits.

August Indira Gandhi's statement to the Indian Congress Parliamentary Board and her statement in the parliament on happenings in Pakistan are construed by the Pakistan government as interference in their internal affairs.

Professor Syed Hameed, vice chancellor of Jawaharlal Nehru University (JNU), visits Pakistan.

26 August India's prime minister sends a letter to General Zia expressing concern over the detention of Khan Abdul Ghaffar Khan.

9–17 September Six relatives of Indian defense personnel who are missing since the 1971 war visit Multan jail to find out whether any of their relatives are there.

11 October Pakistan Foreign Office spokesperson describes as totally false the allegation that Pakistan is providing arms assistance to militants in Punjab.

13 October Dr. Subramaniam Swamy, member of parliament and leader of India's Janata Party, pays a four-day visit to Pakistan.

The government of Pakistan decides to reduce postal rates on all surface letters in pursuance of the decisions taken at the Indo-Pakistan Joint Ministerial meeting.

25 October Additional Secretary Sattar summons Indian Ambassador K. D. Sharma and protests against the alleged anti-Pakistan references made during the Vishwa Sindhi Sammelan in New Delhi.

5 November Pakistan foreign minister Sahabzada Yaqub Khan makes strongly critical references to India in Majlis-e-Shoora, Pakistan's parliament.

Natwar Singh calls Pakistan's Ambassador Piracha to protest against the baseless allegation that

India opposes the anti-government Movement for the Restoration of Democracy in Pakistan.

A group of Hindu *yatris* visit the Katas Raj temple in Pakistan, and another group of Sikh *yatris* visits Sikh shrines in Pakistan.

1984

17 January — Agreed minutes of meetings of Sub-Commission I (economic matters including industry, agriculture, communication, health, scientific, and technological cooperation) and Sub-Commission II (trade) are issued from Islamabad.

21 January — Agreed minutes of Sub-Commission III (information, education including social sciences, culture, and sports) and Sub-Commission IV (travel, tourism, and consular matters) are signed in New Delhi.

A group of 500 Sikh *yatris* from India visits Pakistan.

February — The decision to hang Maqbool Butt, a leader of the so-called Kashmir Liberation Front, leads to protests by POK leaders, Kashmiri students, lawyers, and other groups.

12 February — A three-member Indian delegation, consisting of Haji Sulaiman, member of parliament, G. G. Banatwala, member of parliament, and Iqbal Ahmed, secretary, Delhi Pradesh Muslim League, goes on an 11-day visit to Pakistan. During their stay they call on President Zia, Foreign Minister Sahabzada Yaqub Khan, and others.

1–4 March — India's Foreign Secretary M. Rasgotra and his Pakistan equivalent, Niaz Naik, meet in Delhi and Udaipur. The latter discloses that the former will visit Islamabad from May 12 to resume discussions on Pakistan's offer of a no-war pact and India's proposal for a friendship treaty.

The Acting Chief Justice of Pakistan Mohammad Haleem and Aslam Riaz Hussain, Judge, Pakistan Supreme Court, pay a visit to New Delhi for the Third International Conference of Appellate Judges at the invitation of the chief justice of India.

30 March — A statement is made by P. V. Narasimha Rao in the Lok Sabha on a Calling Attention Notice regarding the situation arising out of the reported nuclear collaboration between Pakistan and China and the reaction of his government.

8 April — A 3,000-strong *jatha* of Sikh *yatris*, led by Sardar Natha Singh, goes on a 10-day visit to Pakistan for Baisakhi Festival at Punja Sahib.

11 April — A three-member delegation, led by the Commissioner for Indus Waters C. S. Hukmani, pays a five-day visit to Pakistan to inspect various dams on the Indus River.

19 April — A five-member railway delegation, led by P. S. Chaudhury, pays a visit to Pakistan to discuss with Pakistan Railway authorities the outstanding liabilities in the field of railways and arrangements for simplifying rail travel between the two countries.

28 April — The Union Agriculture Minister Rao Birendra Singh visits Pakistan with senior officials of the ministry of agriculture to attend the 17th Food and Agriculture Organization (FAO) Regional Conference in Islamabad.

19–23 May — M. Rasgotra leads a seven-member delegation to Islamabad. During the visit, there are discussions on a common text of the noncore articles of a no-war pact and Friendship Treaty and the preamble is evolved on an ad-referendum basis. However, there is no agreement on the two core articles in the Indian draft dealing with bilateralism and the nongrant of bases.

(a) Protocol on Group Tourism signed May 19–23.

(b) Exchange of letters between foreign secretaries of the two countries regarding amendments to the visa agreement of 1974.

26 May A 1,000-strong Sikh *jatha,* led by Guder Singh, exmember of the legislative assembly, goes to Lahore.

Throughout the first half of 1984 the number of apparently indiscriminate intercommunal killings in the Punjaba increases; so, too, do the killings within the Sikhs' community, as prominent moderate Sikhs come under attack from militants.

By the beginning of June over 400 people have been killed and nearly 2,000 injured since the imposition of India's presidential rule in October 1983. The demands of the Sikh agitators include:

- A greater degree of political and religious autonomy for Punjab.
- The incorporation into the state of Chandigarh (a union territory then serving as the state capital of both Punjab and Haryna).
- A greater share of river waters.
- The removal of controversial wording in subclause 2(b) of article 25 of the Indian constitution in which a reference to Hindus is "construed as including a reference to persons professing the Sikh, Jaina or Buddhist religion," this being taken as classifying Sikhs as a sect of Hinduism.

5–6 June During the night of June 5–6, the Indian army, in Operation Bluestar, begins an assault on the Golden Temple in Amritsar. Similar actions are launched simultaneously against 37 other Sikh shrines throughout Punjab. The army suffers heavy casualties in the assault as a consequence of the instruction not to damage the two most sacred parts of the temple, the Hamandir Sahib and the Akal Takht. Ultimately, however troops are unable to avoid causing considerable damage in capturing Akal Takht, which has been reinforced as the stronghold of the militants.

7 June In the basement of the Akal Takht, the bodies are found of S. J. Bhindranwale, Amirk Singh, and Major General Shubegh Singh, a former guerrilla warfare expert in the Indian army who had been dismissed for corruption in the mid 1970s.

Public reactions to the assault on the Golden Temple are widespread and, in some cases, violent, involving civilian disturbances and desertions by Sikhs from army units.

19 June At an Iftar party in Islamabad, President Zia says, "India's allegations accusing Pakistan of involvement in Sikh affairs in East Punjab is totally wrong, without foundation and highly irresponsible. . . ." He added that, even when Muslims are victims in India, he kept quiet, though his heart is bleeding for them because it is India's "internal affair."

Pakistan Labor Minister Ghulam Dastagir Khan, at a reception in London, says, "Those Pakistanis living abroad, who had sent a telegram to the Indian PM Indira Gandhi in which they had requested her to interfere in the internal affairs of Pakistan, should now learn a lesson from what Gandhi is doing in India. Gandhi has massacred thousands of Sikhs in Punjab and thousands of Muslims in Maharashtra."

26–27 June Pakistan Defence Minister Mir Ali Ahmed Talpur says, "What has happened now in the Indian Punjab is more than what happened in the Jallianwala Bagh massacre . . . by praying in the Golden Temple Gandhi cannot wash away the blood stains of these killings on her clothes . . . It is against civilized behaviour to destroy the shrine to flush out extremists."

5 July   An Indian Airlines Airbus A-300 with about 255 passengers on board is hijacked by nine Sikh extremists owing allegiance to Bhindranwale.

7–13 July   Information and Broadcasting Minister H. K. L. Bhagat pays an official visit to Pakistan. General Zia hosts a private dinner for him.

16 July   Pakistan's foreign secretary visits India for talks with the Indian foreign secretary on Pakistan's proposal for a no-war pact and the Indian proposal for a treaty of peace, friendship, and cooperation, scheduled for July 18 and to attend the meeting of the Joint Commission of India, scheduled for early August. Both are postponed at the suggestion of India, because of Pakistan's assistance to Sikh extremists.

26 July   Pakistan's Defence Minister Talpur, in an interview to *Hurmat Weekly,* says, "If for winning the elections genocide is going on 2 August in India, this is not something new. It is part of the game of the so-called democracy. But if Indira Gandhi tries an aggression against Pakistan in order to boost her popularity then we are also not sleeping."

23–25 August   A constitutional amendment permitting the extension of president's rule in Punjab for periods beyond one year is passed by the Indian parliament. (President's rule is extended for a further six months on October 4.)

The hijacking by Sikh militants of two Indian airlines, one in July and the other in August, ends peacefully. Allegations, however, that Pakistan supplied the hijackers with a gun during the second incident intensify Indian accusations that Pakistan is involved in the Sikh's agitation.

24 August   An Indian Airlines Boeing 737, on a flight from Delhi to Srinagar via Chandigarh and Jammu, is hijacked to Lahore by seven Sikh hijackers.

UNICEF Executive Director James Grant, through a Verbal Note to the Pakistan Foreign Office, "deeply regretted" a map in the UNICEF 1984 Annual Report that did not show the correct status of Jammu-Kashmir as a disputed territory.

30 August   Zia remarks in a speech to the Hyderabad Institute of International Affairs that, if Pakistan could refrain from speaking on behalf of 100 million Muslims in India, why should it speak for 10 million Sikhs?

October   A group of 74 Hindu pilgrims pays a visit to Hayat Pitafi temple about 100 kilometers (60 miles) from Sukkur.

9 October   A 16-member Indian cricket team (led by Sunil Gavaskar) pays a visit to Pakistan.

31 October   Gandhi is assassinated in New Delhi on October 31 by two Sikh members of her bodyguard. Her younger son, Rajiv (aged 40), is sworn in as prime minister later that day. As the news of her killing spreads, violence erupts in major cities.

India's armed forces are put on full alert, and security forces are ordered to shoot rioters on sight. After a week the official death toll from anti-Sikh riots in the capital alone is 500.

On receiving the news of Prime Minister Indira Gandhi's death, President Zia visits the Indian Mission and conveys his condolences to the ambassador.

3 November   Sixteen-hundred-strong Sikh *jatha,* led by former premier Singh Laipura visits Pakistan to celebrate the birth anniversary of Guru Nanak Dev at Nankana Sahib. It also visits other Sikh shrines in Pakistan.

4 November   General Zia attends the funeral of Indira Gandhi. President Zia meets India's new Prime Minister Rajiv Gandhi in New Delhi.

25 December   Jasbir Singh, a nephew of Bhindranwale, makes an unsuccessful attempt to enter Pakistan after he is deported from the UK and the UAE.

General Zia sends a congratulatory message to Rajiv Gandhi on his overwhelming victory in India's eighth general elections since independence.

1985

1 January   Non-Muslim banking is abolished in Pakistan.

26 January   Pakistan's President Zia attends the Republic Day reception hosted in Islamabad by India's Ambassador K. D. Sharma.

1 February   A four-member delegation of Agricultural Price Commission (APC) of Pakistan pays a 10-day official visit to India for technical discussions.

9 February   K. D. Sharma is invited to address the Pakistan National Defence College, Rawalpindi. He speaks on "Development of Indo-Pak Relations During the Past Decade, 1974–84."

11 February   The foreign secretaries of India and Pakistan meet at Mali.

25 February   General elections are held for the Pakistan National Assembly.

3 March   Muhammad Khan Junejo is appointed prime minister.

President Zail Singh and Prime Minister Rajiv Gandhi send congratulatory messages to President Zia on his assumption of office as president. The prime minister separately sends a message to Pakistan Prime Minister Mohammed Khan Junejo on his assumption of office.

9 March   Trial of the five hijackers of the Indian aircraft hijacked to Lahore in 1981 commences in Lahore.

13 March   Rajiv Gandhi and General Zia meet in Moscow for K. Chernenko's funeral. They discuss Indo-Pakistan relations.

2 April   The trial of the nine Sikh hijackers, who commandeered an Indian airliner to Lahore on July 5, 1984, gets underway in the Special Court, Punjab (Pakistan).

4–6 April   Foreign Secretary Romesh Bhandari pays a three-day visit to Pakistan as part of his visit to neighboring countries and especially to try for the resumption of dialogue with Pakistan for the normalization of relations.

8 April   A *yatris* of 692 Sikhs, headed by Sardar Gurcharan Singh Roshan, arrives in Pakistan on the occasion of the Baisakhi festival.

14 April   A delegation of women Sikh *yatris* calls on Begum Zia.

20 April   The trial of five Indian nationals, accused of hijacking of Indian airlines plane to Pakistan in 1981, resumes before the Special Court in Lahore.

30 April   A *jatha*, consisting of 75 Hindus led by Sat Pai Mittai, member of parliament, and the Rajya Sabha, visits the Katas Raj temple in Pakistan.

17–25 May   A Sikh *jatha*, comprising 340 pilgrims led by Surinder Singh Joshila, an Akali leader, pays a visit to

Pakistan to pay homage to the late Guru Arjun Dev.

2 June The Pakistan army releases four Indian engineers of J and K Power Development Board who were arrested on May 29 while conducting a survey in the frontier area.

8 June Foreign minister of Pakistan Sahabzada Yaqub Khan says in Islamabad that Pakistan has "categorically rejected" the Indian claim to the Siachen glacier that forms part of the northern area of Pakistan."

12 June Zain Noorani, Pakistan's minister of state for foreign affairs, reportedly states that Rajiv Gandhi has been repeating baseless statements about Pakistan's "peaceful" nuclear program.

Zain Noorani also alleges that Muslims in India are making statements in the National Assembly on the Ahmedabad riots. He expresses the hope that the Indian government will take steps to punish those guilty of inhuman and criminal violence against the minority community.

26 June A 434-strong Sikh *jatha,* headed by Sardar Kulwani Singh Dukhtya, a senior functionary of Akali Dal (Tara Singh group), goes to Pakistan.

2–4 July A 14-member delegation, headed by Sahabzada Yaqub Khan, attends the second round of the Indo-Pak Joint Ministerial Commission meeting in Delhi.

Agreed-on Minutes of Joint Commission, including meetings of four subcommissions, are signed.

Agreement on Agricultural Cooperation is signed at New Delhi, between Buta Singh and Sahabzada Yaqub Khan.

10 September S. K. Singh presents his credentials to President Zia in Rawalpindi.

22 September The Special Court at Lahore resumed its proceedings trying the nine Indians who had hijacked an Indian Airlines aircraft in July 1984.

23 September A high-capacity coaxial cable system is inaugurated in Islamabad.

23 October Rajiv Gandhi and Zia meet in New York for the 40th session of UNGA and discuss Indo-Pakistan relations.

A group of 120 Hindu *yatris* visits the holy temple of Shabani Durbar at Mirpur Methleo (Sindh).

26 October Sahabzada Yaqub Khan states in the Senate that, in the event of any attack on Kahuta nuclear installation, Pakistan will have no option but to retaliate with all its might.

2 November The Special Court at Lahore completes the hearing of the case against five Indian Sikhs who hijacked an Indian Boeing 737 to Lahore on September 29, 1981 and reserves its judgement.

5 November S. K. Singh calls on Khan Abdul Ghaffar Khan and extends to him an invitation from Rajiv Gandhi to attend the centenary celebrations of the Congress.

12 November At a press conference, President Zia says that the exigencies of time are such that the Khokrapara route will not be reopened.

14–16 November Pakistan Minister of Finance, Planning and Coordination Dr. Mahbubul Haq, Ejaz Naik, secretary-general (economic affairs), Mukhtar Masood, commerce secretary, and Dr. M. S. Jilani, Additional secretary (planning), visit India.

18 November Rajiv Gandhi and General Zia meet in Oman on the occasion of its 10th anniversary celebrations and discuss Indo-Pakistan relations.

26 November   Two Indian diplomats are assaulted by Sikh pilgrims at Gurdwara Dera Sahib, Lahore.

3 December   An 18-member delegation of women entrepreneurs, led by Bonti Barooah, goes on a goodwill visit to Pakistan. They call on General Zia.

7 December   Rajiv Gandhi and Zia meet in Dhaka for the SAARC Summit and discuss Indo-Pakistan relations.

17 December   Rajiv Gandhi has discussions with General Zia in Delhi. There is a brief discussion on the clause regarding bases of the proposed friendship treaty, and it is decided that the two foreign secretaries will discuss this when they meet in Islamabad in mid January.

30 December   India's martial law is lifted.

1986

8 January   Indian Finance Minister V. P. Singh, accompanied by finance and commerce secretaries among others, pays a two-day visit to Pakistan.

10–12 January   Talks are held in Rawalpindi between Indian Defence Secretary S. K. Bhatnagar and Pakistan Defence Secretary Syed Ijlal Haider Zaidi to discuss matters regarding the Siachen glacier.

16 January   Romesh Bhandari pays a five-day visit to Pakistan and has talks on important bilateral issues.

Pakistan Muslim League Council passes a resolution stating that relations between India and Pakistan "can be fruitfully normalised only after the Kashmir issue is settled on the basis of UN Resolutions."

18 January   Prime Minister Muhammed Khan Junejo is elected chair of the Pakistan Muslim League.

30 January   Dr. N. S. Randhawa, secretary, department of agricultural research and education, pays an official visit to Pakistan as the head of a five-member delegation.

4–5 February   Meeting of Sub-Commission III and Sub-Commission IV is held at Islamabad.

Correspondence (two letters) is exchanged between the governments of India and Pakistan regarding further amendments in the India-Pakistan visa agreement 1974.

6 February   Agreement is reached on the avoidance of double taxation of income derived from International Air Transport.

18 March   Rajiv Gandhi and Junejo meet in Stockholm for Olaf Palme's funeral and discuss Indo-Pakistan relations.

2–3 April   SAARC Ministerial meeting on international economic issues is held in Islamabad. A 14-point declaration is adopted.

8 April   A 237-member Sikh *jatha* visits Pakistan.

9 April   Vijaya Lakshmi Pandit calls on President Begum Zia in Islamabad.

17 April   Sahabzada Yaqub Khan calls on Rajiv Gandhi.

18 April   Niaz A. Naik and Foreign Secretary Venkateswaran meet in New Delhi.

19 May   A six-member delegation, led by Jaffeer Wafa, Pakistan additional secretary (communications), visits India to discuss modalities for reopening Khokrapar-Munnabao route.

25 May   India's Ambassador presents 3,000 books to President Zia.

30 May   Pakistan Minister of State for Foreign Affairs Zain Noorani meets Indian

Minister of State K. R. Narayanan in New York.

10–12 June
The second round of talks on Siachen glacier between S. K. Bhatnagar and Syed Ijlal Haider Zaidi take place in Delhi. It is agreed to continue the dialogue at a mutually convenient date.

Eight hundred and twelve Sikh pilgrims visit Pakistan.

Six Canadian Sikhs attack four members of the Indian Embassy liaison team at Gurdwar Dera Sahib, Lahore.

19 June
A delegation of the Board of Control for Cricket in India, led by N. K. P. Salve, member of parliament, visits Pakistan.

21 June
A Sikh *jatha* of 500 pilgrims visits Pakistan.

27 June
Tanvir Ahmed, first secretary, Pakistan embassy in New Delhi, is attacked by an unidentified group of persons.

28 June
A delegation of agricultural experts from Pakistan, headed by Amir Mohammad, Chairman of PARC, pays an eight-day visit to India.

1–4 July
A five-member Pakistani delegation of agricultural scientists, led by Dr. Amir Mohammad, chairman, Pakistan Agricultural Research Council, visits India (Hyderabad and New Delhi) to finalize details of an agreement on technical collaboration in various fields between the two countries. An annual work plan on agricultural cooperation is signed at New Delhi. The delegation also calls on Dr. G. S. Dhillon, agriculture minister.

23 July
The National People's Party (NPP) is formed under the chairmanship of Ghulam Mustafa Jatoi.

14 August
The Movement for the Restoration of Democracy (MRD) launches a campaign against the government, demanding fresh general elections.

15 August
The foreign secretaries of India and Pakistan, A. P. Venkateswaran and Abdus Sattar, exchange invitations for bilateral visits at SAARC Council Ministers' meeting in Dhaka.

4–6 October
A Pakistan delegation, headed by Mian Mohammad Javed, visits New Delhi and decides to introduce International Subscribers Dialling (ISD) to enable people to take on ISD for 55 cities in Pakistan and about 200 cities in India.

14 October
An Indo-Pakistan seminar on long-term planning is held at Islamabad under the aegis of the Indo-Pakistan Joint Commission. It is inaugurated by Dr. Mahbubul Haq, federal minister for planning and development. The six-member Indian delegation is led by Dr. Y. K. Alagh, chairman of Bureau of Industrial Costs and Prices

16 November
Rajiv Gandhi and Mohammed Khan Junejo meet during the SAARC summit at Bangalore and decide that the Interior Secretaries of the two countries should meet in Lahore to discuss problems of illicit border crossing, drug trafficking, smuggling, terrorism, and other issues.

19–21 December
A six-member delegation, led by C. G. Somaya, secretary home ministry, visits Islamabad and Lahore for talks with a Pakistan delegation led by S. K. Mahmud, secretary (interior).

22 December
A new federal cabinet is sworn into office by President Zia with Mohammad Khan Junejo continuing as prime minister.

26–28 December
At a meeting of foreign secretaries in Islamabad, A. P. Venkateswaran talks with Abdus Sattar.

1987

6 January
Four Indian trawlers with 60 crew members are seized by the Pakistan Maritime Security Agency (MS). Pakistan Defence Ministry officials claim that India seized 16 trawlers in 1986 and captured 290 Pakistani sailors on suspicion of being spies.

23 January
India's Army is placed on alert in Punjab and Rajasthan following failure of the Pakistan Army to withdraw from their forward positions after their winter exercises.

27 January
Pakistan's Prime Minister Junejo has a telephone conversation with Rajiv Gandhi on the border situation.

30 January–4 February
A five-member Pakistan delegation, led by Foreign Secretary Abdus Sattar and including three senior defense officers, visits India for the first round of talks to deescalate the border situation.

11–19 February
Troops are withdrawn from the Ravi-Chenab sector.

21–23 February
President Zia visits India at the invitation of the Board of Control for Cricket in India. He is accompanied by a delegation of 68 members. The visit is projected in Pakistan as a major diplomatic victory in Pakistan's current efforts to improve relations with India.

27 February
The second round of deescalation talks takes place in Islamabad.

2 March
The Pakistan government and press allege that two Pakistani trawlers were reportedly seized by India and 25 sailors were arrested in the last week of February.

In an interview with Kuldip Nayar, published in about five local newspapers, Pakistan's leading scientist Dr. A. Q. Khan declares the CIA is right in its assessment that Pakistan possesses nuclear capability.

7 March
Pakistan's Maritime Security Agency, Karachi, claims to have seized 11 Indian fishing boats with 96 fishermen on board for poaching in the territorial waters of Pakistan.

11 March
Eleven Indian trawlers are captured by Pakistani authorities. Reportedly, seven Pakistani fishing vessels are detained by Indian authorities.

27 March
An India-Pakistan Friendship Society is set up in New Delhi to promote trust, goodwill, and friendship.

28 March
A three-member delegation of Urban Development Organisations in Pakistan visits India in the last week of March.

7 April
The withdrawal of troops from the exercise area following Operation Brasstacks is completed, and both parties express satisfaction over the pace of withdrawal.

4 May
According to Ansar Burney, 38,362 Pakistani nationals who went to India during 1983–1986 are missing; they have not returned or conveyed any information about their well-being.

21–26 May
The Indo-Pakistan Indus Water Commission meets in Islamabad. The two sides agree to share flood forecasting data recorded at Talal Madhopur and Jammu.

27 May
An explosive device is thrown at India's Consul General Office, Karachi. An asbestos shed is damaged, but there are no injuries and no arrests by Pakistani authorities.

17–19 June
Pakistan foreign minister visits New Delhi to attend the third session of the Council of Ministers of SAARC and call on Rajiv Gandhi.

Pakistan minister for education, sports, and tourism says in the

National Assembly that Pakistan will review the question of its participation in sports with India in view of the behavior of spectators against the Pakistan cricket team at Ahmedabad in March.

24–30 June	Pakistan minister of state for foreign affairs makes statements in the National Assembly about the communal situation in India.
4 July	Khan Abdul Ghaffa Khan is hospitalized.
8 July	According to the BBC, an exchange of fire between Indian and Pakistani border guards at Wagah-Attari border is reported to have occurred July 10–14. A four-member Indian telecommunication delegation visits Islamabad for talks on the improvement of telecommunication links between India and Pakistan.
12 August	The Indo-Pakistan Sub-Commission on Economic Relations and trade meets in New Delhi to sort out differences on expansion of trade.
15 August	President Zia, accompanied by his foreign minister and foreign secretary, attends a reception given by the Indian Ambassador in Islamabad.
16 August	Badshah Khan returns to Pakistan. India's decision to confer Bharat Ratna Award on him arouses sharp controversy in Pakistan.
8–9 September	Joint-staff level talks take place between the two countries at Lahore on evolving new border ground rules.
30 September	Clashes in Siachen area are reported.
1–5 October	Siachen issue hits the headlines: an adjournment motion is disallowed in the National Assembly; Benazir calls for the removal of General Zia

for losing 1,500 square kilometers (579 square miles) of Pakistan territory.

Pakistan FM meets Indian minister of state for foreign affairs at New York for bilateral talks on trade and the regional situation.

A telecom link is established between the two countries.

The first round of official level talks on Tulbul Navigation Project is held at Islamabad.

4 November	Rajiv Gandhi meets Junejo at Kathmandu during the SAARC summit. It is decided to resume foreign secretary–level talks for bilateral discussions between the two countries. Defense secretaries are also expected to meet soon to try to find a solution to Siachen issue.
12–13 November	The second round of official level talks takes place in New Delhi.
30 November	Local bodies elections are held in the four provinces of Pakistan.
8–9 December	A four-member delegation, led by the Pakistan commerce secretary, visits India for talks on trade and economic cooperation.
18 December	Benazir Bhutto is married to Asif Ali Zardari in Karachi.

1988

20 January	Rajiv Gandhi visits Peshawar for 90 minutes on the demise of Khan Abdul Ghaffar Khan. Accompanying the prime minister are Sonia Gandhi; P. V. Narasimha Rao, minister for human resource development; Buta Singh, home minister; Mohsina Kidwai, minister for urban development; Saroj Khaparde, minister of state for health; P. Chidambaram, minister of state for internal security; Khurshid Alam Khan, former minister of state; and Mohammad Yunus.

26 January	President Zia attends the Republic Day reception hosted by the Indian Ambassador. He is accompanied by the Minister of State for Foreign Affairs Zain Noorani and Foreign Secretary Abdus Sattar.
10 February	A five-member Indian delegation arrives in Islamabad and holds talks on the release of fishermen. The Indian delegation is led by Indira Misra, member of the Joint Staff and minister of home affairs, while the Pakistan delegation is led by Anis Ahmad, JS, minister of defense.
	Both countries agree to release all the detained fishermen and vessels as a gesture of goodwill and understanding between the two countries.
23–24 February	The third round of bilateral talks on Tulbul Navigation Project is held at Islamabad. Pakistan delegation is led by Abdul Mahsud, secretary for water and power, and the Indian delegation by Naresh Chandra, secretary in the ministry of water resources.
25 February	Rajiv Gandhi speaks to General Zia on the telephone and invites him to visit Delhi to discuss the Afghanistan issue.
27 February	President Zia requests Rajiv Gandhi to visit Islamabad or send an envoy. The foreign secretaries of India and Pakistan speak by telephone, and an understanding is reached that the foreign secretary will visit Islamabad on March 1 as prime minister's special envoy. However, this is changed to February 29, and later Pakistan reneged on the agreement.
15 March	A 19-member delegation (Sir Syed Society), led by North West Frontier Province (NWFP) Governor Fida Mohammad Khan, commences a weeklong visit to India starting March 15. Fida Khan calls on Rajiv Gandhi during his visit.

Late March	The fourth round of official level talks is held at New Delhi.
	The Pakistan delegation is led by the secretary of the ministry of water and power, Abdul Rahim Mahsud, and the Indian delegation by his counterpart, Naresh Chandra.
10 April	An explosion in the ammunition depot in Ojheri army camp near Rawalpindi and Islamabad kills 100 people, injuring another 1000.
24–25 April	The second meeting of the Indo-Pakistan Committee to combat drug trafficking and smuggling takes place in Islamabad. The Indian delegation is led by B. V. Kumar, director general, narcotics control bureau.
3 May	Foreign Secretary K. P. S. Menon visits Islamabad as a special envoy of Rajiv Gandhi for talks on Afghanistan.
14–16 May	Pakistan Interior Secretary S. K. Mahmud visits India for talks with Home Secretary C. G. Somaya. The two sides agree that the Indo-Pakistan Committee on Border Ground Rules should meet within the next three months to finalize Border Ground Rules on the joint patroling of the border by the BSF and Pakistan Rangers to arrange regular meetings at Commander level Border Security Force (BSF) between the two forces to check smuggling, drug trafficking, and illegal border crossings and to curb the activities of terrorists.
24–27 May	The fifth round of talks on the Tulbul Navigation Project take place in Islamabad. The Indian delegation is led by Naresh Chandra.
	A 15-member delegation of the Indian Cotton Mills Federation, led by its Chairman S. K. Modi, visits Karachi. The delegation calls on the

Sindh governor and visits a textile mill in the province.

29 May | President Zia dismisses the Junejo government, dissolves the National Assembly and orders fresh elections within 90 days.

31 May | President Zia dissolves all provincial assemblies.

1–2 June | Abdul Sattar visits Delhi and calls on Rajiv Gandhi and other ministers. The two delegations hold talks covering a wide range of bilateral issues.

The Indian spokesperson says that Pakistan's abetting of terrorism in Punjab is bound to affect the process of normalization of relations between the two countries.

3–6 June | A three-day Indo-Pakistan convention on "Partners in Prosperity Through Tourism" is held at Lahore. It is jointly organized by Secretary (Tourism) S. K. Mishra from Indian side and Aslam Rahim, secretary for tourism and culture from Pakistan. Both sides indicate their official willingness to consider recommendations to expand tourism between the two countries.

27 June | Secretary (Posts) P. S. Raghavachari leads a two-member delegation on July 1 to Pakistan for talks with Pakistan postal authorities. Both sides discuss various operational details, including the settlement of outstanding postal and postal life insurance dues, and closer operation to improve postal services between the two countries.

Sikh *yatris* visit Pakistan during the month of observance of Maharaja Ranjit Singh's birth anniversary and the martyrdom of Guru Arjun Dev.

3 July | A conference on the Indian Ocean, held in Islamabad, is inaugurated by President Zia. An Indian delegation participates in the conference. The Pakistan minister for science and technology publicly proposes that regional headquarters be established in Pakistan.

5 July | President Zia plays host to two young students of St. Stephen's College–Jitendra Narain and Jaideep Saikia.

17 August | President Zia is killed in a plane crash near Bahawalpur in Punjab, along with other senior officers of the Pakistan Army, including Chairman of the Joint Chiefs of Staff General Akhtar Abdur Rahman and Arnold Raphael, U.S. ambassador to Pakistan. Ghulam Ishaq Khan, chairman of the Senate, is sworn in as acting president. General Mirza Aslam Beg is appointed chief of the Army staff.

India declares a three-day mourning for the death of President Zia.

20 August | President R. Venkataraman attends General Zia's funeral accompanied by External Affairs Minister P. V. Narasimha Rao, Minister for Environment Z. R. Ansar, Minister of State for External Affairs K. Natwar Singh, 11 members of parliament belonging to different political parties, the foreign secretary, and other senior officers.

22–24 September | The fourth round of defense secretary–level talks on Siachen take place in Delhi. Pakistan Defence Secretary Syed Ijlal Haider Zaldi and Indian Defence Secretary T. N. Seshan lead their respective delegations. Zaidi calls on Rajiv Gandhi and Defence Minister K. C. Pant.

2–3 October | Minister of Commerce Dinesh Singh leads a five-member delegation that includes Cabinet Secretary B. G. Deshmukh and Commerce Secretary A. N. Verma for an informal GATT Ministerial meeting held in

Islamabad. Dinesh Singh calls on Pakistan President Ghulam Ishaq Khan and holds talks with Minister for Finance and Commerce R. Mahbubul Haq.

17 November   Elections are held for the National Assembly. The Pakistan People's Party wins 92 out of the 207 seats contested.

30 November   Brigadier Z. I. Abbasi, military attaché, and Mohammad Ashraf Khatib, staff member in Pakistan mission in New Delhi, are expelled after being declared persona non grata. In a retaliatory move, B. D. Sharma, India's consul in Karachi, and a staff member of India's High Commission (HCI), Islamabad, are declared persona non grata by Pakistan's Foreign Office.

A Sikh *jatha* of 3,014 pilgrims from India visits Pakistan on the occasion of anniversary of Guru Nanak.

2 December   Benazir Bhutto is sworn in as prime minister.

12 December   Ghulam Ishaq Khan is elected president of Pakistan.

29–31 December   Rajiv Gandhi, accompanied by Sonia Gandhi, visits Islamabad to attend the Fourth SAARC summit.

India and Pakistan sign three agreements:
1. Agreement on the prohibition of attack against nuclear installations and facilities.
2. Agreement on cultural cooperation.
3. Agreement on avoidance of double taxation of income derived from international air transport.

India's prime minister Rajiv Gandhi and Pakistan's prime minister Benazir Bhutto address a joint press conference. Both describe the talks and agreements as important

confidence-building measures and agreed to hold more frequent meetings.

1989

22 January   A 16-member under-19 Indian cricket team arrives in Pakistan for a six-week tour of Pakistan.

14 February   Ambassador S. K. Singh leaves Islamabad for New Delhi to take over as foreign secretary.

17–21 February   A 13-member delegation of cotton traders from the East Cotton Association visits Pakistan to explore the possibility of buying cotton from Pakistan. The delegation visits Karachi, Multan, and Islamabad.

9 March   A seven-member delegation, led by Pramod Doshi, visits Karachi in the second week of March and meets tea traders in Karachi.

10 March   The Supreme Court rules that the May 29, 1988, dissolution of Pakistan's National Assembly is unconstitutional.

13 March   In the Punjab assembly, Chief Minister Nawaz Sharif wins a vote of confidence in a session demanded by the Pakistan People's Party (PPP).

5–14 April   A *jatha* of over 3,000 Sikh pilgrims visits Pakistan on the occasion of Baisakhi.

16 April   Ambassador J. N. Dixit presents his credentials in Islamabad.

10–12 May   The Director General (Civil Aviation) P. C. Sen. leads a 10-member delegation to Karachi for bilateral talks with Pakistan. The Pakistani delegation is led by the acting Director-General Civil Aviation Authority Ehtashan Akram. The two sides agree to enhance the capacity entitlement of their designated carriers and also to discuss technical matters relating to air traffic service.

11–16 May Adviser (Traffic) Railway Board S. P. Jain leads a five-member railway delegation to Pakistan for talks with Pakistani railway authorities. The Pakistani delegation for the talks, which are held in Lahore and Islamabad, is led by Minister (Traffic) Zahoor Ahmed.

The two sides agree to restore travel for nationals from both countries on all seven days of the week by rail crossing at the Wagah-Attari border.

16–23 May Pakistan's Minister for Tourism Yousuf Raja Gilani leads a four-member delegation to India to participate in the Second Convention of Indian and Pakistani Tour Operators.

21–24 May The Pakistan government approves a 20-year plan for developing nuclear power generation.

The third round of the home secretary–level talks take place in Islamabad. The Indian delegation is led by Home Secretary J. A. Kalyanakrishnan and the Pakistani delegation by Interior Secretary S. K. Mahmud.

2 June The talks between the surveyors general of India and Pakistan, Major General S. M Chadha and Major General Anis Ali Syed, are held on the land and sea boundaries in the Sir Creek. The talks ended in Islamabad without any substantive agreement.

4 June Ghulam Mustafa Jatoi is elected to lead a 94-member opposition coalition in the National Assembly.

14–17 June Defence Secretary Naresh Chandra leads a six-member delegation to Islamabad for the fifth round of talks on Siachen. The Pakistani delegation is led by Defence Secretary Syed Ijlal Haider.

27–29 June India's foreign secretary visits Islamabad for a meeting of the SAARC Standing Committee.

10–11 July The Army Commanders of India and Pakistan (led by Pakistan Director-General, Joint Staff Headquarters Lieutenant General Imtiaz Warrich and India's Director-General of Military Operations (DGMO) Lieutenant General V. K. Singh) meet at New Delhi to discuss points of the redeployment of armies of two countries in Siachen. They agree to meet again in Islamabad in August.

16 July Rajiv Gandhi pays a two-day visit to Islamabad on his way back from Moscow to New Delhi. He is accompanied by Sonia Gandhi, P. V. Narasimha Rao, and senior officials. This is the first bilateral visit of an Indian prime minister to Pakistan since 1960.

18–19 July The India-Pakistan Joint Ministerial Commission holds its third meeting in Islamabad. The delegations of the two countries are led by their foreign ministers.

23–24 July Foreign Minister Sahabzada Yaqub Khan visits New Delhi as a follow-up of his visit to Colombo to resolve the crisis about holding SAARC meetings. He meets Rajiv Gandhi and senior officials and offers Islamabad as a venue for the bilateral discussion between India and Sri Lanka to resolve their differences.

17 August A three-member Indian military delegation, led by DGMO Lieutenant General V. K. Singh, visits Islamabad for the second round of army commanders–level talks on the deployment of forces in the Siachen sector.

21 August A Pakistan embassy official Abdul Shakoor is apprehended in New Delhi for espionage.

20 September	Prime Minister Benazir Bhutto reshuffles her cabinet.
	Pakistan expels a staff member from India's mission, H. C. Pandey. This is in retaliation for the expulsion of a Pakistani High Commission staff member, Abdul Shakoor, by India in August.
1 October	Pakistan rejoins the Commonwealth.
31 October	Prime Minister Benazir Bhutto survives a vote of no confidence by a narrow margin of 12 votes.
11 November	Prime Minister Bhutto includes three members from Islami Jamhoori Ittehad (IJI), the coalition in opposition in her cabinet.

1990

7–11 January	Pakistan's ambassador to Moscow and former ambassador to India, Abdus Sattar, visits New Delhi as a special envoy of Benazir Bhutto.
15–17 January	The seventh Indo-Pak Telecom Operational Coordination meeting is held in Karachi.
21–23 January	Sahabzada Yaqub Khan visits New Delhi and meets Rajiv Gandhi and the external affairs minister in connection with holding a SAARC summit. The Kashmir issue is also discussed.
2 February	Official-level Indo-Pakistan talks on fishermen and fishing boats are held in New Delhi.
2–9 February	A government-sponsored solidarity week on Kashmir is observed in Pakistan.
5 February	A nationwide strike is called by the IJI in support of Jammu-Kashmir. February 5 is declared a national holiday by the federal government of Pakistan.
10 February	Benazir convenes a joint session of parliament, and Sahabzada Yaqub

	Khan proposes a resolution expressing solidarity with the people of Jammu-Kashmir. The resolution is adopted unanimously.
11 February	Six persons are shot by Indian security forces when a mob crosses the LoC in Chakothi in POK.
	Pakistan government sends the following special emissaries to mobilize world public opinion on Kashmir:
	Member for Manpower and Overseas Pakistanis Ghulam Mohd Ahmed Khan Maneka goes to the Middle East and Australia on a seven-day visit.
	Adviser on Foreign Affairs Iqbal Akhund goes to China, Moscow, Washington, and Brussels.
	Law Minister Syed Iftikhar Hussain Gilani goes to Saudi Arabia and Kuwait. He also meets the Organisation of Islamic Conferences (OIC) secretary-general.
	Minister of State for Finance Ehsan ul Piracha goes to Algeria.
	Pakistan's Foreign Secretary Tanwer Ahmed Khan visits Jordan Paris and Ankar between January 30 and February 7.
	Ambassador Happy Minwala visits the United States, France, the United Kingdom, Belgium, and the Netherlands.
	Delegations are also sent out by POK.
13 March	Benazir Bhutto refers to the situation in Kashmir as a *jihad*. During her first visit to POK as prime minister, she gives a highly provocative anti-India speech.
23 March	While addressing the Joint Services parade, President Ghulam Ishaq

Khan criticizes India's defense budget and states that the only possible solution to the Kashmir issue is through UN resolutions.

1 April   Official notification for the setting up of "prime minister's funds for welfare and relief for Kashmiris" is issued.

Benazir again makes an aggressive statement referring to Zulfikar Ali Bhutto's determination to fight over Kashmir for "a thousand years." After Prime Minister V. P. Singh's speech in India's parliament on April 10, President Ghulam Ishaq Khan and Chief of Army Staff M. A. Beg issue statements saying that war is not in the interest of India and Pakistan.

15 April   Foreign Ministers I. K. Gujral of India and Sahabzada Yaqub Khan of Pakistan meet in New York.

24 April   IJI chief, Senator Qazi Hussain Ahimed, stages a *jihad* rally in front of India's High Commission in Islamabad.

A five-member Indian Science and Technology delegation, led by Dr. A. P. Kulshreshta, visits Pakistan for a week.

25 April   Talks are held in New York between Sahabzada Yaqub Khan and I. K. Gujral on the situation in Kashmir.

5 May   A three-member delegation from the Center for Policy Research, India, headed by Pai Panandiker and including I. P. Singh and Dr. Bhabani Sen Gupta, visits Lahore and Islamabad.

14 May   Punjab Chief Minister Nawaz Sharif says that, if India attempts to attack Pakistan, each Kashmiri will dominate 1,000 Hindus.

15 May   An International Conference on Kashmir is organized by Jamaat-i-Islami in Lahore in support of the "freedom movement" of the people of Jammu-Kashmir. This is attended by delegates from Bangladesh, Palestine, Afghanistan, and the Philippines.

24 May   Benazir Bhutto at a press conference says that demand for a separate state for Kashmir was not envisaged in 1947. The proposal for an independent Kashmir could have dangerous consequences for India and Pakistan.

30 May   Ethnic violence in Karachi spreads to a number of areas in the city, bringing the death toll to 103 in four days of fighting.

2 June   Ethnic troubles continue in Karachi, bringing the total number of dead to 200.

18 June   Jammu and Kashmir Liberation Front (JKLF) leader announces the formation of a provincial government of an independent state of Jammu-Kashmir.

22 June   Benazir, in an interview to French daily *Le Figaro,* says that the people of Kashmir should be allowed to decide their own future; neither Pakistan nor India has the right to decide for them.

10 July   Benazir Bhutto arrives in Baghdad, Iraq, at the start of her second mission to the Middle East to solicit support for Pakistan on the issue of Kashmir.

17–20 July   Following an Indian CBM package proposal, the first round of talks by Foreign Secretaries (Muchkund Dubey and Tanvir Ahmed Khan) is held in Islamabad. Little progress is achieved as the Pakistan delegation continued to focus on Kashmir and redeployment of Indian troops.

20 July   The Standing Committee of the Pakistan Senate on Religious and Minorities Affairs, takes "strong note of the continuous violation of the Nehru-Liaquat Agreement."

6 August	President Ghulam Ishaq Khan dismisses Prime Minister Benazir Bhutto, dissolves the National Assembly, and orders national elections for October 24, 1990. Ghulam Mustafa Jatoi, the leader of the opposition in the National Assembly is sworn in as caretaker prime minister.
10–12 August	The second round of foreign secretary–level talks is held in New Delhi.
	Border incidents on August 12 in Kel sector and a speech by V. P. Singh are played up by the Pakistan media.
September	L. K. Advani leads a march (Rath Yatra) beginning in September and lasting several weeks, through northwestern India, culminating in Ayodhya and the destruction of a famous mosque.
	The government of Pakistan imports 500 tons of onions from India. The Indian offer is the lowest; other bidders are Turkey, China, and Spain.
7 October	During a private visit to India, former Information Minister Maulana Kausar Niazi calls on V. P. Singh. He also meets with Rajiv Gandhi.
8 October	Four staff members of CGI, Karachi are expelled.
24 October	Elections are held all over Pakistan; Bhutto's PPP loses in all the provinces to IJI.
3 November	IJI student demonstration set on fire a Hindu temple in NWFP and a Krishna Kali temple in Lahore in the wake of the Ram Janambhumi-Babri Masjid issue. Attacks on other *mandirs* (temples) and Hindu laborers are also reported.
10 November	Nawaz Sharif is sworn in as prime minister of Pakistan.

21–23 November	Nawaz Sharif meets Chandra Shekhar at Male during the fifth SAARC's summit.
25 November	The wife of an official of the Indian High Commission in Islamabad is abducted. Harassment and intimidation of Indian families increase, and a number of unprovoked incidents take place during this month.
29 November	Nawaz Sharif has a telephone conversation with Chandra Shekhar and sends greetings, reiterating his desire to develop cooperative and good neighborly relations with India based on sovereign equality and mutual benefits.
15 December	Pakistan's cabinet, under the chairmanship of Prime Minister Nawaz Sharif, decides to allow the establishment of passenger airlines in the private sector.
18–20 December	The third round of foreign secretary–level talks takes place in Islamabad. Pakistan media report the harassment of five diplomatic officers of Pakistan in Delhi.

1991

5 January	Rallies and demonstrations are held in Pakistan to express solidarity with the movement for self-determination in Kashmir.
	Nawaz Sharif, in his message, pledges that the government and people of Pakistan will continue to extend political, moral, and diplomatic support to Kashmiri Muslims.
	The Pakistani government announces plans to distribute 350,000 acres of its land to the *haris* (landless peasants) in Sind.
9 January	A letter of intent for privatization of Muslim Commercial Bank is handed over to successful bidders.

12 January — A meeting of Council of Common Interests is held under the chairmanship of Prime Minister Nawaz Sharif after a gap of almost 16 years.

17 January — Countrywide rallies are held in protest against U.S.-led attack on Iraq.

18 January — Demonstrations are held all over Pakistan to protest against the bombing of Iraq by the United States and other coalition forces.

27 January — Indo-Pakistan agreement on the prohibition of attacks on each other's nuclear installations and facilities comes into effect.

Pakistan's Senate adopts resolution condemning the United States and United Kingdom for carrying out indiscriminate bombing against Iraq.

1 February — A devastating earthquake hits the Northern Areas of Pakistan. The death toll is estimated at more than 1,000.

5 February — A day of Solidarity with the People of Kashmir is commemorated in Pakistan and POK. Nawaz Sharif declares it a public holiday.

7 February — Nawaz Sharif announces a 25-point foreign exchange reform program.

14 February — Pakistan's National Assembly unanimously adopts a resolution condemning the killing of Iraqi civilians by allied forces.

25 February — POK Prime Minister Rathore states that the Jammu-Kashmir people are not ready to recognize any fictitious LoC, rejecting Dr. Farooq Abdullah's suggestion that the LoC be considered a permanent border in Kashmir.

Film director Randhi Kapoor, accompanied by his unit, visits Pakistan to shoot his film, *Henna*, clearance for which is obtained at prime minister's level.

14 March — Elections are held to Pakistan's Senate. The government coalition, IJI, maintains its control of the upper house.

16–17 March — Federal Interior Minister Chaudry Shujat Hussain, accompanied by his brother-in-law, Ch. Parvaiz Elahi, minister of local government and tourism in Punjab, and by other family members, pays a private visit to Delhi to grieve the death of Delhi-based industrialist Talwar.

21 March — Nawaz Sharif announces an agreement on apportionment of Indus waters.

26 March — Four Pakistanis hijack a Singapore Airlines aircraft en route from Kuala Lumpur to Singapore.

5–7 April — The fourth round of foreign secretary–level talks, headed by Shaharyar Khan and Muchkund Dubey, held in Delhi, is preceded by talks by Major General Arshad Malik, Pakistan Surveyor General, along with his Indian counterpart, on the delimitation of the maritime boundary in Sir Creek.

A high-level military delegation, led by Lieutenant General Shamim Alam Khan, visits Delhi for discussions. Two agreements are signed on "advance notice of military exercises and manoeuvres" and "prevention of air space violations."

11 April — A Shariat Bill is introduced in Pakistan's National Assembly by Minister of State for Law Ch. Amir Hussain.

14 April — Pakistan's Federal Food and Agriculture Minister Lieutenant General (Ret.) Abdul Majid Malik announces a new agricultural policy effective as of April 16.

The Shariat Bill is adopted by Pakistan's National Assembly by 109 votes to 29.

20 April   Nawaz Sharif announces the National Finance Commission Award.

28 April   The Shariat Bill is passed by Pakistan's Senate, 40 votes to 3.

22 May   While on an election campaign in Tamilnadu, Rajiv Gandhi is assassinated by a Sri Lankan. Pakistan's Senate adopts a condolence resolution expressing deep sorrow over this tragic death.

President Ghulam Ishaq Khan and Nawaz Sharif send condolences to Sonia Gandhi. President Ghulam Ishaq Khan visits India's High Commission to sign the condolence book.

24–25 May   Nawaz Sharif visits Delhi, accompanied by Minister Rana Chander Singh. Information Adviser Sheikh Rashid, Foreign Secretary Shaharyar Khan, and others attend the funeral rites of Rajiv Gandhi.

Benazir Bhutto, accompanied by former Federal Ministers Iftikar Gilani and Yusuf Raza Gilani and PPP Information Secretary Salman Taseer, also visits Delhi to attend the funeral rites.

31 May   An Army ammunition depot near Nowshera (NWFP) blows up, killing more than 20 people and destroying approximately 1,000 tons of ammunition.

India's general election is held May–June. Congress emerges with the most parliamentary seats, though still short of a majority, and forms a government headed by P. V. Narasimha Rao.

6 June   In an address to the National Defence College, Rawalpindi, Nawaz

Sharif puts forward a proposal that the United States, the Soviet Union, and China consult and meet with India and Pakistan to discuss and resolve the issue of nuclear nonproliferation in South Asia.

The International Conference on "gross and systematic violation of human rights" in India is held in Islamabad.

JKLF leader Amanullah Khan speaks in favor of placing the entire Jammu-Kashmir under UN trusteeship for a period of five years, following which people would exercise their rights of self-determination.

11 June   Notification is issued announcing Lieutenant General Asif Nawaz Janjua as the new COAS as of August 16 when General Beg retired.

Lieutenant General Shami Alam Khan is appointed chairman of JCSC, effective November 9.

12 June   A summary of the main findings of PDA's white paper on rigging in the previous year's elections in Pakistan is released by PDA Secretary-General Khurshid Mahmud Kasuri.

17 June   Local Pakistani papers report that the Pakistani army has achieved a major victory in Siachen by capturing a post of considerable importance.

2 July   POK Prime Minister Mumtaz Rathore invalidates the June 29 general elections and accuses the government of Pakistan of interfering with the electoral process.

5 July   The GOP sacks caretaker POK Prime Minister Mumtaz Rathore and arrests him under the Maintenance of Public Order Ordinance.

11 July   The Muslim Conference nominates Sardar Qayyum as the new POK prime minister.

16 July	Thirty-seven Indians, held in Pakistan jails, and 39 Pakistanis, held in Indian jails, are exchanged at the Wagah checkpoint.
18 July	Pakistan's National Assembly adopts the 12th Constitutional Amendment Bill, which authorizes the federal government to establish special courts to curb so-called heinous crimes.
19 July	POK's accession day is celebrated in Pakistan to mark the resolution adopted by the All Muslim Congress (AMC) in 1947.
	Nawaz Sharif sends a special message urging the world community to take action to halt atrocities being committed by Indian security forces.
29 July	Sardar Qayyum takes the oath as POK prime minister.
30 July	Fourth meeting of Indo-Pakistan Committee to combat drug smuggling is held in Islamabad.
16 August	Lieutenant General Asif Nawaz is promoted to the rank of general and takes charge as COAS.
18–20 August	Shaharyar Khan visits Delhi as a special envoy of Pakistan's prime minister. During his stay, he calls on prime minister and defense minister and holds meetings with Foreign Secretary Dubey. He also hands over a letter from Nawaz Sharif to Narasimha Rao.
21 August	Nawaz Shariz addresses a rally held to mark the anniversary of the beginning of resistance against the then ruling family of Dogras on August 23, 1947. He reiterates Pakistan's obligation to continue political and moral support to Kashmiris fighting for self-determination.
6–9 September	Samjhauta Express is fired upon by Sikh militants; one Pakistani is killed

	and 20 injured. The Pakistan Foreign Office conveys a strong protest on the incident.
10 September	Nawaz Sharif expands his cabinet, raising its size by 12 new ministers to 50. Seventeen ministers of state and one adviser are sworn in.
24 September	PDA releases a 517-page white paper on rigging in the 1990 elections.
24–27 September	A five-member military delegation, led by DG (Military Operations) Lieutenant General Satish Nambiar, visits Islamabad for talks with Lieutenant General Pirdad Khan, DG (JCSC). Military delegations discuss the recent incident of firing along the LoC and agree to establish contacts between specific sector commanders and to continue future discussions on additional confidence-building measures.
1 October	The fifth round of foreign secretary–level talks is held in Islamabad, headed by Dubey and Shaharyar Khan. Dubey also meets with Ghulam Ishaq Khhan Nawaz Sharif, Minister of State Kanju, and S. G. Akram Zaki.
	It is agreed that the sixth round of foreign secretary–level talks will be held in Delhi in early 1992, preceded by meetings on the Tulbul Navigation project, Sir Creek, and chemical weapons.
7 October	On his return from United Nations General Assembly, Minister of State Kanju in a press conference declares that he has urged Foreign Minister Solanki to accept Pakistan's proposal for deployment of international observers along the LoC.
12 –15 October	The seventh round of secretary–level talks on Tulbul Navigation project, headed by Indian Water Resources Secretary Dr. M. A. Chitale and his Pakistan counterpart, S. R. Poonegar, is held in Islamabad.

17 October   Narasimha Rao has a breakfast meeting with Nawaz Sharif in Harare (Zimbabwe). This is the first meeting between the two prime ministers. It is announced that both sides will continue their dialogue and redouble their efforts to find a solution for all outstanding disputes.

25–28 October   Secretary–level talks on the demarcation of the land boundary in the Sir Creek area and the delimitation of maritime boundary are held in Rawalpindi.

Board of Control for Cricket in Pakistan (BCCP) announces that Pakistan cricket team's tour to India to play five one-day matches has been postponed due to threats from militant Hindus. Earlier Benazir Bhutto has also written to Nawaz Sharif for postponement of the tour in protest against Indian policies in Jammu-Kashmir.

2 November   A Pakistani Foreign Office spokesperson states that the government of Pakistan, GOP, and people are outraged and anguished over the desecration and damage to the Babri mosque.

12 November   High Commissioner J. N. Dixit pays a farewell call on President Ghulam Ishaq Khan. The latter reiterates Pakistan's desire to promote peaceful relations with India on the basis of justice and sovereign equality.

13 November   Nawaz Sharif tells Dixit that SAARC should be made more effective to promote peace and development in the region, when the latter calls on him. Foreign Office Secretary-General Zaki hosts a lunch in honor of Dixit.

14 November   Dixit leaves Islamabad to take up his appointment as India's foreign secretary.

24 November   Pakistan's Supreme Court refuses appeal petition by Sikh hijackers Harminder Singh and Ravinder Singh, who claimed to be citizens of Pakistan on the grounds that they are citizens of Jammu-Kashmir. The two accused participated in hijacking an IAC airbus on a flight from Srinagar to Bombay.

11 December   Jammu and Kashmir Liberation Front Chief Amanullah Khan announces that JKLF will cross the cease-fire line in Kashmir on February 11.

28 December   In an interview with *Hindustan Times*'s editor H. K. Dua, Nawaz Sharif suggests that India and Pakistan commence a dialogue at a high political level to resolve Kashmir and other bilateral issues.

1992

1 January   India and Pakistan exchange lists of nuclear installations and facilities in pursuance of the Agreement on Non-attack of Nuclear Installations.

5 January   Right of Self-determination Day for the Kashmiris is observed in Pakistan and Azad Jammu-Kashmir. Several protest rallies are organized.

23 January   India's new high commissioner to Pakistan, S. K Lambah, presents his credentials to President Ghulam Ishaq Khan.

26 January   India's high commissioner, S. K. Lambah, calls on Prime Minister Nawaz Sharif.

29 January   A presidential ordinance is promulgated establishing the Indus River System Authority.

2 February   Narasimha Rao and Nawaz Sharif meet in Davos, Switzerland.

5 February   In response to a call by Nawaz Sharif, a strike is observed in Pakistan to "express solidarity with the Kashmiris."

6 February	Pakistan's National Assembly adopts a resolution on Kashmir.
11–12 February	JKLF attempts to cross the LoC. Fourteen people are killed and more than 115 injured in the confrontation with paramilitary personnel.
	GOP dispatches the following special emissaries to mobilize world opinion on Kashmir.
	Defence Minister Ghous Ali Shah visits Saudi Arabia and Oman.
	Minister for Food, Agriculture and Cooperatives, Lieutenant General (Ret.) Abdul Majid Malik visits Morocco, Senegal, Cape Verde, and Nigeria.
	Minister for Environment Anwar Saifullah visits Brazil, Ecuador, and Venezuela.
	Minister of State for Foreign Affairs Siddique Khan Kanju visits Malaysia and Indonesia.
	Minister for Science and Technology Ilahi Baksh Soomro visits Egypt.
	Minister for Commerce Malik Naeem Khan visits China.
2 March	Pakistan's Lieutenant General Javed Nasir appoints Director General Inter-Service Intelligence (DGISI) in place of Major General Asad Durrani.
5 March	Sindh Chief Minister Jam Sadiq Ali dies.
7 March	Syed Muzaffer Hussain Shah is elected Sindh CM.
18 March	NPP is expelled from ruling IJI coalition at the center.
25 March	Indian President R. Venkataraman congratulates Pakistani President Ghulam Ishaq Khan on the victory of the Pakistan cricket team in the World Cup Tournament.
30 March	Another attempt is made to cross the LoC on a call given by the JKLF. Firm steps are taken by Pakistan authorities to prevent the crossing.
16 April	Arshad Ali, an official of the Pakistan High Commission in Delhi, is apprehended by Indian authorities for his alleged involvement in espionage activity and is expelled.
24 April	Afghan mujahedeen signs an agreement in Peshawar.
4 May	S. K. Lambah meets Prime Minister Nawaz Sharif.
5 May	Jammat-i-Islami withdraws from the ruling IJI.
	The Imam of Jama Masjid, Delhi, Syed Abdullah Bukhari, pays a two-week visit to Pakistan. Among others, he meets Nawaz Sharif twice.
13 May	Four Pakistani military personnel, who were detained when they crossed over to Indian territory in March 1992, are released.
24 May	Counselor Rajesh Mittal is abducted just outside his house in Islamabad. Allegedly he is tortured by Pakistan intelligence agencies and released after about seven hours of inhuman treatment, including electric shocks. GOP declares him persona non grata for making unfounded allegations.
25 May	Two counselors of Pakistan HC in Delhi, Syed Fayyaz Mahmood Endrabi and Zafar-ul Hassan, are expelled by India.
28 May	GOP announces handing over of law and order responsibility in Sind to the Army for a period of six months.
14 June	The prime ministers of India and Pakistan meet in Rio de Janeiro,

where both are attending the Earth Summit.

15 June Baloch leader Nawab Khair Bux Maqsi returns to Pakistan from exile in Kabul.

9 July Pakistan's Minister of State for Foreign Affairs Muhammad Siddique Khan Kanju meets with Minister of State for External Affairs Eduardo Faleiro in Colombo, where both are attending the 11th SAARC Council of Ministers meeting.

The eighth round of secretary–level talks on Tulbul Navigation project takes place in Delhi.

10 August President of the Awami National Party (ANP) Ajmal Khan Khattak, visits Delhi to participate in the ceremonies commemorating the 50th anniversary of the Quit India Movement and calls on Narasimha Rao.

16 August The sixth round of talks between Shaharyar Khan and Dixit begins in Delhi.

17 August Shaharyar Khan hands over a letter from Nawaz Sharif to Narasimha Rao proposing bilateral negotiations on Kashmir under Article VI of the Simla Agreement.

19 August At the conclusion of the foreign secretary–level talks, the two sides exchange the Instruments of Ratification of the Agreement on Prevention of Air Space Violations by Military Aircraft and Agreement on Advance Notice of Military Exercises, Manoeuvres and Troop Movements. They also sign a Joint Declaration on the Complete Prohibition of a Chemical Weapons and Code of Conduct for Treatment of Diplomatic/Consular Personnel of India and Pakistan.

The Indian side formally hands over a letter of invitation to the chief of Army staff of Pakistan to visit India.

20 August National Democratic Alliance, a new grouping of eight opposition political parties, is launched in Karachi.

27 August The National Assembly adopts a resolution moved by Minister of State for Foreign Affairs Muhammad Siddique Khan Kanju that expresses "deep distress and anguish" over the attempt to desecrate and demolish the Babri mosque.

29 August S. K. Lambah calls on Nawaz Sharif to convey India's strong sentiments and deep concerns at the resolution adopted by the Pakistan National Assembly on Babri Masjid and Pakistan's "undue" interference in India's internal affairs. He also hands over a letter from Narasimmha Rao to Nawaz Sharif in response to the latter's communication of August 17.

3 September Nawaz Sharif and Narasimha Rao meet in Jakarta, where both are attending the 10th NAM summit.

6–10 September Janata Dal leader and former Prime Minister V. P. Singh visits Karachi to participate in a seminar sponsored by the PPP on the Role of Opposition in Asian Societies.

10–30 September Devastating floods hit Pakistan, causing extreme countrywide damage; losses are estimated to be over US$1 billion.

28 September Pakistan Minister of State for Foreign Affairs Muhammad Siddiqui Khan Kanju meets with Minister of State for External Affairs Eduardo Faleiro in New York where both are attending the UNGA session.

30 September India sends two IAF AN-32 aircraft carrying medicines for the flood-affected people of Pakistan.

8 October Pakistan Minister of Education Syed Fakkar Imam visits India in connection with the inaugural ceremony of the First South Asian Festival.

11 October	S. K. Lambah meets with Prime Minister Nawaz Sharif.
15 October	Two Pakistan nationals, Intekhab Zia and Habibullah, are among the six terrorists killed in an encounter with the Indian security forces in Kashmir near the village Kanga Rian in the Jalandhar district.
	Qazi Hussain Ahmed is reelected Amir Jamaat-e-Islami for another five-year tenure.
24–25 October	The opposition POK Democratic Alliance makes an unsuccessful attempt to cross the Line of Control (LoC).
26 October	The Pakistan National Assembly passes a resolution on Kashmir regarding the Line of Control.
28–30 October	A group of demonstrators, led by Advocate Ansar Burney, stages a hunger strike outside the Indian High Commission in Islamabad, demanding the return of the dead bodies of the two terrorists killed in India.
2–5 November	The sixth round of talks on the Siachen issue is held in New Delhi. The Indian delegation is led by Defence Secretary N. N. Vohra and the Pakistan delegation by Defence Secretary Syed Salim Abbas Jilani.
5–6 November	The fifth round of talks on the Sir Creek issue is held in New Delhi. The Indian delegation is led by Nareshwar Dayal, additional secretary, ministry of external affairs, and the Pakistan delegation by Khalid Saleem, additional secretary, ministry of foreign affairs.
18 November	Opposition PDA organizes a so-called Long March from Rawalpindi to Islamabad. Benazir Bhutto is deported to Karachi and excluded from Islamabad for 30 days.
23 November	Benazir Bhutto leads a Long March from Karachi to Rawalpindi.
2 December	The government of Pakistan advises its citizens to avoid traveling to India for "security and safety reasons." Pakistan citizens visiting India are also advised to curtail their visits.
5 December	An official of the Pakistan High Commission Mohammad Ashfaq is apprehended in Delhi while accepting documents from a junior army officer. He is declared persona non grata on December 7.
6 December	Nawaz Sharif expresses a "deep sense of shock and horror" at the Ayodhya developments. Incidents of stone throwing at Shivaji Court in Karachi, which house some members of the staff, take place.
7 December	GOP hands over an aide-memoire protesting the demolition of the Babri Masjid in violation of the interdominion agreement of August 1947 and the Nehru-Liaquat Pact of April 1950.
8 December	Government-sponsored demonstrations are held throughout Pakistan. Several temples, gurudwaras, and churches are attacked and burned. In Karachi, the residence of Consulate-General (CG) Rajiv Dogra is ransacked and burned. Incidents of stone throwing are reported at the houses of members of staff in Islamabad. Huge protests are held in front of missions in Karachi and Islamabad.
9 December	Secretary (West) K. Srinivasan summons Pakistan High Commissioner Riaz Khokhar and lodges India's strong protest at the ransacking and burning of the Indian CG's residence in Karachi and the lack of security arrangements. Families of Indian officials at the Indian Consulate-General Karachi are temporarily sent back home due to the insecure situation in Karachi.

11 December   An aide-memoire is handed over by the joint secretary of the Integrated Programme of Action (IPA) Bhadrakumar to Pakistan Dy. Shahid Malik in Delhi expressing concern at the wanton destruction of places of worship for minorities in Pakistan.

14 December   India asks Pakistan to withdraw another official, Mohammad Anjum for his "unacceptable activities."

15 December   MQM chief Altaf Hussain announces his withdrawal from politics.

17 December   Pakistan declares three Indian officials persona non grata (one from Islamabad and two from the Consul General in Karachi).

24 December   The Pakistan National Assembly adopts a resolution condemning the demolition of the Babri Masjid in Ayodhya and demanding its reconstruction at the original site.

29 December   The Pakistan Foreign Office, interpreting the Code of Conduct unilaterally, asks for the staff strength of CGI Karachi to be reduced from 64 to 20 (including four diplomats and 16 nondiplomats).

1993

4 January   India and Pakistan exchange lists of each other's nuclear installations and facilities for the second consecutive year.

7 January   India's Senate adopts a unanimous resolution on the Ayodhya incident.

8 January   Pakistan's COAS General Asif Nawaz Janjua dies suddenly of a heart attack.

10 January   M. K. Bhadra Kumar, the joint secretary of the Integrated Programme of Action at the Ministry of External Affaires, conveys to Pakistan's Deputy High Commissioner Shahid Malik, GOI's decision to reduce the strength of the Pakistan High Commission in New Delhi to a maximum of 110 personnel by February 10, 1993.

12 January   Lieutenant General Abdul Waheed, commander 12 Corps, Quetta, is appointed as the new COAS at the rank of full general, jumped over some serving officers senior to him.

Benazir Bhutto is unanimously elected chair of the Standing Committee on Foreign Affairs of the National Assembly.

2 February   Nawaz Sharif highlights alleged violations of human rights of Muslims in India in his address to the UN Human Rights Commission in Geneva. Pakistan's attempt to get a resolution passed against India during the conference fails.

4 February   The Pakistan National Assembly adopts a resolution condemning alleged Indian atrocities on Kashmiris.

5 February   JI called for a countrywide strike in Pakistan and POK on the Kashmir issue.

6 February   Asif Zardari (Benazir Bhutto's husband) is granted bail in the Unar case by the Special Court for Suppression of Terrorist Activities and released from prison.

Jamat-i-Islami organizes an All Parties Conference on the Kashmir issue in Lahore.

8 February   Prime Minister Nawaz Sharif announces a program of distributing over 4,000 acres of land among 30,000 landless peasant families of the "Katcha areas" in Sindh.

8 March   The High Court of Azad Kashmir declares the Northern Areas a part of the territory of Azad Jammu-Kashmir in a judgment delivered in Muzaffarabad on a writ petition filed by two residents of Gilgit and advocates from POK.

14 March	Nawaz Sharif sends a message of sympathy to India's Prime Minister on the bomb explosions in Bombay on March 12.
15 March	Pakistan Foreign Office spokesperson regrets the alleged tendency of Indian politicians to blame Pakistan for any unpleasant event in India.
17 March	Two BSF personnel, while patrolling the border in the Ferozpur section, are taken away by Pakistani Rangers.
18 March	The president of the Pakistan Muslim League and former Prime Minister Mohammad Khan Junejo dies in Baltimore, Maryland, where he is undergoing treatment.
19 March	The two BSF personnel are released.
22 March	Prime Minister Nawaz Sharif meets with Pakistan's Ghulam Ishaq Khan amid reports of heightening confrontation between the two leaders.
23 March	K. Srinivasan, secretary (West), MEA, hands over evidence about six members of the Menon family having reached Karachi on March 17 to Pakistan High Commissioner Riaz Khokar. The government of Pakistan is requested to trace them and send them back to India.
27 March	The government of Pakistan refuses permission for a hijacked Indian Airlines aircraft from Delhi to Madras to land at Lahore.
28 March	Three members of the Federal Cabinet, Planning and Development Minister Hamid Naser Chatta, Environment and Urban Affairs Minister Anwar Saifullah, and Adviser to the Prime Minister on Establishment Affairs Asad Ali Junejo resign from the government.
29 March	OIC Foreign Ministers conference concludes in Karachi; resolutions are

suspended on Kashmir and Babri Masjid.

4–5 April	The POK People's Party March to cross LoC ends unsuccessfully.
11 April	The widow of former COAS General Asif Nawaz claims at a press conference that her husband's death is a political assassination caused by slow poisoning.
	Narasimha Rao and Nawaz Sharif meet at Dhaka during the SAARC Summit.
18 April	President Ghulam Ishaq Khan dissolves the National Assembly and dismisses Nawaz Sharif's government. Balakh Sher Mazari is appointed caretaker prime minister.
19 April	India's External Affairs Minister Dinesh Singh makes a personal statement in Lok Sabha on dismissal of Nawaz Sharif's government in Pakistan.
	National Assembly Speaker Gohar Ayub Khan files a written petition in Lahore's High Court challenging the dissolution.
21 April	Union Home Minister S. B. Chavan makes a statement in Lok Sabha on the Bombay bomb blasts, implicating Pakistan.
22 April	Nazeer Ahmed Malik, secretary narcotics control division, is appointed director intelligence bureau, in place of Brigadier (Ret.) Imtiaz, who resigned following the dismissal of the Nawaz Sharif government.
25 April	Nawaz Sharif files a written petition in the Supreme Court challenging the dissolution of the National Assembly.
	Punjab Chief Minister Ghulam Haider Wyne is defeated in the vote of no confidence by a margin of 157

votes to 20. Mian Manzoor Ahmed Wattoo, speaker of the provincial assembly, takes the oath as chief minister of Punjab.

29 April Justice Naseem Hasan Shah is sworn in as chief justice of Pakistan's Supreme Court.

1 May MQM chairman Azim Ahmed Tariq is assassinated in Karachi.

2 May Lieutenant General Javed Nasir and Major General Asad Durrani (both ex-deputy general staff with Inter-Services Intelligence) are prematurely retired from Pakistan's Army.

6 May Pakistan's caretaker Prime Minister Mazari and Indian Vice President K. R. Narayanan have a long conversation in Colombo, when they are seated next to each other during the funeral rites of President Premadasa.

12 May The Commission of Inquiry, set up to probe the death of COAS General Asif Nawaz, submits its report to the law minister.

13–16 May The 77th Meeting of the Permanent Indus Commission is held in New Delhi.

16 May The caretaker Pakistan prime minister, in his meeting with S. K. Lambah, gives a report on the Menon family that admits six of them had arrived in Karachi on March 17, but there is no trace of them thereafter.

17 May At a press conference, India's home minister rejects a Pakistan request for a meeting of the home/interior secretaries of the two countries to discuss the issue of the whereabouts of the Menon brothers.

21 May Jamaat-e-Islami announces the formation of the Pakistan Islamic Mahaz in Lahore with IJI Amir Qazi Hussain Ahmed as its first president.

22 May Baluchistan's Chief Minister Mir. Mohammad Jamali resigns, fearing his inability to defeat a no-confidence motion.

26 May Pakistan's Supreme Court restores the dissolved National Assembly and the dismissed government of Nawaz Sharif.

27 May Pakistan's National Assembly adopts a resolution expressing confidence in Nawaz Sharif by a majority of 123 votes to nil.

Narasimha Rao sends a message to Nawaz Sharif welcoming his restoration as prime minister. The message is personally handed over by S. K. Lambah. He is the first diplomat to be received by Nawaz Sharif after his restoration.

29 May Punjab's provincial assembly is dissolved by the governor on the advice of the chief minister.

30 May Governor of NWFP, Amir Gulestan Janjua, dissolves the NWFP's assembly on the advice of Chief Minister Mir. Afzal Khan.

5 June A written petition challenging the dissolution of the NWFP assembly is filed in Peshawar High Court.

9 June The Lahore High Court temporarily restores the Punjab Assembly and cabinet headed by C. M. Wattoo through interim order. It also places a restriction on any fresh advice to dissolve the assembly or a no-confidence motion until a final decision is reached.

POK government files an appeal against the judgment of the POK High Court, which declared that the Northern Areas are part of Azad Jammu-Kashmir.

20 June The National Assembly adopts a resolution moved by Iftikar Gilani

(PDA) to constitute a committee for the repeal of the 8th Amendment.

A statement issued by an official spokesperson of MEA on the Pakistan High Commission press release of June 18 blames Maharashtra Chief Minister Sharad Pawar and terms the latter tendentious, provocative, and totally contrary to all diplomatic norms.

28 June   The Supreme Court releases a detailed judgment on the constitution petition challenging the dissolution of the National Assembly.

The Lahore High Court restores the Punjab Assembly in its final verdict. However, the Punjab governor again dissolves the assembly on the advice of C. M. Wattoo within minutes of the announcement of the Lahore High Court judgment.

29 June   A joint session of parliament adopts a resolution advising the president to put Punjab under federal rule. Punjab is placed under direct rule under Article 234 (i) of Pakistan's constitution through a proclamation order issued later that night.

30 June   A spokesperson for Pakistan's president issues a handout stating that President Ghulam Ishaq Khan has not received, approved, or signed any proclamation in pursuance of Article 234 of the constitution.

July   Messages are exchanged between the foreign secretaries of India and Pakistan about the possibilities of talks in Cyprus in October during the Commonwealth Summit.

October   Benazir Bhutto returns to office.

16 October   Sixteen armed Kashmiri separatists take over the Hazratbal Muslim shrine in Srinagar. About 150 pilgrims are inside. Ten thousand Indian troops surround the shrine after a tip-off that the militants are

planning to remove a relic—a strand of hair said to be from the Prophet Mohammad—and are threatening to blow up the building. The incident swiftly worsens communal relations in Kashmir. A week later Indian security forces fire into a Muslim crowd and kill about 40 separatists. After month-long mediation, the Srinagar gunmen surrender and the siege ends peacefully, in effect strengthening the authority of the Rao government.

20–21 October   Benazir visits Cyprus for the Commonwealth Summit and makes reference to Kashmir.

22 October   In a meeting between India's Finance Minister Manmohan Singh and Pakistan's Foreign Minister Sardar Farooq Ahmed Khan Leghari, it is agreed to resume foreign secretary–level talks.

25 October   India's Foreign Secretary J. N. Dixit and Pakistan's Foreign Secretary Shaharyar Khan fix dates for foreign secretary–level talks at Islamabad between the first and third of January 1994.

In November the Hazratbal Shrine made prospective Indo-Pakistan talks December uncertain and less likely.

1994

2 January   Although no progress is made in the first high-level talks on Kashmir between India and Pakistan to be held for 30 years, the fact that they take place raises hopes of an eventual agreement.

1–3 January   Foreign secretary–level two-day talks are held in Islamabad between J. N. Dixit and Saharyar Khan. The main issue is Kashmir. The talks fail.

15–16 January   Ministry–level talks take place between India and Pakistan in New Delhi about combating drug trafficking and smuggling.

October

Prime Minister Narasimha Rao reveals that he wants elections to be held in Jammu-Kashmir early in 1995. This state has been under presidential rule for several years, but it is thought that India's army and border security forces had gotten the violence under control. This election plan, fraught with difficulties, is jeopardized, however, when insurgents take crates of electoral rolls from a government building and burn them in a field. Delhi's election plan is to undercut the hard-line militant leaders wanting unity with Pakistan or independence. The release of one leader, Shabir Ahmed Shah, called by Amnesty "one of the longest serving prisoners of conscience in India," signals the change of policy. After being freed, he rejects the election plan.

1995

9 April

India's prime minister sends a message of felicitations to Prime Minister Benazir Bhutto on her assumption of office in October 1993 and offers to discuss all aspects of Kashmir. India's High Commissioner to Pakistan S. K. Lambah tells *The Nation* that India is ready for a dialogue on Kashmir with Pakistan at any time, at any level, and without any conditions.

19 April

India's Foreign Minister Pranab Mukerjee says he is ready for talks with Pakistan at "any place, any time" but that the upcoming South Asian summit is not the forum for such bilateral discussions.

4 May

Pakistan President Farooq Ahmad Khan Leghari rules out the third option of an independent Kashmir as the resolution of the issue because he says it betrays the basic philosophy of the 1947 Partition Plan. India's Prime Minister P. V. Narasimha Rao says that Kashmir issue can be resolved only in a "conducive and congenial atmosphere between India and Pakistan."

17 May

India's External Affairs Minister Pranab Mukerjee says that New Delhi is committed to resolving all its disputes with Islamabad, including those over Kashmir, bilaterally and peacefully. He rules out third-country mediation in Kashmir. Yet another revered shrine is besieged by Indian troops soon after the burning of Charar Sharif.

24 July

Former Pakistan Foreign Secretary Shaharyar M. Khan and J. N. Dixit (India's foreign secretary until 1991) announce at a Wilton Park conference sponsored by the Foreign and Commonwealth Office in London, that a political solution of the Kashmir conflict has to be found, one that also fulfills the aspirations of the Kashmiri people.

1–19 December

The Indian parliament extends federal rule over Kashmir for another six months. (The legislature had been dismissed in 1990.) The Union government wants an election but the electoral commission says the state is still too unstable.

1996

30 January

Pakistani and Indian military officers meet on the cease-fire line dividing Kashmir to ease tension after armed clashes.

7 April

India's Prime Minister Narasimha Rao once again says India is committed to holding a dialogue with Pakistan on all issues, including Kashmir without any preconditions, but rules out third-party mediation.

May

Congress is defeated in the May elections, and a coalition headed by H. D. Deve Gowda is formed.

1997

27 March

Pakistan's Foreign Secretary Shamshad Ahmed takes a firm line when in New Delhi for the first official talks with India in three years. He declares that Kashmir is the core issue on the agenda.

Shamshad Ahmed, due to hold talks with his Indian counterpart Salman Haider during a groundbreaking four-day visit, arrives just hours after a street protest erupts in New Delhi over Pakistan's assistance on Kashmir.

28 March

Pakistan and India sit down at a negotiating table for the first time in three years, with the Kashmir dispute high on the agenda.

A two-hour session, the first official talks since 1994, end in an upbeat mood, with Shamshad Ahmed, who said earlier that Kashmir would be the core issue of the negotiations, saying, "The talks are very cordial and very meaningful and very purposeful. We are very hopeful."

31 March

Pakistan and India complete four days of talks aimed at reducing tension and agree to meet again in Islamabad. "The two foreign secretaries discussed all outstanding issues of concern to both sides in a frank, cordial and constructive manner," according to a joint statement issued after the talks.

April

Another politically weak coalition takes office in India, led by Inder Kumar Gujral.

28 April

Foreign Minister Gohar Ayub Khan asked India to acknowledge the existence of a bilateral dispute over Kashmir, saying such a move is a key to improving relations.

14 May

Addressing the extraordinary summit of the Economic Cooperation Organization (ECO), Prime Minister Muhammad Nawaz Sharif says that Pakistan favors a peaceful settlement of the Kashmir issue in accordance with the resolutions of the United Nations Security Council.

23 May

Secretary General of the United Nations Kofi Annan, in a meeting with Pakistan's Foreign Minister Gohar Ayub Khan, assures him that he is willing to use his good offices to find a solution of the festering 50-year-old Kashmir dispute between Pakistan and India.

22 June

Pakistan and India reach an agreement to set up a mechanism for sustained dialogue on issues between the two countries. Both countries identify eight issues, including the problem of Jammu-Kashmir, to serve as an agenda for future talks.

A joint statement released at the conclusion of the second round of foreign secretary–level talks says that two sides agreed to set up working groups to deal with all outstanding issues at appropriate levels. The problems of peace and security and Jammu-Kashmir would, however, be taken up at the secretary level.

25 June

India rejects Pakistan's interpretation that it has accepted Jammu-Kashmir as a disputed territory after the second round of secretary–level talks is concluded in Islamabad.

17 September

On the second day of the third round of foreign secretary–level talks, the two sides continue diplomatic efforts to "operationalize a mechanism" for future "structured dialogue" on all outstanding issues.

The two sides hold two informal sessions in which different matters relating to the formation of a mechanism of future talks come under discussion. The discussions are essentially on the issue of forming a working group on Kashmir.

November

Gujral's administration collapses and is replaced in March by a BJP-led coalition headed by Atal Bihari Vajpayee.

1998

The American-based Kashmir Study Group (KSG) proposes in its original version the partition of Kashmir into three parts: (1) the Northern Areas and Pakistani Kashmir to stay with

Pakistan, (2) Jammu and Ladakh remaining with India, and (3) the Valley of Kashmir to be reconstituted through a plebiscite as a sovereign entity (but one without an international personality).

May India carries out five nuclear tests. On May 3, three devices are exploded, followed by two more on May 13. On May 28 Pakistan carries out five nuclear tests in the deserts of Baluchistan in response to India's tests earlier in the month. Both sets of tests elicit widespread criticism. Soon after the tests, Indo-Pakistan relations swiftly deteriorate. India blames Pakistan of seeking to internationalize the Kashmir dispute, which it insists must be resolved bilaterally. Pakistan also uses India's tests as a justification for unveiling its own nuclear prowess. Bilateral talks are temporarily postponed while the two countries volley criticism of each other and even exchange shots across their boundaries. Kashmir remains a potential flashpoint, with outside powers watching anxiously the exchanges between the two nuclear novitiates.

Vajpayee and his Pakistani counterpart, Nawaz Sharif, meet in Colombo at the annual summit meeting of SAARC, though they fail to make progress beyond agreeing to resume bilateral talks.

2 June Japan's foreign minister offers to host an international conference involving India and Pakistan in an attempt to resolve their dispute over Kashmir.

4 June India's Prime Minister Atal Bihari Vajpayee announces his readiness to resume talks with Pakistan on all issues, including the core issue of Kashmir, but refuses any third-party mediation.

17 June India's Prime Minister Atal Bihari Vajpayee, in an interview with the

Washington Post, says that his government is ready to settle the Kashmir dispute with Pakistan basically according to the 1972 Simla Agreement.

29 July The prime ministers of Pakistan and India meet on the sidelines of the SAARC Summit in Colombo. The main subject of discussion is the resumption of dialogue on Kashmir. Following a directive of their prime ministers, the foreign secretaries of Pakistan and India meet twice on July 29 and 30, 1998, to overcome the procedural as well as substantive impediments to the resumption of Pakistan–India talks, but they cannot reach an agreement.

4 September Foreign Secretary Shamshad Ahmed and his Indian counterpart K. Raghunath hold several meetings in Durban (during the Commonwealth Summit there) on the issue of the resumption of talks. They arrive at "an understanding, in principle, to operationalise the mechanism for dialogue on all issues as per the agreed agenda."

16–18 October The so-called composite dialogue between India and Pakistan on the issue of peace and security, including CBM and Jammu-Kashmir, is held in Kashmir.

5–13 November Talks between Vajpayee and Sharif resume in New Delhi; they tackle a range of bilateral disagreements as well as Kashmir, their main point of contention. These bilateral issues include the construction of the Wullar Barrage on the Jhelum River in Kashmir, their entrenchments along the inhospitable Siachen glacier, and the demarcation of maritime boundaries around Sir Creek—all without any real progress being made.

1999

February At the conclusion of the Lahore Summit, the Lahore Declaration holds that both India and Pakistan shall:

- Intensify their efforts to resolve all issues, including that of Jammu-Kashmir.
- Refrain from intervention and interference in each other's internal affairs.
- Intensify their composite and integrated dialogue process for an early and positive outcome of the agreed bilateral agenda.
- Take immediate steps to reduce the risk of accidental or unauthorized use of nuclear weapons. (They discussed concepts and doctrines with a view to elaborating measures for confidence building in the nuclear and conventional fields, aimed at prevention of conflict.)
- Reaffirm their commitment to the goals and objectives of SAARC and to concert their efforts toward the realization of the SAARC vision for the year 2000 and beyond with a view to promoting the welfare of the peoples of South Asia and to improve their quality of life through accelerated economic growth, social progress, and cultural development.
- Reaffirm their condemnation of terrorism in all its forms and manifestations and their determination to combat this menace.
- Agree to promote and protect all human rights and fundamental freedoms.

May–July India and Pakistan fight a war along a 2-kilometer (1.2-mile) front in Kashmir at an altitude of over 10,000 feet. This is their fourth war over Kashmir.

2000

18 January The trial begins of Pakistan's former Prime Minister Nawaz Sharif on charges relating to the alleged hijacking in October 1999 of a plane carrying General Pervez Musharraf.

12 May The supreme court of Pakistan endorses the legitimacy of the 1999 military coup.

22 July Pakistan's former Prime Minister Sharif is convicted of corruption, sentenced to 14 years' imprisonment, and banned from holding public office for 21 years.

August Flooding in India's northeastern states, brought about by exceptionally heavy monsoon rains, claims over 300 lives and leaves 4.5 million homeless.

14 August Pakistan's chief executive, General Pervez Musharraf, announces that district elections will be held between December 2000 and August 2001 as the first phase of a "return to democracy."

30 September Renewed exceptional monsoon flooding after September 18 results in a death toll of 758 in India's northeastern state of West Bengal and makes 15 million homeless. In neighboring Bangladesh, at least 250 people die.

12 October India's former Prime Minister P. V. Narasimha Rao is sentenced to three years' imprisonment on corruption charges relating to the bribery of ministers to parliament in 1993.

28 November India's government troops begin a unilateral cease-fire in their confrontation with Kashmiri separatists for the duration of the Muslim holy month of Ramadan.

10 December Pakistan's former prime minister Nawaz Sharif is unexpectedly pardoned, released from prison but sent into exile.

2001

25 January A devastating earthquake strikes the Kutch district of India's northwestern state of Gujerat, killing many thousands, destroying

three towns, and leaving over half a million people homeless.

25 February India's government announces a three-month extension of its unilateral cease-fire in the separatist conflict in the northern state of Jammu-Kashmir.

13 March A sting operation by an Internet news service exposes a culture of corruption among Indian government officials over the awarding of defense contracts, leading to the resignation of Defense Minister George Fernandes.

6 April The Supreme Court of Pakistan sets aside convictions made in 1999 of exiled former Prime Minister Benazir Bhutto for corruption and orders a retrial.

20 June General Pervez Musharraf, who had ruled as Pakistan's chief executive since his military coup in October 1999, assumes the title of president.

14 July A three-day summit meeting in Agra, India, begins between India's Prime Minister Atal Bihari Vajpayee and Pakistan's president, General Pervez Musharraf.

This first top-level meeting between the two governments ends without any agreement as to how to move forward on the Kashmir dispute.

16 July The Agra talks between General Pervez Musharraf and India's Prime Minister Atal Bihari Vajpayee fail to reach any positive conclusion. Musharraf, at a breakfast meeting with senior journalists, says that unless India acknowledges that Kashmir is the main issue of contention between the two countries, no progress can be made.

11 September Major terrorist attacks on the World Trade Center in New York and on the Pentagon in Washington, D.C., come to be widely known as 9/11.

7 October President General Pervez Musharraf extends indefinitely his expiring three-year term as army chief of staff and reshuffles top military commanders to consolidate his hold on power in the face of some vocal domestic opposition to his support for the U.S. campaign in Afghanistan.

December Terrorists, allegedly backed by Pakistan, launch suicide attacks on India's parliament, claiming 12 lives.

21 December The Indian government withdraws its High Commission from Pakistan for the first time since 1971. India mobilizes its army against Pakistan's armed forces.

2002

January Pakistan and India twice pull back from the brink of war with the help of British and American diplomacy.

5 January South Asian leaders conclude a summit overshadowed by a buildup of troops by India on Pakistani borders with no apparent easing of tensions between these nuclear-armed neighbors. Pakistan's President Pervez Musharraf briefly breaks the ice in Kathmandu at the SAARC summit when he walks up to Indian Prime Minister Atal Bihari Vajpayee to extend a hand of friendship—though no substantive talks ensue.

12 January In a landmark television broadcast, Pakistan's president, General Pervez Musharraf, announces the banning of several prominent Islamic militant organizations and offers his country a choice between a progressive moderate Islamic society founded on law, tolerance, and modernity and the divisiveness and destructiveness of sectarian extremism. He rules out compromising over Pakistan as wanted by India and invites Vajpayee for talks.

February A videotape, handed to U.S. consular officials in Pakistan, confirms that a

U.S. journalist, Daniel Pearl, who had been abducted in January, has been murdered by his kidnappers.

27 February   A train full of Hindu activists is halted at Godhrain, the western state of Gujarat, and attacked by arsonists, leading to the deaths of 58 people, the majority of them women and children. The attack sparks a wave of sectarian violence across the state by Hindus against the Muslim minority, leading to at least 60 more deaths.

1 March   Hindu mobs continue a pogrom against Muslims in Gujarat. The intervention of large numbers of troops begins to quell the violence in the latter part of the month.

15 March   The Indian government deploys 37,000 paramilitary troops in Ayodhya, Uttar Pradesh, to prevent further Hindu rites at the former site of the Babri Masjid mosque, destroyed by Hindu militants in 1992. The rites have been banned by India's Supreme Court, pending the resolution of legal disputes over the site.

19 March   In Pakistan five people die in a grenade attack on a Christian church in the diplomatic quarter of Islamabad, the capital. Among the dead are a U.S. diplomat and her daughter. It is thought that the attack is aimed by Islamic extremists both at Westerners and the government of President General Pervez Musharraf, in order to undermine his support for the so-called U.S. war against terrorism.

26 March   Indian's Prime Minister Atal Bihari Vajpayee, while speaking at a function in Himachal Pradesh, states that any talks with Pakistan will have to be held within the purview of the Simla and Lahore Agreements.

31 March   Pakistan's President Pervez Musharraf renews a call for the resumption of dialogue between India and Pakistan to resolve the Kashmir issue and says his government is ready for talks. Musharraf says that the Kashmir issue should be solved according to the wishes of Kashmiris, and his government is ready for talks with India to work out a durable solution. He says this during a conversation with prime minister of Pakistani Kashmir, Sikandar Hayat Khan, in Islamabad.

30 April   Reports prepared for the embassies of EU countries claim that the death toll in communal violence in India's western state of Gujarat has exceeded 2,000 and that the massacre of Muslims is not spontaneous but a long-prepared pogrom in which state officials have connived.

A referendum in Pakistan in which 97.7 percent of voters endorsed the extension of the term of President General Pervez Musharraf by another five years is strongly condemned by opposition parties, the independent Human Rights Commission, and the domestic and foreign press as a stage-managed and fraudulent exercise.

8 May   A suicide bomber in Pakistan's port city of Karachi sets off an explosion that kills 17 people, including 11 French naval engineers working on a project to build submarines for Pakistan's navy. The bombing is blamed on Islamic extremists allied to the Islamic militant al-Qaeda network.

14 May   An attack by Islamic militant separatists on an Indian Army camp in Kashmir causes the death of 34 people, mainly women and children, and brings India and Pakistan close to war with its possible escalation.

June   In the fourth attack on foreign targets in Pakistan since the beginning of the year, a car bomb explodes outside the U.S. consulate in Karachi, killing 13 people and injuring more than 40.

15 July Four men are convicted in an antiterrorist court in Karachi, the capital of Sink province, Pakistan, of the abduction and murder in January of the U.S. journalist Daniel Pearl. One of the convicts, said to be Islamic militant, is sentenced to death, the others to life imprisonment.

16 August Pakistan President Pervez Musharraf vows that Pakistan will never compromise on the Kashmiris' right of determination and rejects polls in occupied Kashmir as a bid to legitimize India's illegal occupation.

In a tough speech at a flag-hoisting ceremony on the country's 55th Independence Day, Musharraf says a referendum on the Kashmiris' political destiny is the key to peace in South Asia. "The struggle for self-determination of our Kashmiri brothers is a sacred trust that can never be compromised," he says.

21 August President Musharraf passes a series of constitutional amendments that ensure a continuing role for the military in government ahead of and despite elections scheduled for October.

8 October Elections begun in September to the state assembly of Jammu-Kashmir are completed. The National Conference (JKNC) Party, traditionally the dominant political force in Kashmir, loses power to a coalition of the People's Democratic Party (PDP) and Indira Congress party.

The new Chief Minister Mufti Hafiz Mohammad Sayeed says that, to end the separatist conflict that had claimed at least 35,000 lives, he will release some political prisoners and seek negotiations with separatist groups.

10 October Legislature elections are held to Pakistan's National Assembly (the lower house of the bicameral federal legislature), fulfilling a Supreme Court order to President General Pervez Musharraf to hold national elections within three years of the October 1999 coup, when Musharraf seized power. The pro-Musharraf Pakistan Muslim League–Qaid-i-Azam (PML-QA) emerges as the largest party with 118 seats in the 342-seat Assembly.

25 October Presiding over a meeting of Pakistan's Kashmir Council, President Musharraf says the Indian troops' role between the two countries, including the Kashmir issue, can be settled through bilateral dialogue.

21 November After prolonged wrangling among Pakistan's major political parties, the National Assembly that was elected in October convenes to choose a new prime minister, electing Zafarullah Khan Jamali, candidate of the PML-Q and an ally of President Musharraf. Jamali's new cabinet is sworn in on November 23.

12 December The Bharatiya Janata Party (BJP), the leading party in India's federal government, wins a landslide victory in elections to the assembly in the western state of Gujarat, the only major state still controlled by the BJP. In his campaign the controversial Chief Minister Narendra Modi exploits local Hindu sentiments that fueled severe anti-Muslim riots earlier in the year.

29 December In an interview with the Indian daily newspaper, *Asian Age,* Pakistan's Foreign Minister Khurshid Mahmud Kasuri dismisses Indian's stand that it would involve only elected representatives in the talks to restore peace in Kashmir. He says, "the talks need not to be exclusive and can involve all shades of opinion, in power or out of power."

2003

12 January — Leaders of the separatist National Socialist Council of Nagaland–Isaac Muivah (NSCNIM) announce that, following a breakthrough in peace talks with the government, they are confident that their guerrilla war for independence, which had started in1954, is effectively over.

10 February — An agreement is signed by the Bodo Liberation Tigers Force (BLTF), the state government of Assam, and the government to end the BLTF's 20-year separatist insurgency and pave the way for the creation of a Bodoland Territorial Council.

25 February — Elections are held for Pakistan's Senate (the upper house of the bicameral federal legislature) by the legislatures of the four provinces. The leading party is the ruling Pakistan Muslim League–Qaid-i-Azam (PML-QA) with 31 seats.

26 February — State assembly elections are held in Himachal Pradesh, Meghalaya, Nagaland, and Tripura in northeast India and produce a modest revival for the opposition Congress (I) party, which in Himachal Pradesh replaces one of only two remaining state administrations of the leading federal governing party, the Bharatiya Janata Party (BJP).

March — In Pakistan police arrest Khaled Sheikh Mohammad, alleged to be the chief of operations of the Islamist al-Qaeda network (and suspected of being the planner of the September 11, 2001, attacks on the United States) in the city of Rawalpindi. Mohammad is thought to have been handed over to the United States after interrogation.

18 April — During a visit to the northern state of Jammu-Kashmir, Indian Prime Minister Atal Bihari Vajpayee makes a surprise offer of dialogue with Pakistan, saying that this is the only way to resolve the long-standing dispute over Kashmir.

12 August — Pervez Musharraf orders a cease-fire along the border of Indian Kashmir and Pakistani Kashmir.

25 August — Two bombs concealed in taxis explode in southern Bombay (Mumbai), killing at least 23 people and injuring more than 150. The victims include both Hindus and Muslims, but suspicion falls principally on Islamic militant groups. On August 31, police in New Delhi, the capital, claim to have foiled a major terrorist attack in the city.

19 September — A court discharges India's Deputy Prime Minister L. K. Advani, from a long-delayed case arising from the destruction in December 1992 of the Babri mosque in Ayodhya in the northern state of Uttar Pradesh.

23 September — At the UN General Assembly, New York, Musharraf renews his call for a cease-fire along the LoC.

22 October — India's Minister for External Affairs Yashwant Singh proposes a set of 12 confidence-building measures, including the start of two new bus services between Srinagar and Muzaffarabad and between Khokarapar (Sindh) and Munabao (Barmer, Rajasathan). Pakistan's response is positive but sets conditions on some of the proposals. Pakistan also suggests an additional confidence-building measure: to provide medical treatment to disabled Kashmiris, widows, and rape victims and 100 scholarships for Kashmiri graduates. Pakistan stresses the need for bilateral dialogue.

23 October — India unveils a plan to move toward "normal" relations with Pakistan, including an offer to talk to Islamic separatist leaders in Kashmir.

23 November — On the eve of Id ul Fitr, Pakistan's Prime Minister Zafarullah Jamali

announces a cease-fire offer to India along the International Border (IB) and the Line of Control (LoC). India proposes that the extension of the cease-fire along the Actual Ground Position Line 9 (AGPL) in Jammu-Kashmir begin at midnight.

25 November   A cease-fire comes into effect at midnight between Indian and Pakistani forces on either side of the LoC in Kashmir. The agreement does not affect India's operations against separatist militants within Kashmir and Jammu.

17 December   Musharraf suggests that he may be willing to back down on the plebiscite demand for Kashmir. This provokes a furious response from Pakistan's hard-line Islamists.

24 December   President General Pervez Musharraf announces several concessions in his Legal Framework Order (LFO) of constitutional matters, resistance to which has paralyzed the legislature for over a year. The most important is that he will step down as Army chief of staff by the end of 2004. On the following day, Musharraf survives an assassination attempt in Rawalpindi that kills 17 people.

2004

1 January   Direct air links between India and Pakistan are resumed on January 1 after a halt of more than two years, with a Pakistan International Airlines (PIA) flight from the city of Lahore to New Delhi. The first Indian Airlines flight from New Delhi to Lahore follows on January 9. The Samijhanta Express train resumes its service on January 15 between Lahore and Attari in Punjab. It is reported that the number of passengers taking the resumed air or train services at first is only moderate, largely because of the strict visa requirements imposed by both countries.

The 12th summit meeting of SAARC is held in Islamabad, Pakistan's capital. Talks are held between Indian and Pakistani officials, culminating in a meeting between Vajpayee and Musharraf and a joint statement on January 6 committing the two governments to beginning a composite dialogue in February.

India's Home Affairs Minister L. A. Advani holds his first talks with the moderate faction of the Kashmir umbrella separate organization, the All-Parties Hurriyat Conference (APHC).

4–6 January   Vajpayee and Musharraf hold their first direct talks for more than two years on January 5. In a joint press statement, Delhi agrees to unconditionally resume the dialogue process with Islamabad after a gap of two and a half years and claims that the"resumption of the composite dialogue will lead to peaceful settlement of all bilateral issues, including Jammu and Kashmir, to the satisfaction of both sides." As an apparent quid pro quo, President Musharraf reassures Prime Minister Vajpayee that "we will not permit any territory under Pakistan's control to be used to support terrorism in any manner."

13 January   India and Pakistan proposes discussions to improve bus services and study technical aspects for the starting of the Muzaffarabad–Srinagar bus service.

19–21 January   India and Pakistan discuss the 450-megawatt power project on the Chenab River in Baglihar during the meeting of Indus Water commissioners held in Islamabad.

22 January   Representatives of the All-Parties Hurriyat Conference (AHPC) and the Indian Deputy Prime Minister L. K. Advani meet and agree to find an "honourable and durable solution" to the Kashmir problem through dialogue emanating from this first meeting.

5 February   Pakistan will never place Kashmir issue in the deep freezer and only discuss trade, travel, and other matters with India, says Shaikh Rashid, minister for information, while speaking at Pakistan's embassy in Washington, D.C., to mark Kashmir Solidarity Day.

16–18 February   Talks are held in Islamabad to agree on a schedule for negotiations to begin in April.

17–18 February   At a meeting of foreign secretaries in Murree, India and Pakistan reach "a broad understanding on the modalities and the time-frame for commencing the composite dialogue."

20 February   The first flag meeting between Indian and Pakistani army units in over three years takes place in the Chorbat La sector organized by the Kargil-based 9th Mountain Division (India).

9–10 March   At a meeting of transport and communications officials in Islamabad, India and Pakistan agree to set up the Munabao–Khokarapar bus service, but it is agreed this can take sometime. No date is given for the second round of talks on the subject.

13 March   Addressing the India Today Conclave 2004 via satellite from Islamabad, Pakistan's President Musharraf says, that if there is no progress by August in the talks with India on Kashmir, he will no longer be a party to the process. General Musharraf says he had made his position clear to India and the United States. "We have to move forward on Kashmir. We have to resolve it," General Musharraf says in comments broadcast on state television.

16 April   Pakistan President Pervez Musharraf tells a meeting of legislators in

Lahore that there is no question of Pakistan's accepting the LoC as the solution to resolve the Kashmir issue. He says there is no question of any sellout on Kashmir.

May–June   The foreign secretaries of the two countries meet for talks on the first two of an eight-point agenda:
1. Peace and security issues, and
2. Kashmir.

In late May, experts meet for talks on nuclear confidence-building measures, and in June they meet for talks on drug trafficking and smuggling.

May   In India's general election, BJP is defeated, and Congress forms a coalition government.

15 May   Pakistani Prime Minister Mir Zafarullah Khan Jamali, while talking to news reporters in Islamabad, says that the change of the government in India will not halt the peace process because the people from both countries need to resolve issues through composite dialogue.

17 May   Addressing the United Nations Security Council, Pakistan's Foreign Minister Khurshid Mahmud Kasuri says that the United Nations Military Observer Group (UNMOGIP) in Jammu-Kashmir can help in promoting a just and peaceful resolution of the Kashmir issue.

20 May   Addressing a press conference in New Delhi, India's incoming Prime Minister Manmohan Singh pledges to push forward the dialogue with Pakistan and to hold talks with all parties over Kashmir.

21–22 June   At a meeting of water and power secretaries held in Delhi, India and Pakistan discuss the construction of a 450-megawatt power project on the Chenab in Baglihar.

23 June

At a meeting of senior officials of the Indian BSF and Pakistani Rangers in Khokhropar, India and Pakistan discuss drug trafficking preventive measures, patroling on the borderline, and complete observation of international laws regarding border security.

July

In July, secretaries of the two countries meet for talks on the six remaining issues:

3. Wullar Barrage
4. Friendly exchanges
5. Siachen glacier
6. Sir Creek
7. Terrorism and drug trafficking
8. Economic and commercial cooperation

In August, the foreign ministers of the two countries meet to review progress.

President Musharraf insists that Kashmir lay at the heart of India–Pakistan confrontation and warns that, if there is no movement toward its resolution, everything will slide back to square one.

28–29 July

At a meeting of water and power secretaries, participants have a dialogue in Delhi about the Wullar Barrage. The two sides confirm their wish to resolve the issue within the provisions of the Indus Waters Treaty.

5–6 August

A meeting of defense secretaries is held in Delhi about the Siachen glacier. The two sides discuss ways of disengaging and redeploying troops from the Siachen glacier and state that talks will continue.

9 August

India and Pakistan carry out an exchange of six prisoners of war at the Wagai border post. Pakistan hands over two prisoners arrested during the Kargil conflict, and India releases four, including one arrested during the Kargil conflict.

10–11 August

During a meeting of home interior secretaries in Islamabad, terrorism and drug trafficking are discussed. The two sides are unable to agree on a definition of terrorism. They agree to strengthen cooperation in tackling drug trafficking by:

• Increasing contacts between narcotics control authorities, and
• Designating officials in the High Commissions to liaise on drug control issues.

15 August

India's Prime Minister Manmohan Singh, in his first Independence Day address, says that India wants a purposive bilateral dialogue with Pakistan to resolve all outstanding issues.

5–6 September

During a meeting of foreign ministers in Delhi, an India–Pakistan joint statement is signed. India and Pakistan review the status of the composite dialogue. The two sides agree on 13 points, indicating a road map for the peace process, including the following Kashmir specific ones:

• Meetings between railway authorities on the Munnabao–Khokhrapar rail link,
• A meeting on all issues related to the commencement of bus service between Srinagar and Muzaffarabad,
• Adding a new category of tourist visa in the visa regime between the two countries and to promote group tourism.

They also recognize the importance of the availability and access to energy resources in the region around South Asia. The ministers of petroleum and gas can meet to discuss the issue in its many dimensions.

It is also agreed that the two foreign secretaries will meet in December 2004 to discuss overall progress, as well as the subjects of peace and security, including CBMs and

Jammu-Kashmir, in the composite dialogue. They will also work out a schedule of meetings on other subjects, that is, Siachen, Wullar Barrage–Tulbul Navigation Project, Sir Creek, terrorism and drug trafficking, economic and commercial cooperation, and the promotion of friendly exchanges in various fields.

24 September   A meeting between Prime Minister Manmohan Singh and President Musharraf takes place in New York on the sidelines of the UN General Assembly. This is their first meeting since Manmohan Singh took office in May.

In a joint statement both leaders agree that CBMs between the two governments should be implemented, keeping in mind practical possibilities. They also address the issue of Jammu-Kashmir and are "agreed that possible options for a peaceful, negotiated settlement of the issue should be explored in a sincere spirit and purposeful manner." The possibility of a gas pipeline via Pakistan to India is also discussed.

25 October   In Islamabad, Musharraf proposes that:
- Pakistan will no longer insist on a plebiscite in Kashmir.
- Since India will not accept a religion-based solution, a solution can be formulated in geographical terms.
- Kashmir can be divided into seven regions, five with India and two with Pakistan.
- A three-stage process should be employed to secure a solution: First, identify the region at stake. Second, demilitarize it. Third, change its status.
- With regard to status, various options can be examined, including "ideas for joint control, UN mandates, condominiums and so on."

November   A scheduled meeting between the petroleum ministers of India and Pakistan is held about the proposed Indo-Iran gas pipeline.

December   A scheduled meeting between foreign secretaries is held to discuss overall progress, as well as issues of peace and security, including CBMs and Jammu-Kashmir, under the composite dialogue.

2005

16 April   India's Cabinet Committee on Security proposes seven CBMs on Jammu-Kashmir:
1. Reviving traditional communication and bus links;
2. Allowing relatives on either side to meet at several points on the LoC, including Poonch, Mendhar, Suchetgarh, Uri, and Tangdar;
3. Promoting and developing international trade across the LoC;
4. Creating a mechanism for permitting pilgrims on both sides to visit Sikh and Hindu temples and Muslim shrines;
5. Promoting cultural interaction and cooperation;
6. Joint promotion of tourism in the area; and
7. Exploring cooperation on issues such as the management of environment and forestry resources.

18 April   India and Pakistan agree on the following CBMs:
- The opening of trade across the LoC,
- Operationalizing the Jammu–Rawalakot route,
- Opening the Karachi and Mumbai consulates by the end of the year, and
- Taking steps to arrange for meetings of divided families along the LoC.

June–August   Muslim separatist leaders from Kashmir cross the cease-fire line and enter Muzaffarabad on June 2. They get a great welcome.

India and Pakistan agree on August 30 to free hundreds of civilians held in each other's jails and to provide better consular access to prisoners. Many are fishermen and others who strayed across poorly marked borders and are accused of spying.

August   During talks held in New Delhi, after successfully concluding an understanding on prenotification of missile tests and on nuclear confidence-building measures, the governments of India and Pakistan agree to a number of conventional CBMs, including the holding of cease-fires on their mutual borders. Both sides agree to:
1. Uphold the ongoing cease-fires;
2. Implement the 1991 agreement between the two countries on air space violations in letter and spirit;
3. Upgrade the existing hotline between the respective DGMOs by the end of September 2005;
4. Not develop any new posts or defense works along the LoC;
5. Hold monthly flag meetings between local commanders at Kargil/Olding, Uri/Chakotie, Naushera/Sadabad, and the Jammu/Sialkot sectors; and
6. Promptly return people inadvertently crossing the LoC and work out a comprehensive framework to that end.

The two sides also agree to report on progress to the respective foreign secretaries, who will decide on the date and venue of the next expert-level meeting on conventional CBMs.

5 September   Prime Minister Manmohan Singh holds talks in Delhi with a delegation led by Chairman Mirmawaiz Omar Farooq of the moderate faction of the Kashmiri separatist group, the All-Parties Hurriyat Conference. In

September the Indian government clears for release 50 people detained previously in Jammu-Kashmir for links with militant groups.

15 September   India's Manmohan Singh and Pakistan's President Pervez Musharraf meet at the UN's World Summit and agree not to allow acts of terrorism to forestall their peace process. They announce that they are committed "to ensure a peaceful settlement of all pending issues, including Jammu-Kashmir, to the satisfaction of both sides." Musharraf says, "our nations must not be trapped by hate and history." Singh, in a meeting with President George Bush immediately beforehand, accused Pakistan of aiding terrorists. Musharraf's spokesperson is reported on India TV as saying that Pakistan still controlled "the flow of terror" into Indian-administered Kashmir.

November   K. Natwar Singh resigns as foreign minister at the beginning of November to combat accusations of corruption. His portfolio is taken over by Prime Minister Manmohan Singh.

28 December   The two countries agree to withdraw troops from their positions on the Siachen glacier, but India's defense minister says that Pakistan does not agree with an Indian proposal that each army should mark its military position before leaving.

2006   At the beginning of the year Pakistan lifts a 40-year ban on Indian films, in a move that it says would lead to joint film productions and greater cultural cooperation. The ban dated back to 1965. Since then cinema audiences in Pakistan had shrunk. From 1,300 cinemas in the 1970s Pakistan had only 270 in 2005. In the 1970s Pakistan produced 300 films a year; in 2005 it made only 18. However, for many years Pakistanis had watched the latest Indian films put out by cable networks.

India and Pakistan also agree to resume, after 40 years, a second cross-border train service, this one between Munabao, India, and Khakrapar.

18–19 January   Two days of talks between India's Foreign Secretary Shyam Saran and his Pakistani counterpart, Rikaza Mohammad Khan, renew a commitment to carry forward the peace process. A few days earlier, President Musharraf said he is disappointed by the lack of progress. There was not much response from India to his ideas for resolving the Kashmir issue. He also accuses India of fomenting insurgency in Baluchistan.

3 February   India announces that it has completed tests and is ready to deploy its latest nuclear-tipped missile, the Agni III (Fire), which can carry a one-ton conventional or nuclear warhead.

March   Ministers from both countries meet in a third round of trade talks in Islamabad and pledge to develop links in banking, freight transport, and soft commodity goods, such as tea and rice.

It is also agreed that there will be moves to open branches of banks in both countries more speedily.

1 May   Twenty-two Hindu villagers are killed in a predawn massacre in Indian Kashmir in the mountainous Doda district. The same day 13 Hindu shepherds are found dead in Udhampur district. These incidents are the worst outbreaks of communal violence in three years, taking place two days before India's Prime Minister Manmohan Singh is to meet leaders of the All Parties Hurriyat conference, consisting of 26 Kashmiri separatist parties.

Talks in and about Kashmir, scheduled to be held between Manmohan Singh and pro-Indian Kashmiri political leaders at the end of May, are boycotted by separatists. Singh admits some abuses by India's security forces and says steps will be taken to stop them.

24 May   A tenth round of the two-year-long talks between India and Pakistan about withdrawing troops from the Siachen glacier break down. About 7,000 Indian and 4,000 Pakistani troops are still deployed in the area.

Talks in May make progress on the long-running demarcation issue involving Sir Creek, a narrow strip of estuary marshland separating India's Gujerat state and Pakistan's Sindh province—the scene of armed clashes in 1965. A joint survey of the Rann of Kutch/Sir Creek is planned.

11 July   Seven bombs rip through the cars of packed rush-hour commuter trains and stations in Mumbai, killing 200 people and injuring over 700. The blasts come within hours of one another, and no organization claims immediate responsibility for what is obviously a well-planned operation. Prime Minister Manmohan Singh says, "No one can make India kneel . . . The wheels of our economy will move on." Suspicions rest on Pakistan-based Kashmiri groups operating in India, especially on the relatively sophisticated, Lashkar-e-Toiba, which quickly denies involvement. Pakistan's President Musharraf condemns the attacks as "despicable" and offers to help any investigation India wants to carry out.

2007

9 March   President Musharraf suspends Iftikhar Muhammad Chaudry, chief justice of Pakistan's Supreme Court for an unspecified misuse of authority. Chaudry appeals.

6 May   Chief Justice Chaudry addresses the largest of a series of rallies in his

support. He criticizes states "which
are based on dictatorships."

2 July
Pakistan's Supreme Court dismisses
evidence against Chief Justice
Chaudry submitted by General
Musharraf's government as
scandalous and bans intelligence
officers from court.

20 July
Chief Justice Chaudry is reinstated by
the Supreme Court of Pakistan.
Charges against him are quashed.

August
India and Pakistan celebrate their
60th anniversaries since
independence with mutual
statements of congratulation.

23 September
The legality of the exiled leader
Nawaz Sharif's decision to return to
Pakistan is upheld by Pakistan's
Supreme Court.

10 September
Former Prime Minister Sharif is sent
back into exile (in Saudi Arabia) only
four hours after his aircraft lands in
Islamabad.

October
Musharraf wins most of the votes in
presidential election. The Pakistani
Supreme Court rules that no winner
can be formally announced until it
rules on Musharraf's eligibility to
stand for election while still army
chief.

Former Prime Minister Benazir
Bhutto returns from exile. Dozens of
people die in a suicide bomb
targeting her homecoming parade in
Karachi.

November
Musharraf declares emergency rule
while still awaiting the Supreme
Court ruling on whether he is
eligible to run for reelection. Chief
Justice Chaudhry is dismissed, and
Bhutto is briefly placed under house
arrest.

A new Supreme Court, staffed with
pro-Musharraf judges, dismisses
challenges to Musharraf's reelection.
Pakistan's chief election
commissioner announces that
general elections are to be held on
January 8, 2008. Nawaz Sharif
returns from exile again. Musharraf
resigns from his Army post and is
sworn in for a second term as
president.

15 December
Pakistan's state of emergency is lifted.

27 December
Benazir Bhutto is assassinated at an
election campaign rally in
Rawalpindi.

Appendices

POLITICAL LEADERS AND SENIOR OFFICE HOLDERS
India

President

1950–1962   Rajendra Prasad
1962–1967   Sarvepalli Radhakrishnan
1967–1969   Zakir Husain
1969   Varahagiri Venkatagiri *(acting)*
1969   Mohammed Hidayatullah *(acting)*
1969–19674   Varahagiri Venkatagiri
1974–1977   Fakhruddin Ali Ahmed
1977   B. D. Jatti *(acting)*
1977–1982   Neelam Sanjiva Reddy
1982–1987   Giani Zail Singh
1987–1992   Ramaswami Venkataraman
1992–1997   Shankar Dayal Sharma
1997–2002   K. R. Narayanan
2002–2007   A. P. J. Abdul Kalam
2007–Present   Pratibha Patil

Prime Minister

1947–1964   Jawaharlal Nehru
1964   Gulzari Lal Nanda *(acting)*
1964–1966   Lal Bahadur Shastri
1966   Gulzari Lal Nanda *(acting)*
1966–1977   Indira Gandhi
1977–1979   Moraji Ranchhodji Desai
1979–1980   Charan Singh
1980–1984   Indira Gandhi
1984–1989   Rajiv Gandhi
1989–1990   Vishwanath Pratap ("V. P.") Singh
1990–1991   Chandra Shekhar
1991–1996   P. V. Narasimha Rao
1996   Atal Bihari Vajpayee
1996–1997   Deve Gowda
1997–1998   Inder Kumar Gujral
1998–2004   Atal Bihari Vajpayee
2004–Present   Manmohan Singh

Pakistan

President

1956–1958   Iskander Mirza
1958–1969   Mohammad Ayub Khan
1969–1971   Agha Muhammad Yahya Khan
1971–1973   Zulfikar Ali Bhutto
1973–1978   Fazal Elahi Chawdry
1978–1988   Mohammand Zia-ul–Haq
1988–1993   Gulam Ishaq Khan
1993   Farooq Ahmed Leghari
1997–2001   Mohammed Rafiq Tarar
2001–2008   Pervez Musharraf

Prime Minister

1947–1951   Liaquat Ali Khan
1951–1953   Khawaja Nazimuddin
1953–1955   Mohammad Ali
1955–1956   (Chaudri) Mohamad Ali
1956–1957   Hussain Shaheed Suhrawardy
1957   Ismail Chundrigar
1957–1958   Malik Feroz Khan Noon
1958   Mohammad Ayub Khan
1958–1973   *No Prime Minister*
1973–1977   Zulfikar Ali Bhutto
1977–1985   *No Prime Minister*
1985–1988   Muhammad Khan Junejo
1988   Mohammad Aslam Khan Khattak
1988–1990   Benazir Bhutto
1990   Ghulam Mustafa Jatoi
1990–1993   Mian Mohammad Nawaz Sharif
1993–1996   Benazir Bhutto
1996–1997   Malik Meraj Khalid
1997–1999   Mian Mohammad Nawaz Sharif
2002–2004   Zafarullah Khan Jamali
2004   Chaudhry Shujaat Hussain
2004–2007   Shaukat Aziz
2007–2008   Muhammad Mian Soomro
2008–Present   Yousaf Raza Gillani

TASHKENT DECLARATION

The Tashkent Declaration was signed in the Uzbekistan Government House in the presence of Alexsei Kosygin, Andrei Gromyko, Marshal Malinovsky, and Madame Yadgardinova, president of the Uzbekistan Soviet Republic. At the request of President Ayub Khan and of

President Shastri, Kosygin opened the proceedings and was a witness of the Tashkent Declaration of January 10, 1966, the text of which is as follows:

The Prime Minister of India and the President of Pakistan, having met at Tashkent and having discussed the existing relations between India and Pakistan, hereby declare their firm resolve to restore normal and peaceful relations between their countries and to promote understanding and friendly relations between their peoples. They consider the attachment of these objectives of vital importance for the welfare of the 600.000.000 people of India and Pakistan.

(1) The Prime Minister of India and the President of Pakistan agree that both sides will exert all efforts to create good-neighbourly relations between India and Pakistan in accordance with UN Charter.

They reaffirm their obligation under the Charter not to have recourse to force and to settle their disputes through peaceful means. They considered that the interests of peace in their region and particularly in the Indo-Pakistan subcontinent and indeed the interest of the peoples of India and Pakistan were not served by the continuance of tension between the two countries.

It was against this background that Jammu and Kashmir were discussed, and each of the sides set forth its respective position.

(2) The Prime Minister of India and the President of Pakistan have agreed that all armed personnel of the two countries must be withdrawn not later than February 25 1966, to the position they held prior to August 2, 1965, and both sides shall observe the cease-fire terms on the cease-fire line.

(3) The Prime Minister of India and the President of Pakistan have agreed that relations between India and Pakistan shall be based on the principle of non-interference in the internal affairs of each other.

(4) The Prime Minister of India and the President of Pakistan have agreed that both sides will discourage any proposals directed against the other country, and will encourage proposals which promotes the development of friendly relations between the two countries.

(5) The Prime Minister of India and the President of Pakistan have agreed that the High Commissioner of India to Pakistan will return to his post, and that the normal functioning of diplomatic relations of both countries will be restored. Both governments shall observe the Vienna Convention of 1961 on diplomatic intercourse.

(6) The Prime Minister of India and the President of Pakistan have agreed to consider measures towards the restoration of economic and trade relations, communications, as well as cultural exchanges between India and Pakistan, and to take measures to implement the existing agreements between India and Pakistan.

(7) The Prime Minister of India and the President of Pakistan have agreed that they will give instructions to their respective authorities to carry out the repatriation of prisoners of war.

(8) The Prime Minister of India and the President of Pakistan have agreed that both sides will continue the discussions of questions relating to the problems of refugees and evictions of illegal immigrants. They also agreed that both sides will create conditions which will prevent the exodus of people. They further agreed to discuss the return of property and assets taken over by either side in connection with the conflict.

(9) The Prime Minister of India and the President of Pakistan have agreed that the sides will continue meetings both at the highest and at other levels on matters of direct concern to both countries. Both sides have recognized the need to set up joint Indo-Pakistan bodies which will report to their governments in order to decide what further steps should be taken.

The Prime Minister of India and the President of Pakistan record their feelings of deep appreciation and gratitude to the leaders of the Soviet Union, the Soviet Government and personally to the Chairman of the Council of Ministers of the U.S.S.R., for their constructive, friendly, and noble part in bringing about this present meeting, which has resulted in mutually satisfactory results.

They also express to the government and the friendly people of Uzbekistan their sincere gratitude for the overwhelming reception and generous hospitality.

They invite the Chairman of the Council of Ministers of the U.S.S.R. to witness this declaration.

(In the Indian document of the Tashkent Declaration, the relevant paragraphs began "The Prime Minister of India and the President of Pakistan" as above; in the Pakistani document these paragraphs began, " The President of Pakistan and the Prime Minister of India.")

Glossary

Ahimsa   Nonviolence.

Akali Dal   Ruling party in the state of Punjab (closely associated with Sikhs) until May 1987 when president's rule was imposed.

Ayurveda   Traditional Indian medicines.

Babri Mosque   Known to Hindus as the Ramjanmabhoomi temple, a mosque built on the site in the state of Uttar Pradesh that is believed to be the birthplace of Lord Rama. Dispute over this site has led to recurrent violence between Hindus and Moslems.

Bandh   Protest through a general strike or closure.

Brahman   Member of a priestly caste.

Dalit   Oppressed (untouchable), literally meaning rained on or trampled.

Desh bachao   Phrase that means save the motherland, a slogan utilized by Rajiv Gandhi as a theme of national unity for the December 1984 parliamentary elections.

Dharmashastra   Code of behavior.

Doordarshan   India's state television network.

Durbar   Celebratory royal ceremony or court.

Gurdwara   Sikh shrine.

Guru   Teacher.

Hajj   Pilgrimage to Mecca

Harijan   Children of god; Mohandas Gandhi's name for untouchables.

Hartal   Strike, including closing shops and businesses.

Hindutva   Hindu-ness.

Jati   Caste or subcaste unit that defines acceptable interactions in marriage, dining and other caste-related practices.

Jihad   Holy war.

Khilafat   Caliphate.

Kisan   Peasant.

Kshatra   Power.

Madrassas   Muslim school or college.

Mahajanapada   Great community.

Maharaja   Great king.

Maharajadhiraja   Great king over other kings.

Millat   Minority religious enclave.

Mleccha   Foreigner, barbarian.

Mohajir   Muslim migrants from India to Pakistan.

Nadu   Local community.

Panch Sheel (or Panch Shila)   Five principles (of peaceful coexistence).

Pir   Sufi master.

Raja   King; chief.

Sabha   Council of elders.

Samsara   Transmigration.

Sati   Widow sacrifice; widow immolation.

Satyagraha   Truth force; nonviolent protest.

Satyagrahin   Person engaging in *satyagraha.*

Scheduled castes   List of untouchable or *harijan* castes and tribes drawn up under the 1935 Government of India Act and subsequently revised. Legislative seats, as well as government posts and places in educational institutions, are reserved for members of these castes.

Sharia   Code of Muslim conduct.

Shiv Sena   Militant nativist communal organization founded in Bombay (Mumbai) in 1966 to agitate against southern Indian immigrants to the state of Maharastra.

Shuddi   Reconversion to Hinduism.

Suba   Mughal province.

Swadeshi   Indigenous, literally "own country."

Swaraj   Independence.

Thagi (or I)   Dacoity, professional criminality. In India or Burma, this term refers to a member of a band of armed robbers.

I   Learned Muslim men.

Unionist Party   An intercommunal party of Muslim, Hindu, and Sikh landlords that dominated Punjab politics in the 1930s. It defeated both Congress and the Muslim League in the 1935 elections.

Varna   Caste, specifically the four broad hierarchical categories of the Hindu caste system. In descending order of the status, the varna are Brahmin, Ksahatriya, and Shudra. Dalits fall below these categories.

Zamindar   Landholder.

Bibliography

Abdullah, Sheikh Mohammad. *Flames of the Chinar: An Autobiography.* Translated by Khuswant Singh. New York: Viking, 1993

Adamec, L. W., and F. A. Clements. *Conflict in Afghanistan: An Encyclopaedia. Roots of Modern Conflict.* Santa Barbara, CA: ABC-CLIO, 2003

Advani, L. K. *Ram Janmabhoomi: Honour People's Sentiments.* New Delhi: Bharatiya Jana Sangh, 1989

Advani, L. K. *Ayodhya Before and After.* New Delhi: Janadhikar Samiti, 1992

Ahmad, Ishtiaq, and A. Bashir. *India and Pakistan: Charting a Path to Peace.* Islamabad, Pakistan: Islamabad Society for Tolerance and Education, 2004

Ahmed, Mushtaq. *The United Nations and Pakistan.* Karachi, Pak.: Institute of International Affairs, 1955

Ahmed, Samina. "Post-Taliban Afghanistan and South Asian Security." In Ramesh Thakur and Oddny Wiggen, eds. *South Asia in the World: Problem-Solving Perspectives on Security, Sustainable Development, and Good Governance.* Tokyo: United Nations University Press, 2004

Ahsan, Aitzaz. *The Indus Saga and the Making of Pakistan.* Lahore, Pak.: Nehr Ghar Publications, 1996

Akbar, M. J. *Nehru: The Making of India.* New York: Viking, 1989

Akram, A. I. "Security and Stability in South Asia." In Stephen P. Cohen, ed. *The Security of South Asia: American and Asian Perspectives.* Urbana: University of Illinois Press, 1987

Ali, Chaudhri Muhammed. *The Emergence of Pakistan.* New York: Columbia University Press, 1967

Ali, S. Mahmud. *Cold War in the High Himalayas: The USA, China and South Asia in the 1950s.* New York: St. Martin's Press, 1999

Ali, Tariq. *An Indian Dynasty: The Story of the Nehru–Gandhi Family.* New York: Putnam, 1985

Ambrose, Stephen E. *Nixon: The Triumph of a Politician.* New York: Simon & Schuster, 1990

Anderson, Benedict. *Imagined Communities: Reflections on the Origin and Spread of Nationalism,* rev. ed. London: Verso, 1991

Anderson, Walter K., and Shridhar Damla. *The Brotherhood in Saffron: The Rashtriya Swayamsevak and Hindu Revivalism.* Boulder, CO: Westview Press, 1987

Anthony, Ian. "Arms Exports to Southern Asia: Policies of Technology Transfer and Denial in the Supplier Countries." In Eric Arnett, ed. *Military Capacity and the Risk of War. China, India, Pakistan and Iran.* New York: Oxford University Press, 1997

Ayres, Alyssa, and Philip Oldengurg, eds. *India Briefing: Take off at Last?* Armonk, NY: M. E. Sharpe, 2005

Ayub, Mohammed. "South-West Asia after the Taliban." In Ramesh Thakur and Oddny Wiggen, eds. *South Asia in the World: Problem-Solving Perspectives on Security, Sustainable Development, and Good Governance.* Tokyo: United Nations University Press, 2004

Azad, Abul Kalam. *India Wins Freedom.* New York: Longman, 1959

Aziz, Sartaj. "South Asia: Melting Pot of Global Faultlines." In Ramesh Thakur and Oddny Wiggen, eds. *South Asia in the World: Problem-Solving Perspectives on Security, Sustainable Development, and Good Governance.* Tokyo: United Nations University Press, 2004

Bahadur, Lal. *The Muslim League: Its History, Activities and Achievements* Lahore, Pak.: Book Traders, 1979

Bajpai, K. Shankar. "Untangling India and Pakistan." *Foreign Affairs* (May–June 2003)

Bajpai, Kanti. "India-US Foreign Policy Concerns: Cooperation and Conflict." In Gary K. Bertsch, Seema Gahlaut, and Anupam Srivastava, eds. *Engaging India: US Strategic Relations with the World's Largest Democracy.* New York: Routledge, 1999

Bandyopodhyaya, J. *The Making of India's Foreign Policy,* 2nd ed. New Delhi: Allied Publishers Ltd., 1979

Barnds, William J. "The United States and South Asia: Policy and Process." In Stephen P. Cohen, ed. *The Security of South Asia: American and Asian Perspectives.* Urbana: University of Illinois Press, 1987

Barton, Sir William. *India's North-West Frontier.* London: John Murray, 1939

Basham, A. L. *The Wonder That Was India.* New York: Macmillan, 1951

Baxter, Craig. *The Jana Sangh: A Biography of an Indian Political Party.* New York: Oxford University Press, 1971

Beckett, F. *Clem Attlee: A Biography.* London: Richard Cohen Books, 1997

Best, Antony, J. M. Hanimaki, J. A. Maiolo, and K. E. Schulze. *International History of the Twentieth Century.* New York: Routledge, 2004

Bhambhri, C. P. *Globalization: India, Nation, State and Democracy.* New Delhi: Shipra Publishing, 2005

Bharatiyajanat Party. *White Paper on Ayodhya and the Rama Temple Movement.* New Delhi: Author, 1993

Bhutto, Benazir. *Daughter of the East: An Autobiography.* London: Hamish Hamilton, 1988

Birdwood, Lord. *A Continent Decides.* London: Hale, 1953

Black, Conrad. *Richard Milhous Nixon: The Invincible Quest.* London: Quercus Publishing, 2007

Black, E. *The Diplomacy of Economic Development.* Cambridge, MA: Harvard University Press, 1961

Bose, Sugata, and Jalal Ayesha, eds. *Modern South Asia Delhi.* New York: Oxford University Press, 1997

Bose, Sugata, and Jalal Ayesha, eds. *Nationalism, Democracy and Development: State and Politics in India.* New York: Oxford University Press, 1997

Bose, Sumantra. *The Challenge in Kashmir: Democracy Self-Determination and a Just Peace.* Thousand Oaks, CA: Sage Publications, 1997

Brass, Paul. *Ethnicity and Nationalism: Theory and Comparison.* Thousand Oaks, CA: Sage Publications, 1991

Brass, Paul. *The Production of Hindu-Muslim Violence in Contemporary India.* Seattle: University of Washington Press, 2003

Brecher, Michael. *The Struggle for Kashmir.* New York: Oxford University Press, 1952

Brecher, M. *Nehru: A Political Biography.* New York: Oxford University Press, 1959

Brines, Russell. *The Indo-Pakistan Conflict.* London: Pall Mall Press, 1968

Brobst, Peter J. *The Future of the Great Game: India's Independence and the Defence of Asia.* Akron, OH: University of Akron Press, 2005

Brown, Judith M. *Gandhi: Prisoner of Hope.* New Haven: Yale University Press, 1989

Burke, S. M., and Ziring L. *Pakistan's Foreign Policy and Historical Analysis,* 2nd ed. Karachi, Pak.: Oxford University Press, 1990

Burki, Shahid Javed. *Pakistan Under Bhutto 1971–1977.* New York: Macmillan, 1980

Buzan, Barry. "A Framework for Regional Security Analysis." In Barry Buzan and Gowher Rizvi, eds. *South Asian Insecurity and the Great Powers.* New York: St. Martin's Press, 1986

Callard, K. *Pakistan: A Political Study.* London: Allen & Unwin, 1957

Caroe, O. *The Pathans.* New York: Oxford University Press, 1958

Caroe, O. "The Geography and Ethnics of India's Northern Frontiers." *The Geographical Journal* (1960)

Cashman, Richard. *Patrons, Players and the Crowd: The Phenomenon of Indian Cricket.* Mumbai: Orient Longmans, 1980

Chambers, Michael R. *South Asia in 2020: Future Strategic Balance and Alliances.* Carlisle Barracks, PA: U.S. Army War College, 2002

Chandhur, Nirad C. *The Continent of Circe: Being an Essay on the Peoples of India.* London: Chatto and Windus, 1965

Chandra, Ramesh. *Scientist to President: President A. P. J. Abdul Kalam.* New Delhi: Gyan, 2002

Chari, P. R. "Security Aspects of Indian Foreign Policy." In Stephen P. Cohen, ed. *The Security of South Asia: American and Asian Perspectives.* Urbana: University of Illinois Press, 1987

Chaturvedi, S. K., S. K. Sharma, and Kumar Madhrendra. *Encyclopaedia of SAARC.* New Delhi: Pragun Publications, 2006

Cheema, Zafar Iqbal. "Pakistan's Nuclear Policies: Attitudes and Posture." In P. R. Chari, Pervaiz Iqbal Cheema, and Iftekharuzzaman, eds. *Nuclear Non-proliferation in India and Pakistan: South Asian Perspectives.* New Delhi: Monohar, 1996

Chopra, V. D. *Genesis of Indo-Pakistan Conflict of Kashmir.* New Delhi: Patriot, 1990

Choudhry, G. W. *Pakistan's Relations with India 1947–1966.* London: Pall Mall Press, 1968

Choudhry, G. W. *The Last Days of United Pakistan.* Bloomington: Indiana University Press, 1974

Clarke, P. *The Cripps Version: The Life of Sir Stafford Cripps.* London: Allen Lane, 2002

Clinton, W. J. *My Life.* New York: Random House, 2004

Cohen, S. P., ed. *The Security of South Asia: American and Asian Perspectives.* Urbana: University of Illinois Press, 1987

Cohen, S. P. *The Pakistan Army.* New York: Oxford University Press, 1998

Cohen, S. P. "The United States, India and Pakistan: Retrospect and Prospect." In Selig S. Harrison, Paul H. Kreisbergm and Dennis Kux, eds. *India and Pakistan: The First Fifty Years*. Woodrow Wilson Center. New York: Cambridge University Press, 1999

Cohen, S. P. *India: Emerging Power*. Washington, DC: Brookings Institution Press, 2001

Cohen, S. P. *The Indian Army: Its Contribution to the Development of a Nation*. New York: Oxford University Press, 2001

Cohen, S. P. "Nuclear Weapons and Nuclear War in South Asia: Unknowable Futures." In Ramesh Thakur and Oddny Wiggen, eds. *South Asia in the World: Problem-Solving Perspectives on Security, Sustainable Development, and Good Governance*. Tokyo: United Nations University Press, 2004

Cohen, S. P. *The Idea of Pakistan*. Washington, DC: Brookings Institution Press, 2004

Coupland, R. *The Indian Problem*. New York: Oxford University Press, 1944

Coupland, R. *India: A Statement*. New York: Oxford University Press, 1945

Cramer, C. *Civil War Is Not a Stupid Thing*. New York: Hurst and Company, 2006

Das Gupta, J. B. *Indo-Pakistan Relations 1947–1955*. Amsterdam: Djambatan, 1958

Deol, Harnik. *Religion and Nationalism in India: The Case of the Punjab*. New York: Routledge, 2000

Dershowitz, Alan M. *Why Terrorism Works: Understanding the Threat. Responding to the Challenge*. New Haven, CT: Yale University Press, 2002

Desai, Moraji. *The Story of My Life*. 2 vols. New Delhi: Macmillan of India, 1974

Desai Sar, R. D., and Anand Mohan, eds. *The Legacy of Nehru: A Centennial Assessment*. Springfield, VA: Massachusetts Nataraj Books, 1992

Deshpande, Ahirudh. *British Military Policy in India 1900–1945: Colonial Constraints and Declining Power*. New Delhi: Manohar, 2003

Dixit, J. N. *Anatomy of a Flawed Inheritance: Indo-Pak Relations 1970–1994*. Delhi: Konark Publishers Ltd., 1995

Durrani, Mahmud Ali. *India and Pakistan: The Cost of Conflict and the Benefits of Peace*. New York: Oxford University Press, 2001

Effendi, M.Y., ed. *The Durand Line: Its Geo-strategic Importance*. Peshawar, Pak.: Area Study Centre, Peshawar and Hanns Seidel Foundation, 2000

Esposito, John. *Islam in Asia: Religion, Politics and Society*. New York: Oxford University Press, 1987

Esposito J. L., ed. *The Oxford History of Islam*. New York: Oxford University Press, 1999

Evans, A. "Forecasting India's Potential." *The Round Table: The Commonwealth Journal of International Affairs* 93, 376 (September 2004): 595–608.

Evans, A. "Kashmir: A Tale of Two Valleys—Kashmir Valley to the Neelum Valley." *Asian Affairs* (March 2005)

Faruqui, Ahmad. *Rethinking the National Security of Pakistan: The Price of Strategic Myopia*. Burlington, VT: Ashgate Publishing, 2003

Fay Ward, Peter. *The Forgotten Army: India's Armed Struggle for Independence 1942–1945*. Ann Arbor: University of Michigan Press, 1995

Feldman, Herbert. *The End and the Beginning: Pakistan 1969–1971*. New York: Oxford University Press, 1975

Finer, S. E. *Man on Horseback*. London: Pall Mall Press, 1963

Frank, Katherine. *Indira: The Life of Indira Nehru Gandhi*. New York: HarperCollins, 2001

Frankel, F. R. *India's Political Economy 1947–1977*. Princeton, NJ: Princeton University Press, 1978

Galbraith, J. K. *Ambassador's Journal: A Personal Account of the Kennedy Years*. Boston: Houghton Mifflin, 1969

Gandhi, Rajmohan. *Patel: A Life*. Ahmedabad, Ind.: Navjivan Press, 1991

Ganguly, Sumit. "India: Policies, Past and Future." In Selig S. Harrison, Paul H. Kreisberg, and Dennis Kux, eds. *India and Pakistan: The First Fifty Years*. Washington, DC: Woodrow Wilson Center Press; New York: Cambridge University Press, 1999

Gauhar, A. *Ayub Khan: Pakistan's First Military Ruler*. Lahore, Pak.: Sang-e-Meel Publications, 1993

George, T. J. S. *Krishna Menon: A Biography*. London: Jonathan Cape, 1964

Ghose, S. *Indian National Congress, Its History and Heritage*. New Delhi: All India Congress Committee, 1975

Gilbert, Martin. *Churchill: A Life*. London: William Heinemann Ltd., 1991

Godbole, Madhav. *Unfinished Innings: Recollections and Reflections of a Civil Servant*. Mumbai: Orient Longman, 2003

Gonsalves, Eric, and Nancy Jettley, eds. *The Dynamics of South Asia: Regional Co-operation and SAARC*. Thousand Oaks, CA: Sage Publications, 1999

Gopal, S. *Jawaharlal Nehru*. 3 vols. London: Jonathan Cape, 1975–1983; Cambridge, MA: Harvard University Press, 1976–1984

Gopal, S. *Radhakrishnan: A Biography*. New York: Oxford University Press, 1989

Gopal, S. *Anatomy of a Confrontation: Ayodhya and the Rise of Communal Politics in India*. London: Zed Books, 1993

Gopal, S., P. Kalhan, and S. Wolpert. *Nehru: A Tryst with Destiny*. New York: Oxford University Press, 1996

Gorbachev, M. *Memoirs*. New York: Doubleday, 1996

Gordon, Sandy. *India's Rise to Power in the Twentieth Century and Beyond*. New York: Macmillan, 1995

Guha, R. *A Corner of a Foreign Field: The Indian History of a British Sport*. London: Picador, 2002

Guha, R. *India after Gandhi. The History of the World's Largest Democracy*. New York: Macmillan, 2007

Gupta, Sisir. *India's Relations with Pakistan 1954–1957*. New Delhi: Indian Council of World Affaires, 1958

Haidar, Salman, ed. *The Afghan War and Its Geopolitical Implications for India*. New Delhi: Manohar, 2004

Hardgrave, R. L., and S. A. Kochanet. *India: Government and Politics in a Developing Nation*, 6th ed. Fort Worth, TX: Harcourt College Publishers, 2000

Harrison, Selig S. *India: The Most Dangerous Decades*. N.J.: Princeton University Press International Institute for Strategic Studies (IISS) 2003

Heimsath, Charles, and Surjit Mansinght. *A Diplomatic History of Modern India*. New Delhi: Allied Publishers, Ltd., 1971

Hersh, Seymour. *The Price of Power: Kissinger in the Nixon White House*. New York: Summit Books, 1984

Hilali, A. Z. *US–Pakistan Relationship. Soviet Invasion of Afghanistan*. Aldershot, UK: Ashgate, 2005

Hilsman, R. *To Move a Nation: The Politics of Foreign Policy in the Administration of John F. Kennedy*. New York: Doubleday, 1967

Horne, A. *Harold Macmillan: The Official Biography*. Vol. I, 1894–1956; Vol. II, 1957–1986. New York: Macmillan, 1989

Huntington, S. *Political Order in Changing Societies*. New Haven, CT: Yale University Press, 1968

Ismay, Lord. *Memoirs*. London: William Heinemann Ltd., 1960

Jalal, Ayesha. *The State of Martial Rule: The Origins of Pakistan's Political Economy of Defence*. New York: Cambridge University Press, 1990

Jalal, Ayesha. *Democracy and Authoritarianism in South Asia. A Comparative and Historical Perspective*. New York: Cambridge University Press, 1995

Jalal, Ayesha. *The Sole Spokesman, Jinnah, the Muslim League and the Demand for Pakistan*. New York: Cambridge University Press, 1985; Lahore, Pak.: Sang-e-Meel Publications, 1999

James, Morrice Sir. *Pakistan Chronicle*. New York: Hurst and Company, 1993

Jansen, G. H. *Afro-Asia and Non Alignment*. London: Faber and Faber, 1966

Jaswant, Singh. *Defending India*. New York: Macmillan, 1999

Jayaprasal, K. *RSS and Hindu Nationalism*. New Delhi: Deep and Deep Publications Pvt. Ltd., 1991

Jenkins, R. *Churchill*. New York: Macmillan, 2001

Johsi, Arun. *Eyewitness Kashmir: Teetering on Nuclear War*. Singapore: Marshall Cavendish Academic, 2004

Jones, O. B. *"Pakistan": Eye of the Storm*. New Haven, CT: Yale University Press, 2002

Kaur, Surinder, and Sher Singh. *The Secular Emperor Babar, a Victim of Indian Partition*. New Delhi: Genuine Publishers, 1991

Kautilya. *Arthasastra*. Translated by R. Shamasastry. Mysore, Ind.: Mysore Printing and Publishing House, 1915; Sirhind, Ind: Lokgeet Prakashan, 1987

Khan, Adeel. *Politics of Identity: Ethnic Nationalism and the State in Pakistan*. Thousand Oaks, CA: Sage Publications, 2005

Khan, Ayub. *Friends Not Masters: A Political Autobiography*. New York: Oxford University Press, 1967

Khan, Hayat A. *The Durand Line—Its Geo-Strategic Importance*. Peshawar, Pak.: University of Peshawar and Hanns Seidel Foundation, 2000

Khilnani, Sunil. *The Idea of India*. London: Hamish Hamilton, 1997

Khrushchev, N. *Khrushchev Remembers*. Boston: Little, Brown and Company, 1970

Kidwai, Rasheed. *Sonia: A Biography*. New York: Viking Penguin, 2003

King, R. *Nehru and the Language of Politics of India*. New York: Oxford University Press, 1999

Kipling, R. *Kim*. New York: Macmillan, 1901

Kissinger, H. *The White House Years*. London: Weidefeld & Nicolson and Michael Joseph, 1979

Kissinger, Henry. *Diplomacy*. New York: Simon & Schuster, 1994

Knight, E. F. *Where Three Empires Meet*. New York: Longmans, 1895

Korejo, M. S. *The Frontier Gandhi, His Place in History*. New York: Oxford University Press, 1993

Krepon, Michael, ed. *Nuclear Risk Reduction in South Asia*. New York: Palgrave Macmillan/Henry L. Stimson Center, 2004

Kumar, Ranjit. *South Asian Union: Problems, Possibilities, and Prospects*. New Delhi: Manas Publications, 2005

Kux, Dennis. *India and the United States: Estranged Democracies, 1942–1991*. Washington, DC: National Defense University Press, 1992

Kux, Dennis. *The United States and Pakistan, 1947–2000: Disenchanted Allies.* Washington, DC: Woodrow Wilson Center Press; Baltimore, MD: Johns Hopkins University Press, 2001

Lamb, Alastair. *The China-India Border.* New York: Royal Institute of International Affairs. New York: Oxford University Press, 1964

Lamb, Alastair. *Kashmir: A Disputed Legacy, 1846–1990.* Hertingfordbury, UK: Roxford Books, 1991

Laqueur, Walter. *Terrorism.* London: Weindenfeld and Nicolson, 1977

Laqueur, Walter. *The Terrorism Readers: A Historical Anthology.* London: Wildwood House, 1979

Laqueur, Walter. *No End to War: Terrorism in the Twenty-First Century.* New York: Continuum International Publishing Group, 2003

Lipton, M., and J. Firn. *The Erosion of a Relationship: India and Britain Since 1960.* Royal Institute of International Affairs. New York: Oxford University Press, 1975

Low, D. A. *The Indian National Congress. Centenary Hindsights.* New York: Oxford University Press, 1988

Low, D. A. *The Political Inheritance of Pakistan.* New York: Macmillan, 1991

Lyngdoh, James M. *Chronicle of an Impossible Election: The Election Commission and the 2002 Jammu-Kashmir Assembly Elections.* London: Penguin, 2004

Lyon, P. *Neutralism.* Leicester, UK: Leicester University Press, 1963

Lyon, P. "Kashmir in International Relations." *The Round Table: The Commonwealth Journal of International Affaires* vol. 3 (2) (October 1966)

Lyon, P. "India's Foreign Policy." In F. S. Northedge, ed. *The Foreign Policies of the Powers.* London: Faber and Faber, 1967

Lyon, P. "Strategy and South Asia: Twenty-five Years on." *International Journal.* Toronto: Canadian Institute of International Affairs, 1972

Lyon, P. "The First Great Post-colonial State: India's Tryst with Destiny." In James Mayall and Anthony Payne, eds. *The Fallacies of Hope: The Post-colonial Record of the Commonwealth Third World.* Manchester, UK: Manchester University Press, 1991

Lyon, P. "Britain and the Kashmir Issue." In Raju G. C. Thomas, ed. *Perspectives on Kashmir: The Roots of Conflict in South Asia.* Boulder, CO: Westview Press, 1992

Lyon, P. "South Asia and the Geostrategics of the 1990s." *Contemporary South Asia* vol. 1 (1992): 25–39.

Lyon, P., and D. Austin. 1993. "The Bharatiya Janata Party of India." *Government and Opposition* 28, 1 (Winter 1993): 36–50.

Maley, William, ed. *Fundamentalism Reborn? Afghanistan and the Taliban.* New York: Hurst and Company, 1998

Malik, I. H. *State and Civil Society in Pakistan: Politics of Authority, Ideology and Ethnicity.* New York: St. Martin's Press, 1997

Malik, I. H. *Kashmir: Ethnic Conflict, International Dispute.* New York: Oxford University Press, 2003

Malik, K. N., and P. Robb, eds. *India and Britain: Recent Past and Present Challenges.* Manchester, UK: Manchester University Press, 1991

Maniruzzaman, T. *The Bangladesh Revolution and Its Aftermath.* Dhaka, Bang.: University Press Ltd., 1988

Marsden, P. *The Taliban: War, Religion and the New Order in Afghanistan.* New York: Zed Books, 1999

Marshall, T. H. *Citizenship and Social Class.* Cambridge, UK: Cambridge University Press, 1950

Masani, Zareer. *Indira Gandhi: A Biography.* London: Hamilton, 1975

Mason, P. *A Matter of Honour: An Account of the Indian Army, Its Officers and Men.* Mason, Philip (pseudo. Woodruff). *The Men Who Ruled India: The Guardians.* London: Jonathan Cape, 1974

Maxwell, N. *India's China War.* London: Jonathan Cape, 1970; New York: Penguin, 1992

Mehrotra, Santosh. *India and the Soviet Union: Trade and Technology Transfer.* Soviet and East European Studies Series. New York: Cambridge University Press, 1990

Mehta, Jagat S. "India and Pakistan: We Know the Past, Must We Live in It?" In Stephen P. Cohen, ed. *The Security of South Asia: American and Asian Perspectives.* Urbana: University of Illinois Press, 1987

Mehta, Ved. *Rajiv Gandhi and Rama's Kingdom.* New York: Penguin, 1995

Menon, V. P. *The Story of the Integration of the Indian States.* Mumbai: Orient Longmans, 1956

Menon, V. P. *The Transfer of Power in India.* Mumbai: Orient Longmans, 1957

Menon, V. P. *The Flying Troika.* New York: Oxford University Press, 1963

Miller, J. D. B. *The Politics of the Third World.* Royal Institute of International Affairs. New York: Oxford University Press, 1966

Mitra, Subrata, ed. *The Post-Colonial State in South Asia.* London: Harvester Wheatsheaf, 1990

Moon, P. *Divide and Quit.* London: Chatto and Windus, 1961

Moore, R. J. *Escape from Empire: The Attlee Government and the Indian Problem.* Oxford, UK: Clarendon Press, 1983

Morris-Jones, W. H. *The Government and Politics of India.* London: Hutchinson & Co., 1964

Mortimer, Robert A. *The Third World Coalition in International Politics.* Westport, CT: Mumbai: Orient Longmans, 1980

Musharraf, P. *In the Line of Fire: A Memoir.* New York: The Free Press, 2006

Nadel, Laurie. *The Biography of Richard Nixon.* New York: Macmillan, 1991

Nanda, B. R. *Gandhi.* London: Allen & Unwin, 1958

Nehru, Brajkumar. *Nice Guys Finish Second.* New York: Viking, 1997

Nehru, Jawaharlal. *An Autobiography with Musings on Recent Events in India.* New Delhi: Allied Publishers Ltd., 1936

Nehru, Jawaharlal. *The Discovery of India.* Kolcatta: Signet Press, 1946

Nehru, Jawaharlal. *India's Foreign Policy: Selected Speeches, September 1946–April 1961.* New Delhi: Government of India, 1961

Noorani, A. G., ed. *The Muslims in India: A Documentary Record.* New York: Oxford University Press, 2003

Oberoi, Harjot. *The Construction of Religion Boundaries: Culture, Identity and Diversity in the Sikh Tradition.* Chicago: University of Chicago Press, 1994

O' Donnell, Charles Peter. *Bangladesh: Biography of a Muslim Nation.* Boulder, CO; Westview Press, 1984

Panagriya, Arvind. "Growth and Reforms During 1980s and 1990s." *Economic and Political Weekly* (Bombay) (June 19, 2004)

Pande, B. N. *Islam and Indian Culture.* Patna, Ind.: Khuda Bakhsh Oriental Public Library, 1987

Pandey, Gyanendra. *Hindus and Others.* New York: Viking Penguin, 1993

Pant, Kusum. *The Kashmir: Pandits.* New Delhi: Allied Publishers Ltd., 1987

Parekh, B., Gurharpal Singh, and S. Vertovee,eds. *Culture and Economy in the Indian Diaspora.* Oxford, UK: Taylor & Francis, 2003

Pimlott, Ben. *Harold Wilson.* New York: HarperCollins, 1992

Probst, Peter J. *The Future of the Great Game: India's Independence and the Defence of Asia.* Akron, OH: University of Akron Press, 2005

Pruthi, Raj. *President A.P.J. Abdul Kalam.* New Delhi: Anmol Publications, 2003

Radhakrishnan. *The Hindu View of Life.* New York: Oxford University Press, 1926

Rahman, M. *Emergence of a New Nation in a Multi-Polar World: Bangladesh.* Dhaka, Bang.: University Press Ltd., 1979

Rai, Mridu. *Hindu Rulers, Muslim Subjects: Islam, Rights and the History of Kashmir.* New York: Hurst and Company, 2004

Rajagopalan, Rajesh. *Second Strike: Arguments About Nuclear War in South Asia.* New York: Penguin, 2005

Rao, Narasimha P. V. *Ayodhya: 6 December 1992.* New York: Viking, 2006

Rappoport, D. C. *Assassination and Terrorism.* Toronto: Canadian Broadcasting Corporation, 1971

Rappoport, D. C. *Inside Terrorist Organizations.* New York: Columbia University Press, 1988

Razvi, Mujtaba. *The Frontiers of Pakistan.* Karachi, Pak.: Dacca National Publishing House Ltd., 1971

Rinehart, R., ed. *Contemporary Hinduism: Ritual, Culture and Practice.* Santa Barbara, CA: ABC-CLIO, 2004

Rizvi, Gowher. "Pakistan: The Domestic Dimensions of Security." In Barry Buzan and Gowher Rizvi, eds. *South Asian Insecurity and the Great Powers.* New York: St. Martin's Press, 1986a

Rizvi, Gowher. "The Rivalry Between India and Pakistan." In Barry Buzan and Gowher Rizvi, eds. *South Asian Insecurity and the Great Powers.* New York: St. Martin's Press, 1986b

Robinson, F. "Jinnah, Mohamed Ali. 1876–1948." *Oxford Dictionary of National Biography,* vol. 30. New York: Oxford University Press, 2004

Rodrigo, Nihal, "SAARC as an Institutional Framework for Cooperation in South Asia," in Ramesh Thakur and Oddny Wiggen eds., *South Asia in the World: Problem-Solving Perspectives on Security, Sustainable Development, and Good Governance.* Tokyo: United Nations University Press, 2004

Rose, Leo E. "India and Its Neighbours: Regional Foreign and Security Policies." In Lawrence Ziring, ed. *The Subcontinent in World Politics: India, Its Neighbours, and the Great Powers,* rev. ed. New York: Praeger, 1982

Rose, Leo E. "India's Regional Policy: Non Military Dimensions." In Stephen P. Cohen, ed. *The Security of South Asia: American and Asian Perspectives.* Urbana: University of Illinois Press, 1987

Roy, Ajit. "West Bengal: Not a Negative Vote." *Economic and Political Weekly* (July 2, 1977)

Saikal, A. "The Changing Geopolitics of Central West and South Asia After 11th September." In Ramesh Thakur and Oddny Wiggen, eds. *South Asia in the World: Problem-Solving Perspectives on Security, Sustainable Development, and Good Governance.* Tokyo: United Nations University Press, 2004

Sankalia, H. D. *Ramayana, Myth or Reality?* New Delhi: People's Publishing House, 1991

Sathasivam, K. *Uneasy Neighbours: India, Pakistan and US Foreign Policy.* Aldershot, UK: Ashgate, 2005

Sayeed, Khalil B. *The Political System of Pakistan.* Boston: Houghton-Mifflin, 1967

Schaffer, Teresita C. *Kashmir: The Economics of Peace Building: A Report of the CSIS South Asia Program with the Kashmir Study Group.* Washington, DC: Center for Strategic and International Studies, 2005

Schlesinger, M. *A Thousand Days: John F. Kennedy in the White House.* Boston: Houghton-Mifflin, 1965

Schofield, Victoria. *Bhutto: Trial and Execution.* New York: Cassell, 1979

Schofield, Victoria. *Kashmir in the Crossfire.* London: I. B. Tauris, 1996

Schofield, Victoria. *Wavell: Soldier and Statesman.* London: John Murray, 2006

Schwartzberg J., ed. *A Historical Atlas of South Asia,* 2nd ed. Chicago: Chicago University Press, 1992

Sen, Amartya. *The Argumentative Indian: Writings on Indian Culture, History and Identity.* New York: Farrar, Straus, and Giroux, 2005

Sender, H. *The Kashmiri Pandits: A Study of Cultural Choice in North India.* New York: Oxford University Press, 1988

Shah, Mehtab Ali. *The Foreign Policy of Pakistan. Ethnic Impacts on Diplomacy 1971–1994.* London: I. B. Tauris, 1997.

Shah, Mehtab Ali. "New Thaw in India-Pakistan Relations." *South Asian Politics.* New Delhi, 2003

Shah, Mehtab Ali. "Sectarianism—A Threat to Human Security: A Case Study of Pakistan." *The Round Table,* vol. 94 no. 385. The Institute of Commonwealth Studies, University of London. Oxfordshire, UK: Routledge, October 2005

Sidhu, Singh Choor. *Amar Shaheed Sant Jarnail Singh Bhindranwale: Martyr of the Sikh Faith.* Chandigarh, Ind.: European Institute of Sikh Studies, 1997

Singham, A. W., and Shirley Hume. 1986. *Non-Alignment in an Age of Alignments.* London: Zed Books, 1986

Singh, Gopal, ed. *Punjab Today.* New Delhi: South Asian Publishers, 1994

Singh, Gurmukh. *The Rise of Sikhs.* New Delhi: Rupa and Company, 2003

Singh, Jasjit, ed. *Nuclear India.* New Delhi: Institute for Defence Studies and Analyses, 1998

Singh, Jaswant. *Defending India.* New York: Macmillan, 1999

Singh, Karan. *Heir Apparent: An Autobiography.* New York: Oxford University Press, 1982

Singh, Mahendra Prasad, and April Mishra, eds. *Coalition Politics in India: Problems and Prospects.* New Delhi: Manohar, 2004

Singh, Manohan. *India's Export Trends and Prospects for Self-Sustained Growth.* Oxford, UK: Clarendon Press, Oxford, 1964

Singh, Ranbir. *Struggle for Justice: Speeches and Conversations of Sant Jarnail Singh Khalsa Bhindranwale.* Dublin, OH: Sikh Educational and Religious Foundation, 1999

Sisson, Richard, and Leo E. Rose. *War and Secession: Pakistan, India and the Creation of Bangladesh.* Berkeley: University of California Press, 1990

Smith, C. *India's Ad Hoc Arsenal: Direction or Drift in Defence Policy?* Oxford: Oxford University Press/Solna, Sw.: Stockholm International Peace Research Institute, 1994

Sorensen, Theodore C. *Kennedy.* Boston: Hodder Headliner, 1965

Spain, James W. *The Way of the Pathans.* New York: Oxford University Press, 1962

Spain, James W. *Pathans of the Latter Day.* New York: Oxford University Press, 1995

Spate, O. H. K. *India and Pakistan: A General and Regional Geography.* New York: Methuen, 1954; 2nd ed., New York: Methuen, 1960

Spear, P. *India: A Modern History.* Ann Arbor: University of Michigan Press, 1961

Srinivasan, T. N. *Eight Lectures on India's Economic Reforms.* New York: Oxford University Press, 2000

Srivastava, C. R. "Lal Bahadur Shastri: Prime Minister of India, June 1964–1966. A Life of Truth in Politics." In *A Dictionary of World History.* New York: Oxford University Press, 1995

Stein, B. *A History of India.* New York: Macmillan, 1998

Subrahmanyam, K. "Prospects for Security and Stability in South Asia." In Stephen P. Cohen, ed. *The Security of South Asia: American and Asian Perspectives.* Urbana: University of Illinois Press, 1987

Swinson, Arthur. *North West Frontier. People and Events 1939–1947.* London: Hutchinson & Co., 1967

Synnott, Hilary. *The Causes and Consequences of South Asia's Nuclear Tests.* International Institute for Strategic Studies (IISS) Adelphi Paper No 332. New York: Oxford University Press, 1999

Talbot, I. *Pakistan: A Modern History.* New York: Hurst and Company, 1998

Talbot, I. *India and Pakistan: Inventing the Nation.* London: Arnold Publishers, 2000

Talbot, Strobe. *Engaging India: Diplomacy, Democracy and the Bomb.* Washington, DC: Brookings Institution Press, 2004

Tanham, George K. *Indian Strategic Thought: An Interpretive Essay.* Report No. R-4207–1USDP. Santa Monica: RAND, 1992

Tatla, Singh Darshan. *The Sikh Diaspora: The Search for Statehood.* Seattle: University of Washington Press, 1999

Taubman, William. *Securing India: Strategic Thought and Practice.* New Delhi: Manohar, 1996

Taubman, William. *Khrushchev: The Man and His Era.* New York: Simon & Schuster, 2004

Taylor, David, and Malcolm Yapp. *Political Identity in South Asia.* Newcastle, UK: Curzon Publications, 1979

Tendulkar, Dinanath Gopal. *Abdula Ghaffar Khan.* New Delhi: Gandhi Peace Foundation, 1967

Thakur, Janardhan. *All the Prime Minister's Men.* New Delhi: Vikas Publishing House, 1977

Thapar, Romila. *Cultural Transactions and Early India: Tradition and Patronage.* New York: Oxford University Press, 1987

Thomas, Raju. *Indian Security Policy.* Princeton, NJ: Princeton University Press, 1986

Thomas, Raju. *Perspective on Kashmir: The Roots of Conflict in South Asia.* Boulder, CO: Westview Press, 1992

Thomas, Raju. "The Shifting Landscape of Indian Foreign Policy." In Steven W. Hook, ed. *Comparative Foreign Policy: Adaptation Strategies of the Great and Emerging Powers.* Upper Saddle River: Prentice Hall, 2002

Tidrick, K. *Gandhi: A Political and Spiritual Life.* London: I. B. Tauris, 2006

Tomlinson, B. R. *The Political Economy of the Raj 1914–1947: The Economics of Decolonization in India.* New York: Macmillan, 1979

Tully, Mark. *India in Slow Motion.* New York: Penguin, 2002

Tully, M., and S. Jacob. *Amritsar: Mrs. Gandhi's Last Battle.* New Delhi: Rupa and Company, 1985

Tully, M., and Z. Masani. *From Raj to Rajiv: 40 Years of Indian Independence.* New York: BBC Books, 1988

Turner, Barry, ed. *Statesman's Yearbook.* Santa Barbera, CA: ABC-CLIO, 1987

Undeland, Charles, and Nicholas Platt. *The Central Asian Republics. Fragments of Empire. Magnets of Wealth.* New York: Asia Society, 1994

Vajpayee, A. B. *Speeches on Ayodhya Issue.* New Delhi: Bharatiya Janata Party, 1992

Vajpeyi, J. N. *The Extremist Movement in India.* Allahabad, Ind.: Chugh Publications, 1974

Van der Veer, Peter. *Religious Nationalism: Hindus and Muslims in India.* Berkeley: University of California Press, 1994

Varshney, A. *Ethnic Conflict and Civic Life: Hindus and Muslims in India.* New Haven, CT: Yale University Press, 2002

Waseem, Mohammad. "Pakistan's Perceptions of the Impact of U.S. Politics on Its Policies Toward Pakistan." In Noor A. Husain and Leo E. Rose, eds. *Pakistan–U.S.Relations: Social, Political, and Economic Factors.* Berkeley, CA: Institute of East Asian Studies, University of California, Berkeley, 1988

Wight, Martin, Hedley Bull, and Carsten Holbraad Wiggen, eds. *South Asia in the World: Problem Solving Perspectives on Security—Power Politics.* Leicester, UK: Leicester University Press, 1978

Wilcox, W. *Pakistan: The Consolidation of a Nation.* New York: Columbia University Press, 1963

Wilcox, W. "India and Pakistan." In S. L. Spiegel and K. N. Waltz K.N., *Conflict in World Politics.* Cambridge, MA: Winthrop Publishers, 1971

Wilkinson, S. *Votes and Violence: Electoral Competition and Ethnic Riots in India.* New York, Cambridge University Press, 2004

Willetts, Peter. "The Non-Aligned Movement and Developing Countries, in 2004." Prepared for the *Annual Register.* www.staff.city.ac.uk/p.willetts /PUBS/AR00-NAM.DOC

Wingate, Lord Ismay. *Memoirs.* London: Heinemann. 1960

Wirsing, R. G. *The Baluchs and Pathans.* New York: Macmillan, 1987

Wirsing, R. G. *Pakistan's Security Under Zia's 1977–1988: The Policy Imperatives of a Peripheral Asian State.* New York: Macmillan, 1991

Wolpert, S. *Nine Hours to Rama.* New York: Random House, 1962

Wolpert, S. *Tilak Bal Gangadhar.* Berkeley: University of California Press, 1962

Wolpert, S. *Jinnah of Pakistan.* New York: Oxford University Press, 1984

Wolpert, S. *Zulfi Bhutto of Pakistan: His Life and Times.* New York: Oxford University Press, 1993

Wolpert, S. *Nehru: A Tryst with Destiny.* New York: Oxford University Press, 1996

Wolpert, Stanley. *Gandhi's Passion: The Life and Legacy of Mahatma Gandhi.* New York: Oxford University Press, 2001

Yasmeen, Samina. "Pakistan and India: The Way Forward." In Ramesh Thakur and Oddny Wiggen, eds. *South Asia in the World: Problem-Solving Perspectives on Security, Sustainable Development, and Good Governance.* Tokyo: United Nations University Press, 2004

Zahab, Abou M., and R. Olivier. *Islamic Networks: The Afghan-Pakistan Connection.* New York: Hurst and Company, 2004

Zahab, Mariam A., and Roy Olivier. *Islamic Networks: The Afghan-Pakistan Connection.* New York: Hurst and Company, 2004

Zaheer, Hasan. *The Separation of East Pakistan. The Rise and Realization of Bengali Muslim Nationalism.* New York: Oxford University Press, 1994

Zeigler, P. *Mountbatten: A Biography.* New York: Alfred A. Knopf, 1985

Ziegler, Philip. *Wilson, the Authorised Life.* London: Weidenfeld and Nicolson, 1993

GENERAL REFERENCES

Armstrong, Robert. Article in George Lord Blake Smith and C. S. Nicholls, eds. *Dictionary of National Biography 1971–1980.* New York: Oxford University Press, 2002

Asian Age (February 23, 2006).

Central Intelligence Agency (CIA). *The World Factbook.* 2003a, www.cia.gov

Central Intelligence Agency (CIA). *The World Factbook: Pakistan.* 2003b. www.cia.gov

Economic and Political Weekly (Mumbai)

Hackett, James. The *Military Balance.* Washington, DC: International Institute for Strategic Studies (IISS), annual

Kapur, A., and Jeyaratnam A. Wilson. *Foreign Policies of India and Her Neighbours.* Kargil Review Committee Report." 1999. http://nuclearweapon-archive.org/India/KargilRCB.html

Kashmir Study Group 1997, *1947–1997: The Kashmir Dispute of Fifty: Charting Paths to Peace.* Kashmir Study Group: New York, 1997

Statesman's Yearbook 1987. New York: Macmillan, 1987. Also Statesman's Yearbook

Stockholm's Institute for Peace Research (SIPRI). Annual publications. http://www.sipri.org/

Who Was Who. 1961–1970. London: A&C Black Publishers, 2007

Who's Who 2005. New York: Palgrave Macmillan, 2005

Yearbook of the North West Frontier Province. Islamabad, Pakistan: Government Press, Annual

Note: boldface page numbers indicate main encyclopedia entries; italic page numbers indicate pictures.

Index